Martin von Cochem

Cochem's Explanation of the Holy Sacrifice of the Masses

Martin von Cochem

Cochem's Explanation of the Holy Sacrifice of the Masses

ISBN/EAN: 9783337286378

Printed in Europe, USA, Canada, Australia, Japan

Cover: Foto ©Lupo / pixelio.de

More available books at **www.hansebooks.com**

HOLY SA[...]

WITH AN APP[...]
FOR [...]

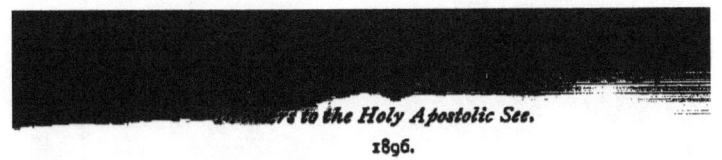
to the Holy Apostolic See.
1896.

PREFACE.

HAVING suggested the translation of Father Martin Cochem's excellent book on the Holy Sacrifice of the Mass, it seems fitting that I should comply with the Publishers' request and introduce it to the American public.

This is a very old-fashioned book; a book written with that sturdy faith and solid devotional feeling which knows no doubt, and acknowledges God's best work with a thankful heart. It will be refreshing reading to our nineteenth-century public, the majority of which lives and acts as if God were not nigh unto us and His saving Sacrifice were not the real immolation of His body and the actual spilling of His blood. In these days of material wonders, we believe in the supernatural life of the Church just as a spoiled child believes in the love of its parents, viz., we take it for granted, and do not bother about it. Some men believe only in a general, abstract way, and go to Mass as a man without appetite goes to the table at the dinner hour—because it is customary.

To bring home to all the divine reality of the incomprehensible Eucharistic act which the Lord Jesus Christ daily reproduces through the ministry of His priests, let us recall, in the words of the Catechism of the Council of Trent, the doctrine which all believing Catholics have to accept as of faith, relying on our pious author to stir up all the more successfully the generous belief of the heart.

"Of all the sacred mysteries bequeathed to us by Our Lord as unfailing sources of grace, there is none that can be compared to the Most Holy Sacrament of the Eucharist."*

The circumstances of its institution by Our Lord Jesus Christ Himself are recorded in the gospels and in the inspired writings of St. Paul.

"The Eucharist was instituted by Our Lord for two great purposes: to be the celestial food of our soul, preserving and supporting spiritual life; and to give to the Church a perpetual sacrifice, by which sin may be expiated and our heavenly Father, Whom our crimes have often grievously offended, may be turned from wrath to mercy, from the severity of just vengeance to the exercise of benignest clemency."

"The Sacrifice of the Mass is one and the same sacrifice with that of the cross: the Victim is one and the same, Christ Jesus, Who offered Himself, once only, a bloody sacrifice on the altar of the cross. The bloody and unbloody Victim is still one and the same, and the oblation of the cross is daily renewed in the Eucharistic Sacrifice, in obedience to the command of the Lord: 'This do for a commemoration of Me.'† The priest is also the same—Christ our Lord; the ministers who offer this sacrifice consecrate the holy mysteries not in their own but in the person of Christ. This the words of consecration declare; the priest does not say: This is the body of Christ, but, 'This is My body'; and thus invested with the character of Christ, he changes the sub-

---

* Catech. of the Counc. of Trent. Part II., Of the Sacrament of the Eucharist.

† Luke xxii. 19; 1 Cor. xi. 24.

stance of the bread and wine into the substance of His real body and blood. The Holy Sacrifice of the Mass, therefore, is not only a sacrifice of praise and thanksgiving, or a commemoration of the Sacrifice of the Cross; but also a sacrifice of propitiation, by which God is appeased and rendered propitious." *

This is a mysterious and awe-inspiring teaching, even to the pious believer. Nor does the Catholic wonder at the hesitating surprise of our non-Catholic Christian brethren who, having been ruthlessly deprived of the life-giving mysteries of Christ, ignorantly believe that the Mass is a mediæval innovation.

For their instruction, as well as for the information of our own people, we here reproduce from the *Apostolical Constitutions* the ceremonies attending the celebration of the Holy Sacrifice of the Mass as prescribed by the apostles themselves on the occasion of the consecration of a bishop. When we have called attention to the fact that these writings are acknowledged to be, at the very latest, of *the third century of the Christian era;* † that the translation here given is the work of a Protestant clergyman who, with the most learned Protestant authorities, acknowledges the genuineness of the original documents —we have given, even to our non-Catholic friends, the most evident proofs which the most exacting and fastidious critics could demand, for the existence of a Christian priesthood ordained for the purpose of offering sacrifice, and of the divine origin of the Holy Sacrifice of the Mass.

The conclusion is rigorous and self-evident. A ministry which does not offer to Almighty God the Sacrifice

---

*Catech. Counc. of Trent. Part II.

† The learned Bunsen claims that the Seventh Book, from which we are to quote, was written not later than the first half of the second century.

of the Mass is not a genuine ministry, is not the priesthood of Christ. A Christian Church which does not recognize the laying on of hands on men set apart to offer sacrifice, and which does not practise that essential act of Christian worship, the Sacrifice of the Mass, is not the true Church of Jesus Christ.

We shall copy only the main features, textually, however, of this apostolical rite, requesting our readers to compare it with the prayers and ceremonies of the Mass to be found in any modern Catholic prayer-book. Those who wish to read it in its entirety will find it in the *Ante-Nicene Christian Library*, vol. XVII., page 212.* For the facility of reference and comparison we shall divide the text into paragraphs corresponding to the usual way of printing the various parts of the Mass in the missals of the laity.

"*After the prayer* [of consecration of the new bishop] *let one of the bishops elevate the Sacrifice upon the hands of him that is ordained.* . . . .

INTROIT, COLLECTS, EPISTLE, AND GOSPEL.

And after the reading of the Law, the Prophets, and our Epistles, and Acts and the Gospels, *let him that is ordained salute the Church, saying:* The grace of Our Lord Jesus Christ, the love of God and the Father, and the fellowship of the Holy Ghost, be with you all. *And let them answer:* And with thy spirit.

SERMON.

And after these words let him speak to the people the words of exhortation. [Then follows the dismissal, so well known in the early Church, of unbelievers, the instruction and dismissal of the catechumens, energumens,

---

*T. & J. Clark, Edinburgh, 1880.

they that are to be illuminated, and penitents. The bishop then prays and salutes the congregation, saying :]

The peace of God be with you all. *And let the people answer:* And with thy spirit.

OFFERTORY.

Let us stand upright before the Lord with fear and trembling to offer. *When this is done let the deacons bring the gifts to the bishop at the altar; and let the presbyters stand at his right hand, and on his left, as disciples stand before their master.*

Let the high priest, therefore, together with the priests, pray over the oblation, that the Holy Spirit may descend upon it, making the bread the body of Christ and the cup the blood of Christ; * *and prayers being ended, let him put on his shining garment, and stand at the altar, and make the sign of the cross upon his forehead with his hand, and say:*

The grace of Almighty God and the love of Our Lord Jesus Christ, and the fellowship of the Holy Ghost, be with you all.

And let all with one voice say: And with thy spirit.

THE PREFACE.

The high priest: Lift up your mind.
All the people: We lift it up unto the Lord.
The high priest: Let us give thanks to the Lord.
All the people: It is meet and right to do so.
Then let the high priest say: It is very meet and right before all things to sing a hymn to Thee, Who art the true God, Who art before all things, "from Whom the whole family in heaven and earth is named," † Who only art unbegotten, and without beginning, and without a ruler; . . . Who didst bring all things out of nothing

---
* Coptic reading. † Ephes. iii. 15.

into being by Thy only-begotten Son, God the Word, the living Wisdom, "the first-born of every creature, the Angel of Thy great counsel," * and Thy High Priest, but the King and Lord of every intellectual and sensible nature, Who was before all things, by Whom were all things. . . . For all these things, glory be to Thee, O Lord Almighty. Thee do the innumerable hosts of angels, archangels, thrones, dominions, principalities, authorities, and powers, Thine everlasting armies, adore. The cherubim and the six-winged seraphim, . . . together with thousand thousands of archangels, and ten thousand times ten thousand of angels † incessantly, and with constant and loud voices, and let all the people say it with them:

SANCTUS.

Holy, holy, holy, Lord of hosts, heaven and earth are full of His glory: Be Thou blessed for ever. Amen.

And afterwards let the high priest say: For Thou art truly holy, and most holy, the highest and most highly exalted forever. Holy also is Thy only begotten Son, our Lord and God, Jesus Christ. . .

CANON.

He [Jesus Christ] was pleased by Thy good will to become man, Who was man's Creator; to be under the laws, Who was Legislator; to be a sacrifice, Who was an High Priest; to be a sheep, Who was a Shepherd. And He appeased Thee, His God and Father, and reconciled Thee to the world, and freed all men from the wrath to come, and was made of a Virgin, Who was in flesh, being God the Word, the beloved Son, the first-born of the whole creation; . . . and He was made in the womb of a Virgin, Who formed all mankind that are born into the

---

* Col. i. 15; Is. ix. 6.   † Dan. vii. 10.

world; He took flesh, Who was without flesh; He Who was begotten before time, was born in time; He lived holily and taught according to the law; . . . He finished the work which Thou gavest Him to do; . . . He was delivered to Pilate the governor, and He that was the Judge was judged; and He that was the Saviour was condemned; He that was impassible was nailed to the cross; and He Who was by nature immortal died; and He that is the giver of life was buried; . . . He arose from the dead the third day; . . . He was taken up into the heavens, and is sat down on the right hand of Thee, Who art His God and Father.

Being mindful, therefore, of those things that He endured for our sakes, we give Thee thanks, O God Almighty, not in such manner as we ought, but as we are able, and fulfil His constitution.

Consecration.

" For in the same night that He was betrayed, He took bread "* in His holy and undefiled hands, and looking up to Thee, His God and Father, " He broke it, and gave it to His disciples, saying: This is the mystery of the New Covenant; take of it and eat.

This is My Body,

which is broken for many for the remission of sins." †

In like manner also " He took the cup " and mixed it of wine and water, and sanctified it, and delivered it to them, saying: "Drink ye all of this, for

This is My Blood

which is shed for many, for the remission of sins: Do this in remembrance of Me. For as often as ye eat this bread and drink this cup, ye do show forth My death until I come."

* 1 Cor. xi.   † Matt. xxvi.; Mark xiv.; Luke xxii.

After the Elevation.

Being mindful, therefore, of His passion, and death, and resurrection from the dead and return into the heavens, and His future second appearing, wherein He is to come with glory and power to judge the quick and the dead, and to recompense every one according to his works, we offer to Thee, our King and God, according to His constitution, this bread and this cup, giving Thee thanks, through Him, that Thou hast thought us worthy to stand before Thee, and to sacrifice to Thee; and we beseech Thee that Thou wilt mercifully look down upon these gifts which are here set before Thee, Thou God, Who standest in need of none of our offerings. And do Thou accept them, to the honor of Thy Christ, and send down upon this sacrifice Thine Holy Spirit, the witness of the Lord Jesus' sufferings, that He may show this bread to be the body of Thy Christ, and the cup to be the blood of Thy Christ, that those who are partakers thereof may be strengthened for piety, may obtain the remission of their sins, may be delivered from the devil and his deceits, may be filled with the Holy Ghost, may be made worthy of Thy Christ, and may obtain eternal life upon Thy reconciliation to Them, O Lord Almighty. We further pray unto Thee, O Lord, for Thy Holy Church spread from one end of the world to another, which Thou hast purchased with the precious blood of Thy Christ, that Thou wilt preserve it unshaken and free from disturbance until the end of the world, for every episcopate who rightly divides the word of truth . . . ; *and let all the people say:* Amen.

Lord, I am not worthy.

Sanctify our body and soul, and grant us the favor to be "made pure from all filthiness of flesh and spirit,"*

* II Cor. vii. 1.

and may obtain the good things laid up for us; and do not account any of us unworthy, but be Thou our comforter, helper, and protector, through Thy Christ, with Whom glory, praise, and thanksgiving be to Thee and to the Holy Ghost forever. Amen.

And after all have said: Amen, *let the deacon say:* Let us attend.

BEFORE COMMUNION.

And let the bishop speak thus to the people: Holy things for holy persons. *And let the people answer:* There is one that is holy; there is one Lord, one Jesus Christ, blessed forever, to the glory of God the Father. Amen.

"Glory be to God in the highest and on earth peace, good-will among men. Hosanna to the Son of David! Blessed be He that cometh in the name of the Lord," being the Lord God Who appeared to us. "Hosanna in the highest!" *

COMMUNION.

And after that let the bishop partake, then the presbyters and deacons, . . . and all the people in order, with reverence and godly fear. . . . And let the bishop give the oblation, saying: The body of Christ. *And let him that receiveth say:* Amen. *And let the deacon take the cup, and when he gives it say:* The blood of Christ, the cup of life; *and let him that drinketh, say:* Amen.

POST COMMUNION.

And when all have partaken . . . let the deacon say: Now we have received the precious body and the precious blood of Christ, let us give thanks to Him Who has thought us worthy to partake of these His holy mysteries, and let us beseech Him that it may not be to us for condemnation, but for salvation, to the advantage of

* Luke ii. 14; Matt. xxi. 9.

soul and body, to the preservation of piety, to the remission of sins, and to the life of the world to come. . . .

THE BLESSING.

Let the deacon say: Bow down to God through His Christ, and receive the blessing. *And let the bishop add this prayer, and say:* O God Almighty, the true God, . . . be gracious to me and hear me for Thy name's sake, and bless those that bow down their necks unto Thee, and grant them the petitions of their hearts, etc. For to Thee belongs the glory, praise, majesty, worship, and adoration, and to Thy Son Jesus, Thy Christ, our Lord and God and King, and to the Holy Ghost, now and always, forever and ever. Amen.

ITE, MISSA EST.

And the deacon shall say: Depart in peace.

These constitutions concerning this mystical worship, we, the Apostles, so ordain for you, the bishops, presbyters, and deacons.

In this fashion the Apostles Peter and John, James and Andrew, and Paul celebrated the Holy Sacrifice of the Mass, and expressed, in the most forcible and solemn language that man can utter, their belief in the real presence of the Lord Jesus Christ in the Holy Eucharist.

Gentle reader, say with Peter: " Lord, to whom shall we go? Thou alone hast the words of eternal life! "

Believe! And that your prayer and mine, " O Lord! strengthen Thou my faith! " be heard, read the book now thrust into thy hand with a request for a *memento* at the Holy Sacrifice.

✝ CAMILLUS PAUL MAES,
Bishop of Covington.

COVINGTON, KY.,
Feast of Our Lady of Mount Carmel, 1896.

NOTICE.

THE writer of this book, the Rev. Father Martin von Cochem, of the Capuchin Order, is the author of several other erudite and edifying spiritual treatises, both in Latin and German. Not one of these, however, according to the opinion expressed at the time of their publication by his superiors, is equal in learning and in practical usefulness to his Explanation of the Holy Mass, which is compiled from the teaching of the holy Catholic Church, of the early fathers, of contemporary theologians and spiritual writers. It is, moreover, written in an agreeable and impressive manner, and the perusal of it cannot fail to give the reader a better acquaintance with the nature of the Mass, to inflame him with devotion for it, and greatly to increase his desire to lose no opportunity of celebrating the Holy Sacrifice or assisting at it, as the case may be.

Father Martin von Cochem was born at Cochem, on the Moselle, in the year 1625, and died at Waghäusel in 1712. Well-nigh two hundred years have now elapsed since his Explanation of the Holy Mass was first published. God alone knows how much good it has done to countless numbers of the faithful. Now, if at that time a book of this description was greatly wanted to bring Christians back to the true well-spring of grace, the right form of divine worship, the need for it is even more urgent in the present day, since, under existing circumstances, Catholics are exposed to still greater dangers than they then were, both in regard to faith and practice. The holy sacrifice of the Mass is, as Father v. Cochem rightly says, an inexhaustible treasury, whence we all, sinners as well as just, may draw the riches we stand in want of. It is the fount of which we all must drink if we would remain steadfast in the practice of virtue or be purged from our sins. But who can appreciate aright, or make any use of, that of which he knows nothing? Wherefore it is to be desired above all things in our own day to make the inestimable treasures that lie hidden in the holy Mass more widely known; and no better means of doing this can be found than by placing within the reach of all this Explanation of the Holy Mass, by Father Martin von Cochem.

It is sincerely hoped that by the blessing of God this new issue may be for the consolation, edification, and eternal salvation of countless souls.

CONTENTS.

	PAGE
PREFACE	iii
NOTICE	xiii

CHAPTER.
I. THE NATURE OF HOLY MASS	11
The Attacks Made by Heretics upon the Holy Sacrifice of the Mass	19
II. THE EXCELLENCE OF HOLY MASS	25
The Dedication of Churches	26
The Manner of Conferring Holy Orders	33
The Great High Priest of the New Testament	41
The Costliness of the Oblation Made in Holy Mass	48
III. THE MYSTERIES OF HOLY MASS	55
Seventy-seven Graces and Fruits to be Derived from Devout Attendance at Holy Mass	66
IV. IN THE HOLY MASS CHRIST RENEWS HIS INCARNATION	72
V. IN THE HOLY MASS CHRIST RENEWS HIS NATIVITY	81
The Joy Caused in Heaven and the Blessings Brought to Earth by the Renewal of Christ's Nativity	89
VI. IN THE HOLY MASS CHRIST RENEWS HIS LIFE ON EARTH	98
VII. IN THE HOLY MASS CHRIST RENEWS HIS INTERCESSION	105

Chapter		Page
VIII.	In the Holy Mass Christ Renews His Passion....................................	114
	The Reason Why Christ Renews His Passion in Holy Mass................................	122
IX.	In the Holy Mass Christ Renews His Death..	129
X.	In the Holy Mass Christ's Blood-shedding is Renewed...................................	137
	The Manner in which the Blood of Christ is Sprinkled upon Us in Holy Mass............	142
	The Manner in which the Precious Blood Intercedes for Us..............................	147
XI.	Holy Mass is the Most Excellent Burnt-offering....................................	154
XII.	Holy Mass is the Most Sublime Sacrifice of Praise..................................	161
XIII.	Holy Mass is the Noblest Sacrifice of Thanksgiving................................	170
XIV.	Holy Mass is the Most Efficacious Sacrifice of Propitiation........................	176
XV.	Holy Mass is the Most Powerful Sin-offering......................................	186
	The Manner in which Holy Mass Effects the Forgiveness of Sin and the Conversion of Hardened Sinners............................	195
	By Means of Holy Mass Venial Sins are Blotted Out....................................	202
XVI.	The Holy Sacrifice of the Mass is the Most Complete Satisfaction for Sin............	208
	The Amount of Temporal Punishment that can be Cancelled by one Mass..................	212
XVII.	Holy Mass is the Most Sublime Work of the Holy Ghost..............................	218
XVIII.	Holy Mass Affords the Sweetest Joy to the Mother of God and to the Saints..........	226
	Holy Mass is the Sweetest Joy of the Saints....	231
XIX.	Holy Mass is of the Greatest Benefit to the Faithful.............................	235
XX.	Holy Mass Procures for Us an Increase of Grace Here and of Glory Hereafter......	243

CHAPTER		PAGE
	Holy Mass Increases the Celestial Glory which shall be Our Portion	251
	Spiritual Communion	254
XXI.	HOLY MASS IS THE MOST SURE HOPE OF THE DYING	258
XXII.	HOLY MASS IS THE UNFAILING SUCCOR OF THE DEPARTED	269
XXIII.	THE MANNER AND THE MEASURE IN WHICH THE PRIEST AND THE ANGELS PRAY FOR THOSE WHO ARE PRESENT AT HOLY MASS	278
	Whether All Masses are of Equal Value	284
	How the Angels Pray for us during Holy Mass	285
XXIV.	HOLY MASS DOES NOT HINDER OUR WORK, BUT HELPS US WITH IT	289
XXV.	GREAT MERIT IS GAINED BY OFFERING MASS IN A RIGHT MANNER	297
	The Infinite Value of the Victim Offered to God in Holy Mass	303
XXVI.	SOME PRACTICAL HINTS CONCERNING THE WAY OF HEARING SEVERAL MASSES AT ONE AND THE SAME TIME	309
XXVII.	AN EXHORTATION TO HEAR HOLY MASS DAILY	317
	The Example of the Saints is an Incentive to Hear Holy Mass Daily	323
XXVIII.	AN EXHORTATION TO HEAR HOLY MASS DEVOUTLY	330
XXIX.	THE DEVOTIONS TO BE PRACTISED AT THE ELEVATION	339
	What Our Behavior Ought to be after the Consecration	345
XXX.	THE REVERENCE WHEREWITH WE OUGHT TO HEAR HOLY MASS	348
XXXI.	THE CEREMONIES OF HOLY MASS, AND WHAT THEY SIGNIFY	353

APPENDIX.

DEVOTIONS FOR MASS ... 371
    First Method of Hearing Mass: For Those Who Wish to Unite Their Prayers with Those of the Priest.. 371

	PAGE
Second Method: Of which the Principal Mysteries of the Holy Sacrifice Form the Subject	382
Third Method: In Honor of Our Lord's Bitter Passion.	392
Fourth Method: For a Mass Offered on Behalf of the Poor Souls	401
DEVOTIONS FOR CONFESSION	410
Before Confession	410
After Confession	413
DEVOTIONS FOR COMMUNION	416
Before Holy Communion	416
After Holy Communion	418
PRAYERS TO GAIN A PLENARY INDULGENCE	422
1. For the Exaltation of the Catholic Church	422
2. For the Conversion of Unbelievers, Heretics, and Sinners	423
3. For Concord amongst Christian Princes	423
4. An Offering of the Indulgence for the Souls in Purgatory	424

EXPLANATION

OF THE

HOLY SACRIFICE OF THE MASS.

CHAPTER I.

THE NATURE OF HOLY MASS.

THE holy Mass is called in Latin *sacrificium*, a sacrifice, by which word a thing far greater and higher than an offering is signified. A sacrifice, in its full and proper signification, is an offering external to ourselves, made to the most high God, and consecrated or hallowed in a solemn manner by a lawfully appointed and duly qualified minister of the Church, to recognize and testify to the supreme dominion of Almighty God over all creatures. From this definition it will be seen that a sacrifice is much more than a simple offering. It represents a lofty and sublime act of worship, due to the infinite God alone, and not to any creature.

That this solemn sacrifice may be offered to none other but God alone is proved by St. Augustine from the universal custom of all nations. Who, he says, has ever been found to assert that sacrifice should be offered to any one save the true God only, or to such false deities as are wrongfully held to be the true God? And in another place he says: The devil would not require sacrifices from his votaries if he did not know this to be a prerogative of the divinity. Many of the great and powerful ones of the earth have arrogated to themselves other acts of homage which are of right paid to God alone; but few indeed have presumed to command that sacrifice should be offered to them. Those who did this desired to be regarded as gods. Hence it may be seen that the offering of sacrifice is an act of divine worship, which it is not fitting to pay to men, to the saints, or to the angels, but to God alone.

St. Thomas of Aquin says: "It is natural to mankind to make sacrificial offerings to the omnipotent God, and man is incited thereto by a natural instinct without an express command or special injunction. This we see exemplified in the case of Abel, Noe, Abraham, Job, and other patriarchs, who offered sacrifice, not in obedience to the law of God, but to the mere impulse of nature. And not only did those persons who were enlightened by God offer sacrifices to Him: the heathen also, simply following the light of nature, sacrificed to their idols, believing them to be true deities. In later times the law given by God to the children of Israel made it obligatory upon them to offer sacrifice to Him daily; on feasts a more elaborate ceremonial was to be observed. They were to offer to Him lambs, sheep, calves, and oxen; and these animals were not to be offered only, they were to be immolated by an anointed priest, with certain prayers and ceremonies. They were to be slaughtered, flayed, their blood was to be poured round about on the altar, and their flesh burnt upon the altar, amid the blowing of trumpets and chanting of psalms. These were the sacred oblations whereby the Jews were wont to pay to God the homage due to Him, and acknowledge Him to be the supreme Ruler over all creatures.

Inasmuch as the idea of sacrifice is so deeply rooted in human nature that all peoples and nations, besides serving God with prayers, hymns, almsgiving, and works of penance, offered some kind of sacrifice whereby they honored the true God or the false deities they venerated as such, it was meet, nay, it was even necessary, that Christ should institute in His Church a holy and divine oblation as a visible service, whereby the faithful should give to God the glory which is His due, and express their own subjection to Him. No sensible man could imagine that Christ, Who ordained everything in His Church in the most perfect manner, should have omitted this highest act of worship, and left it wanting in so all-important a matter. Were it so, the Christian religion would be inferior to Judaism, for the sacrifices of the Old Testament were so glorious that heathens of distinction came from distant lands to assist at them, and some heathen kings, as we read in Machabees (II. iii. 3), even paid out of their revenues the charges belonging to the ministry.

The holy Catholic Church, in the Œcumenical Council of Trent, teaches us what manner of sacrifice or sacred oblation Christ has given to and ordained in His Church.

"Forasmuch as, under the former Testament, according to the testimony of the apostle Paul, there was no perfection, because of the weakness of the Levitical priesthood (Heb. vii. 11, 18), there was need, God, the Father of mercies, so ordaining, that another priest should rise, according to the order of Melchisedech, Our Lord Jesus Christ, who might consummate and lead to what is perfect as many as were to be sanctified. He, therefore, our God and Lord, though He was about to offer Himself once on the altar of the cross unto God the Father, by means of His death, there to operate an eternal redemption; nevertheless, because that His priesthood was not to be extinguished by His death, in the Last Supper, on the night in which He was betrayed —that He might leave to His own beloved spouse, the Church, a visible sacrifice, such as the nature of man requires, whereby that bloody sacrifice, once to be accomplished on the cross, might be represented, and the memory thereof remain even unto the end of the world, and its salutary virtue be applied to the remission of those sins which we daily commit—declaring Himself constituted a priest forever, according to the order of Melchisedech, He offered up to God the Father His own body and blood under the species of bread and wine; and under the symbols of those same things He delivered His own body and blood to be received by His apostles, whom He then constituted priests of the New Testament: and by those words, 'Do this for a commemoration of Me' (St. Luke xxii. 19), He commanded them and their successors in the priesthood to offer them; even as the Catholic Church has always understood and taught." (Session xxii. ch. 1.)

This, and more besides, holy Church teaches us, and enjoins upon us to believe that in the Last Supper Christ did not only change bread and wine into His body and blood: He also offered them up to God the Father, and thus instituted and ordained in His own person the sacrifice of the new covenant. This He did in order to show Himself to be a priest according to the order of Melchisedech, of whom Holy Scripture thus speaks: "Melchisedech, the King of Salem, brought forth bread and wine, for he was the priest of the most high God, and he blessed Abram." (Gen. xiv. 18.) The text does not here expressly state that Melchisedech offered sacrifice to the most high God; but trom the first the Catholic Church has understood this to be meant, and the fathers have thus expounded it. David himself interprets it thus when he says: "The Lord hath sworn, and He will not repent: Thou art a priest forever according to the order of Melchisedech." (Ps. cix. 4.) That both Christ and Melchisedech offered sacrifice is to be inferred from the words of St. Paul, writing to the Hebrews: "Every high priest is appointed to offer gifts and sacrifices." (Heb. viii. 3.) "Every high priest taken from among men is ordained for men in the things that appertain to God, that he may offer up gifts and sacrifices for sins." (*Ibid.* v. 1.) And almost immediately after he adds: "Neither doth any man take the honor to himself, but he that is called by God, as Aaron was. So Christ did not glorify Himself, that He might be made a high priest, but He that said unto Him: Thou art My Son, this day have I begotten Thee. ... Thou art a priest forever according to the order of Melchisedech." And again: "And being consummated, He became, to all that obey Him, the cause of eternal salvation, called by God a high priest according to the order of Melchisedech. Of whom we have much to say, and hard to be intelligibly uttered; because you are become weak to hear." (*Ibid.* v. 4–6, 9–11.)

From these passages it is evident that, since Christ and Melchisedech were high priests, they both offered oblations to the true God. Melchisedech did not sacrifice victims, as did Abraham and the earlier adorers of the true God, but, acting by the inspiration of the Holy Ghost, and at variance with the custom of the times, he sanctified bread and wine with certain prayers and rites, raising them aloft, and offering them to God as a holy, acceptable offering. Thus he became a type of Jesus Christ, and his offering a type of the bloodless sacrifice of Jesus Christ under the New Testament. Now since Christ was not anointed high priest by God the Father according to the order or manner of Aaron, who slaughtered victims, but according to the order of Melchisedech, who presented bread and wine as an oblation, it follows that He also exercised His priestly functions during His lifetime, and offered to God an oblation of bread and wine.

When, we ask, did Christ exercise His priestly office according to the order of Melchisedech? At the Last Supper, when He took bread, blessed it, and said to His disciples: "Take ye, and eat: This is My body." In like manner, taking the chalice with wine, He blessed it, and gave it to His disciples, saying: "Drink ye all of this, for this is My blood. Do this for a commemoration of Me." (St. Matt. xxvi. 26–28; St. Luke xxii. 19.)

On that occasion, therefore, Christ exercised His priestly office after the manner of Melchisedech. For if He did not do so then He never did so at all throughout His whole life, and in that case He would not have been a priest according to the order of Melchisedech. And yet in what exalted language St. Paul describes His priesthood: "The others indeed. were made priests without an oath, but this with an oath, by Him that said unto Him: The Lord hath sworn, and He will not repent: Thou art a priest forever. . . . But this, for that He continueth forever, hath an everlasting priesthood." (Heb. vii. 20, 21, 24.) Hence we see the truth of what the Catholic Church teaches in the Council of Trent: "In the Last Supper He offered up to God the Father His own body and blood under the species of bread and wine; and commanded His apostles and their successors in the priesthood to offer them under these symbols when He said: Do this for a commemoration of Me; even as the Catholic Church has always understood and taught. And this is indeed that clean oblation which cannot be defiled by any unworthiness or malice of those that offer it, which the Lord foretold by Malachias was to be offered in every place clean to His name." (Session xxii. ch. 1.)

The offering of this clean oblation was predicted by the prophet Malachias in the following words: "I have no pleasure in you, saith the Lord of hosts; and I will not receive a gift of your hand. For from the rising of the sun even to the going down My name is great among the Gentiles, and in every place there is sacrifice, and there is offered to My name a clean offering." (Malach. i. 10, 11.) All the fathers of the Church consider this passage to refer to the sacrifice of the Mass. For this prophecy does not find its fulfilment in the Old Testament, but in the New, wherein are also fulfilled the words which were spoken by God the Father to His Son: "Thou art My Son, this day have I begotten Thee. Ask of Me, and I will give Thee the Gentiles for Thy inheritance." (Ps. ii. 7, 8.) This was accomplished when the heathen were converted to the faith by the preaching of the apostles. The sacrifice here predicted by Malachias cannot be that which was offered by Christ on the cross, as non-Catholics assert; for that was made in one place only, on Calvary, not in every place, as the prophet declares. Nor can the supposition be entertained that the prophecy refers to a sacrifice of praise or of good works, for these are no oblation in the proper sense of the word, nor are they always a clean oblation; as the prophet says: "All our justices are before Thee as a filthy rag." (Is. lxiv. 6.)

This prophecy is consequently to be understood as expressly referring to the holy Mass as the one only and true sacrifice of the New Testament; an oblation in itself perfectly pure and holy, which is offered up to God the Father in all times and in all places by Christ Himself through the instrumentality of His priests. Christ is the chief High Priest, our priests are but His servants, and He makes use of their hands and their lips for the offering of a material sacrifice. It is because Christ in His glorified body is not perceptible to our senses, it being at the same time necessary that there should be a visible victim seen by mortal eyes, that He employs the cooperation of the priest in offering up His sacrifice. This oblation will continue to be offered until the end of the world.

It is alleged against us as a reproach by non-Catholics that the word Mass is not found in the Bible. This is unquestionably true, but the same may be said of the word Trinity, yet we are bound to believe that sacred mystery. We are not commanded by Holy Scripture to sanctify Sunday or to baptize infants, yet we know both one and the other to be our solemn duty. In the writings of the early popes and doctors of the Church we frequently meet with the word Mass; witness the writings of St. Clement, the third successor of St. Peter, and those of Popes Evarist and Alexander, who lived in the first century. St. Augustine, St. Ambrose, St. Chrysostom, and other holy fathers of the Church, make use of the word Mass when speaking of the sacrifice of the New Testament. St. Ambrose writes: "I remained at my post, commenced saying Mass, and during the sacrifice I besought Almighty God to come to our assistance." St. Augustine says: "We see, in the lections which are ordered to be read in the holy Mass," etc. Both these doctors of the Church, who lived three hundred years after Christ, employ the word Mass, which shows that it was certainly in common use at that time.

That the apostles were in the habit of saying Mass we learn from Holy Scripture and the lives of the apostles.

St. Matthew was stabbed at the altar whilst offering the holy sacrifice. Tradition relates of St. Andrew that he said to the judge: "I offer daily to the Almighty God upon the altar not the flesh of oxen or the blood of goats, but the spotless Lamb of God." Liturgies for the Mass composed by the apostles St. James and St. Mark are still extant. The Canon of the Mass is ascribed to St. Peter, and other parts were added by some other holy popes. From all that has been said it follows that Mass was celebrated in the Church from the very beginning, and that it has at all times been regarded as the true sacrifice of the New Testament.

THE ATTACKS MADE BY HERETICS UPON THE HOLY SACRIFICE OF THE MASS.

The persecutions which the evil enemy has stirred up at various times against the most holy sacrifice of the Mass are a proof how sacred a thing it must be, and how obnoxious to the devil; otherwise he would not attack it with such violence. In the first ten centuries of the Christian Church teachers of heresy were indeed not wanting, but none of them ventured to assail the Mass, much less did they attempt to do away with it. The heretic Berengarius of Tours was the first who presumed to speak and write against the holy Mass. His erroneous teaching was exposed and triumphantly refuted by the Catholic theologians of the day; it was, moreover, condemned by the General Council of the Church. Before his death the unhappy man abjured his errors, and ended his days as a repentant son of the Catholic Church.

At the commencement of the twelfth century the impious Albigenses appeared in France; amongst other disgraceful tenets they held marriage to be an unlawful state, and encouraged profligacy. They did, it is true, take no exception to the celebration of solemn High Mass in the presence of a large assembly of people, but they would not tolerate Low Mass, at which but few persons assisted. In fact, they prohibited them, under pain of fines and imprisonment. In connection with these heretics Cesar of Heisterbach, who lived about the same time, relates the following incident:

Although the Albigenses had forbidden priests, under heavy penalties, from saying Low Mass, a certain pious priest would not allow himself to be deterred by so unjust a prohibition from saying Mass privately. When this became known, he was arrested and brought before the council, who said to him: " Information has reached us that, in defiance of our prohibition, you have said a Low Mass, and committed a grave offence; we have therefore caused you to be brought before us, to answer for yourself whether it is so." The priest instantly replied without any sign of fear: " I will answer in the words of the holy apostles, who said, when it was inquired of them before the Jewish Council whether they had violated the law by preaching in the name of Christ, ' We ought to obey God rather than man.' (Acts v. 29.) For this reason, therefore, in spite of your unjust prohibition, I said Mass to the honor of God and of His blessed Mother." The judges, greatly infuriated by this bold reply, condemned the pious priest to have his tongue torn out in the presence of all the people. The priest suffered this cruel sentence with the utmost patience; he went straight to the church, his mouth yet bleeding, and, kneeling humbly before the altar at which he had said Mass, poured out his complaint to the Mother of God. Being unable any longer to speak with his tongue, he raised his heart to her with all the more fervor, entreating her that his tongue might be restored to him. So urgent was his supplication that the blessed Mother of God appeared to him, and with her own hand replaced his tongue in his mouth, saying that it was given back to him for the sake of the honor he had paid to God the Lord and to her by saying Mass, and exhorting him diligently to make use of it in that manner for the future. After returning heartfelt thanks to his benefactress the priest returned to the assembled people, and showed them that his tongue had been given back to him, thus putting to confusion the obstinate heretics, and all who had displayed hostility to the holy Mass.

The words of the blessed Father Cesar, in the preface to the little book whence this story is taken, allow of no doubt as to its truth. "I take God to witness," he says, "that I have inserted nothing in this work but what I have seen with my own eyes, or heard from the lips of men who would sooner die than utter a falsehood." Wherefore this true story ought to convince all who think otherwise that the holy Mass is specially pleasing to the most high God.

From the days of the apostles until the present time the holy sacrifice of the Mass has had no more vehement opponent than the unhappy Martin Luther, who not only attacked but decried this divine mystery. He did not do this of himself, nor when he first apostatized, but at a later period, and at the instigation of the devil. In fact the deluded man himself acknowledges in his writings that his teaching comes from the devil, and only at the suggestion of the evil one has he abolished the Mass as an act of idolatry, although he must have known full well that the devil is the hater of all that is good, and teaches mankind naught but what is evil. Besides, Luther might have considered that if the Mass were idolatrous the devil would not oppose it, much less desire that it should be done away with; on the contrary, he would promote it and praise it, because the more Masses were said the more acts of idolatry would be committed, and greater dishonor done to the most high God.

In this wise Satan has deprived not the Lutherans only, but all the Protestant sects that have arisen after him, of the salutary sacrifice of the holy Mass, and thereby done them an irreparable injury. In fact he has made this sublime mystery so repugnant to them that they declare it to be a denial of the sacrifice of the cross, and an accursed worshipping of idols, as we read in the Heidelberg catechism of the Calvinists. Such horrible profanity is enough to fill every pious heart with dread, and cause every good Christian to stop his ears. We will not devote much time to the refutation of such blasphemies; one argument will suffice to overthrow them.

If these heretical doctrines were true, it would follow as a matter of course that from the time of Christ no single person, not even were he an apostle or a martyr, could have been saved. The holy apostles and all their successors in the priesthood celebrated and offered to the most high God the sacrifice of the Mass; all holy martyrs and confessors heard Mass devoutly, and regarded it as the highest act of divine service. Now, if the holy Mass were idolatrous, and a denial of the one sacrifice of Christ, the holy apostles and all the faithful would have been guilty of idolatry, they would grievously have offended the divine Majesty, and rendered themselves worthy of eternal damnation. And since no person of any sense will credit such an assertion, no one can believe the Calvinistic teaching to be true. Rather than to Calvin and Luther, let us listen to St. Fulgentius when he says: " Hold fast the doctrine, and never permit yourself to doubt, that the only-begotten Son of God became man for us, and for us offered Himself to Almighty God, to Whom the Catholic Church throughout the world now offers in faith and charity unceasingly the oblation of bread and wine." Who is most worthy of our belief—a holy and enlightened teacher of the Church, or two apostates such as Calvin and Luther?

To these latter one may apply the words addressed by the learned Peter of Clugny to some other heretics: " If your teaching were universally accepted, that is, if Christians were to abolish the holy sacrifice of the Mass, that would come to pass in this season of grace which never came to pass in the season of wrath: God would no longer be worshipped upon earth. Therefore, O ye enemies of God, listen when the Church of God tells you that a divine sacrifice is essential to her existence, and that in this sacrifice she offers the body and blood of the Saviour, and that alone; and what He did in His death, that she does whenever this offering is made." Such are the words of the aforesaid father.

Let us therefore beware lest the same thing befall us that befell the unhappy heretics. For the evil one robbed them of the holy Mass to their unspeakable injury; but us Catholics, since he could not succeed in depriving us of it, he blinded in great measure so that we might not fully appreciate the magnitude of this holy sacrifice, and its immense potency. Doubtless it was due to Satan's devices that for a considerable period this divine mystery was so seldom made the subject of sermons, that so little was said or written respecting it, and thus Catholics became careless about hearing Mass, or heard it indevoutly.

As a means of preventing this evil the Council of Trent commanded those who had the care of souls frequently to preach about the holy Mass. The decree is as follows: " The holy synod charges pastors, and all who have the care of souls, that they frequently, during the celebration of Mass, expound, either themselves or by others, some portion of those things which are read at Mass; and that, amongst the rest, they explain some mystery of this most holy sacrifice, especially on the Lord's days and festivals." (Session xxii. ch. 8.) If the people are ignorant of the great value of holy Mass they do not love and esteem it as they ought; they never go to Mass on week-days, and on Sundays and holydays they are too often indifferent, irreverent, superficial; they absent themselves on a mere pretext, and without the slightest scruple of conscience.

But if they understand the vast efficacy and value of the holy Mass, they cannot fail to prize more highly this costly treasure, to love it more deeply, and assist at the divine oblation with greater reverence. There is in the Catholic Church no mystery more important, more consoling, more salutary, than this sublime mystery of the altar. If this truth were recognized aright, we should certainly see a larger attendance at Mass on week-days.

CHAPTER II.

THE EXCELLENCE OF HOLY MASS.

THE holy Mass is of such surpassing excellence that not even one of the highest angels can praise it aright. Let us hear what St. Francis de Sales says of it in his *Introduction to a Devout Life:* "Holy Mass is the sun of all spiritual exercises, the mainspring of devotion, the soul of piety, the fire of divine charity, the abyss of divine mercy, and a precious means whereby God confers upon us His graces." It would take long fully to unfold the meaning of these beautiful words, and explain the glorious epithets of which the saint makes use. What he intends to say is this: Let him who desires to be truly pious and devout be assiduous in his attendance upon holy Mass, for this is the best means of obtaining divine grace.

The learned Father Osorius places the holy Mass before all the other mysteries of religion, for he says: "There is nothing in holy Church so sublime and of such inestimable value as the holy sacrifice of the Mass, for in it the adorable Sacrament of the Altar is consecrated, and offered as a sacred oblation to the most high God." Fornerus, some time Bishop of Bamberg, says the same: "The holy Mass far surpasses in dignity all other holy sacraments and rites of the Church." Again he adds: "The holy sacraments are sublime, but more sublime by far is the holy sacrifice of the Mass. For they are vessels of mercy for the living, whereas it is an inexhaustible ocean of divine bounty for both the living and the dead." See how this writer praises and magnifies the holy sacrifice of the Mass, assigning to it a value far beyond that of the sacraments. We will now consider the reasons why the holy Mass is so superexcellent a thing.

First of all, the great excellence of the holy Mass may be inferred from the prayers and ceremonies appointed for the consecration of churches and altars. Any one who has been present at the dedication of a church, who has followed the prayers and understood the ceremonial made use of by the bishop, cannot fail to have been edified by what he witnessed. For the benefit of those who have never assisted at the consecration of churches and altars the ceremonies connected with it shall be briefly described.

THE DEDICATION OF CHURCHES.

The consecrating bishop, who, together with the congregation, has prepared himself by fasting on the preceding day, sets apart overnight the relics to be used in the consecration. On the morning of the day appointed he betakes himself to the place whither they have been carried, and after vesting pontifically recites with the clergy present the seven penitential psalms and the Litany of the Saints. He then goes in procession with the clergy round the outside of the church, the door of which is closed, sprinkling the upper portion of the walls with holy water in the form of the cross, saying: In the name of the Father ✢, and of the Son ✢, and of the Holy ✢ Ghost—the clergy meanwhile singing a responsory. On coming back to the church-door the bishop says a short prayer, and knocks with his pastoral staff at the door, saying: *Attollite portas, principes, vestras*, etc. ("Lift up your heads, ye princes, and be ye lifted up, ye eternal gates, and the King of glory will enter.") He then goes round the church again, sprinkling the lower part of the walls with the same words; and on returning to the door says a different prayer, and knocks with his staff as before. A third time he goes round the church, this time sprinkling the middle part of the walls; he then knocks three times with his staff at the door, saying: "Be opened!" And upon the door being opened he makes a cross with his staff on the threshold, saying: "Behold the sign of the cross; let the spirits of evil depart!" Entering into the church, he says: "Peace be to this house!"

In the middle of the church the bishop kneels down and intones the hymn *Veni, Creator Spiritus;* this is followed by the Litany of the Saints and the canticle of Zachary: *Benedictus Dominus Deus* ("Blessed be the Lord God of Israel.") While these are being sung he forms a cross with the letters of the Latin and Greek alphabets, which he inscribes with his staff on ashes wherewith the floor of the church has previously been sprinkled; then, kneeling before the high altar, he chants three times the words, *Deus, in adjutorium meum intende,* etc. ("O God, come to my assistance," etc.). Thereupon he blesses with the prescribed form of prayer ashes, salt, water, and wine, mixing them together and signing them repeatedly with the cross, and proceeds to consecrate the high altar and the other altars. Dipping his thumb in the preparation which he has just blessed, he makes a cross in the middle and in the four corners of the altar-stone, saying: "Let this altar be sanctified ✢ to the glory of God, of the Virgin Mary, and all the saints, and in the name and commemoration of St. *N.* [naming the patron of the church], in the name of the ✢ Father," etc. These words are repeated five times. Thereupon he goes round the altar seven times, sprinkling it with holy water and reciting the *Miserere.*

He next goes three times round the interior of the church, sprinkling the walls above, below, and in the middle whilst three psalms and antiphons are sung. He also sprinkles the floor of the church in each of the four corners, with certain prayers and the sign of the cross, and returns to the high altar. He then blesses chalk and sand, and mixes them with holy water, thus preparing the mortar for the laying of the altar-stone. Afterwards, going in procession to the place where the relics were deposited on the previous evening, he incenses them, and carries them with lighted tapers and smoking censers round the church. Pausing on the threshold, the bishop makes three crosses on the door, saying: " In the name of the Father✜, and of the Son✜, and of the Holy✜ Ghost, be thou blessed, sanctified, and consecrated."

When the procession reaches the high altar, the bishop makes five crosses with chrism in the cavity of the altar, called the sepulchre, places the case containing the relics in it, incenses them, and closes the repository or sepulchre with a stone that has been blessed and the mortar prepared for the purpose. Thereupon he incenses the altar itself, and hands the censer to a priest, who goes round it incensing every part. Meanwhile the bishop makes five crosses with oil of catechumens on the table of the altar, one in the centre and one in each of the corners, with the same words employed when blessing the water, incenses the crosses, and goes round the altar incensing it. After the prescribed prayer and psalm have been recited he again anoints the altar, making five crosses upon it, saying: " Let this altar be blessed, sanctified, and consecrated." He then again incenses the crosses and the whole altar. This ceremony is repeated a third time, whilst psalms are chanted by the clergy. Finally, the bishop pours oil and chrism over the whole altar, rubbing it in with his hand. He then goes round the interior of the church, and anoints the twelve crosses upon the walls with the chrism, saying: " Let this church be hallowed and consecrated in the name of the Father, etc.," and incensing each cross three times. Returning to the altar, he blesses the frankincense, lays five grains of incense wherever the five crosses were made, forms five small crosses out of wax tapers and lights them. Whilst they are burning, he kneels down, as do all the clergy present, and intones the hymn *Veni, Sancte Spiritus*. This is followed by more prayers and a preface; the clergy chant Psalm lxvii. in thanksgiving for the graces received; the bishop makes a cross with the chrism below the table of the altar, and recites more and longer prayers. After that he rubs his hands with bread and salt, and washes them in water. The clergy wipe the altar with linen, cover it with an altar-cloth, decorate it as best they can, whilst psalms and responsories are sung. In conclusion the bishop incenses the altar three times, and proceeds to celebrate a solemn pontifical High Mass.

All who have been present at the dedication of a church cannot find words to express their surprise at the number of different ceremonies, anointings, benedictions, and prayers that appertain to the ritual. What is the object of all of these? It is in order to render the church a temple meet for the great and holy sacrifice offered up therein to the most high God, and to hallow and consecrate the altars whereon the spotless Lamb of God is to be slain in a mystical manner.

This is sufficient to convince any Christian of the sanctity of our churches and altars, and the great reverence we ought to pay to them. Solomon's temple was but a foreshadow and type of the Christian Church, and yet in what respect it was held both by Jews and heathen! How much the more should we reverence and respect our churches, hallowed as they are by so solemn a dedication! We read in the Third Book of Kings that Solomon, on the occasion of the dedication of his temple, offered up no less than two and twenty thousand oxen, and a hundred and twenty thousand rams. These animals were all slaughtered by the priests, purified, and laid in pieces on the altar. And while the king prayed aloud fire fell from heaven and consumed the victims. The whole temple was filled with a cloud, and the glory of the Lord appeared in the cloud. And all the people, who beheld the fire and the glory of the Lord, filled with awe, fell upon their faces and adored the Lord. Thereupon King Solomon, standing on a high place in the sight of the assembly of Israel, spread forth his hands towards heaven and said: "Is it then to be thought that God should indeed dwell upon earth? For if heaven and the heavens of heavens cannot contain Thee, how much less this house, which I have built!" (III. Kings viii. 27.)

Who, indeed, can fail to be amazed at this, and feel himself unable rightly to comprehend the dignity of that sacred temple? And yet that temple was but a type, an image, of our churches. In that there was nothing but the Ark of the Covenant, which only contained the two stone tables of the law, a basket of showbread, and Aaron's rod that had blossomed. The sacrifices of the Jews were only animals that were slaughtered and burnt, besides offerings of bread, wine, cakes, etc., whereas our churches are dedicated by the bishops with incomparably greater solemnity; they are anointed with holy oil and chrism; they are blessed by being sprinkled with holy water and incensed with frankincense; they are hallowed repeatedly by the sign of the cross, and consecrated finally by the oblation of the most holy sacrifice of the Mass. Instead of the Ark of the Covenant we have the tabernacle, where the true bread of heaven, the adorable Sacrament of the Altar, the body and blood of Christ, is continually reserved. If it is right to hold Solomon's temple in honor, how much more ought we to reverence our consecrated churches, in which God dwells in person.

Our churches are called the house of God, and this in very deed they are, since God Himself dwells in them, and is always to be found in them. He is surrounded continually by a countless host of angels, who serve Him, who adore Him, who worship Him, who praise Him, who offer our prayers to Him. This was foreshadowed by the vision of the patriarch Jacob. Overtaken by night in the open country, he laid down to sleep, and in a dream he saw a ladder standing upon the earth, the top of which reached to heaven. By this ladder the angels of God were ascending and descending, and at the top of it he beheld God Himself. Jacob woke from his sleep trembling, and said: "How terrible is this place! This is no other but the house of God, and the gate of heaven." (Gen. xxviii. 17.) He took the stone on which his head had rested, poured oil upon it, set it up for an altar, and on his return journey he offered sacrifice upon it to God. That was a type of the Christian Church, with its altar, anointed with holy oil and chrism, of which we can in truth say: "How terrible is this place! This is no other but the house of God, and the gate of heaven," for here the angels ascend and descend, and carry up our petitions to heaven. Our churches are the place of which God speaks by the mouth of the prophet Isaias: "I will bring them [the people of the Lord] into My holy mount, and will make them joyful in My house of prayer. Their holocausts and their victims shall please Me upon My altar; for My house shall be called the house of prayer for all nations." (Is. lvi. 7.)

From all this we learn the sanctity of our churches, and the respect we owe to them. It is because they are the house of God, and Jesus Christ dwells in person within them in the Blessed Sacrament, surrounded by innumerable angels, that we know not how to honor them enough, how to be sufficiently devout and recollected in prayer. If we had a living faith, we should enter a consecrated church with trembling; we should worship Christ present in the Adorable Sacrament with deepest reverence, and invoke the assistance of the holy angels who are there. Such was David's custom, as he tells us in the words: "I will worship towards Thy holy temple; I will sing praise to Thee in the sight of the angels." (Ps. cxxxvii. 2, 1.) Therefore to be inattentive in church, or in any other way to displease God by disrespectful behavior, is an insult to the Divine Majesty and dishonor to the house of God. Let us firmly resolve on entering a church not to utter or listen to an unnecessary word, nor to look about us, but to behave reverently, to pray devoutly, to adore the Lord our God, to confess our sins and implore the divine mercy.

Furthermore, we may learn how excellent a thing is the holy Mass from the solemn ordination of priests and clerics. Every priest must be admitted to seven different grades of orders before he is empowered to offer the holy sacrifice of the Mass. The four minor orders indicate that he who receives them is taken into the service of the Church, and may assist the priest who celebrates Mass. But they do not confer the right so much as to touch the chalice, the paten, the corporal, or the purificator; for this the fifth order, that of the subdiaconate, must be received.

Only the subdeacon, the deacon, and the priest are entitled to handle the sacred vessels employed at the altar, or to cleanse them. It is of great importance that all the things that are required for the celebration of the holy Mass should be kept scrupulously clean and in good condition, as they are used in the highest act of divine service, and are brought into contact with the most sacred body and blood of the Lord. It is greatly to be deplored when proper and clean vestments and vessels are not provided, or when the congregation is backward in supplying the priest with the funds requisite for the purpose.

THE MANNER OF CONFERRING HOLY ORDERS.

The three higher grades are the subdiaconate, the diaconate, and the priesthood. This last is conferred during the celebration of Mass, and in the following manner: The deacon who is to be ordained priest, vested in alb, amice, girdle, and stole, the latter being worn over the left shoulder and fastened on the right side, must present himself before the bishop, who occupies a chair on the top step of the altar, and kneel down at his feet. The bishop, in a lengthy and forcible address, sets before him the heavy duties of the office he is about to take upon himself, concluding with the words: " As oft as thou shalt celebrate the mystery of the Lord's death strive to mortify in thy members all evil desires and concupiscences. Let thy doctrine be a spiritual medicine to the people of God; let the sweet savor of thy life rejoice the Church of Christ, so that by thy teaching and example thou mayst edify the house of God, and that both we, for conferring upon thee so weighty an office, as well as thou thyself, for assuming it, may receive from God, not the sentence of condemnation, but rather the reward of good works, which may God operate in thee by His grace. Amen." The bishop then addresses the people, and asks their testimony to the worthiness of the candidate for this high office. If no one alleges anything against him, the bishop kneels down and recites aloud the Litany of the Saints and other prayers, the deacon, who meanwhile lies prostrate upon his face, responding. Afterwards the bishop lays his hands upon his head, repeating a prayer over him, together with a long preface; he then places the stole round his neck and puts the chasuble over his head. Kneeling down, he pronounces another prayer, and the *Veni, Creator Spiritus*. This ended, he resumes his seat, and the deacon, kneeling before him, lays his hands open upon the bishop's lap. The bishop proceeds to anoint the palms with the chrism in the form of a cross; he then touches each finger and both the hands separately, saying: "Vouchsafe, O Lord, to sanctify and consecrate these hands by this anointing and our benediction." He also makes the sign of the cross over them, with a prayer that whatsoever they bless may be blessed, whatsoever they sanctify may remain sanctified, in the name of Our Lord Jesus Christ. He then binds both the hands of the deacon together with a narrow linen cloth, gives him a chalice to hold containing wine and water, also a paten and (unconsecrated) host, saying: "Receive power to offer sacrifice to God and to celebrate Mass, as well for the living as for the dead, in the name of the Lord. Amen." The hands of the newly-ordained priest are unbound; he washes them, the bishop meanwhile proceeding with the celebration of Mass. At the Offertory he delivers a lighted taper to the bishop, whose hand he kisses. Then, kneeling behind him, and holding a missal, he reads with him word for word the Canon of the Mass, receiving from his hand the sacred host at the time of the Communion. The newly-ordained priest has also to recite the Creed, whereupon the bishop confers on him the power to forgive sins by laying his hands upon his head with the words: "Receive the Holy Ghost; whosesoever sins thou shalt remit they are remitted, and whosesoever sins thou shalt retain they are retained." Finally, he takes the oath of obedience to the bishop and his rightful successors, and the ceremony terminates with the following blessing: "The benediction of God the Father, the Son, and the Holy Ghost, descend on thee; and mayst thou be blessed in the order of the priesthood, and mayst thou offer pleasing victims for the sins and offences of the people to Almighty God, to Whom be praise and glory forever and ever. Amen."

Such is the ritual which must be observed in the ordination of priests in the Roman Catholic Church. If these ceremonies be carefully studied, we cannot fail to admire and prize highly the ancient formulæ appointed by the Church for the devout and solemn administration of the Sacrament of Holy Orders. Wherefore should so elaborate a ceremonial be observed at the ordination of a Catholic priest? For this reason, that he may be sufficiently cleansed, sanctified, and made worthy to offer to the tremendous majesty of God the most pure, most holy, most adorable and divine sacrifice of the holy Mass. Wherefore let us hold priests in honor because of their dignity and the consecration they have received; for Christ has said that those who honor them honor Him, and those who despise them despise Him.

The great excellence of the holy sacrifice may furthermore be seen from the number of things that are requisite if it is to be offered. It is necessary to have: (1) An ordained priest, who stands in the place of Christ. (2) A consecrated altar, which must in every church or chapel occupy an elevated position, because it represents the Mount of Calvary, whereon Christ, the guiltless victim, was immolated and lifted up upon the cross. (3) Sacerdotal vestments, namely: (a) The amice, which the priest passes over his head and places round his neck; this represents the linen cloth wherewith in the house of Caiphas the Jews covered Christ's countenance, bidding Him in mockery: Prophesy to us, who is it that struck Thee? (*b*) The alb, which represents the white garment in which He was arrayed in the house of Herod. (*c*) The linen girdle with which the priest girds himself, and which represents the cord wherewith Christ was bound in the Garden of Olives by the Jews. (*d*) The maniple, which, placed on the priest's left arm, represents the bonds wherewith Christ's hands were tied. (*e*) The stole, which, placed around the neck of the priest and crossed upon his breast, represents the chains laid upon Our Lord after He was sentenced to death. (*f*) The chasuble, which represents the purple robe wherewith the impious soldiery clothed Him in derision at the crowning with thorns. The cross upon the chasuble represents the cross to which Christ was nailed; the pillar, the column at which He was scourged. (4) A consecrated chalice, which represents the grave wherein He was laid, or the bitter chalice of His passion, that He drank to the dregs. (5) A pall to cover the chalice; this represents the stone that closed His tomb. (6) A paten, or small silver plate, representing the vases containing the unguents used to anoint the body of Christ before His burial. (7) A corporal, or square of fine linen, which represents the shroud wrapped about His sacred remains. Furthermore, there is (8) the purificator, a small cloth employed to dry the chalice, representing the other cloths that were used at His interment; (9) the veil of silk to cover the chalice, representing the veil of the temple, rent in two from the top to the bottom at the moment of His death; (10) the two cruets, representing the vessels which contained the wine and the gall given Him to drink upon the cross. Besides these it is necessary to have (11) a host; (12) wine; (13) water; (14) two tapers; (15) two candlesticks; (16) a missal; (17) a stand or cushion, to support the missal; (18) three altar-cloths, to lay upon the altar; (19) a lavabo, or napkin, on which the priest dries his fingers after the washing of hands; (20) a bell; (21) a crucifix, to stand in the middle of the altar; (22) a server, to answer the responses. Almost all the things that have been enumerated are essential to the Mass; so much so that the priest who dispensed with any of them, except in case of absolute necessity, would be guilty of a grave sin. We will give an instance of this:

At the time that the Moors had subjugated the greater part of Spain it happened that a certain King of Caravaca, who held captive a large number of Christians, felt his heart touched with compassion for them. He ordered them to be set at liberty, and bade them all appear in his presence. He then asked each one individually what was his trade or handiwork, and gave him permission to exercise it. Amongst the released prisoners there was a priest, who, when asked that question, replied that his calling was that of one who was empowered to bring down Almighty God Himself from heaven to earth. And when the king expressed the desire that he should give proof of this power he replied that it would be impossible for him to do so unless he had everything that was required by Christians for the celebration of the holy Mass. The king then commanded the priest to make a list of everything that was necessary, and he would see that they were provided. The priest wrote down everything with one exception: he quite forgot the crucifix. He did not notice this omission until everything else had been procured, and he was about to begin the Mass. He was much concerned, and hesitated whether he ought to say Mass without it. The king, perceiving that there was something wrong, thought that he was not quite master of his art, and asked why he was troubled. The priest did not conceal the cause of his vexation, but told the king that he had omitted to mention the crucifix, and did not feel certain whether it would be right to celebrate the Mass without it. While he was earnestly entreating the help of God in this difficulty, behold! the vaulted stone roof of the chamber in which the altar had been raised was cleft asunder, and two angels, shining like the sun and clad in costly raiment, descended from above, bearing a glittering crucifix of wood of considerable size. Placing it upon the altar, they bade the priest commence the Mass. The king and all who were present, filled with awe, fell upon their faces on the ground, nor did they dare rise until the celestial visitants, whom they took to be gods, had vanished. Then they no longer doubted that the priest had power to call down from heaven the omnipotent God, and they readily acknowledged the Christian religion to be the true one. Such was the origin of the holy cross still preserved and regarded with great veneration at Caravaca, in Spain. Every year on the anniversary of the event we have just recorded it is exposed for the veneration of the faithful; many sick persons have been cured by drinking water in which it had been dipped. This true story will serve to prove the great excellence of holy Mass, and how important it is that nothing should be wanting of the articles prescribed for the due and proper celebration of this most holy sacrifice.

The ritual which it is obligatory upon the celebrant to observe also gives evidence to the excellence of the holy sacrifice of the Mass. We will enumerate some of the principal ceremonies: Sixteen times does the priest make the sign of the cross on his own person; six times he turns to the people; eight times he kisses the altar;

eleven times he raises his eyes to heaven; ten times he strikes his breast, and as many times he genuflects; no less than fifty-four times he joins his hands; he bows his head or his whole person thirty times; he makes the sign of the cross over the oblation thirty-one times; sometimes he prays with arms extended, more often with folded hands; nine times he lays his left hand upon the altar; eleven times he places it upon his breast; eight times he raises both hands to heaven; eleven times he prays silently; thirteen times he prays audibly; ten times the chalice is covered and uncovered; twenty times the priest moves to and fro before the altar.

These oft-repeated ceremonies and some hundred and fifty others are enjoined upon the priest who celebrates Mass. In addition the rubrics to be followed are four hundred in number; these the priest who says Mass according to the Roman ordo is bound strictly to observe, under pain of sin. For all this ritual has a mystic meaning, and contributes to the proper and reverent performance of this holy and sublime act. On this account Pope St. Pius V. strictly commanded that, in virtue of holy obedience, all cardinals, archbishops, bishops, prelates, and priests should say Mass in this and no other manner, without diverging in any way from it, either by addition or suppression. If a priest willingly and wittingly alters or omits any of these ceremonies, it is not to be reckoned as a slight carelessness on his part, but as a grievous sin, since it is not merely an offence against the honor and dignity of the highest act of worship, but a violation of the express law of the Church. Each time the priest curtails in any way the ceremonial of the Mass a fresh sin is laid to his charge.

Hence we may learn that the faithful owe no slight debt of gratitude to the priest who is bound to observe such strict rules in offering the holy sacrifice for them.

In virtue of this he earns an eternal reward, but we must not forget that a temporal one is also due to him. The customary offering of money must not be withheld, for, as St. Paul reminds us: "They that serve the altar partake with the altar." (1. Cor. ix. 13.)

And if it be asked why the priest says Mass in Latin, an unknown tongue, instead of in the vernacular, we reply: The holy Mass is not a sermon, it is not intended for the instruction of the people, it is the offering for them of the sacrifice of the New Testament. There are good reasons why this should be done in a language which never can change. Some languages are called dead, others living: the former are no longer in common use, and are consequently unchanged; the latter are the modes of speech of the various peoples, and are subject to constant variation. If the Mass were said in one of the living languages, there would be great risk that as the meaning of words changed the original significance of the formulas would change also, and against this danger the Church must guard. As the integral part of religion cannot be altered, so the language of religion must ever remain the same. The unity of doctrine in the Catholic Church throughout the world is beautifully illustrated by the identity of the language she employs. In whatever part of the globe the Catholic finds himself there the great mystery of the faith he professes is celebrated in the same manner, in the same language. And lest the ordinary Christian should remain in ignorance of the meaning of the Latin prayers of the Mass, holy Church, in her maternal care for her children, provides that in the prayer-books they should be translated into the vulgar tongue of each country. She also enjoins, as we have seen, upon every one who has the care of souls frequently to explain to his flock the meaning of the prayers and ceremonies of the Mass, so that no one may fail fully to understand them.

THE GREAT HIGH PRIEST OF THE NEW TESTAMENT.

From what has been said above some idea may be formed of the exalted dignity of the sacrifice of the Mass. We shall, however, comprehend this more fully when we consider who it is who offers this divine oblation. Who, indeed? Is it a priest, a bishop, a pope, an angel, a saint, or perhaps the blessed Mother of God? Not so; it is none other than the greatest of all priests and bishops, the only-begotten Son of the Eternal Father, Jesus Christ, anointed by the Father a high priest, a priest forever according to the order of Melchisedech. This is what gives to the holy sacrifice of the Mass its immense, its all-surpassing excellence, and renders it in very truth a divine oblation.

St. Chrysostom testifies in the following words to the fact that in the Mass Christ Himself, the great High Priest, offers the holy sacrifice: "The priest is only a minister, for He Who sanctifies and transforms the Victim is Christ Himself, Who at the Last Supper changed the bread into His flesh. That He continues to do now. Therefore, O Christian, when thou seest the priest at the altar, think not that it is he who offers the sacrifice, but believe that it is the hand of Christ, invisible to mortal sight." In these words St. Chrysostom asserts unmistakably that Christ in person performs the great act of sacrifice; that He comes down, that is, from heaven, that He transforms the bread and wine into His own body and blood, that He offers Himself to God the Father for the salvation of the world, and as a faithful intercessor pleads for the welfare of His people. Priests are only His servants: they place at His disposal their lips, their voice, their hands, that through their instrumentality He may offer this divine oblation.

And lest any one should, perhaps, refuse to give credence to what St. Chrysostom says, we will adduce other evidence, which no one will dare question, for it is that of the holy Catholic Church, teaching us by the decrees of the Council of Trent: "The sacrifice of the cross and the sacrifice of the Mass are one and the same; the same now offering by the ministry of priests Who offered Himself on the cross." In these words the Church teaches us, and commands us to believe, that priests are but the ministers of Christ, and that Christ immolates Himself upon the altar in like manner as He immolated Himself when hanging upon the cross. How great an honor, how unspeakable a privilege, how inestimable a benefit, it is for us that our divine Saviour should condescend to become our Priest, our Mediator, our Intercessor, and that He should offer and immolate Himself for us in person to God the Father!

Hear how St. Paul speaks of the greatness and glory of this act: "It was fitting that we should have such a high priest, holy, innocent, undefiled, separated from sinners, and made higher than the heavens: Who needeth not daily, as the other priests, to offer sacrifices first for His own sins, and then for the people's: for this He did once, in offering Himself. For the law maketh men priests, who have infirmity: but the word of the oath, which was since the law, the Son Who is perfected for evermore." (Heb. vii. 26–28).

Such is the glowing language in which the Apostle sets before us the great love of our God for us, in that He appoints not a frail, sinful man to be our priest and mediator, but His one and only Son, perfect in sanctity and purity.

Let us now consider the reasons why Christ did not intrust to any mortal man the offering of that sacrifice which is His own. Principally it was because this oblation must be clean and spotless; witness the prediction of the prophet Malachias: "In every place, saith the Lord, there is offered to My name a clean oblation." Concerning this the Church teaches: "This [the sacrifice of the Mass] is indeed that clean oblation which cannot be defiled by any unworthiness or malice of those that offer it." Now if the earthly priest were in reality the one that offered the sacrifice, it might perchance be impure and defiled, and well might we doubt whether such an oblation would be pleasing to God. Therefore God the Father ordained that His most holy Son should retain for Himself the name and office of a priest; according to His own words: "Thou art a priest forever according to the order of Melchisedech." (Ps. cix. 4.) Hence we see that although the priest says the Mass, he is not in reality the one who offers the sacrifice: he is only the representative of the great High Priest Jesus Christ; and just as if a man were to give his servant a sum of money to be offered for him at some shrine, the fact that the servant whom he thus commissioned was in a state of mortal sin could not in any way diminish the value of the gift, so the priest cannot in any wise render that sacrifice unholy or impure which he offers only in the name of Jesus Christ.

But why, it may be asked, did not Christ commission either an angel or a saint to offer this sacrifice—not even His most pure Mother herself, who is immaculate and full of grace; who could not by any possibility render this oblation impure, but would offer it in a perfect manner?

The reason why Christ did not and could not leave the offering of the most holy sacrifice of the Mass to an angel or a saint, much less to a sinful man, but retained the right to do so Himself, was in order that He might daily present to His heavenly Father for the salvation of mankind an oblation which should be ever the same, and should be offered up in so sublime and all-efficient a manner as to be pleasing and acceptable to the Most Holy Trinity.

Hence it follows that each Mass that is said is an act of such supreme dignity, performed by Christ Himself with such piety, reverence, and love, that neither man nor angel can fully comprehend it. This was revealed to St. Mechtilde by Our Lord Himself in these words: "I alone know, and perfectly understand, what this offering is that I daily make of Myself for the salvation of the faithful; it surpasses the comprehension of cherubim and seraphim, and all the hosts of heaven." O my God, how glorious, potent, and beyond all price must be this sacrifice which Christ makes of Himself in the holy Mass, since the highest celestial intelligences are unable to grasp and comprehend it! O adorable Jesus, how unsearchable is this mystery, since Thy divine wisdom and understanding alone can know and appreciate it! Happy the man who assists at holy Mass, and thereby merits to participate in the sacrifice Thou dost offer up for him, the virtue, the efficacy, of which no created intelligence can fathom!

Let us, then, lay this to heart, and consider well of what great profit it is for us to hear Mass, because in the holy Mass Jesus Christ offers Himself up for us, and places Himself as a mediator between the divine justice and the sins of mankind, and either altogether averts, or at least arrests, the chastisement which is the due penalty of our daily offences. Did we but recognize this aright, how we should love holy Mass, how devoutly we should hear it, how reluctant should we be to allow anything to keep us from it! In fact, we should choose rather to suffer temporal loss than to deprive our soul of the benefit of assisting at this sacred and salutary sacrifice. Such was the fervor of the early Christians that they would rather lose their life than omit Mass. Baronius tells a striking story on this subject. The incident occurred about the year 303.

In the town of Aluta, in Africa, all the Christian churches had been destroyed, and the Christian worship proscribed by the emperor's commands. In spite of this prohibition a number of Christians, both men and women, had assembled in a private dwelling to hear Mass. They were surprised by the pagans, seized, and dragged before the judge on the public market-place. The missal, as well as several other books which were found in the captives' possession, were, amid general derision, thrown into a fire kindled on the market-place; they were, however, not consumed, for before the flames could reach them a shower of rain fell with such extraordinary violence as to extinguish the fire. The judge was so struck by this occurrence that he sent the prisoners, thirty-four men and seventeen women, to Carthage, to appear before the emperor. The Christians went quite cheerfully, beguiling the way with psalms and hymns. When they were brought into the emperor's presence, the officer who conducted them said: "These mischievous Christians were apprehended by us, O emperor, in the town of Aluta, where, in defiance of thy decree, they were worshipping their false gods." The emperor immediately had one of the prisoners stripped, placed on the rack, and his flesh torn with sharp hooks. Thereupon one of the others, Telica by name, said aloud: "Why, O tyrant, dost thou torture one alone? We are all Christians, and we all have heard Mass as well as he." Then the emperor caused this man also to be stripped, and subjected to the same torment. "Whose doing was it that you held this meeting?" he asked. "It was the doing of Saturninus, the priest, and of us all," was the reply; "but remember thou art acting contrary to all justice in torturing us on account of it." "Thou oughtest to have obeyed our mandate, and abandoned the practice of thy false worship," the emperor rejoined. But Telica answered: "I owe obedience to no command that is contrary to the commands of my God, for which I am ready to die." Then the emperor ordered the martyrs to be unbound, and cast into prison without food or drink.

Meanwhile the brother of one of the prisoners, himself a heathen, came forward, and accused a senator of the name of Dativus of having been the means of inducing his sister, whose name was Victoria, to hear Mass. But Victoria spoke up for herself: "It was by no man's persuasion, but of my own free will," she said, "that I went to that house to attend holy Mass; for I am a Christian, and my crime is that I follow the law of Christ." Her brother answered: "You are demented, and speak like a fool." "I am no fool," she replied, "but a Christian." The emperor then asked if she would return home with her brother, but she answered that she recognized those as her true brethren and sisters who suffered for the name of Christ; nor would she abandon them, for she, too, had been present at Mass, and with them had received holy communion. The emperor urged her to save herself by following her brother's counsel, for he wished to spare her, as she was a woman of rare beauty, and a member of one of the first families in the town; but, finding he prevailed nothing, he ordered her to be placed in confinement, and no effort to be spared to induce her to give up her faith. The parents of this maiden had desired her to marry against her will, and rather than submit to this she had sprung out of a high window, and, going to Saturninus, the priest, entreated him to admit her into the number of consecrated virgins.

Finally, the tyrant addressed Saturninus himself, and inquired whether in defiance of the imperial decree he had assembled those people for worship. Saturninus replied: "I assembled them by God's command, for His divine service." "Wherefore didst thou do that?" the emperor asked. "Because it is obligatory upon us to offer the holy sacrifice," the priest answered. And upon the emperor inquiring further whether it was at his instigation and persuasion that the people assembled for this purpose, he acknowledged that it was so, and that he had himself said the Mass. The judge then sentenced him to be stripped, and torn with hooks until his bowels protruded through his flesh; afterwards he was thrown into the dungeon where the other prisoners were confined.

Emericus, another of the captives (who was subsequently canonized), was next led before the emperor. On being asked who he was he said that he was the one who was responsible for this meeting, for it was in his house that the Mass was celebrated; and he had caused it to be done for the sake of his brethren, because they could not be deprived of holy Mass. Thereupon he met with the same fate as the others. Then the emperor, addressing the remaining prisoners, said: "It is to be hoped that you will take warning by the punishment inflicted on your fellow-Christians, and not throw your lives away in like manner." But they all answered as one man: "We are Christians: we are resolved to keep the law of Christ, though it cost us our blood." Singling out one of those before him, Felix by name, the emperor said: "I do not ask thee whether thou art a Christian, but whether thou wert present when the Mass was celebrated." "That question is quite superfluous,"

Felix replied; "a Christian cannot exist without holy Mass, any more than Mass can be celebrated without Christian people. I boldly avow that we met together with pious devotion, and offered our prayers during the time the Mass was being said." At this the tyrant flew into such a rage that he caused the holy martyr to be thrown to the ground and beaten to death.

After all the captives had been most cruelly tortured they were thrust together in one large dungeon, and their jailers were strictly ordered to give them no food whatsoever. Their relatives, hearing this, came to the prison, bringing provisions with them, but the jailers searched them, took everything from them, and ill-treated them into the bargain. The inhuman tyrant never relaxed his barbarity; thus the servants of Christ were left to perish of hunger and thirst in the prison.

This story, which Baronius takes from the ancient records, proves beyond a doubt that in the early Christian Church Mass was said, and that the faithful were present at it. We may also learn from it how great was the devotion which the pious Christians of the first centuries had for holy Mass, so that rather than desist from hearing it they were willing to suffer agonizing torture and the most cruel death. And whence was this fervor? It arose from their appreciation of the sovereign virtue of holy Mass, and their keen desire to share in its fruits. Let their example be a lesson to us, inciting us to hear Mass with greater devotion and more profit to our souls

THE COSTLINESS OF THE OBLATION OFFERED UP IN HOLY MASS.

All that has been said of the excellence of the holy sacrifice of the Mass is inadequate to express the worth of the victim which is offered up to the Most Holy Trinity in the Mass. St. Paul says: "Every high priest is appointed to offer gifts and sacrifices" (Heb. viii. 3); therefore, as Christ has been anointed high priest by His Father, He must of necessity have a victim to sacrifice. The Apostle does not go on to say what Christ has to offer upon the altar; he leaves us to reflect upon it. Let us therefore ask what is the victim which Christ, in His character of high priest, immolates to God the Father.

The victim must be no mean oblation, but one of immense and priceless value; otherwise it would not be worthy to be offered to the infinite Deity. For in proportion to the greatness of him to whom it is presented must be the excellence of the gift that is offered. He who should offer a worthless and contemptible gift for the acceptance of a monarch, far from earning his thanks, would only merit his displeasure. Now we know Almighty God to be the sovereign Lord of heaven and earth, exalted far above all earthly kings and princes. Hear what the Wise Man says of Him: "For the whole world before Thee is as the least grain of the balance, and as a drop of the morning dew, that falleth down upon the earth." (Wis. xi. 23.) If the whole world is only as a drop of dew in God's sight, what can be found in the whole wide world meet to be offered to His majesty? What is there in heaven or on earth that Christ can offer as a worthy and acceptable sacrifice to the Most Holy Trinity except a victim that is divine?

What, then, is it, do you imagine, that Christ offers up to Almighty God in the holy Mass? Listen, and marvel. In all the universe He found but one gift, one alone, meet to be offered up to the infinite Deity, and that was His sacred humanity, holy and immaculate, His adorable body and blood, His most pure soul. Concerning this St. Chrysostom says: "Christ was and is both priest and victim; He is the priest according to the spirit, the victim according to the flesh. He is both the sacrificer and the thing sacrificed." St. Augustine says much the same in his commentary on Ps. xxvi.: "Christ alone was a priest in such wise as to be at the same time the victim; for He sacrificed naught else but Himself"; since all the treasures of heaven and earth could furnish no victim fit to be sacrified to the Most Holy Trinity.

The sacred humanity of Our Lord was the greatest and highest work of divine omnipotence. This the Mother of God revealed to St. Bridget in these explicit words: "Of all things that exist, or that have ever existed, nothing is so estimable and precious as the sacred humanity of Christ." For the bountiful hand of God endowed the human nature of His Son with treasures so rich and so innumerable of grace and virtue, of sanctity and wisdom—in a word, with such perfection, that nothing more or greater could be added to it. And this not because God's power in the bestowal of rare and priceless gifts is limited, but because Christ's human nature was incapable of receiving anything greater. The Mother of God is possessed of a beauty, holiness, and excellence that surpasses our conception, yet in comparison to Christ's sacred humanity she is but as a burning torch to the midday sun. And on account of this supreme excellence Christ's sacred humanity is adored not only by pious mortals, but by the holy angels upon earth; and in heaven it is also the object of unceasing adoration, second only to God Himself, in virtue of the exalted graces and perfections wherewith Christ, as the head of the human race, has invested His human nature in a degree surpassing that of any other creature.

God, in His bounty and liberality, endowed the angels at their creation with great sanctity and other glorious attributes; He has also, out of pure charity, bestowed on many good people and eminent saints from their birth gifts and graces of no ordinary kind; above all, He conferred upon the Blessed Virgin Mary, both at her creation and throughout her life, extraordinary graces, privileges, and perfections in great abundance. But in the sacred humanity of Christ all these gifts and graces meet together, besides other inestimable prerogatives and celestial favors without number, which the Holy Ghost implanted in it at its creation. Hence we may judge how noble, how excellent, how glorious beyond all comprehension is Our Lord's humanity, and what an unfathomable ocean of perfections it contains within itself.

The most holy and exalted humanity of Christ is the precious oblation which the great High Priest, the only-begotten Son of God, daily in every Mass that is said, presents and offers up to the Most Holy Trinity. Nor does He offer this alone; with it He offers all that in this same sacred humanity He did and suffered during three and thirty years, to the greater honor and glory of the ever-blessed Trinity: all His fasts, vigils, prayers, journeyings; all His penances, preachings, mortifications; all the persecutions, calumny, contempt, the outrages to which He was exposed; the pains, the scourging, the crowning with thorns, the wounds, the torture and anguish He endured; His tears, His sweat of blood, the water that flowed from His side, and the crimson tide of His blood. All this Christ places before the Holy Trinity in every Mass that is celebrated, offering it up in no less valid a manner than He did when on earth in His holy life and bitter sufferings.

But the essential value of this sacrifice consists in this, that Christ does not offer up His sacred humanity alone, but in union with His divinity. For although in the holy sacrifice of the Mass it is not the divinity but the humanity of Christ that is offered up to the Holy Trinity, yet the perfection wherewith this oblation is made is owing to the hypostatic union. Through this union the humanity is divinized, enriched with endless treasures of grace, and given a worth beyond all price. Hence we conclude how inestimable is the sacrifice which the Redeemer offers to the most high God in every Mass, since He offers up His sacred humanity in a marvellous and incomprehensible manner.

Finally, we must not fail to observe that Christ does not offer up His humanity glorified as it is in heaven, but in the lowly form under which it is upon the altar. The angels in heaven tremble before the glorified humanity of Jesus Christ, and they are lost in amazement when they behold the abasement of this same humanity upon our altars. Here it lies hidden, imprisoned, as it were, under the species of bread and wine. For so closely do these outward forms surround and conceal the sacred humanity of Our Lord that if they are moved to another place it is removed with them, and as long as the forms continue it remains present beneath them, no mortal power availing to separate it from them. Under so small, so humble, so lowly a form does Christ present Himself to the ever-blessed Trinity, offering Himself up in a manner which inspires all the heavenly host with profound admiration.

What impression can we suppose to be made upon the ever-blessed Trinity by the sight of this humiliation of Christ's glorious humanity? Great honor accrues to the heavenly Father from this extreme abasement on the part of His well-beloved Son. It imparts great virtue to the holy sacrifice of the Mass, for that is the means whereby this divine mystery is accomplished. It is a source of salvation and of vast profit to mankind, for whose sake this most holy sacrifice is offered. It affords no slight solace and refreshment to the suffering souls in purgatory, for whose release Mass is frequently said.

This knowledge may serve to make us appreciate and value more highly the holy sacrifice of the Mass, and assist at it more frequently, with greater joy and deeper devotion. For the Masses offered daily are the weapons of divine grace, the fount of divine mercy, the sacrifice of atonement which is all-powerful, if we assist at it devoutly. On this account our heartfelt thanks are due to our adorable Saviour for having instituted for our sakes this efficacious and salutary sacrifice, wherein He offers Himself up for us daily, nay, hourly, to the Holy Trinity. We ought indeed to thank Him for having given us so powerful a weapon, whereby we may win divine graces, and, as it were, take by storm the citadel of His mercy.

In order to impress more deeply upon our minds the excellence of the holy sacrifice of the Mass let us recollect how Christ Himself consecrated the Chapel of Our Lady in the church at Einsiedeln. It is related in the life of St. Meinrad that eighty years after the death of that pious recluse, at the request of Eberhard, a man of noble lineage, Conrad, Bishop of Constance, came to consecrate the Chapel of St. Meinrad. During the night preceding the day appointed for the ceremony, Conrad, going into the church to pray, heard the voices of the angelic choirs chanting the antiphons and responsories of the ritual for the dedication of churches. On entering the edifice he beheld Christ the Lord in person, clad in sacerdotal vestments, attended by multitudes of saints and angels, performing the ceremony of dedicating the chapel. At this wondrous sight the saintly bishop could hardly believe himself in possession of his senses. Yet he heard and saw distinctly all that went on, and observed that Christ made use of exactly the same formulas and ceremonies which are appointed to be employed by bishops in the consecration of a church, while some of the saints acted as acolytes. The blessed Mother of God, in whose honor the altar and the chapel were consecrated, appeared above the altar resplendent with celestial glory, brighter than the sun, more dazzling than the light. The dedication ended, Our Lord Himself offered the holy sacrifice.

At the conclusion of the Mass all the heavenly company vanished from sight, and the bishop was left alone, entranced with joy and spiritual delight. When he awoke from his rapture, the footsteps which he perceived in the ashes strewn upon the floor, and the walls anointed with chrism, testified to the reality of what he had seen. The next morning the clergy and people assembled, awaiting the commencement of the ceremony. But the bishop declared he could not dedicate the church, as this had already been done by the denizens of heaven. As, however, every one thought he was laboring under a delusion, he was compelled to begin to perform the ceremony, when he was arrested by a voice from on high, which said three times, in the hearing of all present: "Cease, brother, the chapel has been divinely consecrated!" Thereupon St. Conrad desisted from his purpose, and sent a report of the miraculous occurrence to Rome.

This marvellous story bears fresh witness to the sanctity of the holy Mass, since Our Lord Himself condescended to celebrate it. Would that we could have been with Bishop Conrad at that time, and could have witnessed what he witnessed! What would have been our amazement, our delight, our devotion! But at any rate we may rejoice in the knowledge that Christ celebrated Mass in the same manner in which we are accustomed to celebrate it.

CHAPTER III.

THE MYSTERIES OF HOLY MASS.

NOW that I am about to speak of the mysteries of holy Mass, many and exalted as they are, I cannot but exclaim with David, the prophet king: "Come and behold ye the works of the Lord: what wonders He hath done upon earth." (Ps. xlv. 9.) Many indeed are the wonders and signs Christ has done upon earth, but amongst them all He has done nothing greater or more marvellous than the institution of the holy Mass at the Last Supper. It is an epitome, so to speak, of all the wonders God has wrought, and in itself so replete with mysteries that St. Bonaventure does not hesitate to say of it: "The holy Mass is as full of mysteries as the ocean is full of drops, or as the sky is full of stars, and as the courts of heaven are full of angels. For in it so many mysteries are daily performed that I should be at a loss to say whether greater or more lofty wonders have ever been accomplished by divine omnipotence."

This statement does indeed appear strange and almost beyond belief. Can it really be true that the mysteries contained in the holy Mass cannot be numbered? Sanchez agrees with St. Bonaventure on this point, for he says: "In holy Mass we receive treasures so wonderful and so real, gifts so divine and so costly, benefits so many appertaining to this temporal life, hope so certain for the life which is to come, that without faith it would be impossible for us to believe these assertions to be the truth." By these words he means to say that the good things, both for the present and for the future, which we receive through holy Mass surpass our natural powers of belief; and did not God grant to us the gift of supernatural faith, by which we are enabled to believe what we cannot understand, we should never credit the inestimable benefits we derive from holy Mass. The same writer adds: "Just as one may take from the sea or from a river all the water one needs, not only without exhausting it, but even without in the least diminishing its volume, so is it with the holy Mass. So immeasurably great is it that it can suffer no diminution, much less exhaustion of its plenitude." This comparison teaches us that holy Mass is an ocean of grace and glorious mysteries, whence we may daily obtain all manner of good things both for our souls and our bodies.

The following remarkable incident will serve to illustrate what has just been said, and to kindle in the reader greater devotion toward holy Mass. We read in the life of St. John of Facundo, a noted member of the Augustinian Order, that he never on any account omitted saying Mass, and in fact, urged by his great longing to offer the holy sacrifice and receive Our Lord, he said it every morning at the earliest hour possible. He was, however, so slow in celebrating that the server used to go away and leave him at the altar, and at last no one could be got to serve his Mass. The saint then went to the prior, and entreated him to order the brothers to do so. But the prior spoke sharply to him, saying, "Why do you give the brothers so much trouble by being so long over your Mass? I shall rather enjoin upon you henceforth to say Mass like other priests." John did as he was commanded, but obedience cost him so much that he went again to the prior, and, throwing himself at his feet, begged him to withdraw his command. The prior would not consent to do this until John had confided to him, in confession, the reasons which made it impossible for him to say Mass more quickly. Having heard them, he no longer hesitated to tell the brothers that they must serve Father John's Mass, even though their patience was somewhat taxed. Furthermore, the prior, having obtained permission from the saint, communicated his secret to another father, to whom he said: "You may believe me when I say that the reason why our Father John says Mass so slowly is because God reveals to him the profound mysteries that are accomplished in the Mass—mysteries so sublime that no human intelligence is capable of grasping them. The secrets he disclosed to me concerning them were of so tremendous a nature that I was overwhelmed with awe, and almost swooned. It is certain that Christ frequently manifests Himself visibly to this father, speaking with him as one speaks to a friend, and showing him His five sacred wounds, whence proceeds a light of exceeding brightness, which, shed upon the saint, quickens both body and soul, so that he experiences no need of earthly nourishment. He also beholds the body of Christ shining like the sun at noonday, and perceives its infinite beauty and glory. Such are the lofty and divine things he is privileged to know, mysteries which it is not given to man to fathom, much less to utter. Since I have thus been made aware of the immense benefits accruing to mankind by the celebrating or assisting at Mass I have made a firm resolution never to omit saying or hearing Mass, and to do my utmost to induce others to do the same." From these noteworthy words which the prior uttered we see clearly that solemn mysteries are contained in the holy Mass, and we ought to reverence it most profoundly.

But before proceeding to explain these mysteries further I will next show how various types of the Old

Testament are fulfilled and, as it were, renewed in the holy Mass.

The first type of the holy sacrifice of the Mass was the sacrifice of the pious and just Abel, who offered a burnt-offering of the firstlings of his flock to the Lord his God, out of true devotion and as a recognition of his subjection to the Divine Majesty. That this oblation was pleasing to Almighty God we learn from the words of Scripture: "The Lord had respect to Abel, and to his offerings." (Gen. iv. 4.) Or, as it has been otherwise translated: "The Lord kindled Abèl's sacrifice." That is to say, when the pious Abel had laid his oblation, together with the wood, upon the altar, and by his prayers offered it up to God, fire descended from heaven, and consumed the flesh of the lamb that had been slaughtered. So it is in the holy sacrifice of the Mass; when the priest has offered the oblation of bread and wine upon the altar, and pronounced the words of consecration over them, the Holy Ghost, the divine fire, descends from heaven and consumes the oblation of bread and wine, changing it into the true body and blood of Christ. Abel's sacrifice found favor in the sight of God Almighty; the Christian sacrifice is incomparably more pleasing in His eyes. For when the officiating priest elevates the host and offers it up to God, the heavenly Father utters the same words which He spoke at the baptism of Jesus: "This is My beloved Son, in Whom I am well pleased." (St. Matt. iii. 17.)

The second type of the holy sacrifice of the Mass was the sacrifice offered by the patriarch Noe, of which we read in Holy Scripture: "Noe built an altar unto the Lord, and taking of all cattle and fowls that were clean, offered holocausts upon the altar. And the Lord smelled a sweet savor, and said: I will no more curse the earth for the sake of man." (Gen. viii. 20, 21.) Now if

Noe's sacrifice was so acceptable to God that His wrath was appeased, and He promised no more to destroy the earth with a deluge, how much more acceptable to Him will the sacrifice of the priest of the New Testament be, wherein His only Son is offered as a sweet victim.

We find a third type of the holy sacrifice of the Mass in the various sacrifices of the holy patriarch Abraham, who once offered his son Isaac, and of whom it is frequently said in Holy Scripture: " Abraham built also an altar to the Lord, and called upon His name." (Gen. xii. 8.) The same is likewise said of Isaac and Jacob, who were faithful servants of God, and, like all His servants, were wont to offer burnt-offerings and sacrifices unto the Lord of lords. All priests of the New Testament have been imitators of the great patriarchs of old, and have closely followed their example by devoutly offering to the supreme Deity, at different times and in different places, the most acceptable sacrifice of the holy Mass. This practice is continued unto the present day with even greater zeal, since it is now customary for every priest who is truly devout to offer the holy sacrifice to God daily.

The fourth type of the holy Mass was the sacrifice of Melchisedech, the king and high priest, who, when the patriarch Abraham returned victorious from the slaughter of his enemies, as an act of thanksgiving offered to God Almighty a new oblation, consisting of bread and wine, presented with special forms and ceremonies. Melchisedech is pointed out in Holy Scripture as a type of Christ, as was said in the first chapter of this book.

The sacrifice offered by Aaron and all other priests of the Mosaic law formed a fifth type of the holy sacrifice of the Mass. Before the institution of this law, which was given by God Himself, the just men of the Old Testament, guided by the light of nature, had offered holocausts and burnt-offerings to God. In the law of Moses God appointed three kinds of sacrifices to be offered to Him by the whole Jewish nation. These were burnt-offerings, peace-offerings, and sin-offerings. Two lambs without blemish were to be immolated to Him daily in the temple at Jerusalem. These sacrifices of the Jews lasted until the time of Christ, and all clearly foreshadowed the sacrifice of the cross. After the death of Christ they ceased; for the Jewish sacrifices were merged in the Christian, that is, in the holy sacrifice of the Mass.

All these ancient sacrifices, especially the sacrifices of Abel, Abraham, and the high priest Melchisedech, receive special mention in the Mass. After the Consecration the priest says: "We offer unto Thy most excellent majesty the holy bread of eternal life, and the chalice of eternal salvation. Upon which vouchsafe to look with a propitious and serene countenance, and to accept them, as Thou wert graciously pleased to accept the gift of Thy just servant Abel, and the sacrifice of our patriarch Abraham, and that which Thy high priest Melchisedech offered to Thee, a holy sacrifice, an immaculate host." By these words of her liturgy the Church declares with sufficient plainness that the sacrifices of the Old Testament were types of the holy sacrifice of the Mass, and as such were acceptable and pleasing to the most high God.

Some devout Catholics, and many who are not Catholics, take exception at this prayer, and are even scandalized by it, because they consider it to imply that the priest calls upon God graciously to accept his sacrifice in the same manner in which He vouchsafed to accept the sacrifices of Abel, Abraham, and Melchisedech; whereas it cannot be denied that the sacrifice of the Mass, in which the sacred body and blood of Christ are offered to God the Father, is far more pleasing to Him than the animals or the bread and wine offered to Him by the patriarchs of old. It must, however, by no means be overlooked that the priest does not beseech God Almighty to look propitiously upon the victim he is offering, because that which he offers to Him, Jesus Christ, His well-beloved Son, is incomparably more precious in His sight than any created being. All that the priest asks of God is that He will graciously accept this sacrifice, the way and manner in which he offers it, in other words, the devotion with which he celebrates Mass, just as He accepted the worship paid to Him when Abel, Abraham, and Melchisedech offered sacrifices. Thus the point in question is not the worthiness of the victim, for that is beyond dispute, but the devotion of the officiating minister and of the congregation who unite their prayers to his.

In regard to the mysteries of holy Mass, it must above all be borne in mind that the principal mysteries of Our Lord's life and passion are represented and set before us in it. David foretells this when in his prophetic spirit he says: "He hath made a remembrance of His wonderful works, being a merciful and gracious Lord." (Ps. cx. 4). And in order that we may have no doubt that in this passage he refers to the sacrifice of the Mass upon our altars, he says in another psalm: "I will compass Thy altar, O Lord, that I may hear the voice of Thy praise, and tell of all Thy wondrous works." (Ps. xxv. 6, 7.) The same is signified by Christ when, at the institution of the Holy Eucharist, He said to His apostles: "Do this for a commemoration of Me"; just as if He would say: Since the time is now approaching when, after accomplishing the redemption of mankind, I shall leave you and go to My heavenly Father, I institute the holy Mass as the one sacrifice of the New Testament, wherein all the mysteries of My whole life and of My passion are represented, and placed before the eyes of all believers, in order that you may never forget Me, but have Me ever in your remembrance.

We will now prove the truth of these words, and briefly explain how all the mysteries of Christ's life and passion are contained in the Mass. First of all, the adorable mystery of the incarnation is not merely represented, but actually repeated. For just as the Blessed Virgin Mary offered herself to God, body and soul, to be instrumental in the incarnation of the Son of God, and, by the operation of the Holy Ghost, the Word was in her made flesh, so the priest offers to the heavenly Father bread and wine, which, when the words of consecration are uttered, are changed by the power of the Holy Ghost into the true body and blood of Christ. Thus the divine mystery of the incarnation is renewed, and the priest as truly holds Christ in his hands as the Mother of God bore Him in her virginal body. Is not this the greatest and most astounding of miracles?

In like manner the adorable mystery of the birth of Jesus Christ is renewed and clearly placed before us in the holy Mass. For just as Christ derived His human existence from the Blessed Virgin, so in the Mass, at the word of the priest, He again comes upon earth in the garb of humanity, and the celebrant, when the last words of the prayer of consecration have passed his lips, actually holds God made man in his anointed hands. In proof of this, kneeling, he humbly adores his God and his Creator; he reverently elevates Him, displaying Him with joy to the assembled people. Just as the blessed Mother of God showed her new-born infant, wrapped in swaddling-clothes, to the simple shepherds who came to adore Him, so the priest holds up that same infant Christ, not, indeed, wrapped in swaddling-clothes, but concealed under the form of bread, to the sight of the people, that they may see and worship Him as their Lord and their God. And those who do this with heartfelt love and reverence perform a greater act of faith than did the pious shepherds; for they, beholding with their eyes the humanity of Christ, believed in His divinity, whereas we only see the outward forms of bread and wine, and yet firmly believe that both the divinity and humanity of Christ are concealed beneath them.

In holy Mass that same child is also present Who was adored by the three kings, taken by Simeon in his arms, and presented by the blessed Mother of God in the temple to the Eternal Father. We can imitate the example of those holy personages, and offer to Christ acceptable worship, and merit an everlasting reward. Furthermore, we hear Christ proclaiming to us by the mouth of the priest His holy gospel, to the profit and salvation of our souls. As the Mass proceeds we behold Him exercising His miraculous power, transforming wine into His sacred blood, a miracle far greater than that of Cana, where He changed water into wine. Or we see Him, as at the Last Supper, changing the elements of bread and wine into His very flesh and blood. Finally, at the elevation we see Christ lifted up upon the cross; with the ears of our spiritual sense we hear Him interceding for us: "Father, forgive them, for they know not what they do." (St. Luke xxiii. 34.) They know not, that is, how deeply they have outraged Thy divine majesty by their transgressions. We do not, it is true, behold all these things with our bodily eyes, we discern them by the light of supernatural faith, and by this our faith we merit a greater recompense than did those who witnessed them with the organs of the body. This we know on the authority of Our Lord Himself, Who said: "Blessed are they that have not seen and have believed." (St. John xx. 29.) The higher and more incomprehensible are these mysteries the more meritorious is our faith, and the greater will be our reward in heaven. In regard to this Father Sanchez writes: "If Christians did but know how to profit by these things, they might, by hearing one single Mass, acquire a greater store of riches than could be found in all created things."

Furthermore, in holy Mass Christ fulfils that most true and consoling promise which is recorded by the evangelist St. Matthew: "Behold, I am with you all days, even to the consummation of the world." (St. Matt. xxviii. 20.) These words are not to be understood as referring only to His divinity, in virtue of which He is everywhere present, but also to His sacred humanity, in which He dwells among us, present in the Mass and in the adorable Sacrament of the Altar, ready at all times to listen to our prayers, to afford us assistance in our need. It must, moreover, be observed that in the Mass Christ is not merely present in person, as in the adorable Sacrament of the Altar: He is there as our victim, our mediator, as the atonement for our sins. For since Christ exercises in the Mass His sacerdotal functions, by right of His office it belongs to Him, as St. Paul says: "That He may offer up gifts and sacrifices for sins" (Heb. v. 1); that He may, that is, offer up Himself to His heavenly Father for the sins of the people, as He offered Himself up to Him upon the cross.

What are the chief reasons, it may be asked, why Our Saviour will be with us day and night until the consummation of the world?

1. Because He is the head of His Church, and the members of that Church are His spiritual body; and since the body cannot be in heaven with its head, it is fitting that the head should remain on earth with the body.

2. Christ is the bridegroom and the Church is His

bride, to whom He is united far more closely than any earthly spouses can be united; consequently His love impels Him to remain continually with His beloved bride. St. Paul, in his Epistle to the Ephesians, beautifully describes the nature of the love that Christ bears to His spouse: "Husbands, love your wives, as Christ also loved the Church, and delivered Himself up for it, that He might sanctify it, cleansing it by the laver of water in the word of life, that he might present it to Himself a glorious Church, not having spot or wrinkle, or any such thing, but that it should be holy and without blemish." (Eph. v. 25-27.) Through holy Baptism we are made members of the Church, and adorned beautifully as are the angels. The love of Christ for a soul that is pure far exceeds that of any earthly bridegroom for his bride, however fair she may be. And therefore He cannot bear to be separated from her, but declares that He will abide with her until the end of the world. It is, however, in an invisible manner that Christ abides with His Church, His bride. His union with her belongs not to the material, but to the spiritual, order, and is effected by faith, as He tells us in the words of the prophet Osee: "I will betroth thee to Me forever; and I will betroth thee to Me in justice, and judgment, and loving kindness and tender mercies. And I will betroth thee to Me in faith, and thou shalt know that I am the Lord." (Osee ii. 19, 20.) Now, as Christ espouses the Church to Himself in faith, He must needs remain hidden, in order that His bride, that is, the souls of the faithful, may have opportunity for the exercise of faith, and thereby earn a rich reward in heaven.

3. Since Jesus Christ is the bridegroom of the Church, it is fitting that He should guide and govern His spouse, that He should provide for her sustenance, that He should interest Himself in her safety and her welfare.

This, and much more besides, He does in holy Mass and in the sacraments, thereby proving Himself to be a fond and faithful lover, who allows His spouse to lack nothing that is needful for her in time and in eternity.

Remember, O Christian, if thou livest in mortal sin thou art a prey of the devil, a slave of Satan. Whereas if thou art in a state of grace, thou art the spouse of Jesus Christ, beloved by Him, amply provided by Him with all the means that are conducive to thy salvation. How numerous are the graces and benefits this loving bridegroom offers to thee in holy Mass! How numerous the means He places within thy reach of acquiring virtue, of insuring thy salvation! Every time thou hearest Mass in a state of grace, with devout attention and in a spirit of recollection, Our Lord, of His loving kindness, makes thee to participate in no less than seventy-seven graces and fruits. Well mayst thou marvel at this; it is, however, true, as we shall proceed to show. An enumeration of these graces may, perhaps, assist thee to believe in and recognize them.

SEVENTY-SEVEN GRACES AND FRUITS TO BE DERIVED FROM DEVOUT ATTENDANCE AT HOLY MASS.

1. For thy salvation God the Father sends His beloved Son down from heaven.
2. For thy salvation the Holy Spirit changes bread and wine into the true body and blood of Christ.
3. For thy sake the Son of God comes down from heaven and conceals Himself under the form of the sacred host.
4. He even abases Himself to such an extent as to be present in the minutest particle of the sacred host.
5. For thy salvation He renews the saving mystery of the incarnation.

6. For thy salvation He is born anew into the world in a mystic manner whenever holy Mass is celebrated.

7. For thy salvation he performs upon the altar the same acts of worship that He performed when on earth.

8. For thy salvation He renews His bitter passion in order that thou mayst participate in it.

9. For thy salvation He mystically renews His death, and sacrifices for thee His precious life.

10. For thy salvation He sheds His blood in a mystic manner, and offers it up for thee to the Divine Majesty.

11. With this precious blood He sprinkles thy soul, and purifies it from every stain.

12. For thee Christ offers Himself as a true burnt-offering, and renders to the Godhead the supreme honor which is its due.

13. By offering this act of worship to God thou dost make reparation for the glory which thou hast failed to give Him.

14. For thee Christ offers Himself to God as a sacrifice of praise, thus atoning for thy omissions in praising His holy name.

15. By offering to God this oblation which Christ offers thou givest Him greater praise than do the holy angels.

16. For thee Christ offers Himself as a perfect sacrifice of thanksgiving, making compensation for all failures on thy part to render thanks.

17. By offering to God Christ's act of thanksgiving thou dost make ample acknowledgment of all the benefits He has bestowed on thee.

18. For thee Christ offers Himself as the all-powerful victim, reconciling thee to the God Whom thou hast offended.

19. He pardons thee all thy venial sins, provided thou art firmly resolved to forsake them.

20. He also makes reparation for many of thy sins of omission, when thou didst leave undone the good thou mightest have done.

21. He removes many of the imperfections attaching to thy good deeds.

22. He forgives thee the sins, unknown or forgotten, which thou hast never mentioned in confession.

23. He offers Himself as a victim to make satisfaction for a part at least of thy debts and transgressions.

24. Each time thou hearest Mass thou canst do more to pay the penalty due to thy sins than by the severest work of penance.

25. Christ places to thy credit a portion of His merits, which thou mayst offer to God the Father in expiation of thy offences.

26. For thee Christ offers Himself as the most efficacious peace-offering, interceding for thee as earnestly as He interceded for His enemies on the cross.

27. His precious blood pleads for thee in words as countless as the drops which issued from His sacred veins.

28. Each of the adorable wounds His sacred body bore is a voice calling aloud for mercy for thee.

29. For the sake of this propitiatory victim the petitions proffered during Mass will be granted far sooner than those that are proffered at other times.

30. Never canst thou pray so well as whilst present at Mass.

31. This is so because Christ unites His prayers to thine, and offers them to His heavenly Father.

32. He acquaints Him with thy needs and the dangers to which thou art exposed, and makes thy eternal salvation His particular concern.

33. The angels also, who are present, plead for thee, and present thy poor prayers before the throne of God.

34. On thy behalf the priest says Mass, by virtue of which the evil enemy will not be suffered to approach thee.

35. For thee and for thy everlasting salvation he says Mass, and offers that holy sacrifice to God Almighty.

36. When thou hearest Mass, thou art thyself in spirit a priest, empowered by Christ to offer the Mass both for thyself and others.

37. By offering this holy sacrifice thou dost present to the Blessed Trinity the most acceptable of all oblations.

38. Thou dost offer an oblation precious indeed, of greater value than all things in heaven and earth.

39. Thou dost offer an oblation precious indeed, for it is none other than God Himself.

40. By this sacrifice thou dost honor God as He alone is worthy to be honored.

41. By this sacrifice thou dost give infinite satisfaction to the Most Holy Trinity.

42. Thou mayst present this glorious oblation as thine own gift, for Christ Himself gave it unto thee.

43. When thou hearest Mass aright, thou dost perform an act of highest worship.

44. By hearing Mass thou dost pay the most profound reverence, the most loyal homage, to the sacred humanity of Our Lord.

45. It is the best means whereby to venerate the passion of Christ, and obtain a share in its fruits.

46. It is also the best means of venerating the blessed Mother of God, and increasing her joy.

47. By hearing Mass thou canst give greater honor to the angels and saints than by reciting many prayers.

48. By hearing Mass devoutly thou canst also enrich thy soul more than by aught else in the world.

49. For in this act thou dost perform a good work of the highest value.

50. It is a signal exercise of pure faith, which will receive a great reward.

51. When thou dost bow down before the sacred host and the sacred chalice, thou dost perform a supreme act of adoration.

52. For each time that thou dost gaze reverently upon the sacred host thou wilt receive a recompense in heaven.

53. Each time thou dost smite thy breast with compunction some of thy sins are remitted to thee.

54. If thou hearest Mass in a state of mortal sin, God offers thee the grace of conversion.

55. If thou hearest Mass in a state of grace, God gives thee an augmentation of grace.

56. In holy Mass thou dost spiritually eat the flesh of Christ, and drink His blood.

57. Thou art privileged to behold with thine eyes Christ hidden under the sacramental veil, and to be beheld by Him.

58. Thou dost receive the priest's benediction, which is confirmed by Christ in heaven.

59. Through thy diligence in hearing Mass thou wilt also obtain corporal and temporal blessings.

60. Furthermore, thou wilt be preserved from many misfortunes that would otherwise befall thee.

61. Thou wilt also be strengthened against temptations which would otherwise have vanquished thee.

62. Holy Mass will also be to thee a means of obtaining the grace of a holy death.

63. The love thou hast shown for holy Mass will secure for thee the special succor of angels and saints in thy last moments.

64. The remembrance of the Masses heard in thy lifetime will be a sweet solace to thee in the hour of death, and inspire thee with confidence in the divine mercy.

65. They will not be forgotten when thou dost stand before the strict Judge, and will incline Him to show thee favor.

66. Thou needest not fear a long and terrible purgatory if thou hast already to a great extent atoned for thy sins by frequently assisting at holy Mass.

67. One Mass devoutly heard will do more to mitigate the pains of purgatory than any act of penance, however difficult of performance.

68. One Mass in thy lifetime will be of greater service to thee than many said for thee after death.

69. Thou wilt attain a high place in heaven, which will be thine to all eternity.

70. Thy felicity in heaven will, moreover, be increased by every Mass thou hearest on earth.

71. No prayers offered for thy friends will be as efficacious as a single Mass heard and offered on their behalf.

72. Thou canst amply recompense all thy benefactors by hearing Mass for their intention.

73. The best help, the greatest consolation, thou canst afford the afflicted, the sick, the dying, is to hear Mass for them.

74. By this same means thou canst even obtain for sinners the grace of conversion.

75. Thou canst also earn for all faithful Christians saving and salutary graces.

76. For the suffering souls in purgatory thou canst procure abundant refreshment.

77. And if it is not within thy power to have Mass said for thy departed friends thou canst by devout assistance at the holy sacrifice release them from the tormenting flames.

What dost thou now think of holy Mass, O Christian? Can it be supposed that in the whole world there is any other good work whereby so many graces and fruits are placed within our reach? It is no longer possible to question the truth of the words of Father Sanchez quoted above: "If Christians only knew how to profit by holy Mass, they might acquire greater riches than are to be found in all the things God has created." We have indeed a precious storehouse in the Mass: happy he who can earn treasures so great at the cost of so little labor! Who would willingly miss Mass? Who would not delight in hearing it? Let us resolve never to lose an opportunity of hearing Mass, provided the duties of our state of life do not prevent us from doing so.

To omit hearing Mass daily merely from carelessness or indolence would be a proof that we were either ignorant of, or indifferent to, the divine treasures it contains. God grant that those who read this book may in future appreciate more fully this pearl of great price, value it more highly, seek it more diligently!

CHAPTER IV.

IN THE HOLY MASS CHRIST RENEWS HIS INCARNATION.

IN the preceding chapter the mysteries of holy Mass were but slightly touched upon; we will now take each in turn, examining it more closely and explaining it more fully.

The sublime mystery of the incarnation is the first to claim our attention. I will begin by adducing the testimony of the learned and pious Marchantius to prove that every time Mass is said the incarnation of the Son of God is renewed. He writes: "What is the Mass if not a forcible and complete representation, nay, renewal, of the incarnation, the birth, the life, the sufferings, and the death of Christ, and the redemption that He wrought?" With this statement, wonderful as it is, and almost past our comprehension, some persons will perhaps not agree. In order, therefore, to prove beyond doubt that it is true we will proceed to show, in this chapter, after what manner Christ becomes incarnate anew whenever holy Mass is celebrated.

We know how great, how vast, how inexpressible was the benefit God in His loving kindness bestowed on mankind when the Eternal Word, for the sake of man and of his salvation, came down from heaven, by the operation of the Holy Ghost became incarnate in the womb of the Virgin Mary, and took upon Himself our human nature. This incomprehensible mystery it is which the priest adores when, in the Creed, at the words: *Et incarnatus est* (" He was made man "), he does not merely bow his head: he bends his knee in reverent awe, returning thanks to the Giver of all good for vouchsafing thus deeply to abase Himself.

Holy Church in her wisdom has ordained that every year, throughout the season of Advent, all the faithful should meditate upon this infinite benefit, devoutly adore the mystery of the incarnation, and render thanks to God for His goodness, as is indeed our bounden duty. For in thus becoming incarnate Christ won for us such great graces, in His human body He did and suffered so much for us, that eternity will not be long enough to render Him the thanks that are His due.

But, marvel of marvels, Christ did not content Himself with merely becoming man once for all. In order daily and hourly to renew and increase the satisfaction which His Eternal Father and the Holy Ghost have, before all time, derived from the contemplation of this mystery, in the fulness of His divine wisdom He devised and instituted the sublime mystery of the Mass, in which His incarnation is renewed as definitely as if in reality it again took place; nay, it does actually take place again, although in a mystic manner. For this we have the authority of the Catholic Church, for in the secret prayers for the ninth Sunday after Pentecost we read: "As often as the remembrance of this victim is celebrated, so often is the work of our redemption carried on." The words are not: So often is the work of our redemption represented, but, So often is the work of our redemption carried on. And what is this work of our redemption but the incarnation, the birth, the passion, and the death of Jesus Christ? all of which are in reality accomplished and renewed every time the Mass is celebrated.

To this St. Augustine also bears testimony. "How great the dignity of a priest," he says, "in whose hands Christ again becomes man! O celestial mystery, wrought in so marvellous a manner by God the Father and by the Holy Ghost through the instrumentality of the priest!" St. John Damascene says: "If I am asked how bread is changed into the body of Christ, I answer: The Holy Ghost overshadows the priest, and operates that in the elements which He effected in the womb of the Virgin Mary." Again, we find the same clearly stated by St. Bonaventure in these words: "God appears to do no less a thing when He deigns daily to descend from heaven upon our altars than He did when He came down from heaven and took upon Himself our human nature." These remarkable words of the seraphic doctor, the meaning of which it is impossible to mistake, warrant us in asserting that Christ performs as great a miracle in every Mass that is celebrated as He did when He became man, more than 1800 years ago.

This is confirmed by the Ven. Alanus de Rupe, who

puts the following words into the mouth of the Saviour: "As I once became man at the sound of the angelic salutation, so in each Mass I again become man after a sacramental manner." That is, as the Divine Word became flesh through the overshadowing of the Holy Ghost when the *Ave Maria* was spoken, so the same Divine Word, when the words of consecration are uttered, becomes man in the hands of the priest, in a different manner, it is true, but through the self-same divine power.

Here we may well exclaim with St. Augustine: "How great is the dignity of a priest, in whose hands God again becomes man!" How great, we may add, is the dignity of the Catholic, for whose salvation Christ Jesus daily in holy Mass again becomes man in a mystic manner! This enables us to understand what Holy Scripture says: "God so loved the world as to give His only-begotten Son." (St. John iii. 16.) O sweet consolation for us miserable mortals to know that the love of our God for us is so great that every day He comes down from heaven again, and again becomes incarnate for our sake! How we ought to rejoice in the solace thus afforded us!

In the *Imitation* we find the following passage: "As often as thou sayest or hearest Mass it ought to seem to thee as great, as new, and as delightful as if Christ, that same day first descending into the womb of the Virgin, had been made man." (Bk. iv. ch. 2.) What inexpressible comfort it would afford us if Christ now for the first time became man, if we heard that the divine Child would be born of His holy Mother! Who but would hasten with joy to worship the Christ, to implore of Him grace and mercy? Then why, since He becomes man in a mystic manner upon our altars, do we not hasten no less gladly to hear Mass, implore no less earnestly His mercy and pardon? It is because we have no living faith, and consequently no true appreciation of this great gift of God.

We will now consider in what wise Christ renews His incarnation, and what are the wonders He works in this act. Our religion teaches us that when the priest holds the host in his hands previous to the consecration he holds nothing but a piece of bread; but as soon as he pronounces the words of consecration, at that same moment the host is changed by divine power into the true body of Christ. And since without blood the body cannot live, so the blood of Christ is also present in His sacred body. Thus in the place of the bread which a moment before the priest held in his hands he now holds Jesus Christ, the Son of the most high God. This is indeed a mystery exceeding great, a miracle beyond all understanding, in which not one alone but many and great ones are contained.

Is it not a wonder beyond all wonders that bread can become the real body of Jesus Christ, and wine His true blood? Is it not a wonder beyond wonders that although the bread and the wine are no longer present, the outward forms of both bread and wine remain? They retain the shape, the color, the taste they possessed before the consecration. Is it not a wonder beyond all wonders that these outward forms, or accidents, remain, independent of all else, and preserved only by supernatural means? It is no less a miracle than if all the walls of a house were to fall away, and the roof to re- remain suspended in the air without any support. Is it not a wonder beyond all wonders that Christ can reduce His human body into so small a compass as to be contained within a little host, nay, within the most minute particle of one?

All these and many other great miracles which will not be enumerated here are wrought by Christ in every

Mass at the moment of the consecration for our salvation. The benefits He thereby confers upon us are immeasurably vast. This was made known to St. Gertrude, as we read in her revelations. On one occasion when she was hearing Mass, just before the consecration, bowing down to the ground, she said to Our Lord: "O sweet Jesus, the work which Thou art about to accomplish is so inestimable, so surpassingly sacred and sublime, that one so abject and lowly as I am may not dare to look upon it. I will, therefore, take refuge in the lowest depths of humility, and there await my share of the salvation which this mystery is to bring to all Thy elect." Thereupon Our Lord answered her: "If thou wert to direct all thy hardest labors and toils in My service to this end, namely, that this sacrifice, which is profitable for all Christians, whether living or dead, may have an effect proportionate to its great dignity, thou wouldst greatly assist Me in the work that I have to accomplish."

In like manner we should consider, before the consecration, how extraordinary a miracle God works upon the altar for our salvation, and awaken within our hearts a lively desire that by our cooperation the sacrifice at which we are assisting may be for the greater glory of God, and for the good of the faithful. To this end we may pray in the words of St. Gertrude:

"O sweet Jesus, the work which Thou art about to accomplish is so sublime that one so lowly and abject as I am may not dare to look upon it. I will therefore take refuge in the abyss of my own nothingness, and will there await my share of the salvation which this mystery is about to bring to all Thy elect. Would to God, O sweet Jesus, that I could cooperate in this glorious work! How gladly would I spend all my strength and endure the heaviest toils in order that this sacrifice, which is offered for all Christians both living and dead, may be productive of results proportionate to its great dignity. I beseech Thee to grant Thy grace to all who say or who hear Mass, that they may offer the most holy sacrifice to Thy greater glory and for the benefit of all the faithful. Amen."

We will now proceed to consider how vast is the authority conferred by Christ, not upon angels, but upon men, when He empowers the priest to perform the greatest of miracles with a few short words, to change the bread and wine into His sacred body and blood. Concerning this the Ven. Alanus de Rupe says: "So great is the power of God the Father that He could call the heavens and the earth into being out of nothing; so great is the power of the priest that he can call down the Son of God Himself to be a sacrifice and a sacrament, and can dispense to mankind by means of this sacrifice and this sacrament the treasures the Saviour won for them. Herein consists to a great extent the majesty of God, the joy of His blessed Mother; this forms the felicity of the blessed, the surest help of the living, the chief solace of the souls in purgatory."

Wonderful and admirable indeed is the mighty power of the words of consecration, the renewal of Christ's incarnation in the hands of the priest! Rejoice, moreover, and exult that we are privileged, in the holy sacrifice of the Mass, as we know on the authority of Christ Himself, to magnify our heavenly Father, to cause great joy to our blessed Lady and all the saints in glory. Holy Mass is, besides, the best help of the living, the sweetest consolation of the departed.

Here, again, we may exclaim: "God so loved the world as to give His only-begotten Son, that whosoever believeth in Him may not perish, but may have life everlasting." (St. John iii. 16.) God first manifested this unspeakable love to the world when He sent His Son from heaven to take upon Himself the nature of man. He now daily manifests anew this same love by sending His Son from heaven again to become man in the Mass. And as His first incarnation caused joy in heaven and brought salvation to earth, so is it with His daily incarnation upon the altar. By His first incarnation Christ earned treasures inestimable of divine grace: by the renewal of that incarnation He distributes those celestial riches to all those who say or hear Mass devoutly. The following example will illustrate this:

It is recorded in the annals of the Franciscan Order that blessed John of Alvernio was accustomed to say Mass with extraordinary devotion, so much so that he often experienced an ineffable sweetness almost too great for his frail powers to endure. On one occasion, when he had to sing the High Mass on the feast of the Assumption, no sooner had he begun the Mass than his soul was flooded with bliss so rapturous that he feared he should be unable to finish the function. It was as he anticipated. For when he got to the consecration, and the exceeding greatness of the love of Christ was borne in upon him, which impelled Him to come down from heaven to assume human nature, and which still continually impels Him to renew the same act in holy Mass, the heart of the good priest melted within him, his strength forsook him, and he was unable to finish the prayer of consecration. The father guardian, perceiving this, hastened to the altar with another father to assist him to finish the consecration. The other monks and the rest of the congregation were much alarmed, for they thought the priest had suddenly been taken ill. At length, putting a great force upon himself, he finished the words of consecration. And behold! the host he held in his hands was changed into the form of a smiling infant, and blessed John saw the divine Child as a newly-born babe resting in his priestly hands. At that moment so keen an appreciation was given him of the profound humility of Our Lord in becoming man for us, and daily renewing His incarnation, that this knowledge was too much for him, his forces gave way, and he would have fallen had not the father guardian and some of his brethren supported him in their arms. Nevertheless he contrived to proceed with the Mass until the communion. But when he received the consecrated elements he became completely unconscious, and had to be carried into the sacristy, where for some hours he lay like one dead. In fact the people already began to lament and bewail his loss. When he came to himself again, his brethren entreated him for the love of God to tell them what had happened thus to overwhelm him at the altar. Unable to resist their importunity, he answered: "When, immediately before the consecration, I thought upon the love of Christ, which once in time past induced Him to become man, and induces Him daily to become anew incarnate in holy Mass, I felt my heart melt like wax, and my limbs lose their power, so that I could not stand upright, or pronounce the words of the prayer. And when, by a great effort, I uttered them I saw in my hands no longer the sacred host, but a lovely child, the very sight of which pierced my soul and consumed my bodily strength, so that I swooned away, and fell into a sweet ecstasy of love." This is what the father related to his pious hearers, to make known to them the unfathomable love of Our Lord to us poor sinners, since for us, and for our salvation, He daily renews the mystery of His incarnation, and imparts to us the fruits of that mystery in abundant measure.

From this incident it may be seen what joy comes down from heaven to earth when the source of all celestial felicity vouchsafes to descend upon our altars. Many a time have saintly souls tasted this bliss, and we too might have been privileged to taste it had we assisted at Mass with more devout recollection, more lively faith. We may also learn of what great profit to us is this renewal of Christ's incarnation, since those who hear Mass are made partakers in the merits of His first incarnation. By this profound abasement of Himself He appeases the just anger of God, and averts the chastisement we deserve so well. We cannot thank Him enough for all the benefits He bestows on us; especially for this, that He has instituted holy Mass for our sake, and renewed in it not His incarnation alone, but also all the mysteries of His life and death. We can show Him our gratitude in no better way than by devoutly hearing Mass every day, or at least as often as we can, and offering it to the Most Holy Trinity in thanksgiving for the mercies we have received.

CHAPTER V.

IN THE HOLY MASS CHRIST RENEWS HIS NATIVITY.

"IN that day the mountains shall drop down sweetness, and the hills shall flow with milk." (Joel iii. 18.) Thus the holy Church throughout the world speaks of the sweet mystery of Our Saviour's birth. And, indeed, on that day of days, when the only-begotten Son of God, clothed in human flesh, was born into this world, it may truly be said that the mountains dropped down sweetness, and the hills flowed with milk and honey. For He Who is sweeter far than milk and honey, Who is Himself the plentiful source of all sweetness, by His entrance into the world made all things sweet; He brought true joy from heaven, He brought peace to men of good will; He brought comfort to the afflicted, to the world the dawn of a new and brighter day.

Oh, how great was the joy of the heavenly Father in that night when He beheld His well-beloved Son, begotten from all eternity, born of the pure Virgin, whom He vouchsafed to call by the endearing name of daughter! How great the gladness of the Son of God when He beheld Himself clad in the vesture of our humanity, possessing now not only a Father in heaven, but a Mother on earth besides! How great the satisfaction of the Holy Spirit on beholding Him Whom He had united to the Father from all eternity in the closest bond of a perfect love now by His operation joined so intimately to human nature that the two natures, so infinitely distinct and diverse, were united together in the one person of the God-Man! How great the sweetness which filled the soul of the Blessed Virgin when, gazing on her new-born babe, she told herself that the infant she held in her arms was not her Son alone, but also the Son of the Eternal Father, the most high God!

How great, moreover, was the happiness of those who were privileged to look upon the fairest of all the children of men, and to hold Him in their embrace! We read in the life of St. Joseph of Cupertino that it was revealed to him that, after the return of the three kings to their own country, crowds of pilgrims flocked from all parts of the land to Bethlehem to see the newly-born King of the Jews, to feast their eyes on His wondrous beauty. He adds that they entreated the Mother of Jesus to permit them to take the lovely infant in their arms, and press Him to their heart. This our blessed Lady graciously allowed them to do, noticing to her astonishment that the gentle Child lovingly caressed the good, whilst He held Himself aloof from the evil.

Although we rightly count those privileged persons happy, yet it must not be forgotten that we are even more privileged than they, since we may daily gaze with the eye of faith on that tender infant, and may share in the gladness attending His birth. Listen to the words of Pope Leo I.: "Our minds enlightened and our love enkindled by the record of the evangelists and the utterances of the prophets, we do not seem to regard the birth of Christ as an event of the past, but as one present to our sight. For we hear proclaimed to us what the angel announced to the shepherds: 'Behold, I bring you tidings of great joy; this day is born to you a Saviour.' Every day we may be present at this happy birth, every day our eyes may behold it, if we will but go to Mass. For then it is in very deed renewed, and by it the work of our salvation is carried on."

The same is told us in the revelations of the Abbess Hildegard: "At the moment when, in the Mass, the bread and wine are changed into the body and blood of Christ the circumstances of His incarnation and birth are mirrored before us as clearly as when these mysteries were accomplished by the Son of God when He was on earth." This testimony has been confirmed by the Church; she bears witness to the truth that the birth of Christ is renewed and represented afresh in the sight of Heaven, just as when it took place more than 1800 years ago. In what manner and by whose agency Christ is born in holy Mass St. Jerome tells us in these words: "The priest calls Christ into being by his consecrated lips"; that is to say: Christ is born into the world at the bidding of the priest when his lips utter the words of consecration. Pope Gregory XV. declares the same in the prayer he enjoins upon the priest to recite before saying

Mass: " I am about to celebrate holy Mass, and to call into being the body and blood of Our Lord Jesus Christ."

Holy Church herself teaches us that the birth of Christ is effected anew after a spiritual manner in the Mass, for she places on the lips of the officiating priest the self-same song of praise which the angels sang on Christmas morn: " Glory to God in the highest, and on earth peace to men of good will." (St. Luke ii. 14.) Let us, when these words sound in our ears, imagine ourselves listening to the angel who thus spoke to the shepherds: " I bring you good tidings of great joy; for this day is born to you a Saviour, Who is Christ the Lord. You shall find the Infant wrapped in swaddling-clothes, and laid in a manger." (St. Luke ii. 10–12.) Suppose our angel guardian were to say to us: " Rejoice, my child, for now, in this Mass, thy Saviour will be born for thy salvation; thou wilt see Him with thine eyes under the form of the sacred host." If our guardian angel does not say this to us, our faith tells it to us, and ought we not to rejoice on this account? And if we really believe this, we shall adore the divine Child at holy Mass with the same reverence and affection as did those who were privileged to behold Him with their bodily eyes.

In the life of the fathers we read that a certain priest named Plegus, who habitually said Mass with great devotion, conceived a special desire to know in what manner Christ was present under the veil of bread and wine; not that he in any way doubted his Lord's real presence there, but love prompted the wish to see Him with his bodily eyes. One day when he was saying Mass, immediately after the elevation, this desire was so strong within him that he fell upon his knees, and said: " I beseech Thee, Almighty God, that Thou grant to me, unworthy as I am, to behold the bodily form of Jesus Christ in this sacred mystery; that as Simeon of old took Him in his arms, so I may see Him with my eyes, and touch Him with my hands." While he thus prayed, an angel appeared at his side, and said to him: " Behold, and see Christ here present in bodily form, as when He was an infant on His Mother's knee." Startled by these words, the priest raised his head, and there, lying upon the corporal, he saw the Son of God in the shape of a beautiful babe, that looked at him smilingly, and stretched out His tiny hands to be taken in his arms. But out of reverence the priest ventured not to do this, until the angel said: "This is Jesus, the Son of God, Whom a few moments ago thou sawest under the form of bread; He is now present as He really is; fear not, but rise up, and take Him in thy arms, and let thy heart rejoice in God thy Saviour." Encouraged by these reassuring words, he rose from his knees, lifted the Child in his trembling hands, and caressed Him fondly. Then, gently laying Him again upon the corporal, he again knelt down, and humbly prayed Him to resume His former shape, in order that he might receive Him in holy communion, and bring the Mass to an end. When after this prayer he again stood up, he saw the Blessed Sacrament once more in the form of the consecrated wafer, and consumed it with singular devotion.

This instance has been given in order that we may know and believe that in holy Mass Christ is not present to the imagination alone, or in a purely spiritual manner, but really and truly, and in a bodily form: the self-same infant Christ to Whom the Mother of God gave birth at Bethlehem, and Whom the three kings came to adore. Here, as there, His countenance is concealed by swaddling-clothes, that is, by the external shape of the consecrated host which we see with our eyes. But the tender child Who lies hidden beneath those outward forms can only be perceived by the interior sight of faith, the faith that believes undoubtedly that Our Lord is in truth concealed beneath this lowly form. The reasons why He thus conceals Himself from our view are many; the principal one is this, to give opportunity for the exercise of faith in so momentous a matter, and enable us to acquire merit every time we hear Mass. Numerous instances might be adduced in which Our Lord, for the confirmation of our faith in His personal presence, has permitted devout Christians, nay, more, Jews and unbelievers, to see Him in bodily shape. We will give one.

Albertus Krantius relates at some length the efforts repeatedly made by the Emperor Charlemagne to convert the pagan Saxons to the Christian faith. Although he more than once completely subjugated them by force of arms, and compelled them to abjure their idolatrous practices, again and yet again, under the leadership of Wittekind, their chief, they fell away from their Christian profession. It was in the Lent of one year when, for the twelfth time, the emperor entered their land at the head of a large force. Easter approached, and all the soldiers of the imperial army were ordered to prepare themselves for the reception of the sacraments, and for the devout celebration of the festival in their camp. At that time Wittekind, the Saxon chieftain, went to the German intrenchments with the object of witnessing the Christian ceremonies. In order to escape recognition he disguised himself in the rags of a mendicant, and in this character, without any companion, he entered the camp, and begged alms of the soldiers. Meanwhile he carefully observed all that was going on, and obtained all the information he could. He noticed how on Good Friday the emperor and all the soldiers went about with a mournful mien, kept a strict fast, and spent a considerable time in prayer; how on Holy Saturday they went to confession, and on Easter Day received holy communion. Whilst he was assisting at the Mass, at the moment of the consecration he distinctly saw in the hands of the priest a beautiful child of most engaging aspect, the sight of which filled him with a joy and happiness which he had never before felt. During the remainder of the Mass he could not take his eyes off the priest. His astonishment was still greater when, on the soldiers going up to receive communion, he saw the priest give the same beautiful child to each communicant, by whom it was received, though not always in the same manner. For to some the child went with evident delight; from others He turned away, resisting with all His might, and only going to them under compulsion. The Saxon chief did not know what to make of the unheard-of marvels which he witnessed. At the conclusion of the Mass he left the church, and took his stand amid a swarm of beggars, who solicited alms from the congregation as they passed out. The emperor gave to each mendicant with his own royal hand, and as Wittekind extended his hand to receive the coin destined for him one of the emperor's servants recognized him by the peculiar formation of one of his fingers. The man whispered to his royal master: "That is Wittekind, the Saxon leader; I know him by his crooked finger." The emperor had the stranger brought to him in his tent, and asked him why he, the Saxon chieftain, had come there disguised as a beggar. Wittekind was terribly afraid lest he should be taken for a spy, and treated as such, so he told the truth to the emperor. "Do not be angry with me," he said; "I only did this in order to have a better opportunity of acquainting myself with the Christian worship." The emperor then inquired what he had seen, and Wittekind replied: "I have beheld wonders greater than any I have ever before seen or heard of; wonders far beyond my comprehension." He then told him what he had observed on Good Friday, on Holy Saturday, and what he had witnessed at Mass that same morning, requesting that these mysteries might be explained to him. The emperor was amazed to hear that God had granted to this obdurate heathen the grace to behold the divine Child in the sacred host, a grace He had given to but few saints. He then explained to the Saxon the reason why they were sorrowful on Good Friday, why they fasted, why they went to confession and communion; and so deeply was the heart of the heathen touched that he renounced his worship of idols, accepted the Christian faith, and, when sufficiently instructed, received the Sacrament of Baptism. He took some priests back with him to his people, and by their ministry the dukedom of Saxony was gradually converted to Christ.

This true story, which was the cause of the conversion of the Saxons, proves beyond a doubt that the infant Christ is truly present in the consecrated host, and has been seen in bodily shape not only by certain of the faithful, but even by heathens. He conceals the ineffable beauty of His glorified body from our sinful sight, but it is not hidden from the eyes of God the Father, and all the company of heaven; on the contrary, in every Mass it is displayed to them in such unspeakable loveliness that the Most Holy Trinity is glorified by it, while the blessed Mother of God, the angels and saints, experience a joy and happiness that no words can adequately describe. For, as Christ is reported to have said to the Ven. Alanus, nothing contributes more towards magnifying God, rejoicing His blessed Mother, and causing the felicity of the saints than the holy sacrifice of the Mass.

When the holy angels look upon this new-born infant, they prostrate themselves before Him in lowly adoration,

This is what St. Paul refers to when he says: " Let all the angels of God adore Him." (Heb. i. 6.) In the night of the nativity God the Father brought His only-begotten Son for the first time into the world; but whenever Mass is said He brings Him anew into the world, on to our altars, that He may sacrifice Himself for us, and impart to us the fruits of His birth. Then the angels fall down and worship Him; as the Church says in the preface: " The angels praise, the dominations adore, and the powers fear Thy majesty: the heavens also, and the heavenly forces, and the blessed seraphim glorify it in common exultation." Thus in the night when He was born they sang: " Glory to God in the highest, peace on earth to men of good will." We too, together with the heavenly host, will praise and glorify the divine Child, Who comes anew from heaven, and takes upon Himself the form of an infant for our salvation, and grants to all who assist at Mass an abundant share in the merits He has won for us.

THE JOY CAUSED IN HEAVEN AND THE BLESSINGS BROUGHT TO EARTH BY THE RENEWAL OF OUR LORD'S NATIVITY.

We need the intelligence of the angels to explain aright this sublime mystery, for it surpasses human understanding. We cannot conceive an idea of the joy which it causes to the Most Holy Trinity; but we know it to be one of the truths of our holy religion that the three sacred Persons of the Trinity are all-sufficient in themselves, and each communicates to the others His own ineffable bliss. Holy Scripture speaks of the uncreated Wisdom, the Son of God, in these words: " He is the brightness of eternal light, and the unspotted mirror of God's majesty, and the image of His goodness." (Wis. vii. 26.) This mirror has been from all eternity before the eyes of the heavenly Father; in it He beholds Himself reflected most clearly, and finds in it infinite satisfaction; for in it He has always seen, He sees now, and will ever see His own boundless power and sovereign perfections as they are, and as they will remain to all eternity. This knowledge of Himself and the continual contemplation of this divine mirror are the essence of His infinite and perfect felicity, so that in default of all else, these alone would suffice to constitute His perfect happiness to all eternity.

This spotless mirror is placed before the Eternal Father in a new and different manner in the mystery of Christ's nativity, for the divine mirror was then arrayed in the garb of our humanity, and decked with all virtues and perfections as with rare and costly jewels. The contemplation of it afforded the Eternal Father (to speak after the manner of men) a new pleasure, one in which all the company of heaven took part. Wherefore, in the exuberance of their delight, the blessed spirits raised their voices in that melodious song, the *Gloria in excelsis*, the strains of which reached earth, and filled the pious shepherds with unspeakable joy, and before the *Gloria* was ended the angelic choirs came down to Bethlehem, and prostrated themselves before the newborn Babe, paying lowly homage to Him as their sovereign Lord.

All this, which happened on the night of the nativity, still takes place daily in every Mass, for then the firstborn Son of God again becomes man in the hands of the priest, and at his word is born anew. It is no new Christ Who is called into being by the prayer of consecration, no multiplication of His person takes place: He only becomes personally present in a place where previously He was not. He is indeed but one Christ, and remains ever one and indivisible; yet it is not merely in a spiritual manner, but in a corporate manner also, that He is truly present on the altar. And in the sacred elements He remains present so long as they continue intact. When, however, the elements undergo a change, Christ's personal presence within them ceases, and ceases so completely that were He present in no other place, but only beneath those forms, He would cease to exist, and there would be no Christ either in heaven or upon earth.

Now, when this first-born Son of God is born again at the word of the priest, when this bright mirror, adorned with all divine perfections, is lifted up, and offered both by priest and people to God the Father, what, thinkest thou, is the joy the heavenly Father feels? Certainly it is a joy equal to that which He felt in His beloved Son on the night of His nativity, for then, as now, He beheld the same Son of Whom He said: " This is My beloved Son, in Whom I am well pleased." (St. Matt. iii. 17.) There is but this difference, that then Christ was clothed with a mortal body, whereas now, in holy Mass, He is decked in His glorified body, and His five sacred wounds shine like costly jewels. Then He was born with a visible and material body; now, on the contrary, He is born in a spiritual, though not less real, manner.

Furthermore, we must consider that God the Father does not only take pleasure in the contemplation of this divine mirror, but that this mirror is His own living and beloved Son, Who loves Him with filial affection, and causes Him inexpressible delight. The felicity which the Godhead finds in the humanity of Jesus Christ is a felicity far surpassing that which accrues to it from the praises of the angels, the adoration of the saints, the worship of the faithful. For only the sacred humanity of Christ, united in His one Person to the Godhead, and thereby divinized, is capable of rendering to the Godhead a tribute of praise, of love, of glory worthy of its infinite majesty. Christ alone, as He told St. Mechtilde, knows perfectly how that sacrifice of Himself is daily offered upon the altar for the benefit of the faithful. In like manner He alone knows how the Godhead is to be duly praised and magnified in the daily sacrifice of the Mass. This He accomplished in so beautiful, so admirable a manner that neither cherubim, nor seraphim, nor any of the powers of heaven are capable of fully comprehending, much less of themselves performing, this act. All the heavenly hosts look on with amazement and admiration; their intelligence cannot fathom this source of infinite felicity. And since we know it to be repeated every day in thousands of Masses, who can find words to express the magnitude, the extent of the joy which the ever-blessed Trinity derives from the Masses that are daily celebrated?

My God, I fervently rejoice at the thought of this felicity, and fain would I increase it by my heartfelt homage. I beseech Thee, O Jesus, that in the holy sacrifice of the Mass Thou wouldst perform my part in loving and magnifying the Most Holy Trinity, and defray, in my behalf, the debt of love and veneration which I have neglected to pay.

Finally, let us consider the unspeakable blessings brought to a sinful world by the daily renewal of Our Lord's birth in the holy sacrifice of the Mass. The prophet Isaias, speaking of the nativity of the Saviour, says: "A child is born to us, and a son is given to us." (Is. ix. 6.) The same may be said of His spiritual birth: whenever Mass is said, a child is born to us, a son is given us. How precious, how invaluable is this gift! It is none other than the most precious of all celestial treasures, none other than the Son of the Eternal Father, in Whom all riches dwell. He descends from paradise on every altar when Mass is said, bringing with Him riches immeasurable and celestial treasures. The chief amongst these are: divine grace and mercy, contrition and forgiveness of sins, remission of the penalty due to our sins, amendment of life, the grace of a good death, a greater degree of glory in heaven; besides many temporal favors —preservation from accidents, from sin and shame, the blessing of God on all we do. These and many other graces He is ready to communicate freely to those who hear Mass devoutly, and He will bestow them abundantly.

If we consider more attentively the prophecy of Isaias, we shall find in it something further for our encouragement. He says expressly that a child is born to us, a son is given us. If the child Jesus is thus born to us in holy Mass, and given to us, He is our very own; all that He has is ours, all that He does belongs also to us. The honor, the thanksgiving, the worship, the satisfaction He renders to the Blessed Trinity, is ours as well. What can be a greater consolation to us poor sinners when we hear Mass than to know that not the Mass only, but the infant Christ Himself, is all our own? Hadst thou been present in the stable the night of the nativity, and hadst thou been able to take the tender Babe in thy arms, and offer Him to God the Father, with the earnest entreaty that for the sake of this sweet child He would have mercy upon thee, would He not, thinkest thou, have shown thee favor, and forgiven thee thy transgressions? Well, then, do so whenever thou hearest Mass. Approach in spirit to the altar, take the divine Child in thine arms, and offer Him to God the Father.

Another point remains to be noticed, which is most noteworthy and needs explanation, namely, that Christ is not merely born mystically upon the altar, but He there assumes so lowly a form that both heaven and earth are amazed at it. St. Paul in his Epistle to the Philippians describes the abasement of the Saviour in His first incarnation and birth in these forcible words: " Brethren, let this mind be in you, which was also in Christ Jesus: Who, being in the form of God, thought it not robbery to be equal with God: but emptied Himself, taking the form of a servant, being made in the likeness of men, and in habit found as a man. He humbled Himself, becoming obedient unto death, even to the death of the cross." (Phil. ii. 5–8.)

Such are the emphatic words in which St. Paul declares to us the profound humility of Christ, and directs our attention to His annihilation of Himself. But he who considers the spiritual birth of Our Lord in the Mass will find in it a far greater and more profound depth of humility. For in His temporal birth He was made like unto man, and took upon Him the form of a fair and beauteous child; in His mystic birth, however, he assumes the form of bread, and appears to the outward vision as a piece of bread. Nay, more, so entirely does He abase and annihilate Himself as to conceal Himself in the minutest particle that the eye can discern.

This is indeed unparalleled humility and unheard-of self-renunciation! The words which the prophet-king spoke of Christ are most applicable here: " I am a worm, and no man: the reproach of men, and the outcast of the people." (Ps. xxi. 7.) For who heeds a crumb of bread? Who recognizes it as his God? Who renders Him honor and glory? Where is the splendor that appertains to His glorified body? Where is His omnipotence? Where His sovereign majesty, before which heaven and earth tremble and are afraid? He has laid all this aside, and clothed Himself with the garment of the deepest abasement. He Who is the divine and eternal

Word cannot utter a syllable. He Who made the heavens and the earth is unable to move hand or foot. He Whom the heaven of heavens cannot contain is confined, imprisoned, as it were, in a little wafer. He Who is seated at the right hand of the Father lies upon the altar bound as a sacrificial lamb, ready to be slain anew in a spiritual manner as a victim for our sake. Behold the infinite humiliation of the sovereign Lord of heaven and of earth! Behold the unspeakable charity of this faithful lover towards the children of men!

Furthermore, in His humility and self-abasement Jesus Christ becomes subject in holy Mass to the officiating priest, and this not only to the good and fervent, but to the lukewarm and indifferent, permitting them to deal with Him according to their will. Nay, what is even more astonishing, He does not refuse to receive their benediction, although St. Paul says: "Without all contradiction, that which is less is blessed by the better." (Heb. vii. 7.) How, then, can Christ, Who is so incomparably greater than the priest, take the blessing of one so infinitely His inferior? Yet the priest blesses the host not only before but after the consecration, and this no less than fifteen times, so profound is the self-abasement of Our Lord. We are told that when Christ came unto John to be baptized by him "John stayed Him, saying: I ought to be baptized by Thee, and comest Thou to me?" (St. Matt. iii. 14.) In like manner the priest ought to shrink back in fear, and say: "I, O my Lord, ought to receive Thy blessing, for how canst Thou, the most high God, receive the blessing of a miserable sinner like myself?" This is indeed most astonishing, and we are led to inquire the reason why Christ stoops so low.

One of the chief reasons to be alleged is this: in order by His extreme abasement to appease the wrath of an angry God, and avert from sinful men the just chastisement of their iniquities. There is no surer way of conciliating an enemy than to humble one's self before him and beg his forgiveness. We learn this from the example of the impious King Achab, of whom it is recorded in Holy Scripture that when the prophet Elias foretold to him, by God's command, that on account of his evil doings the Lord would chastise his wife and children, so that they should not be buried, but their dead bodies become the food of dogs and of the birds of the air, "Achab rent his garments, and put hair-cloth upon his flesh, and fasted, and slept in sack-cloth, and walked with his head cast down. And the word of the Lord came to Elias the Thesbite, saying: Hast thou not seen Achab humbled before Me? Therefore, because he hath humbled himself for My sake, I will not bring the evil in his days, but in his son's days will I bring the evil upon his house." (III. Kings xxi. 27–29.)

Now if the godless King Achab, of whom it is said that he did evil above all that were before him, through humiliation and self-abasement so far prevailed with Almighty God that He did not send upon him the threatened punishment, what will not the extraordinary humiliation of Christ upon the altar avail with His heavenly Father? For the sake of sinners, who have provoked the just God to vengeance by their pride and their malice, Christ humbled Himself far more profoundly than Achab ever did. For Christ lays aside His glorious apparel, He conceals Himself under the form of the sacred host; He does not merely "walk with His head cast down," He lies upon the altar, a patient victim, and from the bottom of His heart calls upon God the Father to pardon and spare the sinner. Will not God Almighty say to His angels as He said to the prophet of old: "Have you not seen how My Son humbleth Himself before Me?" And the angels will answer: "Yea, we see and are amazed at the deep abasement of our Lord and God." And God will then reply: " Because My divine Son has thus annihilated Himself, and humbled Himself before Me to plead for sinners, I will spare them, and turn away from them the chastisement their transgressions deserve."

Listen, then, O sinner, hear what God says to thee, and thou wilt understand how it is that thy life has been so far prolonged, and thou hast not been punished according to the measure of thy iniquities. For my part, I think that it is principally because thou hast often heard Mass, and hast thus shared in the intercession of Christ. On the altar He has made thy interests His own, He has humbled Himself before God on thy behalf, He has averted the penalty thou hast deserved. Wherefore return humble thanks to thy faithful advocate, and say to Him in the gratitude of thy heart:

" Praise and glory be to Thee, O most sweet Jesus, for the infinite love wherewith Thou dost vouchsafe to descend from heaven in the holy Mass to change bread and wine into Thy sacred flesh and blood, to conceal Thyself under these contemptible appearances and by means of this boundless humility to appease the just wrath of God and avert the chastisements due to us. With our whole hearts we thank Thee for this inestimable benefit. With all the powers of our soul we praise and magnify Thee, and we beseech the hosts of heaven to unite their voices to ours and compensate for what is defective in our giving of thanks. We humbly pray Thee to enlighten our minds, that we may clearly comprehend the saving mysteries which Thou dost daily enact upon our altars, that we may venerate them aright, and profit by them for our eternal salvation. Amen."

CHAPTER VI.

IN THE HOLY MASS CHRIST RENEWS HIS LIFE.

IF we were to contemplate attentively the great mysteries of holy Mass, and impress forcibly upon our minds that the officiating priest as the representative of Jesus Christ, arrayed in the garments of gladness, reproduces before our eyes the mysteries of the wondrous life and death of the Saviour, we should surely hasten to church at the first stroke of the bell, eager to assist at this consoling spectacle, because, as Sanchez says: " In this sacred drama the merits of our Redeemer are bestowed upon us and given us for our very own."

If our eyes were enlightened by faith, this sacred spectacle would fill us with intense joy. For holy Mass is a brief compendium of the whole life of Christ, and a renewal of all the mysteries comprised in it; not, indeed, a fictitious portrayal of past events, but a real and actual repetition of all that Christ did and suffered upon earth.

Thus in holy Mass we have the same child lying before us Whom the shepherds beheld wrapped in swaddling-clothes, but under a form still more lowly, that of bread and wine; yes, the same child to Whom the three kings paid homage, and Whom Simeon took in his arms, is before us upon the altar, and we may adore Him piously and embrace Him lovingly, as did they. In the course of the Mass the Gospel is preached to us; it is, indeed, the voice of the priest that we hear, but the words have the same weight as if Christ Himself uttered them. Furthermore, we see Him perform a greater miracle than the one He wrought at Cana in Galilee; for there He changed water into wine, here He changes wine into His sacred blood. In the Mass the scene of the Last Supper is reenacted, for the bread and wine undergo a change similar to that they then did. Christ is also slain anew by the hand of the priest, and by him offered up to God most high. Father Sanchez, writing on this subject, says: " He who desires to profit by holy Mass will be able to obtain forgiveness of sins and the gift of divine grace just as readily by assisting at it devoutly as if he had in person witnessed all these mysteries." Hence it will be seen how salutary is this solemn service, and how much may be gained by those who are present at it.

Let us hear how Denys, a pious Carthusian, explains the representation of the mysteries of Our Lord's life in holy Mass. He says: " The whole life of Christ which He led upon earth was one long celebration of Mass, He being Himself the altar, the priest, the victim."

It may be said that Our Lord put on the sacerdotal vestments when, hidden from sight in His Mother's womb, He took our flesh and assumed the garb of mortality. Issuing thence, on the night of the nativity, as from the sacristy, He began, on His entrance into the world, the *Introit*, which is the commencement of the Mass. The cries He uttered in the crib were the *Kyrie Eleison*. The *Gloria* was sung by the angels who appeared to the shepherds and accompanied them to the stable at Bethlehem. The *Collects* represent the petitions He offered when He spent the night in prayer, imploring for us the mercy of God. The *Epistle* represents the instructions He gave on the prophecies of Moses and the prophets, showing how they were fulfilled in Himself. He read the *Gospel* when He traversed the country of Judea proclaiming His divine doctrine. The *Offertory* was when He daily made an oblation of Himself to God the Father for the redemption of mankind as a propitiatory victim. The *Preface* represents His daily tribute of praise to God the Father, His thanksgiving for the benefits conferred upon man. The *Sanctus* was sung by the Hebrew people on Palm Sunday, when they cried: "Blessed is He that cometh in the name of the Lord: Hosanna in the highest!" (St. Matt. xxi. 9.) The *Consecration* took place at the Last Supper, when He changed bread and wine into His body and blood. The *Elevation* was when He was lifted up upon the cross and made a spectacle to angels and to men. The *Paternoster* represents the seven words He uttered upon the cross. The *Breaking of the Host*, the separation of His sacred soul and body. The *Agnus Dei* was spoken by the centurion and those who were with him when, smiting their breasts, they said: "Indeed this was the Son of God." (St. Matt. xxvii. 54.) The *Communion* represents the anointing of Our Lord's body and laying it in the tomb. The *Blessing* at the conclusion of Mass represents the benediction He gave to His disciples when about to ascend into heaven.

Such was the great act of worship which Christ performed upon earth, and which He enjoined upon His apostles and their successors to repeat daily, in a short form. Fornerus says: "Holy Mass is a brief epitome of Our Lord's life; a recapitulation in one short half hour of what He did during the thirty-three years He spent upon earth." Thus we, who have the opportunity of hearing Mass, may deem ourselves equally fortunate with the contemporaries of Our Lord; nay, more fortunate than they, since they could only hear and see one Mass, and that a very long one, whereas we may hear more than one every day, and, at small cost to ourselves, share in the fruits of Christ's life and passion. In further explanation of the manner in which Our Lord reenacts in holy Mass the mysteries of His life on earth, we will relate the following anecdote. It occurs in the writings of Thomas of Cantiprat, Suffragan Bishop of Cambrai.

In the year 1267, a priest at Douai, whilst giving communion at Easter in the Church of St. Amatus, suffered one of the hosts to fall to the ground. To his great amazement he saw it rise from the ground and remain suspended in the air. Taking it in his hand, he carried it to the altar, and, kneeling humbly before it, he begged pardon of Christ for the indignity that had been done to Him. Whilst he was devoutly contemplating the Adorable Sacrament, he was astounded to see the form of the host disappear, and the form of a beautiful child take its place. So great was his emotion that he could not restrain his sobs and tears. The clergy present in the choir drew near to ascertain what was the matter, and they too saw the fair infant. Deeply touched by the sight, they broke out into exclamations of joy and delight. Then the congregation in their turn approached to behold the miraculous appearance, which afforded such convincing proof of Christ's real presence upon the altar. But lo! another wondrous change took place! The people could not see what the clergy had seen, for they had beheld a tender child, whereas now Christ stood before them in the form of a man, in the splendor of His divine majesty. Fear and amazement fell upon all, the sanctuary was thronged with eager spectators. For a considerable time Our Lord remained thus visible in His sacred humanity; He then withdrew His corporal presence, and the host was deposited by the priest in the tabernacle. The report of what had happened spread far and wide, and reached the ears of the bishop, who relates the occurrence. He immediately went to Douai, and inquired of the dean whether what he had heard was true. The dean replied: "It is not only true that Christ was seen by a great number of persons in the sacred host, but He is still seen by many in His human form." "Then"—thus the bishop writes—"a burning desire to see this same sight took possession of me: I begged the dean to show me the miraculous host. We went together to the church, followed by a multitude of persons, who hoped that Our Lord would again show Himself to them. The dean unlocked the tabernacle with trembling awe; he reverently took out the Blessed Sacrament, and with it blessed the people. Marvellous to relate, they all began to sob and cry aloud: 'Jesus, Jesus!' I asked what all this meant and they said: 'We see our Lord and Saviour with our bodily eyes.' But I saw nothing, only the host unchanged; and I felt deeply grieved, for I thought some sin had rendered me unworthy to behold my Saviour. I examined my conscience, without, however, finding anything special wherewith to reproach myself, so with tears I besought Our Lord to vouchsafe to show Himself to me. My petition was granted; I too was privileged to see, not, as many of those present did, the form of a child, but that of a full-grown man. After I had gazed for a short space of time upon the Saviour in the surpassing beauty of this appearance, my heart being meanwhile suffused with joy and happiness on account of the kindness wherewith He regarded me, a change took place, and I saw Him before me as the Man of sorrows. I beheld Him wearing the crown of thorns, disfigured by the streams of blood that veiled His sacred countenance. Overcome with compassion at this sorrowful sight, I shed bitter tears over the sufferings of my Redeemer; so vividly did I realize them that it seemed as if the thorns that crowned His head pierced my own temples. A confused murmur ran through the multitude who had assembled, for each one saw something different at the same moment. Some perceived Our Lord in the form of a lovely infant, others beheld Him as a beautiful boy, as a youth just attaining man's estate, as a man in the prime of years, or, again, as He was at the time of His passion. The emotions that stirred the hearts of the people, the feelings that were kindled in their breasts, the tears that flowed from their eyes, must be left to the imagination of the reader, for words fail to describe them."

This beautiful, encouraging, and consoling story cannot but lead each one of us to wish that we had been privileged to witness so touching a spectacle; to desire that the grace of seeing the Saviour with our bodily eyes under these several appearances had been granted to us also. What would have been the joy, the consolation, the sweetness we should have experienced! O Lord Jesus, although I have never seen Thee in bodily shape in the sacred host, yet I firmly believe that Thou art present there, and dost present Thyself before the Eternal Father under the varied appearances Thou didst assume on earth. And as Christ in a marvellous and incomprehensible manner assumed those mortal shapes, so in every Mass does He reproduce all the mysteries of His life and passion in the sight and to the satisfaction of God the Father and God the Holy Ghost, of His blessed Mother and all the choirs of angels and the saints, just as when these solemn mysteries were enacted during His lifetime on earth. Thus there is incomparably more joy in heaven on account of one single Mass than because of any other good work or act of worship in the world.

This joy is not occasioned simply by the vivid representation of the life and passion of Christ, but also by the honor which the sacred humanity renders to the Godhead in holy Mass. For in every Mass that is said, with all the might of His divinity, with all the power of His humanity, with all the force of His human heart, Christ honors, praises, loves, worships, and magnifies the adorable Trinity in so sublime and incomprehensible a manner that the glory rendered to the Godhead by angels in heaven, by saints on earth, is immeasurably inferior to the glory which He then renders to it. Hence we see how exalted an act of worship holy Mass is, and how much we can prevail with God every time that we celebrate or assist at it.

Before concluding this chapter let us consider the great profit and spiritual advantages we may gain from holy Mass. Christ, our precious Saviour, during the three and thirty years in which He labored upon earth, laid up a vast store of merits, not for Himself, but for us, His children. Nor are His labors yet at an end, as He Himself testifies: "My Father worketh until now, and I work." (St. John v. 17.) He continues His work, not that He may earn more, but that He may qualify us to receive what He has earned for us. On this account He renews His sacred life in every Mass that is celebrated, and in each one enacts afresh what it took Him thirty-three years to accomplish. This He presents to the Eternal Father, to effect our reconciliation with Him. By it God is well pleased, and His wrath at our transgressions is appeased. He offers all His merits to God in payment of our debts, and when we hear holy Mass He bestows on us as much as we are capable of receiving, that we may thereby make atonement for our sins.

Give thanks, therefore, O Christian, to this thy true friend, Who has labored for thee and laid up for thee so rich a store of treasures. Acknowledge His great charity towards thee in offering these treasures for thy acceptance, and bestowing them upon thee freely. See that thou hear Mass daily, if possible, in order to appropriate to thyself a large portion of these riches. Thou wouldst spare no pains and grudge no time if thou couldst acquire temporal riches as easily as thou canst acquire wealth for thy soul. Why, then, remain so careless in regard to the eternal treasures, and by thy indifference allow them to escape thy grasp? May God enlighten thy blindness, convert thy sloth into diligence, and inspire thee with true fervor; and when this happy change is effected thou wilt then hear Mass frequently and to thy soul's profit.

CHAPTER VII.

IN THE HOLY MASS CHRIST RENEWS HIS INTERCESSION.

ST. JOHN, the beloved disciple of Our Lord, says in his first Epistle: "We have an advocate with the Father, Jesus Christ the just, and He is the propitiation for our sins." (1. St. John ii. 1, 2.) What a comforting assurance of our salvation these words afford us, since Holy Scripture expressly tells us that the Son of God Himself, the Judge of the living and the dead, is our defender and our intercessor.

The question now arises, When and where does Christ fulfil this His office? The Catholic Church believes and teaches that not only in heaven, but also on earth, in the holy Mass, Christ pleads for us, and commends us to the mercy of God. The learned Suarez says: "As often as the sacrifice of the Mass is offered, so often does Christ plead both for those who offer it and those for whom it is offered." He pleads, that is to say, for the priest who officiates, for the people who unite their prayers to his, and for all those for whom priest and people offer the holy sacrifice.

St. Laurence Justinian thus describes the manner in which Christ offers this intercession: "When Christ is spiritually slain upon the altar, He calls upon His heavenly Father, He shows Him His wounds, that in virtue of His earnest supplication man may escape eternal damnation." These are consoling words, for they show how faithfully Christ intercedes for us, how deeply He interests Himself in our behalf. During His sojourn upon earth, He took our salvation so much to heart that He oftentimes spent the whole night in prayer and watching, as St. Luke expressly tells us: " He went out into a mountain to pray, and He passed the whole night in the prayer of God." (St. Luke vi. 12.) This was no infrequent occurrence, as we learn from the same evangelist: "In the daytime He was teaching in the temple; but at night, going out, He abode in the mount that is called Olivet." (*Ibid.* xxi. 37). And in the following chapter he adds: " He went, according to His custom, to the Mount of Olives." (*Ibid.* xxii. 39.) These words testify unmistakably that Jesus was accustomed to go out to the Mount of Olives, and remain all night long at prayer under the open vault of heaven. For what or for whom did He pray? St. Ambrose answers this question: "Not for Himself did the Lord ask anything, but for me." It was not, therefore, on His own behalf that the Saviour spent whole nights in prayer: it was on man's behalf, that we might be saved from everlasting perdition. And since He foresaw how many millions of human beings would be eternally lost in spite of His having suffered and died for them, we may believe that the loss of these souls caused many tears to flow from His pitying eyes, many a sigh to rise from His compassionate heart.

These fervent prayers which our blessed Saviour offered when on earth He renews and repeats in every Mass that is celebrated, setting them before God the Father, as it were, in a brief summary. but just as definitely as if they were all said over again. Moreover, He bids Him behold the bitter tears which He shed for the salvation of sinners; He counts over to Him the sighs that rent His breast on account of man's transgressions, the nights He spent in watching and prayer for those who had wandered far from God. All these He offers for the salvation of the world, but more especially for the salvation of each individual who is present at Mass. Consider what must be the sanctity, the fervor, the cogency of these prayers, uttered by the Holy of holies, Jesus Christ the Son of God, in person, in all the power of His divinized humanity ! How all-powerful must such a prayer be with God ! How pleasing in His sight ! How efficacious for those on whose behalf it is offered! How acceptable to the Most Holy Trinity, to Whom it is addressed !

Furthermore, observe that Christ does not confine Himself to pleading from the altar for all who are present, but, to enhance the potency of His prayer, He sacrifices Himself to God on their behalf. Who can rightly estimate the power, the efficacy, of this sacrifice ? In the revelations of St. Gertrude it is stated that, at the elevation of the host, the saint saw Christ with His own hands lifting on high His heart in the form of a golden chalice, presenting it to His heavenly Father, and offering Himself for His Church in an ineffable manner, which it surpasses human understanding to comprehend.

Consider well, and lay to heart, how sublime a mystery, how exalted and divine a sacrifice, is holy Mass. Consider well, and admire profoundly, the inscrutable manner in which our blessed Redeemer immolates Himself in every Mass for the safety of all believers. Neither saint nor angel, not even the Mother of God herself, can fully penetrate this mystery. Our Lord Himself told St. Mechtilde (as has already been said) that no created intelligence could fully understand this daily sacrifice He makes of Himself. From His words we see how fervently and powerfully He pleads from the altar for His people, especially for those who assist at Mass; nor does He plead only, He makes an oblation of Himself in a manner so unspeakably sublime that the highest powers of heaven are incapable of fully comprehending it. How great the grace, how great the salvation, herein vouchsafed to us!

In addition to this it must be remembered that in holy Mass Christ does not offer Himself up in the splendor of His divine majesty, but in a state of abasement so complete that no parallel can be found to it. For upon the altar He is present not only in the whole undivided host, but in the minutest particle of it; and He can well apply to Himself the words of David: "I am a worm, and no man: the reproach of men, and the outcast of the people." (Ps. xxi. 7.)

In this contemptible form, in this extreme abasement, He speaks from the altar in a voice so powerful that it pierces the clouds, rends the heavens, and awakens the divine mercy. We read in the prophecy of Jonas that when the King of Ninive heard that in forty days the city would be destroyed he rose from his throne, laid aside his regal robes, clothed himself in the garment of penance, and commanded his subjects to cry to the Lord with all their strength. This humiliation and penance on the part of the king had the effect of turning away the wrath of God, and inducing Him to revoke the sentence, and spare the guilty city. If by humbling himself this heathen king obtained mercy for his city, what will not Jesus obtain from God, since He does far more in holy Mass? For He descends from His celestial throne, He lays aside His regal glory, He conceals Himself under the insignificant appearance of the host, and calls with all His strength upon Almighty God for mercy for His people addressing Him in words such as these:

"Behold, O heavenly Father, the profound humility and deep abasement wherewith I cast Myself before Thee, in the semblance of a worm rather than of a man. It is on behalf of these unhappy sinners that I plead, entreating Thee to pardon and to spare them. They have revolted against Thee, but I humble Myself before Thee. They have provoked Thee to anger by their iniquities: I desire to appease Thee by My humility. They have incurred Thy just vengeance: let My earnest petitions avert from them that vengeance. Spare them, O My Father, for My sake, and chastise them not according to their misdeeds. Deliver them not over to Satan, let them not go into everlasting perdition. I cannot let them be lost: they are Mine, purchased at a great price with My own blood. Especially I pray for those who are here present, for whom once again I give My life and shed My blood, that through the merits of that sacred blood and cruel death they may be preserved from eternal death."

To what lengths, O Jesus, does Thy love for us carry Thee, impelling Thee to interest Thyself so deeply in us, to do so much for us, to intercede so fervently on our behalf! Who but would rejoice to hear Mass if he knew that Christ Himself was pleading for his salvation—pleading not with words alone, but, in order to give weight to His petition, offering Himself upon the altar, and renewing His passion in a mystical manner?

Who could fail to place confidence in such an intercessor? Who would not desire to have this intercessor for his own? This desire can easily be fulfilled. We can readily make Him our own, by hearing Mass devoutly. We know beyond a doubt that Christ, when hanging upon the cross, commended those of His followers who stood by the cross in a special manner to His heavenly Father, and applied to them the fruits of His passion; He even promised paradise to the thief on His right hand. No less is it beyond a doubt that Christ does the same for those who are present at holy Mass, above all if they entreat Him to intercede for them, and grant them a share in His sacrifice of Himself. He then pleads as powerfully for them as He did for His enemies upon the cross. Can we question the efficacy of such a prayer? Nothing can serve to strengthen our hope more than the knowledge that the only-begotten Son of God vouchsafes daily to intercede for us, and makes the affair of our salvation His own.

If the Blessed Virgin Mary were to come down from heaven, to appear to thee, and speak to thee these consoling words: "Fear not, my child; I promise thee to take upon myself the important work of thy salvation, to entreat my Son on thy behalf, to persist in my entreaties until He promises to make thee a partaker of eternal felicity," would not thy heart overflow with happiness? Wouldst thou not exult and rejoice at this favor on the part of the blessed Mother of God, and no longer entertain a doubt of thy salvation, since she had assured thee of her all-powerful intercession?

If, then, we have (as is only right) such great confidence in the intercession of the Mother of God, why have we not the same, nay, even yet more, confidence in the most potent advocacy of the all-glorious Son of God, Who does not merely promise to be our mediator with His Father that we may attain the bliss of heaven, but actually does intercede for us in every Mass at which we are present in person, and restrains the execution of divine justice, so that we may not be punished as our misdeeds deserve, but be saved through grace? Not with words alone does He plead; His tears speak too; the five wounds of His adorable body, each drop of blood that fell from those wounds, every throb of His Sacred Heart, every sigh that escaped His breast—all these are voices eloquent on our behalf, voices whose cry ascends on high, which reach the throne of God, and move to compassion the tender heart of our Father in heaven. What is the grace which prayers such as these cannot obtain? What the evil which they cannot avert? What the favors they are impotent to procure?

Since the foregoing pages will have sufficed thoroughly to convince us that Christ intercedes in holy Mass after a special manner on behalf of all who are present, why do we not go to Mass more frequently, in order to have a share in His intercessory supplications? We are often heard to complain and deplore that we pray but ill; although if we go to Mass Christ will pray for us, and make amends for all our deficiencies. Hear how kindly He invites us: "Come to Me, all you that labor and are burdened, and I will refresh you." (St. Matt. xi. 28.) This He said when He was on earth; and now from the altar He seems to say: "Come to Me, all you who cannot pray for yourselves, and I will pray for you." Why do not we, miserable sinners, avail ourselves of this invitation, and hasten to Him in holy Mass? We are accustomed when misfortunes overtake us to go to our fellow-creatures, to acquaint them with our trouble, and ask for their prayers. If we trust to the prayers of men to help us, should we not place far more confidence in the all-efficacious, all-powerful prayer of Christ? No one can be certain of his salvation; when the disciples asked Our Lord: "Who, then, can be saved?" He answered: "With men it is impossible, but not with God." (St. Mark x. 26, 27.) Since we hear from Christ's own lips that it is impossible of ourselves to insure our salvation, let us take refuge in holy Mass from the dangers that surround us, and Christ will intercede for us, and obtain for us an eternity of bliss.

Do not, then, lament, and say: "Wretched sinner that I am, I do not deserve, I am not worthy, that Christ should plead for me," but rather rest assured that if at holy Mass thou dost breathe but one sigh to Christ He will pray for thee; in fact He is bound to pray for thee. For St. Paul says in the Epistle to the Hebrews: "Every high priest is ordained for men in the things that appertain to God, that he may offer up gifts and sacrifices for sins." (Heb. v. 1.) Now since Christ has been appointed by God the Father to be our high priest, and since He fulfils His priestly functions in holy Mass, He is bound in virtue of His office to pray for the people, and offer the holy sacrifice of the Mass. Nor does He only offer it for the congregation taken as a whole, but for every individual member of it; just as He died for the whole world, and for each believer personally; as also He watches over all mankind in general, and over each one of us in particular. Therefore doubt no longer that Christ prays for thee, but believe it confidently if thou dost hear Mass with due devotion.

From all that has been said we now understand full well how powerful and how earnest is the prayer Christ offers for us upon the altar, and how beneficial is its effect upon us. Only one thing yet remains, that we should unite our prayer to His, or rather should implore Him to make it one with His. For this union will render it so powerful that no other prayers can compare with it.

"The prayers said at Mass," Bishop Fornerus tells us, "offered in union with the holy sacrifice, have infinitely more value than any other prayers, however long, however fervent, more even than ecstatic contemplations, in virtue of the merits of Christ's passion, the power of which is manifested in holy Mass by a superabundance of celestial gifts and graces. For as the head is the noblest portion of the body, no other member being comparable to it, so does the prayer offered by Christ, our head, when He prays for us in the Mass surpass in dignity the prayers of all Christian people, who are His members."

Therefore, if we unite our poor petitions which we offer during the Mass to the perfect prayer of Our Lord, they will, like a copper coin immersed in molten gold, be beautified and ennobled, and rendered meet to be borne to heaven, together with Our Lord's prayer, and with it presented to God as a precious oblation. Hence it follows that prayers which are said at Mass-time, even if less good in themselves (provided this be not through our own fault), will have far more value than more fervent prayers said at home. How foolish, then, and blind to their own interests are they who choose to say their prayers in their own house when they might go to Mass, and thus greatly enhance their merit! For if they were to perform their ordinary devotions whilst the holy sacrifice was being offered, with the intention of assisting at it, only interrupting their prayers at the consecration to adore the sacred body and precious blood of the Saviour, they would merit far more than if they said the same prayers at home or out of doors. For they would be made partakers in all the graces that have been enumerated in these pages, and lay up a store of treasures in heaven. Wherefore take heed, O pious reader, that, as often as is possible, thou dost unite thy petitions to those of our blessed Lord in holy Mass.

CHAPTER VIII.

IN THE HOLY MASS CHRIST RENEWS HIS PASSION.

AMONG all the mysteries of the life of Christ there is not one which can be meditated upon with greater profit, or which has a greater claim on our adoration, than His bitter passion and death, by means of which our redemption was effected. The fathers of the Church tell us that those who meditate upon and venerate Our Lord's passion will obtain a rich reward. There are many different methods of doing this, each profitable in its way, but none can be better than that of hearing Mass attentively; for then the bitter passion is in reality suffered anew, reiterated for our benefit, and consequently we can meditate upon it more easily, and represent it to ourselves more forcibly.

That the passion of Christ is renewed in holy Mass must be clearly apparent to every one. Everything recalls it and points to it, and preeminently the sign of the cross, which meets our eye continually. In the altar-stone five crosses are engraven, and in consecrating it the bishop made the sign of the cross more than a hundred times. The sacred vessels and the sacerdotal vestments are all marked with the cross. During the celebration of Mass the priest crosses himself sixteen times, and blesses the oblation with the same sign twenty-nine times. What is this constant reiteration of the sign of the cross intended to signify if not that the sacrifice of blood offered by Christ upon the cross, that is, His bitter passion and death, is represented, repeated, renewed upon the altar?

Although Our Lord at the Last Supper expressly said: "Do this for a commemoration of Me," yet the holy sacrifice of the Mass is not simply a commemoration, but a renewal, of the passion of Christ. Holy Church teaches: "Whosoever shall say that the sacrifice of the Mass is only a remembrance of the sacrifice of the cross, let him be anathema." And in the same session of the Council of Trent (xxii. ch. 2) she states: "In this divine sacrifice which is celebrated in the Mass that same Christ is contained and immolated in an unbloody manner Who once offered Himself in a bloody manner on the altar of the cross." Had we no other authority than this, it ought to content us, and remove all doubt from our minds. For what the Catholic Church, under the guidance of the Holy Spirit, teaches and sets before us for our acceptance, that we are bound to believe firmly, and never in any wise to gainsay. Now the Church definitely declares that the same Christ Who in times past made the sacrifice of Himself upon the cross in a painful manner, with shedding of blood, is now truly present in holy Mass, and is immolated afresh, but after a bloodless and painless manner.

In proof and corroboration of this the Church further asserts: "For the victim is one and the same; the same now offering by the ministry of priests Who then offered Himself on the cross, the manner alone of offering being different." That is to say: in both these sacrifices, that of the cross and that of the Mass, the same victim is offered, and He Who offers the sacrifices, both the one and the other, is the same, even Christ; but the manner in which He offers Himself in the one place and in the other is different. On the cross He offered Himself, a sacrifice of blood, although He was put to death by the hands of the executioners; on the altar He likewise offers Himself, this time by the hands and the ministry of priests, by whom He is immolated, but in a bloodless manner.

The word immolate, from the Latin *immolare*, to slay, is frequently employed by the Church in the Ordinary of the Mass. St. Augustine also makes use of it when he says: "Christ was indeed only once immolated in person, yet He is immolated every day for the people in the sacrament or in holy Mass." The word is a peculiar one; it is constantly employed in the Scriptures in reference to the slaughter and sacrifice of the victims that were offered upon the altar. Now by employing the same word in speaking of the Mass the Church intends to indicate that Christ is offered up in holy Mass not merely by the word of the priest, nor by the elevation of the Adorable Sacrament, but that, as the sacrificial lamb, He is mystically made to suffer, immolated and slain, as we shall proceed to show more explicitly.

St. Cyprian tells us: "The sacrifice we offer is the passion of Christ." By this he evidently meant to say: When we say Mass, we reiterate what was enacted in Christ's passion. St. Gregory enunciates this truth still more plainly: "Although Christ dies not again, yet He suffers again for us in the sacrifice of the Mass after a mysterious, mystical manner." Theodoret speaks no less plainly: "We offer no other sacrifice but that which was offered upon the cross."

It would be easy to quote many other authorities in proof of this, but for sake of brevity we will pass them by and content ourselves with the infallible testimony of the Church, who dictates to us the following prayer amongst the *secreta* for the ninth Sunday after Pentecost: "Grant us, we beseech Thee, O Lord, worthily to frequent these mysteries; since as often as the remembrance of the victim is celebrated, so often is the work of our redemption carried on." Here the question arises: What may the work of our redemption be? This every child can answer; for if you ask him, By what are we redeemed? he will answer: Through the sufferings of Christ. Thus, if the Church declares that this work is carried on in every Mass, it follows that the passion of Christ is renewed in every Mass. We find the same truth expressed in the secret prayer for the festival of some martyrs (Nov. 8): "May Thy plentiful blessing descend, O Lord, upon us, and both render our gifts agreeable to Thee, and be to us a sacrament of redemption." These words must not be understood to mean that we are redeemed over again in holy Mass, but that in the Mass the fruits of our redemption may be communicated to us, as the Church says elsewhere: "May the effect of our redemption be applied to us through this sacrament."

Another writer says: "What else is holy Mass than a renewal of our redemption?" Again Molina beautifully formulates the same truth: "Holy Mass is infinitely superior to any other oblation that is offered; for it is not merely an image of our redemption: it is the very work itself, wrapped in mystery, but truly carried on." The testimony which has been adduced will amply suffice to convince every one that holy Mass is a renewal of Christ's passion, and that the gentle Lamb of God is mystically slain anew in every Mass which is celebrated. The following instance will illustrate this truth:

A Saracen prince named Amerumnes had occasion to send his nephew to the town of Amplona in Syria, where a splendid church had been erected and dedicated to St. George. As soon as the Saracen descried this church from afar he told his servants to stable the camels there and put their provender upon the altar. On arriving they prepared to execute these orders; but the priests interposed, warning the prince against such a desecration of the house of God. No heed was paid to their remonstrance; the camels were driven into the church; as soon, however, as they crossed the threshold they fell down dead. This alarmed the Saracen, and he commanded his followers to remove the bodies of the camels from the church.

The day on which this occurred happened to be a festival, and a large congregation had assembled to hear Mass. The priest was almost afraid to begin, for he dreaded some act of profanation on the part of the Saracen, who stationed himself near the altar that he might observe the ceremonies of the Mass. He watched them attentively; and when the celebrant, according to the Greek rite, divided the consecrated host into four parts with a knife, it appeared to the interested onlooker as if he were cutting the flesh of a beauteous child, whose blood flowed into the chalice. Roused to indignation at this sight, he would have run the priest through with his sword on the spot had not curiosity as to what would ensue restrained him. When, at the time of communion, the priest consumed the sacred elements, to the eyes of the Saracen they bore, not the semblance of bread and wine, but of real flesh and blood. In every host which was administered to the communicants he observed the same appearance. "What barbarians these Christians must be!" he said to himself. "At their idolatrous rites they slay a child, whose flesh they eat. I will surely avenge the cruel murder of this innocent babe, and put these savage monsters to a miserable end." At the conclusion of the Mass the priest distributed the eulogia, or blessed bread, to the people, and gave a piece to the stranger. "What is this?" he angrily asked. The priest answered: "It is blessed bread." Then the unbeliever exclaimed aloud: "Is this what you offer upon the altar, inhuman wretch? Have I not myself seen you slay a sweet child with your own hands, eat His flesh and drink His blood? and did you not afterwards give it to others?" The priest, amazed beyond expression, replied humbly: "My lord, I am a sinner, unworthy to look upon mysteries so sublime; since you have been privileged to behold them, you must enjoy great favor with God." The Saracen then asked whether it had not been as he had seen. The priest replied that so indeed it was; but to the eyes of sinful man it was not given to penetrate this deep mystery, and he saw nothing more than bread and wine, which by the words of consecration were changed into the body and blood of Christ. So deeply was the Saracen impressed by what he had seen and heard that he expressed the wish to become a Christian, and begged to be baptized. But the priest, fearing the anger of the prince's uncle, refused to comply with his request, bidding him, if he were really in earnest, to betake himself to the bishop on Mount Sinai and relate to him what he had witnessed; the bishop would then instruct him in the Christian faith and admit him to holy Baptism. Thereupon the Saracen returned to his followers, without, however, telling them a word of what had passed; under cover of night, disguised in a palmer's weeds, he secretly took his departure, and made his way to Mount Sinai, where he acquainted the bishop with the cause of his conversion. He was duly instructed and baptized, the name of Pachomius being given to him. Later on he became a monk. After three years spent in austere penance he returned, with his superior's permission, to his home, in the hope of converting his father. He was, however, put to cruel torture and finally stoned to death.

This miracle proves to us not only that the body and

blood of Our Lord are really present in the Adorable Sacrament, but also that He is truly immolated upon the altar, mystically, although not actually. To the Saracen it was given to see the priest in the Mass apparently dividing the flesh of a child, in order that he who was a complete unbeliever might, by his astonishment at what he beheld, be led to inquire, and to embrace the Christian religion. Moreover, God willed that this occurrence should be recorded, and handed down to posterity, to increase our knowledge, and confirm our faith in this transcendent mystery. For although in holy Mass Christ does not suffer physical pain or death, yet He displays Himself to His heavenly Father under the same pitiable appearance which He presented when scourged, crowned with thorns, and crucified; and this as distinctly as if He were again enduring these tortures in reality for the sins of the world.

On this subject Lancicius says: " Holy Mass is a representation of the sufferings and death of Christ, not only in words, as anything may be reproduced upon the stage, but in deed and reality; hence the fathers of the Church call the Mass a repetition of Christ's passion, and allege that in it after a mystical manner He again suffers and is crucified." These are the words of a spiritual writer, the author of learned works on the mysteries of the Mass. We will give another instance in corroboration of what has been said.

In the lives of the fathers we read of an old, unlettered hermit, who could not grasp the truth of the real presence of Our Lord in the Blessed Sacrament. He used to say: "In the Holy Sacrament of the Altar we have not the body of Christ, but His image." Two other aged hermits, hearing this, went to him and endeavored to show him his error, expounding to him the teaching of the Catholic Church, and supporting their arguments by passages from the Holy Scriptures. But he would not be convinced: nothing short of a miracle, he said, could make him believe it. The hermits spent the week in prayer; when Sunday came, and they were all three present in the chapel at Mass, they saw, after the consecration, a child of great beauty on the altar in the place of the host. This sight filled them with holy joy. But their joy was changed to horror when, just at the breaking of the host, they saw an angel pierce the child with a knife, and collect in the chalice the blood which flowed from the wound. And when the man who refused to believe the doctrine of transubstantiation approached the altar to receive communion, as the priest was about to administer to him the Adorable Sacrament, he saw that it was blood-stained, and bore the appearance of flesh. Thereupon he cried aloud: " O Lord Jesus, I acknowledge my unbelief, and deplore my obstinate continuance in it. I steadfastly believe the consecrated bread to be Thy sacred body, the chalice Thy sacred blood. I beseech Thee again to conceal Thyself under the form of the host, that I may receive Thee to my soul's profit." His prayer was heard; he devoutly received communion, returned thanks to God and to the two fathers who had shown him his error, and proclaimed to all around what he had been privileged to behold in holy Mass.

Here we have additional evidence that Jesus Christ is not merely present in person and in reality in the sacred host, but that in holy Mass He renews His bitter passion. " Just as He once took upon Himself the sins of the whole world, that He might wash them away with His blood, so are our sins now laid upon Him, the same lamb Who is to be immolated upon the altar to atone for our transgressions." These words give the reason why Christ renews His passion and death in every Mass that is said;

we will, however, proceed to elucidate the subject somewhat more fully.

THE REASON WHY CHRIST RENEWS HIS PASSION IN HOLY MASS.

The cause wherefore Christ suffered His bitter passion cannot be better expressed than in the following words of Father Segneri, S.J.: "When Christ was upon earth, by His divine omniscience He foresaw that, in spite of His bitter passion, many millions of mankind would not participate in the redemption He purchased for them, and consequently would be doomed to eternal perdition. In the infinite love which He, as our elder brother, bore to us, and in His desire for our salvation, He offered Himself to His heavenly Father, declaring Himself willing to hang upon the cross, not three hours only, but until the end of time, in order that the tears He shed, the blood that flowed from His veins, His fervent prayers and sighs, might assuage the severity of divine justice, and move the divine compassion and loving-kindness to ordain some means whereby the loss of so vast a number of souls might be prevented."

St. Bonaventure, in his meditations, also says that Christ was ready to remain upon the cross until the end of the world, and other theologians concur in this opinion. Our Lord Himself has, furthermore, revealed to many saints that He would suffer over again all that He suffered for the whole world for the sake of one sinner.

The Eternal Father did not accept the offer made by the Saviour to prolong His passion upon the cross until the last day; the three hours of His crucifixion were amply sufficient; and in His omniscience He knew that whosoever failed to share in the merits of the sacred passion would have only himself to blame for the loss of his soul.

Far from quenching the ardor of Christ's love for man, this sentence only kindled it the more, and strengthened His desire to rescue us unhappy sinners from eternal damnation. Therefore in His divine wisdom He devised a means whereby He could remain on earth after His death, continue His saving passion, unceasingly plead with God for man as He did when nailed upon the cross. What was this wondrous means? None other than the most holy sacrifice of the Mass, wherein He daily, continually, suffers mystically upon the cross; suffers for us, pleads for us, calls upon God for grace and mercy on our behalf with irresistible urgency.

In the Bollandists' life of St. Colette (6th March), who was remarkable for her great devotion to holy Mass, it is said: On one occasion, when she was assisting at the Mass said by her confessor, she was heard, at the consecration, to exclaim: "O my God, my Jesus! O angels and saints, O men and sinners, what marvels are these that we see and hear!" After Mass her confessor asked what had made her cry aloud in this manner. She replied: "When your reverence elevated the sacred host, I beheld Christ upon the cross, the blood flowing from His precious wounds; at the same time I heard Him thus address the Eternal Father: Look upon this body of flesh, in which I hung upon the cross, in which I suffered for mankind. Look upon My wounds, look upon the blood that I shed, consider My sufferings, consider My death. All this I endured to save sinners. Now, if Thou dost consign them to perdition on account of their iniquities, and deliver them over to the devil, what compensation shall I have for My bitter passion, for My cruel death? The reprobate sinners will render Me no thanks; on the contrary, they will curse Me to all eternity. But if they were saved they would praise and magnify Me forever in gratitude for My sufferings. For My sake, therefore, spare these sinners, O My Father, and preserve them from eternal damnation."

By this we may understand how earnestly Our Lord intercedes for us in holy Mass, and implores His heavenly Father to have mercy upon us. For since the Mass is a renewal of His passion, while it is celebrated that must be enacted over again which was carried on upon the cross. On the cross Jesus cried with a loud voice: "Father, forgive them, for they know not what they do." (St. Luke xxiii. 34.) In like manner in holy Mass He cries from the altar, asking forgiveness for all sinners indeed, but yet more especially for those who are present at Mass. The voice with which He cries is so powerful, so persuasive, that it pierces the clouds, and reaches the heart of the Eternal Father. Thus Christ fulfils His office of mediator; as St. John says: "We have an advocate with the Father, Jesus Christ the just; and He is the propitiation for our sins." (1. St. John ii. 1, 2.) And St. Paul writes: "Christ Jesus that died, yea, that is risen also again; Who is at the right hand of God, Who also maketh intercession for us." (Rom. viii. 34.) He intercedes for us in heaven, but more especially He intercedes for us at the altar, because there He exercises His sacerdotal functions, and, as St. Paul says, it appertains to the priest to offer sacrifices for the sins of the people. (Heb. v. 1.)

St. Laurence Justinian bears the same testimony when he says: "When Christ is immolated upon the altar, He speaks to His Father, He shows Him the marks of the wounds on His sacred body, that by His intercession we may be saved from eternal torment." How much is done for our welfare by Christ's prayers from the altar! How often would calamities have befallen us had they not been averted by His prayers! How many thousands of the blessed, now happy in heaven, would be in hell had not Christ by His intercession saved them from that place of torment! Let us, therefore, go frequently and gladly to Mass, in the hope that we may have a share in His intercession, be preserved from evil, and, through that omnipotent mediator, obtain from God that which of ourselves we cannot obtain.

We have now seen the principal reason why Christ renews His passion in holy Mass; it is in order to be able to intercede for us with as much efficacy as when He hung upon the cross, and to move His heavenly Father to compassion by the sight of His sufferings.

Another reason of the renewal of Christ's passion in the Mass is this: in order to apply to us the fruits of His sacrifice of Himself upon the cross. We shall understand this better if we bear in mind that, throughout the whole course of His life, and preeminently on the cross, He earned an infinite store of merits, of which only a few pious persons, who were found worthy to receive them, were then made partakers. He now communicates these treasures daily on many occasions, but chiefly during holy Mass. A pious writer tells us: " That which on the cross was a sacrifice of redemption is in holy Mass a sacrifice of appropriation, whereby the virtue and the power of the sacrifice of the cross is applied to each one individually." These are joyful and reassuring words for the sinner. It has not been our privilege to stand beneath the cross on Calvary, and share in the fruits of that stupendous sacrifice; but if we hear Mass with attention the virtue and power of the sacrifice of the cross will be applied to our souls, not, indeed, in quite the same manner, yet to each one in particular according to the depth of his devotion.

Now see what an immense benefit it is for us that Christ renews His passion in holy Mass for our sakes, bestowing upon and applying to us the merit of it! And why, thinkest thou, does He do this? Principally that we may take for our own the merits of that passion, and offer them to Almighty God, to the great profit of our souls. St. Mechtilde tells us of what advantage this offering is to us. To her Christ once said: "Behold, I bestow all My bitter sufferings upon thee, that they may be thine own, and thou give them back, and offer them to Me." And that we might know that this gift is made to us preeminently in holy Mass Our Lord added: "He who offers up to Me My passion, which I have made his, shall receive twofold for all that he gives, as I have said: He shall receive a hundredfold, and shall possess life everlasting."

These words are indeed full of comfort. Happy above measure are we in possessing holy Mass, since in it Christ bestows on us treasures of great price, which it is within our power to increase and augment. If we do but say to Our Lord: "I offer Thee, O Jesus, Thy bitter passion," He replies: "My child, I give it back to Thee in twofold measure," and if we offer Him His precious blood the answer is the same, for whatever portion of His sufferings we present to Him He returns us double for all we offer. This He will do as often as we offer to Him as our own any part of His passion. Truly this is good usury, an easy method of acquiring spiritual riches!

There is yet another reason for the renewal of Christ's passion in holy Mass. He does this in order that the faithful, for whom it is impossible to have assisted at the sacrifice of the cross, may, by assisting at Mass, earn the same graces and merits as if they had actually stood beneath the cross, provided they do so with the same devotion. This is saying a great deal, for it is tantamount to saying: See how great a sacrifice is ours! It is not merely a memorial of the sacrifice once offered upon the cross: it is one and the same, and will always be the same. Moreover, the fruits it produces are identical with those produced by the sacrifice of the cross. This assertion appears almost incredible. Can it possibly be that the holy sacrifice of the Mass is the self-same sacrifice that was offered on Calvary? Can it possibly produce the same effects as Christ's passion? That this is so proves how admirable and how efficacious a sacrifice it is. Listen to the words of Molina on this point.

"Christ has ordained that His Church should perpetually offer the same sacrifice which He offered upon the cross, the identical sacrifice although it be offered not in a bloody, but an unbloody, manner. I say the same sacrifice, yet the Mass contains infinitely more graces and excellencies. As it is the same sacrifice as that of the cross, it must possess the same potency, and the same merit, and be equally acceptable to God. That it is really and essentially the same may be seen from the fact that the victim is the same, the priest is the same; it is offered to the same God, with the same object. The only difference consists in this, that the manner of offering is not the same; for then upon the cross Christ was immolated with pain and shedding of blood, whereas now in a painless and unbloody manner."

Ponder then, O Christian, these forcible words; consider the priceless value of the sacrifice of the Mass, its great dignity, its immense potency. Not only do we know this from the teaching of pious and learned men: Holy Church declares expressly that the sacrifice of the cross and the sacrifice of the Mass are one and the same.

Hence we see clearly that we can do as much to please Our Lord, and acquire as much merit for ourselves, when we hear Mass as we should have done had we been present on Calvary, if we are no less devout and recollected than we should have been standing beneath the cross. Ought we not to consider ourselves supremely fortunate in being able daily to witness Christ's passion in holy Mass, and apply the fruits of it to our souls? Fortunate indeed in that we can in spirit stand beneath the cross of the dying Saviour, that we can behold Him with our eyes, speak to Him with our lips, tell Him our troubles, obtain from Him help and consolation, just as those did who were present in person at the crucifixion. How highly we ought to prize the favors Christ thus daily places within our reach; how anxious should we be to claim a share in the graces He thus holds out to us!

CHAPTER IX.

IN THE HOLY MASS THE DEATH OF CHRIST IS RENEWED.

THE evangelist St. John tells us that Christ once said: "Greater love than this no man hath, that a man lay down his life for his friends." (St. John xv. 13.) There is nothing dearer or more precious to a man than his soul or his life; therefore in giving this up for a friend he gives up what is most valuable to him. But Christ went further than this; in His love for mankind he gave His life, not only for His friends, but also for His most inveterate enemies. Therefore His was no ordinary soul, but one which was holy and noble beyond compare. In the Gospel of St. John Our Lord says: "I lay down My life for My sheep." (*Ibid.* x. 15.) These words have apparently a special meaning; for Our Lord does not say: "I will lay down My life for My sheep," nor, "I have laid it down," but, "I lay down My life for My sheep"; that is to say, "I continue constantly to give My life for believers." This He does daily in holy Mass, wherein His death is renewed. The manner in which this is effected will now be explained.

In old times it was customary in Lent to act a passion-play, to place before the minds of the people more vividly the sufferings of Christ. A young man used to be fastened to a cross, and after hanging there for some time he used to feign the outward signs of approaching dissolution, as if expiring of agony, so that the spectators were moved to tears. Now in holy Mass no one plays the part of the Saviour; He offers Himself, He expires in person. He does not commission an angel or a saint to act for Him, for they could not do what He does as He does it. Day after day He re-enacts His passion in the sight of heaven and earth, that it may always be had in remembrance by God in holy Mass as it was enacted on Calvary. We will give an anecdote in illustration of this, and then confirm it by the teaching of theologians.

Cesar of Heisterbach relates that in his monastery there was a father named Gottschalk who, whilst saying the midnight Mass at Christmas at a side-altar, with much devotion and tears, beheld after the consecration a child of wondrous beauty in his hands instead of the sacred host. He clasped the child in his arms and kissed it, his soul meanwhile being filled with ineffable sweetness. In a few moments the child vanished, and the priest ended his Mass. Before his death, which occurred shortly after, he related to the bishop what he had seen. The bishop was much struck with it, and gave an account of the apparition to one of his priests who thought rather lightly of the sacerdotal office. This priest listened to it attentively, and at the end said with a sigh: "Alas! why does God reveal these things to saints and men who are perfect in faith? He ought rather to permit unhappy sinners like myself, who are apt to doubt the reality of His presence in the Blessed Sacrament, thus to see behind the veil." Not long after, while he was one day standing at the altar, it was given to this same priest to see what good Father Gottschalk saw. As he was in the act of breaking the sacred host before the *Agnus Dei* he beheld a child of striking loveliness in his hands. Covered with confusion at the sight, he turned the sacred host, and lo! there was Christ upon the cross, His head bowed down, apparently at the point of death. The priest was deeply touched; he nearly fainted; tears streamed from his eyes as he gazed on the figure of the dying Saviour, and he knew not whether to proceed with the Mass. But the vision quickly vanished, the host regained its former shape, and the Mass was concluded amid many tears. The congregation in the interim were anxious to know what had befallen their pastor, why he had been such a long time over the Mass, and why he had wept so freely. Conscious of this, he immediately went up into the pulpit, and told them of the vision he had had of the infant Christ and of the dying Saviour. The impression he had received was deep and permanent; he amended his life, did penance for his former negligence, and to the day of his death was in every respect a model for the imitation of his parishioners.

This vision shows us to a certain extent how our Redeemer, in holy Mass, places His cruel death before God the Father and God the Holy Ghost, besides the whole company of heavenly spirits, in such a manner as not to give them grief, but to acquaint them with the immensity of the love which led Him thus to suffer for the redemption of the world. Could we for once be privileged to see as that priest did our expiring Lord in the sacred host, how willingly, how attentively, should we hear

Mass! how profoundly should we compassionate Our Saviour in His agony! We may behold this if we will, not with our bodily eyes, it is true, but with the eyes of faith. As often as we kindle within us such faith we please Our Lord and earn a rich recompense for ourselves. For the purpose of enabling us to believe more firmly Christ gives us some clear and plain signs of His death in the Mass, which are thus expounded to us by those who are learned in the divine science:

When, at the Last Supper, Jesus converted bread and wine into His sacred body and blood, He did not change both at the same time, nor under one form, but changed each separately, and under two distinct forms. He might have said the words: "This is My body and My blood," over the bread; had He done so, the bread would have been truly His living body and blood, but He would not thus have manifested His death to us in so clear a manner. He chose, therefore, first to change the bread only, by virtue of the words of consecration, into His sacred body and give it to His disciples to eat, and afterwards the wine into His sacred blood, and give it also separately to His disciples. And by the guidance of the Holy Spirit He has taught His Church to ordain that the priest should first change the bread into His sacred body, and elevate it, and then proceed to change the wine into His blood, and elevate that also separately, to bring His death more definitely before the minds of the people.

On this subject Lancicius says: "Because, in the order of nature, dissolution follows upon the total separation of the blood from the body, this being the immediate cause of Christ's death upon the cross, the manner in which He chose to accomplish the sacrifice of Himself, therefore in the holy sacrifice of the Mass His death is likewise set forth by the separation of His blood from His body. Thus by the words of consecration His body becomes present under the form of the bread, His blood beneath that of the wine, each distinct and apart from the other." This is a true immolation of Christ, wherein the substances of bread and wine are changed and annihilated.

In explanation of this Gervase says: "The victim offered in holy Mass is Christ; not, indeed, under the form He wears in heaven, but as He is under the form of the bread and of the wine, as it were dead: for He is in a condition of immobility and inaction, as far as all the powers of the body are concerned. But at the same time He can exercise all the powers of the soul, the understanding, the will, etc."

The mind of man cannot fully conceive, nor the tongue of man adequately express, how acceptable to Almighty God is this representation and reproduction of Christ's passion. Yet we must endeavor to form some idea of it. When Christ thus places His death before God the Father in the Mass, He renders Him the same perfect obedience which He formerly rendered to Him. In every respect His obedience was perfect, but never did it cost His human nature so dear as when He submitted to the death upon the cross. St. Paul thus speaks of this act: "He humbled Himself, becoming obedient unto death, even to the death of the cross." And that we might know how pleasing to God the Father this obedience, so difficult to flesh and blood, was, and how richly it was recompensed, he adds: "For which cause God also hath exalted Him, and hath given Him a name which is above all names." (Phil. ii. 8, 9.) This perfect obedience Christ offers to His Father in holy Mass, and with it He offers the heroic virtues that marked His passion and death: His spotless innocence, His profound humility, His invincible patience, the ardent charity He displayed not only towards His Father, but towards His executioners, His enemies, and towards us, ungrateful sinners that we are.

Furthermore, He places before Him the pain He suffered, the blows His tender heart received, the fear of death that disquieted Him, the dislocation of all His bones, finally, the thrust of the lance that pierced His sacred side. All these He places before Him as vividly as if all were happening over again at the present time, thus awakening anew the satisfaction God the Father experienced at the death of His beloved Son, when He saw how willingly He endured the bitterness of death out of love to Him and for His greater glory. And as Christ then appeased His Father's anger, obtained pardon for transgressors, and reconciled the world to God, so He does now in every Mass, procuring for us blessings for which we can never be grateful enough.

Let us now hear what pious and learned men say respecting the immense benefits which come to us by this renewal of Christ's death. First of all let us listen to Pope St. Gregory: "This victim preserves souls from eternal perdition in a special manner, for it represents the death of the only-begotten Son of God." What consolation do not these words convey to the heart of those who on account of their sins are apprehensive concerning their eternal salvation. For St. Gregory, whose writings were inspired by the Holy Ghost, expressly states that because the Mass reproduces mystically the death of Christ it thereby possesses in an especial manner the power of preserving souls from everlasting death. Let us, therefore, be diligent in hearing Mass, let us venerate the death of Christ, and offer it as an oblation to God the Father, that we may escape eternal perdition.

The learned Mansi expresses himself in the following

instructive and encouraging manner: "Since the only-begotten Son of God, Who offered Himself as a victim upon the altar of the cross, is sacrificed afresh in the Mass, it follows of necessity that the sacrifice of the Mass is of as great value as the sacrifice of the cross." We shall proceed to show the truth of this saying, and how it is to be rightly understood.

No less reassuring is what Cardinal Hosius says: "Although in holy Mass we do not crucify Christ afresh, yet we make ourselves partakers in His death as much as if this were the case. In the sacrifice of the cross His death was with shedding of blood; in the sacrifice of the Mass His death is bloodless and mystical, yet it produces the same fruit as the sacrifice of blood, just as if the latter were now being carried on." Does it not seem strange, this that we are taught, that the reproduction of Christ's death in an invisible manner should produce the same effects as His actual and visible death? Yet so the cardinal declares, for he adds: "For we are made to participate in the Mass in the fruits of Christ's death just as if He were expiring before our eyes." As this is so, who can estimate the power and efficacy of holy Mass, the blessings it contains for those who piously assist at it? Hadst thou stood, O reader, upon Calvary beside thy dying Saviour, how great the graces, the spiritual treasures, thou wouldst have carried away with thee thence! Thou wilt find no less rich a store, which thou canst make thine own, in holy Mass, if thou hearest it in the same spirit as if thou wert in the presence of thy dying Redeemer.

Concerning this the Abbot Rupert remarks: "Just as Christ when hanging upon the cross granted forgiveness of sins to all who came to Him, even so when present under the form of bread and wine He grants the same forgiveness of sins to all the faithful." These words encourage us to hope that by hearing Mass piously we may work off a good portion of the penalty due to our sins.

In the writings of Father Segneri this forcible passage occurs: "The sacrifice of the cross wrought the remission of sin in general; in holy Mass the virtue of Christ's blood is applied to this and that person individually. By His death and passion Christ collected the riches which in the Mass are dealt out to us. His death is a treasury, Mass the key that unlocks it." Hence, when we go to Mass, Christ puts, as it were, into our hand the key of His well-stored treasury, and allows us to enter and carry away graces in proportion to the devotion of our heart.

The same writer says further: "Observe, therefore, what it really means to say or to hear Mass. To do so is equivalent to causing God, Who once died for all mankind, to die over again, in a mystical manner, for me, and thee, and each one present, just as if He suffered death for the sake of each one individually." Lay these words to heart, O Christian reader; consider the love wherewith Christ requites thee when thou hearest Mass for love of Him. He repays thy service so liberally that He is ready to give His life for thee, and to bestow on thee the merits of His death. He does in fact die for thee spiritually, and would die again for thee corporally, and with the same suffering as of yore, were this possible and necessary.

Our Lady once spoke thus to an eminent servant of God: "So great is the charity of my Son towards those who assist at holy Mass that He would, if needful, die for each one as many times as that individual had heard Mass; but this is not necessary, because His merits are infinite." So astonishing is this statement that one seems hardly able to believe it; yet it is in harmony with the infinite charity of Christ, which urges Him daily to sacrifice Himself, not once, but many thousand times, in a spiritual manner for hapless sinners. Let us resolve, therefore, to hear Mass daily with devout attention, to go in spirit with Christ to Calvary, to stand by him during His passion and at His death. The author of the *Imitation* bids us do this in the passage already quoted: " As often as thou sayest or hearest Mass it ought to seem to thee as great, as new, and as delightful as if Christ, that same day first hanging on the cross, was suffering and dying for the salvation of men." (Bk. iv. ch. 2.). Yes, He truly suffers and dies in a mystical manner for each one who hears Mass, and that with the same charity wherewith He sacrificed Himself in His body upon the cross for all the human race.

What unfathomable charity, what boundless grace, is this that Jesus Christ, the Son of God, should die in a mystic manner for those who hear Mass, as He once died visibly for the whole world! How profitable, how salutary, is this for us! How great are the merits we may gain! Hadst thou been present on Calvary, and hadst thou there offered to God the Father the sufferings of His Son in His last agony, thinkest thou not that thou wouldst have obtained the pardon of all thy sins? The loving Father would doubtless have granted thee, a repentant sinner, full remission of thy guilt and its penalties for the sake of His dear Son Who died for thee. Well, then, thou canst ask this forgiveness in holy Mass, because Jesus is truly present there, in the same sacred humanity in which He suffered and died.

CHAPTER X.

IN THE HOLY MASS THE SHEDDING OF CHRIST'S BLOOD IS RENEWED.

ST. PAUL, in his Epistle to the Hebrews, thus describes the custom under the Old Dispensation of sprinkling the people with the blood of the sacrificial victim, that by this sprinkling all might be purified and sanctified: " When every commandment of the law had been read by Moses to all the people, he took the blood of calves and goats with water and scarlet wool and hyssop, and sprinkled both the book itself and all the people, saying: This is the blood of the testament, which God hath enjoined unto you. The tabernacle also, and all the vessels of the ministry, in like manner, he sprinkled with blood. And almost all things, according to the law, are cleansed with blood: and without shedding of blood there is no remission." (Heb. ix. 19–22.) This shedding of blood and sprinkling were a type of the shedding of Christ's blood, and the sprinkling of that divine blood upon us, which is far more efficacious for the washing away of sin than the blood of the Jewish rite. For St. Paul says in the same chapter: " If the blood of goats and of oxen sanctify such as are defiled, to the cleansing of the flesh, how much more shall the blood of Christ cleanse our conscience from dead works, to serve the living God?" (*Ibid.*)

But some one reading this may perhaps say: " Christ shed His sacred blood in His passion, and the believers living at that time were sprinkled with it; we, however, were not born then, and thus we are deprived of this great grace." Distress not thyself on this account, O Christian; the blood of Christ was then shed just as much for us as for the faithful of that day. Besides, of His divine wisdom Christ devised another means by virtue of which He daily sheds His precious blood, and applies it for the cleansing of our souls. Dost thou ask when and how this is done? I answer, Whenever Mass is celebrated, as shall now be explained.

The first authority to be quoted is St. Augustine, who says: "The blood of Christ is shed for sinners in holy Mass." These words are so plain that they need no elucidation, and they are uttered by one so trustworthy that no one can gainsay his testimony. We will next listen to St. Chrysostom, who expresses himself thus: "The Lamb of God is immolated for thee, His blood flows mystically upon the altar; the blood contained in the chalice is drawn for thy cleansing from His sacred side." This passage has been expounded as follows: "Once for all Christ shed his blood in a visible and painful manner, but at this we could not be present. This shedding of blood is, however, repeated daily in an invisible manner: His hands are wounded, His feet are transfixed, His side is pierced, His blood is made to flow, but in a manner of which our senses cannot take cognizance. We can appropriate to ourselves His infinite merits by our glowing desire, by our contrition and sorrow, by holy communion, but above and beyond all by hearing Mass." These words deserve attentive consideration; they are those of a learned theologian, and he expressly tells us that by no means can we participate in the merits of Christ so surely as by assisting at Mass, adding these words: "In the Mass the priest by the prayer of consecration draws, as it were, the blood from the Saviour's side, in order to apply it to thee for thy cleansing, thy sanctification, the forgiveness of thy sins." Many other authorities might be cited in confirmation of this statement, but we will content ourselves with the testimony of the learned Father Natali, who says: "The same blood which flowed from the side of Christ is in the chalice after the words of consecration have been spoken, and it is shed for us for the remission of sins."

The formula of consecration is, however, this: "This is the chalice of My blood, . . . which shall be shed for you and for many, to the remission of sins." These are Christ's own words, whereby He changed the wine into His precious blood. By His command the priest utters the same words; he does not, however, utter them as if he merely meant to proclaim from the altar what the words were which Christ made use of, but as asserting it to be true that the wine is changed into the blood of Christ, as is in fact the case.

Now the priest does not content himself with saying: "This is the chalice of My blood"; he continues: "which shall be shed for you and for many, to the remission of sins." As the first part of the sentence is certainly fulfilled, with no less certainty will the latter part be fulfilled. Consequently the sacred blood of Christ is verily and indeed shed in the Mass "for you and for many"; that is, for you who are present, and for the many who are absent; for those who hear Mass and for those who would gladly do so if they could, and who therefore desire a memento in it. These are the "many" for whom Christ's blood is shed in holy Mass for the remission of sins.

This proof is of greater force than any other, for the authority upon which it rests is none other than the truth which comes from the lips of God Himself. How sublime a mystery is this! How unspeakable is the love of Christ to us poor sinners! Is it really possible that our adorable Jesus, Who shed His blood to the last drop for us, should shed it again and again for us, daily, hourly, for the remission of our sins and for our eternal salvation? How great are the graces, the blessings they receive who assist at holy Mass! "As oft as the blood of Christ is shed," says St. Ambrose, "it is shed for the remission of sins." What greater inducement can we have to hear Mass than the assurance that by doing so we can obtain remission of our sins? We are not left in doubt as to whether the chalice really contains Christ's blood, for God has revealed this truth and made it evident by numerous miracles, of which one will now be narrated.

We read in the writings of Cesar of Heisterbach that about the year 1220 there lived in the archdiocese of Cologne a female recluse who had retired from the world and taken up her abode in a kind of cell built on to the wall of a church, where she led a life of contemplation and penance. This recluse had a special devotion for holy Mass, and a small window was constructed in the wall of her dwelling to enable her to assist at it. But the evil enemy, finding her on other points proof against his assaults, contrived to instil into her mind a tormenting doubt as to the transubstantiation of the wine into the blood of Our Lord. This temptation was so strong that it quite overthrew her faith, and she even communicated her doubts to some women with whom she held intercourse through a window. But God had compassion on His servant and wrought a visible miracle to deliver her from error. One day, when the priest of a neighboring parish was saying Mass, through carelessness (or perhaps by the special permission of Providence) he overturned the chalice after the consecration. He was horrorstruck, but still more so when he observed that the wine which was spilt had assumed the appearance and color of blood. At the conclusion of the Mass he tried in every way to wash the stain out of the corporal, but all was in vain. When the next Sunday came, he took the blood-stained corporal up into the pulpit, told the congregation what had occurred, and with tears held up the corporal to their view. This made a great impression upon the people, who were much touched at the sight of the Saviour's blood, and the conviction was borne in upon the priest that the miracle was intended to confirm the faith of those who were tempted to doubt. Accordingly he made it known far and wide; at length he went to the dwelling of the recluse of whom we have spoken, told her all that had happened, and exhibited the blood-stained corporal to her also. As soon as she saw the marks of the precious blood she fell to the ground, bewailed her fault with bitter tears, and humbly begged the pardon of all who were present. She then made aloud a profession of faith, saying: "I steadfastly believe that in the consecrated chalice the true, natural blood of Christ is really present, the same that was shed for us upon the cross; and in this belief I hope to live and die." The priest returned home, and on again placing the corporal in water he found to his astonishment that the stains instantly disappeared. When the recluse heard this, she perceived that God in His mercy had worked this wonder for her good, and this conviction served to establish her still more firmly in faith.

Something similar is told of Father Peter Cavagnelas, a monk of the Order of St. Jerome. For a long time he was a prey to terrible doubts as to whether the blood of Christ was present in the sacred host. One day when, in saying Mass, he came to these words of the canon: "We most humbly beseech Thee, Almighty God, command these things to be carried by the hands of Thy holy angel to Thy altar on high, in the sight of Thy divine majesty," and, according to the rules of the rubric, bowed down profoundly, behold, a cloud descended upon the altar and concealed both the host and the chalice from his sight. The priest felt much alarmed, for he knew not what this thing meant. He made an act of sincere contrition and lifted up his heart in fervent prayer to God. After a time his petition was heard, the cloud lifted, and he saw the sacred host suspended over the chalice. While he gazed upon it with reverence, he perceived that blood was dropping from it; this continued until there was exactly the same quantity as there had been wine in the chalice. Joy filled his heart; all his doubts vanished; thenceforth nothing ever obscured his firm faith in the presence of the blood of Christ in the sacred host.

These two stories show that the body and blood of Christ are both present at the same time in each of the elements, although by virtue of the prayer of consecration the body of Christ is principally under the form of bread in the sacred host, His body under the form of wine in the sacred chalice. Here we may pause, and endeavor to realize what an immense grace it is for us to possess the adorable blood of Christ in the Mass. The Catholic Church owns no greater, more costly treasure; for a single drop of this blood which is united to the person of the Divinity outweighs in value all the riches of heaven and of earth. This precious blood is not only present with us in the Mass, we have it for our very own (as was said in Ch. V.), and as our own we may offer it to Almighty God.

THE MANNER IN WHICH THE BLOOD OF CHRIST IS SPRINKLED UPON US IN HOLY MASS.

Hitherto we have been inquiring in what way the precious blood of Christ is shed in holy Mass; we will now see how it is sprinkled. For we know that as the precious blood is really shed when Mass is celebrated, so it is likewise sprinkled upon all who are present, and poured out upon their souls. Of this we have a clear type in the Old Testament, to which St. Paul refers when he says how Moses sprinkled the blood of calves and goats upon all the people, saying: "This is the blood of the testament, which God hath enjoined unto you." (Heb. ix. 20.) The words Christ employed when He consecrated the chalice at the Last Supper are almost identical: "This is the new testament in My blood." (St. Luke xxii. 20.) St. Paul adds, in the passage already quoted: "It is necessary, therefore, that the patterns of heavenly things should be cleansed with these: but the heavenly things themselves with better sacrifices than these." (Heb. ix. 23.) By this he meant to say: The Jewish synagogue, which was a type of the Catholic Church, was cleansed by the sprinkling of the blood of calves and goats, whereas the Catholic Church is cleansed by the blood of the Lamb of God. Now in order that anything be cleansed either with blood or with water it must be sprinkled or moistened with blood or water. Thus, if our souls are cleansed by the blood of Christ in the Mass, they must be sprinkled therewith, as we will now proceed to show.

St. Chrysostom says: "Thou seest that Christ is immolated in the Mass, thou seest that the people present are sprinkled and marked with the crimson blood from His veins." In this passage this great doctor of the Church expressly asserts that in holy Mass the blood of Christ is not merely poured out for us, but poured out upon us. Marchantius says the same: "The precious blood is shed in the Mass as a holy oblation, and the souls of the faithful who stand around are sprinkled with it." It would be impossible to employ plainer language than this. St. John likewise speaks no less clearly:

"Jesus Christ hath loved us, and washed us from our sins in His own blood." (Apoc. i. 5.) Observe, the Apostle does not say that Christ sprinkles us with His blood, but that we are actually washed in it.

St. Paul bears the like witness when he says: "You are come to Jesus the mediator of the New Testament, and to the sprinkling of blood which speaketh better than that of Abel." (Heb. xii. 24.) Here it may be asked: When do we come to Jesus, our mediator? In holy communion we approach very near to Him, and receive Him into our hearts. But we do not come to Him as to our mediator then: we receive Him as our spiritual sustenance. It is in holy Mass that we come to Him as our true mediator and intercessor, for in this He is Himself the real high priest, Whose office it is to make intercession for the people. Now if we come to Him in the Mass as to our mediator, at the same time we come, as St. Paul says, to the sprinkling of blood. This sprinkling takes place whenever Mass is celebrated; our bodies are not sprinkled, but our souls. In His passion the blood of Christ was shed, but it fell upon the stones and upon the ground. In holy Mass the self-same blood is shed; it does not, however, fall upon the earth, nor upon the bodies of men: it is applied to the souls of those who are present. Just as Moses sprinkled the Jews with the blood of the sacrificial victims, and the priest sprinkles Christian people with holy water, so Christ spiritually sprinkles the souls of the faithful with His blood, which is shed for them in the Mass.

This spiritual sprinkling is far more beneficial to us than the material sprinkling. Hear what St. Magdalen of Pazzi says concerning it: "This blood, when applied to the soul, imparts to it as much dignity as if it were decked in a costly robe; it imparts to it such brilliance and splendor that couldst thou behold the effulgence of thy soul when sprinkled with that blood thou wouldst fall down to adore it." Remarkable words indeed! Happy the soul which is adorned with such beauty! Happy the man who is privileged to gaze upon it! Go often to Mass, dear reader, that thou mayst then be sprinkled with the blood of Christ and arrayed in rich apparel, which will render thee glorious forever in the sight of angels and saints. For the purpose of strengthening thee in the belief that Christ's blood is applied to our souls in holy Mass I will relate an instance to the point.

In the life of Pope Urban IV. we read that about the year 1263, in the town of Bolsena, near Rome, there was a priest to whom one day, while he was saying Mass, just after the consecration, the devil suggested doubts as to whether Our Lord was really present in the sacred host. He said within himself: "I neither see nor feel anything to make me think this is Christ's veritable body. It cannot be so; this is nothing more than it appears, a mere wafer-bread." Thus he did not only doubt Christ's presence, he actually denied it, and fell into the sin of heresy. However, he proceeded with the Mass, and elevated the host as usual, and lo! a wonderful miracle occurred. When the host was lifted up, blood began to trickle from it like a gentle shower from heaven. The priest was so terrified that he did not know what he did. The people who were present saw the miracle, and could not refrain from exclaiming aloud: "O sacred blood! O blood of our God! For whose sake art thou shed?" and again: "O blood from the Saviour's veins, fall upon our souls, cleanse them from the stains of sin! Precious blood, forgive us our sins, and call upon God for mercy!" The voices of the congregation recalled the priest to himself; he thought to lay the sacred host upon the corporal, but it was soaked with blood to such an extent that there was scarcely a dry place left. Then tears burst from his eyes, and he bitterly repented his unbelief. He went on with the Mass, although hardly able to do so from weeping. After the communion he folded the blood-stained corporal together and laid it aside, thinking to conceal the wonderful occurrence. But after Mass the people came to him and questioned him about what had happened, as they knew not whether their eyes had deceived them. So he was obliged to exhibit the corporal to them; and at the sight of it they were so deeply moved that they fell on their knees, struck their breasts, and with tears besought the mercy of God. The report of this spread far and wide; an innumerable multitude of devout people came to Bolsena, desirous to see the proof of the miracle. When Pope Urban IV. heard of it, he bade the priest present himself before him, bringing the corporal with him. The priest obeyed; trembling, he fell at the feet of the Pope and the cardinals and ecclesiastics who were present, confessed the doubts that had assailed him, related what had happened, and showed the corporal soaked with the precious blood. The Pope and the whole assembly forthwith venerated upon their knees the precious blood, and later on a splendid church was erected at Bolsena in honor of the precious blood by order of His Holiness, who, furthermore, enjoined that the miraculous corporal should be deposited there, and every year, on the anniversary of the day when the miracle occurred, it should be solemnly carried in procession round the church.

That which was seen at Bolsena six hundred years ago comes to pass every day in every one of our churches at every Mass, only in an unseen manner. When the priest, offering the highest act of worship, elevates the sacred host and the chalice, the blood of our God distils from them like a gentle rain from the clouds, bedewing not the earth, not the bodies of men, but the souls and minds of all who are present. Nor is its gracious influence confined to the good and pious: it is extended also to the evil. The souls of the just it purifies and embellishes; it makes them fruitful in good works, it strengthens them when they are weak, it subdues the force of temptation, it effects in them all the good of which each one is capable. Those who are not devout Christians it seeks to convert, to soften their hard hearts, to correct their evil inclinations; while to all who are enemies of God it offers peace and reconciliation. And for the sinner who, in his obduracy, resists the proffered grace, the precious blood pleads with God for him and arrests the arm of justice.

See how great are the benefits which accrue alike to the just and to the sinner through this life-giving blood! Hence learn how profitable it is for both the one and the other to go regularly to Mass. For there the just will be cleansed from their sins, as St. John says: "The blood of Jesus Christ, His Son, cleanseth us from all sin." (1. St. John i. 7.) And for the sinner it obtains the grace of conversion. Consider, then, O thou who truly lovest God, how signal a grace is this, that in holy Mass thy soul should be sprinkled, purified, beautified, by the sacred blood of Christ, thy Saviour. Couldst thou see thyself thus adorned, thus beautified, how heartfelt would be thy joy, thy gratitude towards God! How unremitting wouldst thou be in thy attendance at holy Mass!

THE MANNER IN WHICH THE PRECIOUS BLOOD INTERCEDES FOR US.

Amongst the many gifts and graces wherein those participate who hear Mass devoutly one of the principal is this, that the blood of Christ, shed upon the altar, pleads for us with God, and obtains mercy for us. How profitable, how salutary, for the sinner is this voice of impetration, how powerful is it in averting the wrath of God! All the grievous sins we commit cry to God for vengeance, and excite His anger against us, as we learn from Holy Scripture. For in the Book of Genesis God says: "The cry of Sodom and Gomorrha is multiplied, and their sin is become exceedingly grievous. I will go down and see whether they have done according to the cry that is come to me." (Gen. xviii. 20, 21.) Again, St. James says: "Behold the hire of the laborers who have reaped down your fields, which by fraud hath been kept back by you, crieth; and the cry of them hath entered into the ears of the Lord of Sabaoth." (James v. 4.) The prophet Isaias represents God as denominating all sins of whatever nature as a cry. Hence we perceive that our sins, as a great clamor, ascend continually to God, and challenge Him to manifest His just wrath against the world.

Who, then, is there who can allay the anger of God, who can turn aside His awful vengeance? There is no one in heaven or on earth who can do this; only when the blood of Jesus Christ speaks it is all-availing. For although the cry sent up by innumerable sins is so loud that it is heard in the height of heaven, yet the voice of the blood of Christ is still more powerful; it is almighty and infinite, it does not merely pierce the clouds, it reaches the heart of God the Father. And how greatly soever the frightful and horrible clamor of a world's sins and iniquities may anger and irritate the heart of God, the blood shed by Jesus Christ speaks in accents so sweet and pleasing that He forgets His wrath, for the pleasure He derives from the voice of Christ outweighs the displeasure caused by the clamor of sin.

The reader may perhaps ask: How can it be said

that this sacred blood cries to Heaven, as one hears nothing of it? In answer I ask: How could the blood shed by Abel cry to Heaven, as Abel was dead, and his blood flowed out of the wounds he had received? Yet we know God said to Cain: "The voice of thy brother's blood crieth to Me from the earth." (Gen. iv. 10.) This was no audible voice, yet it was so powerful that it rose from earth to heaven, it entered into the ears of God the Father, and called upon Him to avenge the fratricide. The voice of the blood shed by Jesus Christ in holy Mass is likewise mystic, yet it, too, is so powerful that it compels an angry God to show mercy. We know that this sacred blood cries to God in holy Mass from the words of St. Paul to the Hebrews: "You are come to Jesus the mediator of the New Testament, and to the sprinkling of blood which speaketh better than that of Abel." (Heb. xii. 24.) This passage implies that if we come to Jesus, sprinkled with blood, it cries to God for mercy upon sinners with a voice that will take no denial.

This precious blood, shed in the Mass, calls upon God with a loud, penetrating voice after this wise: "Behold and consider, O just God, how I, the precious blood of Thy first-born Son, have been shed, copiously and willingly, amid circumstances of pain and ignominy. Behold and consider the violence, the scorn, the cruelty, shown me; how I have been despised, spit upon, anathematized, trodden under foot. All this I endured with the utmost patience, that by my means sinners might be sanctified and saved. But Thou, O strict Judge, wilt condemn them on account of their sins, and cast them into the abyss of hell. Who will compensate me for the indignities I suffered? The sinners who are condemned will in their devilish hate heap maledictions upon me. If they were saved, they would bless and give thanks to me for all eternity. Hear my cry, therefore, O merciful God, and for my sake grant to sinners the grace of conversion and amendment, to the just the grace of final perseverance."

When the precious blood of Christ intercedes for us in this manner, it is impossible that God should turn a deaf ear to such an entreaty. For if the blood of innocent Abel cried from the ground with so loud a voice that it was heard in heaven, and God Himself was compelled to look down from heaven upon the earth, and avenge the fratricidal act, as we are told: "The voice of thy brother's blood crieth to Me from the earth. Now, therefore, cursed shalt thou be upon the earth, which hath opened her mouth and received the blood of thy brother at thy hand" (Gen. iv. 10, 11.)—if, I say, Abel's blood when shed availed so much, what will not the power of Christ's blood be, shed as it is daily upon our altars, and offered up to God! Abel's blood cried for vengeance; the blood of Christ cries for mercy. Now we know that God is far more inclined to show mercy than to do vengeance; as the Church says in one of her prayers: "O God, Whose property is ever to have mercy and to spare." St. Peter repeats the same in one of his epistles: "The Lord is not willing that any should perish, but that all should return to penance." (II. St. Pet. iii. 9.) Thus the blood of Christ obtains mercy with greater ease than Abel's blood obtains vengeance.

In the circumcision, the sweat of blood, the scourging, the crowning with thorns, the carrying of the cross, and the crucifixion the blood of the divine Saviour cried to Heaven for the reconciliation of mankind with God. It did not cry in vain; witness the words of St. Paul: "God indeed was in Christ, reconciling the world to Himself." (II. Cor. v. 9.) The same divine blood cries to God every day in holy Mass, not with one voice only, but with as many as He shed drops from His sacred body. It calls with a powerful, far-reaching voice; it cries with all the force of His divinity and His humanity; and this not in one Mass alone, but in every one of the thousands that are daily celebrated. And with it at the same time the wounds of Christ cry with as many tongues as there were wounds on His body; the heart of Christ cries, its every throb an entreaty; the lips of Christ cry, their every sigh a prayer. Can we suppose it possible that a cry so manifold should fail to touch the heart of the Eternal Father? Even had it been already determined that the sinner should receive the just reward of his deeds, so powerful, so adorable, is the blood of Christ that divine justice cannot refuse to fulfil its request.

In corroboration of what has been said I will relate a remarkable occurrence. In former times, in the archdiocese of Mayence, there was a small town called Walldürn. Now it happened in the year 1330 that the parish priest of that place was so careless as to overturn the chalice after the consecration, so that the sacred blood was poured out upon the corporal. Immediately there appeared upon the corporal the image of Christ crucified, and around it eleven representations of the head of the Saviour, with the crown of thorns and disfigured with blood. In his confusion and alarm the priest concealed the corporal under the altar-stone, fearing the chastisement of God and the reprimand of his ecclesiastical superiors. But his conscience left him no peace, and he took the matter so much to heart that he fell into a mortal sickness. In his last agony, which was long and painful, he sent for a neighboring priest, confessed his carelessness in overturning the chalice, and told him where the corporal was hidden. He also gave him permission to make the miraculous occurrence public. After his death, which took place within a short time, the priest took out the corporal, kissed it reverently, and exhibited it to the people, giving, at the same time, a full account of the incident. Sometime later he took the corporal to his bishop; he sent him to Rome, where Pope Urban V., who then occupied the chair of Peter, confirmed the miracle, and granted an indulgence to the faithful who should visit Walldürn to venerate the sacred blood.

Here the question arises why the precious blood that was spilt should assume the shape of a crucifix and eleven representations of the head of the Saviour. In my opinion, amongst other reasons this one is to be noted, because the blood thus spilt calls to God for mercy. The number eleven probably corresponds to the number of drops that fell out of the chalice. These drops cried and called to God not for vengeance and chastisement, but for mercy and pardon, both for the priest himself, and for all those who should venerate the sacred blood. It implored and obtained for the priest the grace to repent and confess his fault before his death, and for the people it continues to implore a similar grace, since experience proved that hardened sinners, who for long years had neglected confession, in presence of the sacred blood were struck with contrition and humbly confessed their sins.

In addition to the all-prevailing cry which the blood of Christ sends up to Heaven, there is something else peculiar to it, whereby the anger of God is appeased, namely, the sweet odor which ascends from that blood when it is shed upon the altar. Referring to the Jewish burnt-sacrifices, God says: "The morning holocaust you shall always offer every day of the seven days for the food of the fire, and for a most sweet odor to the Lord, which shall rise from the holocaust, and from the libations of each." (Numbers xxviii. 23, 24.) Now if the odor arising from the burnt flesh of animals and the effusion of their blood was agreeable to Almighty God, what will not the most sweet odor of Christ's precious blood effect, when offered upon the altar as a holocaust worthy of His divine majesty!

When the priest offers the chalice, he says: "We offer unto Thee, O Lord, the chalice of salvation, beseeching Thy clemency, that in the sight of Thy divine majesty it may ascend with the odor of sweetness for our salvation, and for that of the whole world. Amen." The priest makes use of these words because the wine contained in the chalice will be changed into the precious blood of Christ. St. Paul says: "Christ hath loved us, and hath delivered Himself for us, an oblation, and a sacrifice to God for an odor of sweetness." (Eph. v. 2.) When this precious holocaust was offered upon the cross, with shedding of blood, at the cost of great pain, so delicious was the fragrance that ascended to heaven that it counteracted the evil odor that arose from the many and grievous sins of mankind. For the death of Christ, the shedding of His blood, was more pleasing to God than the iniquities of the world were displeasing to Him. And when this divine Victim is sacrificed and His blood shed mystically upon our altars, a sweet and agreeable odor daily ascends thence unto the Lord. Thus, if with a contrite heart thou dost offer the precious blood of Christ to God in holy Mass, not only dost thou dispel the stench of thy sins by the perfume of His blood, but thou dost more to please God than thou hast done to displease Him by thy misdeeds.

When the patriarch Isaac, whose eyes were dimmed with age, had kissed his son Jacob, dressed in the garments of his brother Esau, Holy Scripture tells us that on smelling the fragrant smell of his garments he blessed him, and desired for him every kind of temporal prosperity. The most sweet odor of Christ's blood has a like effect; so that God looks with favor upon the pious worshipper who offers it to Him in holy Mass, and bestows upon him His divine benediction, with an increase of grace and of celestial gifts. All the saints, too, rejoice when Mass is celebrated, when the perfume of the sacred blood rises in clouds of fragrance from the altar, filling the courts of heaven, to the joy and refreshment of all its blessed denizens. Let it, therefore, be our endeavor when present at Mass to adore the precious blood with devout veneration, to implore its intercession, to offer it to God for our salvation.

CHAPTER XI.

HOLY MASS IS THE MOST EXCELLENT BURNT-OFFERING.

UNDER the Old Law there were four principal kinds of sacrifices: (1) The burnt-offering, in recognition of the supreme majesty of God; (2) the offering of praise and thanksgiving, in acknowledgment of the benefits received from God; (3) the peace-offering, or propitiatory sacrifice, to propitiate the divine favor; (4) the sin-offering, or expiatory sacrifice, to obtain forgiveness of sin and remission of the penalty of sin. Each one of these sacrifices had its own special ceremonial, and it was not permissible to offer sacrifices of a different nature in one and the self-same manner.

From the commencement of the world until the coming of Christ innumerable victims were offered to God Almighty, which from the testimony of Holy Scripture we know to have been acceptable to Him. According to the Mosaic law, the Jews were commanded to immolate daily two lambs of a year old as a burnt-offering, one in the morning, and one in the evening; on the Sabbath Day two were to be offered both morning and evening. At every new moon seven lambs, two calves, and one ram were prescribed for the burnt-offering, and the same number at Easter and Pentecost during seven consecutive days. At the feast of Tabernacles for a whole week fourteen lambs, thirteen calves, two rams, and one goat were to be offered. In addition to these costly sacrifices each individual brought an oblation on his own account, such as oxen, calves, sheep, lambs, rams, doves, wine, bread, incense, etc., to be offered according to one of the four ways above mentioned.

All this is stated here in order that those who read this book may know what costly and burdensome sacrifices it was obligatory upon the ancient patriarchs and Jewish priests in olden times to offer. Yet, notwithstanding the expense and trouble attaching to those sacrifices, they gave but little glory to God, and obtained no great reward for the persons who offered them. If, in spite of this, Holy Scripture tells us that these offerings were a sweet odor before God, the reason is this, because they were typical of the sacrifice of Christ. Hence we may learn how far happier we Catholics are than were the Jews of old, since Jesus, of His infinite goodness, has appointed for us a burnt-offering, the offering of which is attended with no difficulty, a sacrifice which of all others is most acceptable in God's sight, which is a source of the greatest joy in heaven, the greatest profit to mankind, the greatest solace to the souls in purgatory.

If it were possible for any one person, with his own hand and with profound devotion, to have immolated and offered to God as a burnt-offering all the victims which have been sacrificed since the beginning of the world until the coming of Christ, that individual would doubtless have paid much honor to God, and caused Him much satisfaction. But the service rendered and the satisfaction occasioned would be in no wise comparable with the glory, the felicity, derived by the divine majesty from one single Mass. How can that be possible, O my God? This we shall understand when we hear what manner of burnt-offering the Catholic Church has in holy Mass.

The Christian burnt-offering is a visible, material oblation, which is offered to God only by a duly qualified minister, as an acknowledgment of His supreme dominion over all creatures. St. Thomas says: "By this burnt-offering we testify that God is the primary source of all creation, the final end of all our felicity, the sovereign ruler of all things, Whom we adore, and to Whom, in evidence of our just subjection, we offer a visible victim, worthy of His august majesty." These words explain briefly what a burnt-offering essentially is; this will be made plainer by what follows.

The burnt offering is, by God's ordinance, reserved for Him alone, for He says by the lips of Isaias: "I the Lord, this is My name; I will not give My glory to another." (Is. xlii. 8.) Hence may be gathered the singular excellence of the burnt-offering, since it may be offered to no creature, not even to the Mother of God, or to any saint, without idolatry; to God alone may it be offered. God permits us to praise, to love, to honor, to invoke, His saints, but He has never given us permission to offer to them our sacrifice, the holy sacrifice of the Mass. The Council of Trent, speaking on this subject, says: "Although the Church has been accustomed at times to celebrate certain Masses in honor and memory of the saints, not, therefore, however doth she teach that sacrifice is offered unto them, but unto God alone, Who crowned them; whence neither is the priest wont to say: 'I offer sacrifice to thee, Peter, or Paul'; but, giving thanks to God for their victories, he implores their patronage, that they may vouchsafe to intercede for us in heaven whose memory we celebrate upon earth." (Session xxii. ch. 3.) Thus the Church teaches us that the Mass cannot be offered to any saint, but that it may be offered to God for the greater glory of the saints.

We will now speak of the nature and character of the burnt-sacrifice in order that its excellence may be better understood. According to the Jewish ritual, in the burnt-offering all the flesh of the victim was consumed by fire, whereas in other sacrifices only a portion was burnt, the remainder being eaten by the priests and those who offered the oblation. The reason why the whole of the victim was consumed in the burnt-offering was to show that all things belonged to God, and must be offered in His service. In strict justice God has a right to demand the life of every man as He commanded Abraham to slay and sacrifice his son Isaac. He was, however, content with Abraham's prompt obedience. In the law of Moses He commanded every first-born child to be sanctified to Him, saying: "They are all Mine." (Ex. xiii. 2.) He did not go so far as to require them to be immolated; it sufficed that the mother should present her child in the temple, and ransom it with money.

The only-begotten Son of God was accordingly presented by Mary, His Mother; and although she offered the customary oblation for Him, with this God was not satisfied: she had to offer Him again, to be tortured and put to death, in order that by His precious death all men might be released from the obligation of giving their life as a sacrifice to God. Concerning this St. Paul says: "If one died for all, then all were dead, and Christ died for all." (II. Cor. v. 14, 15.) For the life of Christ was far nobler than that of all men living; consequently His death was of more value in the sight of

God than the death of all mankind. And since Christ is thus offered up to God in every Mass that is celebrated, more glory is given to God, a greater act of worship is performed in one Mass than if every dweller upon earth laid down his life in honor of Him.

Gervase declares the holy sacrifice of the Mass to be of all acts of piety and devotion the noblest and the best. Why is this? Because in it we testify, not by word so much as by deed, that God has every right to demand from us the sacrifice of our life. Thus under the Old Dispensation the Jewish priest, at the time of sacrifice, was accustomed to say: "As I immolate this animal to the glory of God, so God, the supreme Lord, could, should He so will, destroy us all, one with another. Thus, when I slay this victim, it is to signify that it would only be His due were we to sacrifice our lives to His glory, and therefore I offer Him the life of this animal in the place of our own."

In like manner Sanchez observes: "The homage we pay to God, the glory we give Him in holy Mass, is so great that no greater service, no greater honor, could be shown Him upon earth. For thereby we testify that in His sovereign majesty He is worthy that not the blood of calves and goats, but the most precious blood of His first-born Son, should be offered to Him in sacrifice."

Meditate upon what these two learned men say respecting the value of holy Mass, and the infinite honor it enables us to pay to God Almighty. Ought we not to hasten with joy to Mass in order to unite with the priest in performing this highest act of homage to Him Who is our rightful God and Lord? For by neglecting to hear Mass for any frivolous reason we defraud Him of the honor we could, and ought to, have shown Him.

Hear, too, what Marchantius says: "What is holy

Mass but an embassy sent daily to the ever-blessed Trinity with a gift of priceless value, which we present to the three divine Persons in recognition of their dominion over all creatures, and of our dependence upon them? The life and death of Jesus Christ is a daily tribute paid to God, the Author of life and death, by the Church militant in cooperation with, and in presence of, the Church triumphant, in order that to Him, the Triune God, the highest honor may be paid by all His creatures, and that His might, His wisdom, His love, His endless perfections, shining forth in this mystery, may be duly honored by all. What can be more pleasing to the most high God than when heaven and earth unite to laud and magnify His wondrous power and majesty?"

This explanation of the true burnt-offering is so necessary that it ought to be taught to the people, and impressed upon them continually. Heaven and earth do indeed meet together in order to give to God, in holy Mass, praise and thanks worthy of Him. The holy angels carry our oblation on high, and present it before God.

But the chief honor which is given to God by the holy sacrifice of the Mass comes not from men nor from angels, but from Christ Himself. He alone can estimate aright the infinite greatness and grandeur of the divine majesty. He alone knows how infinite is the glory due to it. Therefore He alone, and none other, can pay to God honor worthy of His sovereign majesty, and this He does in every Mass that is celebrated. Although both angels and men can do much for the glory of God, it is as nothing in comparison with what Christ does.

Supposing the Turks were to conquer our country, and threaten us that, if we did not deny Christ, we should all be barbarously tortured and finally burnt alive. And supposing we all answered unanimously that we would rather suffer anything than be faithless to Our Lord, and submitted in a body to torture and death, would not this heroic deed be most pleasing to God, would it not tend vastly to His greater glory? Doubtless it would. And yet this glory would be trifling and insignificant in comparison with the glory which is due to the divine majesty. But when the first-born Son of God abases Himself to the dust before the Most Holy Trinity, when He makes Himself a worm and no man, and in this state of humiliation offers to God the highest reverence, the glory rendered to the Most Holy Trinity cannot be surpassed.

Meanwhile the Son of God gives Himself into the power of man, to be by him immolated as an innocent lamb in a mystical manner, and offered to the triune God as a true burnt-offering, thereby making it possible for us to perform an act of homage and of praise worthy of the Divine Majesty to Whom it is offered. Hence it follows that in this sacrifice alone have we the means of rendering such service, such glory, to God Almighty as will be worthy of His sovereign dignity, and therefore well-pleasing in His sight. Had not Christ placed it within our power to offer this noblest of sacrifices, we should ever have remained debtors to God, and should have departed out of this world laden with guilt. What greater benefit could Jesus have bestowed on us, what greater love could He have shown us, than He did by instituting this superexcellent sacrifice? Do we not owe Him hearty thanks, and ought we not to avail ourselves of this means of obtaining the remission of our many and heavy debts? Let us endeavor to spare time from our other occupations to hear Mass frequently, and offer to God this most acceptable burnt-offering in payment of the debt we owe Him.

CHAPTER XII.

HOLY MASS IS THE MOST SUBLIME SACRIFICE OF PRAISE.

THE nature of God is so infinite and incomprehensible that no created intelligence is capable of grasping it and describing it. His sanctity is unfathomable, His glory is immeasurable, His riches are beyond compare. He is in Himself strictest justice, gentlest mercy, superabundant loving-kindness, the most attractive beauty. Although the angels and saints love Him with their whole heart, yet they tremble before His awful majesty, and worship Him prostrate upon their faces in lowly adoration. With all their powers they laud, magnify, and bless His infinite perfections; nor do they ever weary of His praise. This praise God demands from them; it belongs to Him as their sovereign Lord, and is justly due to His endless sanctity.

From all eternity, before anything was made, God magnified Himself, and the three divine Persons rejoiced in their majesty and grandeur. God the Father magnified the unsearchable wisdom of His Son; God the Son magnified the bounteous goodness of the Holy Ghost, and God the Holy Ghost magnified the infinite power of the Eternal Father. This is shown in the revelations of St. Mechtilde, to whom Christ said: "If thou desirest to honor Me, praise and magnify Me in union with that most excellent glory wherewith the Father in His almighty power and the Holy Spirit in His loving-kindness have glorified Me from all eternity; in union with that supreme glory wherewith I in My unsearchable wisdom have glorified the Father and the Holy Spirit from all eternity, and wherewith the Holy Spirit, in His ineffable goodness, has magnified the Father and Me from all eternity."

Urged by His infinite bounty and love, God created heaven and earth, angels and men, creatures animate and inanimate, in order that they might praise and glorify Him as was His due, and as much as in them lay. That such was His original intention we learn from Holy Scripture, which says: "The Lord hath made all things for Himself" (Prov. xvi. 4); that is to say, in order to be known, praised, and glorified by His creatures. This the angels did from the first moment of their creation, this they do now, and will do to all eternity. The irrational creatures also, wild beasts and tame animals, trees and plants, minerals and stones, each in its own way and according to its capacity, contribute to enhance the glory of the Creator, to Whom they owe their being. This may be proved by the words Christ addressed to St. Mechtilde: "When the priest says in the Mass: 'Through Whom the angels praise Thy majesty,' do thou join thy voice to theirs in that celestial hymn of praise whereby the ever-blessed Trinity magnifies itself and is magnified, and wherein the Blessed Virgin Mary and all the angels and saints do participate. Wherefore say a *Pater*, and offer it to Me in union with that hymn of praise with which heaven and earth and all created things glorify Me."

Now if all irrational creatures praise their Creator, how much the more is it incumbent upon man to extol and magnify Him, since to this end he was created and endowed with reason. Under the Old Dispensation David felt this obligation; the psalms and prayers he composed consist of little else than the praises of God, and of motives whereby he incites himself to magnify His holy name. If the Jews were so assiduous in praising God, much more is it the bounden duty of Christians to do the same, since it is for this that we are made the children of God, as St. Paul distinctly tells us : " Who hath predestinated us unto the adoption of children ... unto the praise of the glory of His grace." (Eph. i. 5, 6.) That is to say, God has adopted us Christians as His children in order that we may laud and magnify His greatness and His grace. This is the chief duty of all mankind, and he who neglects it sins grievously against God. But who can fulfil this duty aright, since the majesty of God is infinite and incomprehensible, above and beyond the praise of both angels and men?

Seeing that our poor human powers were incapable of giving to God the glory due to Him, our blessed Lord, at the Last Supper, instituted the holy Mass, which is an eucharistic sacrifice, and as such is offered to God by the Church daily and hourly, by day and by night. In the Mass the celebrant says: " We offer to Thee, O God, a sacrifice of praise." Previously to that he utters this song of praise: " Glory be to God on high; we praise Thee, we bless Thee, we adore Thee, we glorify Thee," etc. In the preface he says: " Holy, holy, holy, Lord God of Sabaoth ; heaven and earth are full of Thy glory; hosanna in the highest. Blessed is He that cometh in the name of the Lord ; hosanna in the highest." What a glorious hymn of praise is this ! The seraphim in heaven sang the *Sanctus, Sanctus, Sanctus;* the little Hebrew children on earth were inspired to sing the *Hosanna in excelsis*. Thus these words of praise resound partly from heaven, partly from earth; the Church, moreover, repeats them thousands of times every day in the Mass, thus praising the Lord our God by the mouth of His priests.

St. Laurence Justinian expresses this well when he

says: "It is certain that nothing gives God greater glory than the spotless victim of the altar, which Christ ordained to be sacrificed in order that His Church might offer praise to God." In these words the saint implies that we can magnify God in no better way than by celebrating or assisting at holy Mass. Molina explains how this is. "In holy Mass," he says, "the first-born Son of God is offered up to the Father, with all the praises and glory which He rendered Him on earth." Thus the praise God receives is infinite, for it is the praise His divine Son offers to Him. From our altars Christ praises God in a manner really worthy of the divine majesty, and this neither angels nor saints, much less men, are capable of doing. Hence it follows that the praise rendered to God in one Mass far exceeds that which He receives from the angels and the redeemed in heaven.

St. Irenæus tells us of a maiden who desired most earnestly to praise God with all her powers. Many were the sighs she breathed forth to Heaven, exclaiming: "Would that I had a thousand tongues wherewith to praise Thee, O my God! Would that I had the hearts of all men in my power that I might incite them to Thy praise! Fain would I give understanding and affections to all irrational and inanimate creatures, and engage them to praise Thee incessantly! Were it possible for me to create new heavens, and fill them with seraphim, I would strain every nerve to accomplish this. Happy indeed should I be were I endowed with such powers of soul and body as would enable me to adore, praise, honor, and magnify Thee more than all the choirs of angels, the company of the blessed!" Such were the fervent desires that filled this loving soul, and over flowed in ardent aspirations. One day, when inflamed more hotly than usual with the flames of this holy fire, she heard a celestial voice speaking to her. "Hail, beloved daughter!" it said; "know that I derive more praise from one Mass than all you could give Me were your wishes accomplished. Go diligently to Mass, and offer to Me that sacrifice of praise, and you will thereby praise and magnify Me to the utmost of your desire."

Hence learn, O Christian, what a sublime sacrifice holy Mass must be, since thereby greater glory is given to the most high God than by the adoration of all the heavenly host. If all the powers of heaven were to unite to form a solemn procession in honor of the Holy Trinity, at the head of which would be the Mother of God, the chief of all creatures, surrounded by the nine choirs of angels, followed by innumerable companies of the saints and blessed, singing with the sweetest voices, playing on the most melodious instruments, this triumphant procession would doubtless be to the praise and glory of God, and would be pleasing in His sight. But if at the close of the procession the Church militant were to commission one single priest to say one Mass in honor of the ever-blessed Trinity, this one priest, with his one Mass, would offer an incomparably higher tribute of praise than that grand procession had done. Nay, it would be as far superior in glory and sublimity as the Son of God is exalted above all created beings.

This being so, we perceive how much we ought to love and honor Christ for having given us in holy Mass a means at once simple and sublime of honoring and magnifying the Divine Majesty in a manner commensurate with His great dignity. This consideration ought to awaken in us a keen desire to hear Mass frequently, and acquit ourselves satisfactorily of the duty and obligation to praise God. That it is our bounden duty to praise Him has already been shown in the commencement of this chapter. It was there stated, besides, that to fulfil this obligation aright it was necessary to comprehend the divine nature in all its dignity and vastness; and of this no created beings, not even the angels, are capable. Only the sacred humanity of Christ understands perfectly, by reason of the hypostatic union, how infinitely great the Godhead is, how infinitely worthy of praise. Accordingly the humanity of Christ lauds and magnifies the Godhead everywhere, but more especially on our altars during Mass. There only is God praised in a fitting and worthy manner, because Christ is there present in His humanity, and there He offers the most costly sacrifice of praise to the glory of God the Father. Now mark this well: Christ offers the tribute of praise which He pays to the Godhead on the altar principally in the name of those who are present, supplying what is wanting to their praise. Nay, more, He gives it to them, to be offered to God as their own, that they may thus defray the debt they owe Him. He who thus offers to God the sacrifice of His divine Son does more to praise Him than all the angels and saints are in a position to do; for their praise is finite and imperfect, whereas he who hears Mass with this object offers to Him praise which is both infinite and divine.

In support of this assertion we will hear what certain pious and learned men say on this subject. Father John Angelo, a priest of great enlightenment, speaking of holy Mass, says: "When I meditate upon the mysteries of the Mass, it appears to me that the praise, glory, and joy accruing to God the Father by the mystical sacrifice of His Son is so superexcellent that the praise of all the choirs of angels and the company of the saints bears no comparison to it. For the works of creatures, however noble and excellent, contribute nothing to the work of the Creator. Although the angels and saints serve God in an admirable manner, and worthily sing His praise, yet of what value is what they do compared with the glory accruing to the ever-blessed Trinity from holy Mass? For since the priest and the people offer to the Eternal Father the Incarnate Word and His tribute of praise, their oblation is that of a God, and the praise, honor, and thanksgiving is infinite."

These noteworthy words serve to corroborate what has already been said, that God is more praised by the sacred humanity in holy Mass than by all created things in heaven and earth. That the hosts of heaven join in praising God at holy Mass we may gather from the legend which records that Satan, having entered into a woman, and being exorcised, was asked what was the power possessed by a priest. "Great, indeed," he answered, "are the dignity and power of a priest, for when he changes the substance of the bread and wine upon the altar the heavens are opened, and all the celestial court descends to earth." The truth of the foregoing assertion is attested by the revelations of St. Bridget, which have been formally approved by the Church. The saint says: "One day when I was hearing Mass, when the priest came to the consecration, it appeared to me as if sun and moon, the stars and planets, all the orbs of heaven in their course, chanted a sweet harmony. To these were added multitudes of celestial singers, whose entrancing notes our ears could not catch, much less our tongues frame. The choirs of angels gazed at the priest, and bowed low before him in reverence. The devils on the other hand shuddered, and fled in dismay. As soon as the words of consecration were spoken the bread was changed into a living lamb that had a human face. All the angels, of whom there were as many as there are motes in a sunbeam, worshipped and adored it. A great number of holy souls were also present, who joined in praising God and adoring the Lamb."

This remarkable vision tells us how numerous a company of heavenly spirits are present at Mass, and how rapturous the song of praise they sing to Almighty God, a song in which the material orbs of heaven join. In the midst of angels and saints thou dost stand, O devout Christian, when thou hearest Mass; thou dost join with them in praising thy God. Think how greatly He must be honored and glorified by holy Mass. Theologians tell us that it is a sacrifice so royal, so pleasing to God, that all the virtues and good works, the praise, the honor, the adoration, of angels and men, fall far short of it in value. For since Christ is both victim and priest, no one can deny that the exalted nature of the sacrificed and the sacrificer renders the oblation of praise and glory infinitely superior to that which any and every created being can offer.

Hence it is clearly seen how transcendent is the praise, the love, the thanksgiving, offered to the Holy Trinity in every Mass, and how amply the debt we owe to the Divine Majesty—a debt we ought to, but do not, pay—is defrayed for us; nay, more, reparation is made for the blasphemies and insults daily uttered against God. Were it not for this, a world could no longer subsist in which Almighty God is daily a thousand times blasphemed. We know how terribly these insults offend Him, for He says in the prophecies of Isaias: " Now what have I here? ... My name is continually blasphemed all day long." (Is. lii. 5). How can I remain any longer in a world where I am incessantly outraged, blasphemed, reviled? I will therefore withdraw My presence, and deliver the world over to the power of Satan. Nay, I will destroy it, and cast all the blasphemers into hell. God would indeed have reason to do this, for we know one mortal sin is enough to destroy the whole world. Why does He not do it? What restrains Him from executing His dread purpose? Most decidedly it is the holy sacrifice of the Mass which averts this calamity. For although the divine majesty is continually blasphemed by ungodly men, on the other hand it is continually honored by priests in thousands of Masses, and worthily blessed by Christ Himself. This tribute of praise far outweighs the blasphemies of the reprobate, and makes amends to God for the indignities shown Him.

We have indeed reason enough, and it is our bounden duty to give heartfelt thanks to Christ for having, of His pure mercy, instituted the sacrifice of the Mass, whereby the world, despite its iniquities, is preserved from destruction, blasphemers are rescued from the abyss of hell, the negligence of the just is compensated for, and the infinite God receives the praise and honor which belong to Him.

All glory and thanks be to Thee, therefore, most loving Jesus, from me and from all children of the Church, nay, from all creatures in heaven and on earth, for the inestimable benefit which Thou hast conferred, and dost daily confer, upon us by the institution of holy Mass. How can we better express our sense of this benefit than by regular and devout attendance at Mass, by participating in the oblation of praise and thanksgiving which Thou dost offer to the Godhead in it? Would to God that I could incite all men to hear Mass frequently, to hear it devoutly! Do Thou do what I cannot do; pour into my heart and into the hearts of all the faithful the spirit of devotion, so that we may ever increase in our love for holy Mass, and may daily join in offering this sacred oblation.

CHAPTER XIII.

HOLY MASS IS THE NOBLEST SACRIFICE OF THANKSGIVING.

IMMEASURABLE indeed are the benefits which have been bestowed, and are daily bestowed, upon us by the divine liberality. For God the Father is our Creator; He has given us our five bodily senses and made us sound of limb; He has created our soul after His own image, cleansed it by the operation of the Holy Ghost in the laver of Baptism, purified it and chosen it for His spouse. He has appointed to each one of us an angel guardian for our protection; He sustains us as His children, forgives us our sins in confession, feeds us with His sacred body and blood in holy communion, bears patiently with us when we fall into sin, awaits with long-suffering our return to Him, gives us good inspirations, prevents us with His grace, teaches us by His divine word, delivers us from evil, grants our humble prayers, comforts us in tribulation, strengthens us in temptation, protects us from disgrace, graciously accepts our good works, and confers on us innumerable benefits.

Many and great as are these and other favors which God in His bounty has lavished on us, they are not all; for to these He adds this grace, that of adopting us for His children. St. John the Evangelist extols this inestimable benefit in the following words: "Behold what manner of charity the Father hath bestowed upon us, that we should be called, and should be, the sons of God." (I. St. John iii. 1.) And St. Paul says: "And if sons, heirs also; heirs indeed of God, and joint-heirs with

Christ." (Rom. viii. 17.) Is not this an unspeakable favor, that Almighty God should call us poor beggars His children, and make us rightful heirs to His kingdom?

To all this He adds another, a stupendous, benefit. When by reason of our sins we had come under the dominion of Satan, He ransomed us from that slavery by His own Son. Christ wished to impress upon us the magnitude of that benefit when He said: "God so loved the world as to give His only-begotten Son" (St. John iii. 16) not only to take upon Him our nature, but to suffer a cruel death for us. Nor was this infinite benefit conferred only on the friends of God: His enemies also were included in it, as St. Paul says: "God commendeth His charity towards us, because when as yet we were sinners Christ died for us." (Rom. v. 8, 9.) For love so surpassing as this we can never make an adequate return. If the great God and Lord of all had but once vouchsafed to look kindly upon us, poor worms of earth, we could never be grateful enough to Him. How, then, can we thank or requite Him for having endured a life of poverty and suffered a death of shame for our sakes?

Osorius says: "If any one has conferred a great boon upon thee, thou art bound to make ample returns, lest thou appear wanting in gratitude to thy benefactor." Since we have received benefits so innumerable from the hand of God, we are bound to requite them fittingly. Wherefore let us say with the Royal Prophet: "What shall I render to the Lord for all the things that He hath rendered to me?" (Ps. cxv. 3.) And with the prophet Micheas: "What shall I offer to the Lord that is worthy?" (Mich. vi. 6.) What these holy men said and did it is our duty to say and do. We are under the greatest obligations to our God; if we make Him no return, we are guilty of the basest ingratitude and incur a grievous sin.

What, then, wilt thou do, who art poor and destitute? How wilt thou defray thy heavy debt? Listen to the counsel David gives thee: "Offer to God the sacrifice of praise, and pay thy vows to the Most High." (Ps. xlix. 14.) Now the noblest offering of praise, as was shown in the preceding chapter, is the holy sacrifice of the Mass. Consequently thou canst find no better means of giving thanks to God, the greatest of all benefactors, than by frequently hearing Mass, and offering it to Him in return for all His mercies. St. Irenæus says: "For this holy Mass was instituted, that we might not appear thankless towards our God." That is to say: If it were not for the sacrifice of the Mass, we should have nothing in the whole world wherewith we could adequately render thanks to God for the benefits we have received from Him. Christ, therefore, had this object in view when He instituted the Mass, namely, to provide us with an efficacious act of thanksgiving whereby to express our gratitude towards God.

The words of the Mass are of themselves sufficient evidence that it is justly termed a sacrifice of thanksgiving. What is it but a hearty giving of thanks when the priest says in the *Gloria in excelsis:* "We praise Thee; we bless Thee; we adore Thee; we glorify Thee; we give thanks to Thee for Thy great glory, O Lord God, heavenly King, God the Father Almighty," etc.? And in the preface he calls upon all present to give thanks, saying: "Let us give thanks to the Lord our God; it is truly meet and just, right and salutary, that we should always and in all places give thanks to Thee, O holy Lord, Father Almighty, Eternal God, through Christ Our Lord," etc. No more sublime hymn of praise can be offered to God than the Church utters in the preface.

And when the priest comes to the consecration he says these words: "Who took bread into His holy and venerable hands, and with His eyes lifted up towards heaven, to God, His almighty Father, giving thanks." How touching is this lifting up of the eyes of our dear Lord! How all-powerful His giving of thanks, transcending by far that of all angels and all men! Had we been able of ourselves to give God due thanks, it would not have been necessary for Christ to come to our assistance. What He did at the Last Supper He repeats daily upon our altars, where, raising His eyes to His Father, He gives Him hearty thanks for all His benefits. And since this thanksgiving is from the lips of One Who is divine, it cannot be otherwise than infinite; and since it is infinite, God can require nothing more; and since He can require nothing more, it must needs give Him infinite satisfaction.

Therefore, when thou hearest Mass, unite thy heart and thy will to the heart and the will of Christ, and give God thanks with all thy powers. And in order that this giving of thanks may be the more efficacious and acceptable, offer to the Eternal Father that superabundant thanksgiving which His divine Son, under the species of bread and wine, offers to Him, for all the benefits He has bestowed on thee.

If from thy earliest childhood up to this hour thou hadst thanked God upon thy knees for all His gifts and graces, if thou hadst called upon all devout persons to join with thee in thy life-long tribute of thanks, nay, if thou hadst invoked the company of angels and saints to come to thy aid, and they in union with thee and all good men had incessantly thanked and praised God, the tribute of gratitude paid to Him would be less than that rendered to Him by His Son in one single Mass.

We will now inquire into the reason of this. Philosophers tell us that the finite bears no relation to the infinite, for the infinite transcends the finite in an infinite degree. Now the thanksgiving of all creatures both in heaven and on earth is finite, and consequently finite in power and finite in value. But the thanksgiving of the Son of God, what He renders to His Father in holy Mass, is infinite, in virtue of His divinity, and therefore infinite in power and in value. Accordingly it is infinitely more pleasing to God the Father than the thanksgiving of all the finite beings in the universe. Christ offers this infinite thanksgiving to His Father for thee, if thou dost hear Mass devoutly: He gives it thee for thine own, and as such thou canst offer it to Almighty God. Do this, and the thanks thou wilt render to God will be no finite and human thanksgiving, it will be infinite and divine.

Would to God that we appreciated aright the immense treasure which we possess in holy Mass! How happy should we then be! How attentively we should hear Mass! To us may be applied the words of St. Paul: "I give thanks to my God always for you, for the grace of God that is given you in Christ Jesus, that in all things you are made rich in Him, . . . so that nothing is wanting to you in any grace." (1. Cor. i. 4, 5, 7.) Truly by the holy Mass we are made rich in Christ, and no grace is wanting to us; on the contrary, from it, as from a perennial fountain, we may draw abundant supplies of grace, for in it lies hid a wealth of celestial riches above all that the world could ever contain.

Thus in holy Mass we have the noblest burnt-offering, the sublimest sacrifice of praise and of thanksgiving. It is the believer's greatest treasure, the devout Christian's dearest joy. It is a salutary atonement for the sinner, a powerful support for the dying, the surest earnest of deliverance for the departed. We may truly say that in holy Mass we are made rich in Christ Jesus, so that no grace is wanting to us.

In conclusion I will recapitulate what has been said on

this point by Segneri: "Consider, O Christian, how indebted we are to Our Saviour for the institution of holy Mass; for without it we could never thank God aright for His benefits. It was the plenteousness of His love that induced Him not only to load us with benefits, but to place within our reach the best means of giving Him thanks for those benefits. Would that we appreciated our privileges and turned them to good account! When we hear Mass, Christ, Who is immolated for us to God the Father, becomes our own, and with Him we become possessed of His infinite merits, and are able to offer them to God the Father, to lighten the heavy load which weighs us down to the ground."

Let us lay these words to heart, and profit by them. They show clearly how deeply we are indebted to Christ, not for instituting the Mass alone, but for constituting it so excellent an act of thanksgiving, whereby we may give thanks to God abundantly for all the benefits He has conferred on us.

Praise and thanks be to Thee, O Lord Jesus Christ, from me and from all created things, because of Thy pure love to us Thou hast instituted holy Mass, and made it a channel of countless graces and mercies to us. As a fitting acknowledgment of Thy favors I offer to Thee, and through Thee to the Holy Trinity, all the praise and thanksgiving rendered to Thee in all Masses until the end of time. I beg the choirs of angels and the company of the redeemed to laud and magnify Thee with us to all eternity. Amen.

CHAPTER XIV.

HOLY MASS IS THE MOST EFFICACIOUS SACRIFICE OF PROPITIATION.

IN the law of Moses God enjoined upon the Jews to offer not only burnt-offerings in recognition of His sovereign dominion, but also peace-offerings for obtaining temporal good and averting calamities. These peace, or propitiatory, sacrifices were much valued by the Jews, for through them they gained many blessings and were delivered from many evils. It is recorded in the First Book of Kings (ch. vii.) that when the Philistines were about to attack the children of Israel the latter entreated Samuel to cry to God for them. Samuel took a lamb, and offered it as a holocaust to the Lord, and cried to the Lord for Israel. Then God struck terror into the ranks of the Philistines, and they were overthrown by the Israelites. We also read of David that when the land was visited by a pestilence he offered holocausts and peace-offerings, and the plague was stayed from Israel. (II. Kings xxiv.) Many similar instances occur in the pages of Holy Scripture.

If God gave to the stiff-necked Jews so efficacious a sacrifice of propitiation, will He not have given to Christians one far more powerful? If under the Old Covenant a lamb, immolated as a peace-offering, was the means of procuring for those who offered it many blessings from God, what will not the sacrifice of the Lamb of God avail when, under the New Dispensation, it is offered an innocent victim upon our altars, and with it an inexhaustible store of merit?

The Christian Church does indeed enjoy far greater privileges than the Jewish synagogue. Each sacrifice of the Old Law could only be offered for one object: the burnt-offering was appointed solely in recognition of the sovereignty of God; the sacrifice of atonement was for the remission of sin; the peace-offering to obtain some favor from God. And for each of these there was a distinct ceremonial, so that it could not be celebrated in a two-fold manner. Now holy Church, although she has but one sacrifice, can offer that one sacrifice with various intentions, and by it more can be effected than by all the different sacrifices of the Jews.

The Council of Trent speaks very clearly on this point. It teaches us that: "If any one saith that the sacrifice of the Mass is only a sacrifice of praise and of thanksgiving, or that it is a bare commemoration of the sacrifice consummated on the cross, but not a propitiatory sacrifice; or that it profits him only who receives; and that it ought not to be offered for the living and the dead, for sins, pains, satisfactions and other necessities, let him be anathema." (Sess. xxii. C. 3.) These words contain an article of faith, which no man must gainsay, and which must be accepted on pain of forfeiting all title to eternal salvation. Hence it may be certainly affirmed that one Mass may be offered for various intentions, and that by one Mass many things may be asked and obtained from God. One may celebrate or hear Mass, or have it offered, for the greater glory of God, in honor of His blessed Mother, of the angels and saints, for one's own welfare and salvation, to obtain health, preservation from misfortune, forgiveness of sin, amendment of life, the grace of a good death. All these blessings may be asked for one's self or for one's friends, and at the same time the Mass may be offered for the deliverance of the suffering souls in purgatory. In fact the more numerous our intentions the more abundant our merits.

Theologians tell us how potent holy Mass is as a propitiatory sacrifice. Marchantius says: "This sacrifice possesses an infinite potency to obtain what we ask, because of the infinite value of the victim, the infinite dignity of the priest. There is no gift, no grace, which it does not avail to obtain. However numerous are the persons for whom it is offered, this sacred victim can procure the fulfilment of their petitions; and for these reasons: because Christ, the great high priest, is infinitely well-pleasing to God; because the merits which He offers to God the Father are infinite; because His passion, His blood, His wounds, are all-prevailing."

From these words we learn whence the Mass derives its immense potency. It is from the exalted dignity of the person of Christ, Who, as the great high priest, Himself offers this sacrifice, and presents to God the merits of His passion and death, which are infinite in value. And since Christ offers to His Father far more than He asks of Him, how can He refuse His request? In regard to the value of holy Mass St. Laurence Justinian says: "There is no sacrifice so excellent, so profitable, so acceptable to the Divine Majesty as the holy sacrifice of the Mass, in which the wounds of our Redeemer, the humiliations He endured, the scourging and other tortures, are offered up to the Father. In it He beholds the sacred humanity of His Son, Whom He sent into the world that through His intercession sinners might find pardon, the fallen might be raised up, the just might receive the gift of eternal life."

Wherefore when the priest, and the people who hear his Mass, present to the Eternal Father the sufferings and merits of Christ, in virtue of these gifts their petitions will be granted.

In the law of Moses God forbade the judges to take a gift: "Thou shalt not accept person nor gifts; for gifts blind the eyes of the wise and change the words of the just." (Deut. xvi. 19.) This prohibition was on account of the frailty of human nature, which renders it almost impossible for the judgment not to be biassed by gifts of value. But when Holy Scripture says, "Gifts blind the eyes of the wise," this does not apply to the all-wise God, Whose eyes cannot be dazzled by gifts. And yet we are not wrong in asserting that the offering of the holy Mass leads God to alter His judgment and revoke His verdict. In fact we are assured that on receiving from our hands a gift of such intrinsic value divine justice concurs with divine mercy in listening to our petitions and granting our requests.

A devout writer says: "In holy Mass we do not merely ask as suppliants of the Divine Mercy: we offer an equivalent for the favors we implore; we purchase them with a great price, the sufferings of Jesus Christ." Consider how costly are the gifts we offer in holy Mass; how dearly we purchase from God the graces we seek. We offer the sacred humanity of Christ, which for the greater glory of God was scourged, crowned with thorns, and crucified. We offer the same humanity which was personally united to the Godhead, and by this union ennobled in the highest degree. We offer the wounds that sacred humanity received, and the tears and blood that were shed.

As a matter of fact what we offer to God in holy Mass is more than what we ask of Him in prayer; therefore it seems almost impossible that we should meet with a refusal. For we ask for what is created and earthly; but what we offer is divine and of priceless value. Can we imagine that God, Who cannot be outdone in generosity, Who promises to recompense even a cup of cold water, will make us no return when we present to Him the chalice of the blood of His first-born Son, shed anew in the Mass, which cries to Him for grace and mercy on our behalf?

After the Last Supper Our Lord said to the apostles: "Amen, amen, I say to you, if you ask the Father anything in My name, He will give it you." (St. John xvi. 23.) What more suitable time for presenting our petitions to the Father in the name of His Son than during Mass, when we present that divine Son in person, when we offer Him to the Father, and with Him all the supplications which He uttered upon earth? St. Bonaventure says: "When a great general is taken prisoner, he is not set free unless a heavy sum is paid for his ransom." So we, who hold Christ a prisoner in holy Mass, will not let Him go until He gives us forgiveness of sin and the promise of eternal felicity. When the priest elevates Our Lord in the sacred host, it is as if he called thus upon the people: " Behold, He Whom all the universe cannot contain is a prisoner in our hands. We will not let Him go until He grants our petitions." We may in this case follow the example of Jacob, and take his words upon our lips: "I will not let Thee go except Thou bless me." (Gen. xxxii. 26.) We will now give an instance of how much may be obtained by means of holy Mass.

In the chronicles of the Capuchin Fathers we read of a pious lady, the wife of a very bad man, who treated her cruelly, and every day put some fresh affront upon her. After enduring this miserable state of things for several years she began almost to despair. One day two Capuchins knocked at her door and asked an alms. She gave them what they asked, and then with tears told them how afflicted she was. The religious did their utmost to console her, advising her to go to Mass every day, and offer up her trials to Almighty God; through the power of the Mass they doubted not her husband would be softened, and treat her more kindly in future. The woman thanked them for their good advice, and promised, if possible, to act upon it. But her husband was such a tyrant that he never would allow her to go to Mass on week-days, so that the woman, much to her distress, was unable to follow the counsel of the good religious. However, not long after it happened, in the good providence of God, that her husband had occasion to go on a long journey, and during his absence his wife gladly embraced the opportunity thus afforded her of hearing Mass every day. Earnestly she commended herself and her godless consort to God during the holy sacrifice, imploring Him to bring her husband to a better mind. Unfortunately the latter returned home sooner than he was expected, just at the time that his wife was at Mass. When, in answer to his questions, the servants informed him that their mistress was at church, and that, while he was away, she had been in the habit of going to Mass daily, the scoundrel flew into a rage, and with sundry imprecations vowed he would kill her. This was no empty threat; on her reappearance he seized her by the throat, and tried to strangle her. The hapless woman thought her last hour was come; raising her heart to God, she besought Him, in virtue of the Mass she had just heard, to come to her rescue. The divine assistance did not tarry: the man's hands became suddenly benumbed. This infuriated him the more; he declared his wife was a witch, and put forth all his strength to execute his evil purpose. But in vain; his hands were rigid and cold as marble. Then at last he recognized the divine justice; bitterly he bewailed his sins, promising to amend his life and conduct himself properly towards his wife in future. Then they both appealed to the mercy of God, made vows and promises, not desisting until their supplications were heard, and the man regained the full use of his hands. This severe chastisement had the effect of inducing him entirely to abandon his impious course of life, treat his wife kindly, and frequently accompany her to holy Mass.

The story of these two people shows the great blessing connected with the holy sacrifice. The lady had doubtless often called upon God for help in her sore distress, but her prayers had not been granted. But when she went to Mass, and there poured out her sorrow before God, she was not merely consoled, but the cause of her affliction was removed. This proves the truth of Molina's words: "Through the sacrifice of the Mass, so costly in itself, so acceptable to God, all that is necessary for our salvation may be obtained from God, from His blessed Mother, and from the saints. And by no other means can we obtain that which has been denied to us in holy Mass." Enough has been already said to confirm this statement. For in the Mass we do not pray alone: the priest, the angels, Christ Himself, intercede with us and for us. Nor do we only proffer petitions, we present to God a gift equal to Himself. If, under such circumstances, our request is denied, when and where can we hope that it will be granted? Thus it is true that we can obtain by no other means that which the holy sacrifice has not procured for us.

Here it may be asked how it is that, seeing the immense value of holy Mass, the petitions of those who offer it are not always granted. Father Gobat explains this in the following manner: "All do not obtain what they desire, for, although by no other act of worship do we so readily obtain from God the fulfilment of our wishes as by holy Mass, yet the efficacy of the Mass depends upon certain conditions which are not found in most men." Cardinal Bona speaks more explicitly on this point: "It belongs to the nature of a petition to suppose that the person asked is at liberty to withhold the thing for which he is asked. When we pray for anything to be given to us, we put forward a reason which we think will have weight with God, but He is by no means thereby compelled to grant our request. At the same time it may be certainly affirmed that holy Mass is never offered in vain. If we do not receive the very thing for which we asked, we infallibly receive something else that is more beneficial for us. And if this is not bestowed upon us immediately it will be given us in God's good time. Many graces are, besides, of such magnitude that not only one or two, but several, Masses are required if we would obtain them."

We gather this from the answer Our Lord gave to St. Gertrude when she asked Him how it was that her prayers were so seldom granted. He replied: "If I, the unsearchable Wisdom, do not always grant thy petitions according to thy desire, I give thee something more profitable, for by reason of human frailty thou art unable to tell what is best for thee." Another time the saint asked Our Lord: "What good do I do to my friends by praying for them so much, since I perceive no improvement in them?" He replied: "Do not wonder at seeing no apparent fruit of thy prayers; I, in My eternal wisdom, dispose of them so that they will be most productive of good. I say to you, every prayer that is offered for any one augments his eternal happiness; no sincere prayer ever fails of its effect, although the eye of man may not be able to perceive in what way or manner."

Every one must content himself with this answer, and take comfort from the assurance Christ gives that no pious prayer fails in its object or passes without reward. And if no prayer fails of its object, how much less holy Mass, the best of all prayers? Lay to heart these words of Our Lord: "No sincere prayer fails of its effect." The sincere prayer is one which is offered with confidence and fervor. He who prays without confidence receives little or nothing at all, as the following example will show.

We read in the life of the Abbot Severinus that a vast swarm of locusts having alighted on a certain part of the country, where they were devouring all the produce of the soil, the inhabitants of the region thus devastated betook themselves to the abbot, and entreated him to pray for the removal of this scourge. Compassionating their distress, the holy man bade the people assemble in the church, and in a forcible address set before them the necessity of penance and of prayer. In conclusion he said: "I know no better means of intercession than the holy sacrifice of the Mass; I will therefore offer it, that you may be spared the loss of your crops. Do you on your part unite with me in fullest confidence in offering it to God for this object." The people did as they were admonished, with the exception of one farmer, who said: "You are fools to hope you will mend matters in this way. If you heard twenty Masses and prayed all day long, it would not help you to drive away a single locust." Then he went his way to his work, while the others devoutly heard Mass and implored Almighty God to deliver them from the plague of locusts. Immediately after they went out into the fields; and behold! their prayer was already answered: the locusts had risen and were taking flight. The people raised their hands to God in joy and gratitude, and the unbelieving farmer, who was there too, could scarcely believe his eyes. His want of faith was not to go unpunished, however, for the swarm of locusts when they had got some distance whirled round, descended like a thick cloud on his land, and began to consume everything with their proverbial voracity. The unlucky man cried to God for help, but he cried in vain; the locusts did not depart until every green leaf had disappeared.

This story teaches us the potency of holy Mass, and the guilt of despising it. It ought to inspire us with the firmest confidence, so that we may follow the injunction of St. Paul: "Let us go, therefore, with confidence to the throne of grace; that we may obtain mercy, and find grace in seasonable aid." (Heb. iv. 16.) What is the throne of grace which the Apostle exhorts us to approach? It is the sacred altar, whereon the Lamb of God is immolated, whereon He gives His life for us, that we may find grace and mercy. We ought to go daily to this throne of grace to implore help in our necessity. We ought to go with devotion, reverence, and confidence, for it is a throne of grace, not of vengeance; a throne of mercy, not of justice; a throne where we shall find aid and shall meet with no rebuff. When, therefore, we pray for anything special at holy Mass, let us say with confidence:

"Behold, O Father of mercy, in this holy sacrifice I come in confidence to Thy throne of grace to obtain pardon of my sins and help in my misery. I place my whole trust in this holy sacrifice, hoping thereby to obtain from Thee all I need. For the dignity of the victim is infinite, the oblation is of infinite value, and the power of the sacrifice is infinite. On these three grounds Thou canst not refuse, O my God, to grant me the favor I ask, provided it be for Thy glory and for my good. Through the infinite satisfaction which this holy sacrifice affords Thee I ask in all confidence that Thou wouldst bestow on me the grace I implore for Thy greater glory, and wouldst increase the confidence wherewith I approach this throne of grace."

CHAPTER XV.

HOLY MASS IS THE MOST POWERFUL SIN-OFFERING.

THE light of reason suffices to teach us that the infirmity of human nature, so prone to sin, needs a sacrifice of atonement, and of this the patriarchs who lived before the time of Moses were conscious. For we read of holy Job, who lived by the light of natural religion, that he was accustomed every seven days to call his ten children together to sanctify them, and offer holocausts for every one of them. For he said to himself: " Lest perhaps my sons have sinned [in their feasting] and have blasphemed God in their hearts." (Job i. 5.) Thus we see that the prompting of reason led the patriarchs to offer expiatory sacrifices to God Almighty, and implore His pardon. In the law of Moses God Himself appointed a sacrifice of atonement for the person who sinned, saying: "Let him do penance for his sin, and offer of the flocks an ewe-lamb or a she-goat, and the priest shall pray for him and for his sin. But if he be not able to offer a beast, let him offer two turtles or two young pigeons to the Lord, one for sin and the other for a holocaust, . . . and the priest shall pray for him and for his sin, and it shall be forgiven him." (Lev. v. 5, 6, 7, 10.)

If the Old Law, which was but a shadow of the New, appointed an expiatory sacrifice for the consolation and spiritual welfare of the Jews, how much the more needful that the Church should provide a sacrifice of atonement for her children—a new sacrifice, as far superior to the old as the Christian Church is to the Jewish Synagogue. The sacrifice of blood, offered upon the cross, was once offered, and could not be repeated; it was therefore necessary to institute another, which should be offered daily for our daily transgressions. On this point the Church teaches us: "Although Christ was about to offer Himself once on the altar of the cross, there to operate an eternal redemption; nevertheless, because that His priesthood was not to be extinguished by His death, at the Last Supper He offered up to God the Father His own body and blood, under the species of bread and wine, and commanded His apostles and their successors in the priesthood to offer them." (Council of Trent, sess. xxii. ch. 1.)

Such are the words in which the holy Catholic Church declares to us that Christ at the Last Supper instituted the Mass, and commanded His apostles and priests to celebrate it. The reason of this is also given: "That He might leave to the Church a visible sacrifice, whereby that bloody sacrifice might be represented, and its salutary virtue be applied in remission of the sins we daily commit." This passage contains an article of faith, which no one must venture to contradict; and it shows us that holy Mass is a sacrifice of atonement, since it was instituted by Christ in order that His Church might have a sacrifice for the remission of daily sins. What a salutary, what an all-prevailing, sacrifice of atonement! Happy the Church who possesses such a sacrifice!

That the Mass is indeed a veritable sacrifice of atonement, offered in expiation of the sins of the people, is shown by the action of the priest, who, at the commencement of the Mass, humbly bowing down, says the *Confiteor*, or general confession, striking his breast three times; and after the server has done the same in the name of the congregation he pronounces the absolution: "May Almighty God have mercy upon you, forgive you your sins, and bring you to life everlasting." Then, signing himself with the sign of the cross, he says: "May the almighty and merciful Lord grant us pardon, absolution, and remission of our sins." He next invokes the mercy of God for the forgiveness of sin, saying the *Kyrie eleison:* " Lord, have mercy on us; Christ, have mercy on us! Must not this humble and devout ejaculation, rising to heaven, reach the ear of God, and move His divine heart to pity?

The priest also says many collects, secret prayers and other prayers, which contain a petition for forgiveness of sin. Presently he repeats three times, aloud: " Lamb of God, Who takest away the sins of the world, have mercy upon us!" All this leaves no doubt that the Mass is a sacrifice of atonement, offered for the remission of sin.

On this subject Marchantius says: "As Christ upon the cross took upon Himself the sins of the whole world, to atone for them with His blood, so we lay our sins upon Him as upon a victim about to be immolated upon the altar, that He may expiate them. It is to indicate this that the priest at the commencement of the Mass bows down at the foot of the altar, and in the spirit of humility presents himself as if laden with the sins of the people before the Eternal Father, in order to prevail on Him to have mercy. In this position he also personates Christ upon the Mount of Olives, Who, bowed down under the burden of the sins of the whole world, which were laid upon Him, fell upon His face, His sweat becoming as drops of blood, and prayed earnestly to His heavenly Father. So the priest, Christ's representative, prays for his own sins and those of all persons present, for whom the price of our redemption was once paid, and is daily renewed and offered afresh to operate the remission of sin."

These beautiful and consoling words cannot fail to infuse courage into the heart of every sinner, and inspire him with joyous ardor in hearing holy Mass; for they tell him that Christ has taken upon Himself all the transgressions of which he is guilty, and will atone for them with His blood; they tell him that Christ in the sinner's place implores the mercy of God the Father, offering to Him the great price of our redemption, to obtain for us remission of sin.

Let us now hear what the fathers of the Church say with respect to this expiatory sacrifice, and how they explain it. St. James in his liturgy says: "We offer Thee this unbloody sacrifice, O Lord, for our sins and the ignorance of the people." Here observe that we commit many sins of which we take no heed, which we do not confess, but for which we shall yet have to give account. That these unrecognized sins are accounted as transgressions we learn from David, who prays that they may be forgiven: "The sins of my youth and my ignorances do not remember." (Ps. xxiv. 7.) And again: "Who can understand sins? From my secret ones cleanse me, O Lord, and from those of others spare Thy servant." (Ps. xviii. 13, 14.) In order that we may not appear before the judgment-seat of God with these secret sins upon our soul, let us be diligent in hearing Mass, of which St. James, the first Bishop of Jerusalem, says: "That it is offered for the ignorances of the people."

Marchantius also says: "The holy sacrifice of the Mass, offered to Almighty God, serves to atone for mortal sins, but preeminently for secret sins, those, that is, which after careful examination of conscience we cannot recall to mind." Holy Mass does not actually cleanse from sin, but it obtains for us the grace of contrition, not only for known sins, but still more for those that are unknown or forgotten. St. Gregory says: "Just persons do not tremble on account of known sins, because they have confessed and done penance for them. Their chief cause for apprehension lies in the sins of which they are not conscious; as St. Paul says: 'I am not conscious to myself of anything, yet am I not hereby justified: but He that judgeth me is the Lord' (1. Cor. iv. 4.), and the Lord has sharper eyes than I have." We miserable mortals shall indeed have cause to quake in the judgment on account of our secret sins. Wherefore we shall do well to offer all the Masses we hear to the divine justice for the remission of our secret sins. This is expressed in the words the Church places on the lips of the priest in the prayers for the fifth Sunday after Epiphany: "We offer unto Thee, O Lord, sacrifices of propitiation; that, taking compassion on us, Thou wouldst absolve us from our sins." The sins of which we are not conscious we cannot confess to the priest; therefore we confess them in general to God, and offer to Him the Mass as a propitiatory sacrifice, beseeching Him to absolve us from them.

Furthermore, let us hear what Pope Alexander I. says concerning this sacrifice of propitiation: "By the offering of this victim the Lord is appeased, and forgives all, even the most grievous sins." The holy pope and martyr Julius writes : "All sins and iniquities are blotted out by the offering of this oblation." What comfort these words bring to the heart of the sinner, assuring him, as they do, that all sins, without exception, may be purged away by holy Mass! Again, St. Athanasius says : "The offering of the unbloody sacrifice is the expiation of our crimes." Passages of this kind from the fathers might be multiplied, but we will content ourselves with the pronouncement of holy Church on the subject: "The holy Synod teaches that this sacrifice is truly propitiatory, and if one draw nigh unto God, contrite and penitent, He will be appeased by the offering thereof, and, granting the grace and gift of penitence, forgive even heinous crimes and sins." (Sess. xxii. ch. 2.) Words of solace, which show us what blessings and graces flow to us from this noblest of sacrifices! What praise and gratitude we owe to Christ for having given us so efficacious a means of propitiating an offended God!

It may perhaps be asked, What need have we of a propitiatory sacrifice, since without it we can appease the wrath of God by sincere repentance? I answer: Doubtless we can appease the divine anger by sincere contrition; but how is the sinner to obtain sincere contrition? It will not spring up of itself within his breast, for we might as well expect the dead to come to life again as a sinner of his own self to awake to penitence. If it were possible for him to do this, there would not be many doomed to eternal perdition; for almost everyone, feeling his end draw near, would excite in himself contrition and sorrow, and die in the grace of God. A sermon, or a pious book, may perchance be instrumental in awakening a sinner to repentance, but not without a special grace from God. God, justly offended by our crimes, is by no means bound to give us this grace, and He does not give it lightly, unless He is specially moved thereto. Now, there is nothing in heaven or on earth which has so much power with God to induce Him to grant this grace, as holy Mass. As Father Gobat says: "Holy Mass is for all those who hear it an expiatory sacrifice of such value that for the sake of it God grants them power to do all that is necessary to obtain pardon of the mortal sins they may have committed; that is, He gives them grace to acknowledge and bewail their sins, and to make a good confession."

The words Our Lord addressed to St. Gertrude show

how easily we may obtain remission of sin, through offering holy Mass to this end. It was one Holy Week, while the antiphon, "He is sacrificed because He Himself willed it," was being sung, that He said to her: "If thou believest that I am offered up to God the Father upon the cross because it was My will to be offered in this manner, believe also and doubt not that every day I desire, with the same love and strength of desire, to be sacrificed for every sinner upon the altar, as I sacrificed Myself upon the cross for the salvation of the world. Therefore there is no one, however heavy the weight of sin wherewith he is burdened, who may not hope for pardon, if he offers to the Father My sinless life and death, provided he believes that thereby he will obtain the blessed fruit of forgiveness."

These words, coming as they do from the lips of divine Truth, are indeed full of sweet consolation. Can it possibly be true that the charity of Christ is so exceeding great that He desires daily to be offered to God the Father in holy Mass for each individual sinner, with the same desire that urged Him to suffer upon the cross for the world's redemption? If so, fulfil, O sinner, this ardent desire of thy Lord; offer daily, nay, many times a day, the passion, the death of His well-beloved Son to God the Father, trusting to receive remission of thy sins according to the promise of Jesus Christ. This oblation can be made not only at Mass, but at other times besides; not only with the lips, but also with the heart. For in the words quoted above, Our Lord makes no mention of holy Mass, nor of vocal prayer.

Now, if the unspoken offering of the heart is so efficacious, what must not the efficacy be of the actual material oblation, which is daily offered in holy Mass? For in the Mass Christ is not offered merely by words, or in a spiritual manner: He is offered actually and corporally by the hands of the priest, and what the priest offers we offer. For it is not in his own name alone that the priest offers the body and blood of Christ, it is in the name of all present, of all faithful Christians. After the consecration he employs these words: "Wherefore, O Lord, we thy servants, as also Thy holy people, offer to Thy most excellent Majesty a pure host," etc.

Before leaving the subject of the expiatory sacrifice, let me add the words Our Lord spoke to St. Mechtilde: " Such is My long-suffering, when I come at the time of Mass, that there is no sinner, how great soever, there present, with whom I do not bear patiently, and to whom, provided he desire it, I do not gladly grant forgiveness of sin." These words, ineffable in their charity, tell us how potent is holy Mass as an expiatory sacrifice, since it is the means of reconciling us to Christ so completely that, far from repulsing the sinner who comes to Mass, He stretches out His arms to him, He embraces him as a dear friend, He gladly forgives his offences, if only he gives signs of true penitence for his sins.

A beautiful instance of this is given in the lives of the fathers. A saintly recluse, named Paul the Simple, had received from God the gift of reading the secrets of the heart. When the hermits came to church on Sundays, he used to stand by the door, and if he perceived that one of them had some sin upon his conscience he would tell him of it in private, and exhort him to amend. One day, while he was thus standing at the church door, he saw a man approaching whose countenance, as indeed his whole person, was of a dark hue. Two devils walked on either side of him, pulling him hither and thither with the chains wherewith they had bound him; his guardian angel followed, sorrowfully, at some distance. The holy man began to weep and strike his breast, for he was grieved on account of the miserable condition of this unhappy sinner. The hermits begged him to come inside the church to hear Mass, but he remained upon the threshold, not ceasing to weep and lament. When the monks issued from the chapel after Mass, he watched anxiously for the object of his concern; and see! he came towards him with a bright and beaming countenance, his angel guardian at his side, while the devils withdrew discomfited. Then Blessed Paul sprang to his feet, and exclaimed aloud: " How inexpressible is the goodness of God! How unfathomable is the divine mercy!" Standing upon the steps of the church, he called to the others: " Come, brethren, listen, hear what has happened, and marvel at the wonders worked by our God. I saw this man enter these portals black as ebony, surrounded by demons; but when he comes out he is fair and white, and his angel walks beside him." Turning to the individual in question, he said to him: " Give the glory to God, and tell us the condition of thy soul." Then the man declared in the hearing of all: " I am a grievous sinner; for a long time I have been leading a licentious life. But when, just now in the church, I heard those words of the prophet Isaias read for the epistle: 'Wash yourselves, be clean, take away the evil of your devices from My eyes. If your sins be as scarlet, they shall be made as white as snow' [Is. i. 16, 18]—I breathed forth a prayer to God, saying: 'O Thou Who camest into the world to save sinners, fulfil Thy promise to me, a poor sinner.' During the whole of the Mass I kept repeating these words: 'I promise Thee, O my God, never again will I commit so great a sin; O Lord, receive me, miserable transgressor that I am.' And I left the church fully resolved to lead a new life." And all who were present praised God, saying: " How glorious are Thy works, O Lord, Who by the power of holy Mass dost bring the sinner to repentance, and admit him to Thy favor."

Well may we exclaim with these pious hermits: "How great is the power of this most holy sacrifice of the Mass! How mightily does it operate in the conversion of sinners! How many a hardened sinner is by it moved to repentance, rescued from eternal perdition!" Let us render continual thanks to our loving Saviour, Who at so great a cost to Himself appointed this salutary sacrifice of propitiation, thereby making it easy for us to reconcile ourselves to an offended God, and acquit ourselves of the debt we owe Him. How privileged we are in contrast to the Jews of old, who, for all their costly sacrifices, had not one which could avail for the remission of a single sin; as St. Paul says: "It is impossible that with the blood of oxen and goats sins should be taken away." (Heb. x. 4.) If we lived under a dispensation like to that of the Jews, our sins would probably be unatoned for, and we should be lost forever, since now, when we possess a sin-offering of such surpassing virtue, we absent ourselves from it on such slight pretexts, and assist at it so carelessly. Bethink thyself, O sinner, how greatly against thy own interests thou art acting in neglecting Mass, and putting off to a future life the expiation of thy sins. See that thou correct thyself in this respect; rouse thyself from thy tepidity, and frequently offer to God the atoning sacrifice of the Mass.

THE MANNER IN WHICH HOLY MASS EFFECTS THE FORGIVENESS OF SIN AND THE CONVERSION OF HARDENED SINNERS.

St. Thomas Aquinas asserts the Mass to be a powerful means of atonement when he says: "The special effect of the holy sacrifice of the Mass is that it operates our reconciliation with God." In explanation of this he gives the following illustration: "Just as a man will forgive the wrong done him by his fellow-man on consideration of a valuable gift which is presented to him, or a service which is rendered to him, so the anger of God may be appeased by the acceptable service thou dost render Him when thou hearest Mass, and by the priceless gift which thou dost offer Him in the oblation of the body and blood of Jesus Christ." This doctrine of the angelic doctor coincides with the opinion of all theologians and with the teaching of Holy Scripture.

We are told that the patriarch Jacob, fearing that his brother Esau, enraged at finding that he had defrauded him of his birthright and his father's blessing, would seek to revenge himself on him, said within himself: "I will appease him with presents, afterwards perhaps he will be gracious to me." (Gen. xxxii. 20.) Accordingly he sent him a quantity of camels, cows, oxen, sheep, goats, in view of conciliating him. Now, when in holy Mass we offer to the God against Whom we have offended the virtues, the merits, the life, passion, and death of His Son, His anger will be far more quickly appeased than Esau's was, because these gifts are of infinite value, and highly pleasing to God the Father. It is true our transgressions still cry for vengeance, but the blood of Christ calls for mercy on our behalf. The voice of this blood is, however, all-powerful. Therefore it prevails over the cry of our sins. Hence Albertus Magnus says: "By this inestimable gift the divine indignation and anger are fully appeased."

No one will doubt that holy Mass has power to reconcile the repentant sinner to God; but whether it also avails to reconcile the unrepentant is quite another question, and one which must be answered in the negative, for only by sincere contrition can the sinner pass from a state of wrath to a state of grace. Consequently if an unrepentant sinner hears Mass, or Mass is said for him, it does not reconcile him to God, nor readmit him to grace.

Is holy Mass of no benefit to him, then? It is of great benefit to him, both temporally and spiritually. It profits him temporally, because for the sake of the Mass God preserves him from some misfortune, or bestows on him some favor. And the reason of this is because God, of His ineffable bounty, never leaves the least service unrewarded. Every time we hear Mass we merit an eternal recompense; but the unrepentant sinner is not capable of receiving an eternal recompense. Therefore God, of His pure mercy, gives him a temporal reward, such as preservation from some calamity, or the bestowal of some good thing in this life.

But the spiritual profit accruing to him is much greater. For, according to the teaching of theologians, God gives in holy Mass preventing grace, by virtue of which the sinner is brought to the knowledge and abhorrence of mortal sin. This divine assistance, merited by the Mass heard or celebrated, does not, however, produce the same effect in all. There are hardened sinners, and sinners who are inclined to penance. The latter will by the holy Mass be brought to true contrition and penance, and through them be reconciled to God; but the former, though the same grace is offered them, will reject it in the obduracy of their evil heart.

We must not, however, conclude that the Mass is not a propitiatory sacrifice because the hardened sinner will not accept, but rejects God's preventing grace; it is, and always will be, a propitiatory sacrifice, and we are bound to regard it as such. The Church teaches: "If any one saith that the sacrifice of the Mass is not a propitiatory sacrifice, let him be anathema." (Sess. xxii. c. 3.) It is termed propitiatory because through the merits of Christ assistance is given to the sinner to recognize and repent of his sins. This succor is specially given to those who assist at Mass. Were it not so, the Mass would possess no peculiar power of making us participators in Christ's redemption over and above that of any other good work which may be offered up on behalf of a sinner. We know that this cannot be the case, for in the Mass Christ bequeathed to us a special antidote against the poison of sin.

It is by no means indispensable that the effects of the Mass should be immediately apparent; it is enough that they should come in God's own time. We know that Christ upon the cross pleaded with tears on behalf of sinners, and offered for them His cruel passion and death; yet of all the thousands present how few struck their breasts in contrition and said in firm faith: "Indeed this was the Son of God." (St. Matt. xxvii. 54.) The others continued obdurate, and thrust from them the proffered grace and divine assistance. Not until Pentecost did the prayer of Christ and His sacrifice upon the cross produce their effect; then three thousand persons were converted by the preaching of St. Peter. In like manner the holy sacrifice of the Mass does not always effect the conversion of the sinner at once: it works gradually, when God softens the hard heart of the sinner by degrees, and disposes it to receive the influence of grace. This gradual conversion is preeminently due to holy Mass, since it gives time for the sinner to hear several Masses or have them said for him. Marchantius says the same: "Holy Mass does not blot out sin, but it produces contrition, or the desire of true contrition. Sometimes this contrition is given during the celebration of the Mass which is said on behalf of a particular person, sometimes at a later period, but always in virtue of that Mass. Oftentimes it happens that by a special grace the sinner is converted after the lapse of some time, and is not aware that he owes his conversion to the potency of the holy sacrifice. And when the sinner is not converted it is because he rejects the divine assistance which is offered to him, and abuses the means of grace instead of using them aright."

The words of this learned man testify to the immense power which the holy Mass possesses for the conversion of hardened sinners. The Church also teaches us that when a repentant sinner offers the holy sacrifice to God, with the intention of conciliating Him, the grace of conversion and reconciliation with God will certainly be granted him. "If we draw nigh unto God, contrite and penitent, and with sincere heart and upright faith, with fear and reverence, offer the holy Mass to God, the Lord, appeased by the oblation thereof, and granting the grace and gift of penitence, forgives even heinous crimes and sins." (Sess. xxii. ch. 2.) What consolation these words contain for the heart of the sinner! With what hope do they not inspire the pusillanimous and despondent! They are assured that by the oblation of the Mass they can so far appease the anger of God that He will turn aside His wrath, will forgive them their transgressions, and admit them to His grace and friendship. Thus is fulfilled what Sirach says "The oblation of the just maketh the altar fat, and is an odor of sweetness in the sight of the Most High" (Ecclus. xxxv. 8); that is to say, when a miserable sinner offers to the Eternal Father His only-begotten Son as an expiatory sacrifice, and implores His mercy in virtue of Christ's merits. The Wise Man says: "A secret present quencheth anger: and a gift in the bosom the greatest wrath." (Prov. xxi. 14.) What is the secret gift here spoken of but the body of Christ under the form of bread? Let us in holy Mass offer this secret gift, this costly present, and we shall thereby quench the anger of God and appease His wrath.

This, as St. Bonaventure reminds us, the priest does in

the name of all present when he elevates the sacred host, as if to say: "We miserable sinners have transgressed and grievously offended Thee, O heavenly Father; but look upon the face of Thy Christ, Whom we here present to Thee, hoping to change Thy anger into mercy. Turn not away Thy face from Thy Son, of Whom Thou saidst: 'This is My beloved Son, in Whom I am well pleased.' For His sake turn us to Thee, and be not angry with us anymore." By such supplications and the oblation of the Mass many sinners have obtained the grace of repentance, which otherwise they would not have done. Holy Church would not place upon the lips of the priest the following prayer (secret for the fourth Saturday of Lent) were she not well aware that the offering of this expiatory sacrifice has the power to soften the hard heart, to convert the obstinate sinner: "Be appeased, we beseech Thee, O Lord, by our offerings which Thou hast accepted; and graciously compel our wills, even though rebellious, to turn to Thee.' Wherefore let the sinner, although he may have sunk so low in the defilement of sin that he must needs almost despair of his conversion, go to Mass, and repeat that prayer, humbly imploring the God of mercy to convert him by means of the great power of holy Mass.

But here an objection may perhaps be raised: What will such a prayer avail, how will it profit the sinner, since Holy Scripture says: "He that turneth away his ears from hearing the law, his prayer shall be an abomination" (Prov. xxviii. 9)? The angelic doctor St. Thomas Aquinas thus answers this question: "Although it is clearly stated in several passages of Scripture that the prayer of one who is in mortal sin cannot be pleasing to God, yet of His ineffable bounty He does not reject that prayer which is prompted by good motives, but graciously listens to it."

But even supposing that God would not accept the prayer of a hardened sinner, nevertheless He would most assuredly accept the holy Mass, so pleasing in His sight, which the suppliant offers. I do not mean that the prayer which the sinner offers during the Mass is pleasing to God, but that the Mass offered by the hardened sinner is most acceptable to Him. Can it be doubted that the just God will graciously accept the precious gift of the body and blood of His Son, even when offered by a sinner who in himself is hateful to Him? Will He not say: "Although this man is My enemy and abhorrent to Me, yet the gift which he offers to Me with a good intention is surpassingly valuable and agreeable to me. Since he thus honors Me, I will in return for this gift offer him My grace; and if he accepts it I will overlook the affront he has done Me, and restore him to My friendship and favor."

This assertion does not rest on my opinion alone, but upon the authority, as has already been seen, of the Council of Trent, which teaches that the offering of the holy sacrifice is a means of reconciling the sinner to God, and of obtaining the remission of all, even heinous, crimes and sins. Listen, O sinner! to this consoling truth. Take from it fresh hope of thy salvation, fresh courage for the amendment of thy life; disentangle thyself from the net of despair, and trust in this all-powerful sacrifice of atonement. Although Holy Scripture says: "To God the wicked and his wickedness are hateful alike" (Wis. xiv. 9), yet do thou go diligently to church, and there join in offering the holy sacrifice to God. For even if thou didst hear Mass in a state of mortal sin, thou wouldst not commit another mortal sin, as priests do if they celebrate unworthily, or the laity if they communicate unworthily; on the contrary, thou dost obtain help to return to the state of grace.

The same effect is produced if a good man hears Mass

on behalf of an evil-doer, offering it to God for his conversion. We learn this from the revelations made to St. Gertrude. One day, when the saint was earnestly entreating God at the time of Mass to prevent with His grace those souls who were destined to be converted and saved, and in virtue of the holy sacrifice to anticipate the time fixed for their conversion, she longed to plead also for those reprobate sinners who appeared to be doomed to eternal perdition, so great was the compassion she felt for them. She restrained herself, however, fearing that she would pray in vain. Our Lord, desiring to correct this pusillanimity on her part, said to her: "Do you suppose that My spotless body and precious blood, here upon the altar, is not sufficiently powerful to bring those who are in the way of perdition to a better course of life?" St. Gertrude, amazed at the excess of lovingkindness evinced in these words, felt emboldened, while pondering them in her heart, to cry to the all-merciful Saviour, imploring Him by His precious body and blood, by the holy Mass then being celebrated, by His perpetual oblation of Himself upon the altar for the salvation of sinners, to bring at least some of those sinners who were in the way of damnation back to a state of grace. Our Lord graciously received her fervent petition, and assured her that it should be granted. Let this testimony to the potency of holy Mass to save sinners induce us to hear it frequently and devoutly, and offer it for our own conversion and that of other sinners.

BY MEANS OF HOLY MASS VENIAL SINS ALSO ARE BLOTTED OUT.

Through the holy sacrifice of the Mass venial sins also are atoned for—sins which are highly displeasing to God, far more so, in fact, than we unhappy sinners are wont to imagine. The following simile may help us to appreciate the malice of venial sin. A man had a son who made him angry every day: he was careless at his work, idle, given up to pleasure; he made a bad use of his father's money, and paid no heed to the admonitions addressed to him. The father complained bitterly of his son's conduct. But the latter excused himself on the plea that he never raised his hand against his father, or did him any mortal injury. In like manner we conduct ourselves towards God by the venial sins we daily commit.

If we had no expiatory sacrifice wherewith to appease the wrath of our heavenly Father, to what a miserable end we should come! Even though our daily sins are venial, not mortal, we yet stand in great need of a sacrifice of atonement, lest the divine anger at length get the upper hand and He drive us out of His house as unworthy to be His sons.

In order to provide against so miserable a fate our loving Saviour has appointed for us a powerful means of atonement in holy Mass, wherein the oblation of the divine victim is offered for the blotting out of venial as well as mortal sin. This is expressly stated by holy Church in the decrees of the Council of Trent: "Christ instituted the holy Mass in the Last Supper that its salutary virtue be applied to the remission of those sins which we daily commit." (Sess. xxii. ch. 2.) These words, which are too clear to need elucidation, prove beyond a doubt that the Mass is intended for the forgiveness of daily venial sin.

A learned writer expresses the same truth at greater length; he says: "This sacrifice is repeated daily because we sin daily, and the sins we commit are such as are inevitable to human frailty. Wherefore so long as the Christian falls daily, so long will Christ be immolated daily in a mystical manner." Christ has, it is true, given us many other means of expiating our venial sins, such as making acts of contrition, prayer, patience in suffering, etc., but none of these is so efficacious as holy Mass.

On this point Suarez says: "It may be assumed that those who offer the holy sacrifice with the intention of obtaining the remission of their venial sins obtain it at least by reason of their prayer, because their will is opposed to venial sin.' By this he intends to say: Since contrition for sin is indispensable to forgiveness, if a man hears Mass with the object of obtaining the pardon of his venial sins, it is a sure sign that he feels contrition for them, and desires to be delivered from them. Father Gobat says: "Holy Mass is so essentially a sacrifice of atonement for those who hear it that by virtue of this holy sacrifice they obtain the remission of all their venial sins, even though they feel as yet no lively contrition for them. And provided they hear Mass in view of obtaining this remission, it is granted immediately and in full force." This assurance, given us by learned writers, that if we offer holy Mass in order to obtain forgiveness of venial sin it will be granted to us, even if our contrition be but weak, is indeed most consoling. It affords a fresh motive for going to Mass, since we have therein so easy a means of blotting out our daily offences.

Again, speaking of the immense power inherent in holy Mass for the pardon of venial sin, Suarez says: "Christ instituted this divine oblation, and attached to it the virtue of His death, which is applied to us for the remission of our daily sins." That is to say: Christ forgives our venial sins by virtue of His death, inasmuch as in holy Mass His death is renewed in a mystic manner. Osorius also remarks that not only is the penalty of sin done away with in holy Mass by virtue of Christ's passion, but the guilt of venial sins is also cancelled by this holy sacrifice.

"The fruit of the Mass," says Father Stratius, "is exceedingly plenteous, for it renders us participators in the superabundant riches of Christ's merits and satisfaction for sin. Such is the power of holy Mass that our sins melt away before it as wax before the fire, and the penalties we have incurred are turned aside from us." Wherefore, at the time of the *Confiteor*, at the commencement of the Mass, do thou pray thus: "O most just God, with contrite heart and steadfast hope I lay my sins upon this sacred altar, in order that they may be consumed by the flames of Thy divine charity, purged away by the precious blood of Jesus, and fully atoned for by His infinite merits. Amen."

What has been said above may be summed up in these words of Marchantius: "It is evident that, in accordance with the object of its institution, the holy sacrifice of the Mass blots out venial sin. For Christ, knowing well how weak our nature is and how prone to evil by reason of original sin, provided us with a suitable remedy, and ordained a daily sacrifice for daily sins." How can we sufficiently thank our loving Redeemer for this unspeakable benefit, how can we appreciate it aright? If we had not this divine oblation, or if we were to make no use of it for the expiation of our venial sins, alas! what a weight of sin should we not carry with us before the tribunal of the Eternal Judge! How long, how severe, would be the atonement required from us in another world! for these are the sins of which David speaks when he says: "My iniquities are multiplied above the hairs of my head." (Ps. xxxix. 13.) And again: "Who can understand sins?" (Ps. xviii. 13.) They are the sins of which the Church says: "My transgressions are more in number than the sands of the sea." These sins often escape our observation altogether, so that we do not confess or atone for them. We may, however, purge away and expiate them by means of the all-prevailing sacrifice of propitiation which the greatest of all benefactors has graciously bestowed upon us in holy Mass.

Wouldst thou obtain forgiveness of thy venial sins by virtue of that holy sacrifice, then imitate the example of St. Gertrude, of whom it is recorded that "during holy Mass, which is the most true and efficacious atonement for the guilt of man, when the sacred victim was immolated by the priest, she offered it to the Most High for the cleansing away of her sins. God the Father received the oblation graciously and admitted the saint to His embrace." These words, taken from the revelations of the saint, may well make us marvel at the wonderful power of this holy sacrifice. For when St. Gertrude, at the elevation of the adorable host, fervently prayed: "Holy Lord God, I offer to Thee this sacred host for the remission of my sins," these few words were effectual not merely to cleanse her soul from the stains it had contracted, but to render it worthy to be admitted to the bosom of God the Father.

In imitation of the saint, see that thou, with a devotion and an emphasis like hers, at the elevation of the host, offer to God the Father the sacred oblation of the body and blood of His Son for the complete atonement and cleansing away of thy sins, both mortal and venial, saying: "Most merciful Father, since this sacred victim is the most true and worthy atonement for the guilt of mankind, vouchsafe to receive it in expiation of my sins, and grant me remission of the chastisement due to them. Amen." The more often, the more earnestly, thou dost this, the greater the number of venial sins which will be blotted out. For if thou dost ponder what has been said in this book of the supernatural power of the holy sacrifice of the Mass, thou wilt not doubt that it can avail to cancel all thy sins and shortcomings.

Consider, furthermore, that holy Mass does not only

deliver from venial sin, it also cleanses our souls from their stains. St. John Damascene teaches us this when he says: "The immaculate and unbloody sacrifice of the Mass is for the healing of all wounds and the purification of all stains." This God foretold by the mouth of the prophet Ezechiel of old: "I will pour upon you clean water, and you shall be cleansed from all your filthiness." (Ezechiel xxxvi. 25.) The cleansing here spoken of is effected by means of the sacred stream which flowed from Our Lord's pierced side; we read in St. John's Gospel: "One of the soldiers with a spear opened His side, and immediately there came out blood and water." (St. John xix. 34.) This was done by the special permission of God, for the divine Saviour desired to receive this wound in His side, and that it should remain open after His death, that it might become for us "a fountain of water, springing up into life everlasting." (*Ibid.* iv. 14.)

The existence of this fountain was foretold by the prophet Zacharias: "There shall be a fountain open to the house of David and to the inhabitants of Jerusalem." (Zach. xiii. 1.) Out of this life-giving source the precious stream of blood and water flows perennially, and to it all have free access, that they may quench their thirst and wash their stains away. The cleansing fount only flows, however, for those who go to it; it only profits those who draw from it water to wash away the stains of sin. In every Mass that is celebrated this salutary stream flows over all who are present, for the wound of Christ's side is then opened afresh. Happy we for whose cleansing this fountain ever flows! How many unhappy sinners have gone thither, and thence with joy drawn the waters of grace, as the prophet Isaias foretold: "You shall draw water with joy out of the Saviour's fountains." (Is. xii. 3.) And those sinners who neglect to repair to this fountain He kindly invites to do so: "All you that thirst, come to the waters; and you that have no money, make haste, buy and eat; come ye, buy wine and milk without money and without any price." (Is. lv. 1.) In like manner St. John in the Apocalypse invites us: "The spirit and the bride say: Come. And he that heareth, let him say: Come. And he that thirsteth, let him come; and he that will, let him take the water of life, freely." (Apoc. xxii. 17.)

Behold how earnestly the prophet Isaias and the apostle John invite us to this health-giving fountain, which flows in holy Mass, because they both know how salutary is this water from the Saviour's side. For this fountain is a healing bath wherein our souls are washed, purified, and sanctified. Let us with the greatest joy and eagerness betake ourselves to this fount of grace, open to us in holy Mass, and hear Mass with contrition and devotion, in order to cleanse our souls from guilt and stain.

CHAPTER XVI.

THE HOLY SACRIFICE OF THE MASS IS THE MOST COMPLETE SATISFACTION FOR SIN.

FOR the right comprehension of what follows it is necessary to bear in mind that the consequences of every sin are twofold: there is its guilt and its penalty. The guilt, or withdrawal of God's favor, and the eternal punishment are remitted by contrition and confession; the temporal punishment is likewise remitted by contrition, confession, and penance, but mostly only in part; that is to say, the deeper the contrition, the more sincere the confession, and the more severe the penance the larger the amount of temporal punishment of which they obtain the remission. The remainder of our debt must either be paid by means of tears, prayers, vigils, fasts, alms-giving, confession and communion, pilgrimages, Masses, and indulgences, or by the fire of purgatory. Such works of penance are most repugnant to our senses, and on that account many refuse to perform them. What remains to be done, then, if we desire to escape the pains of purgatory, and yet will not do penance?

We must do as did the servant in the Gospel of whom Our Lord speaks: "The kingdom of heaven is likened to a king, who would take an account of his servants. And when he had begun to take the account, one was brought to him that owed him ten thousand talents. And as he had not wherewith to pay it, . . . falling down, he besought him, saying: Have patience with me, and I will pay thee all." (St. Matt. xviii. 23–26.) Must we not wonder at the boldness of this self-confident servant, who craves not the forgiveness of his enormous debt, or even of a part of it, but merely asks permission to postpone the payment of it? It was impossible for one in his position to find the means of defraying such a debt, even could he have lived another hundred years in his master's service.

Let us remember that the story here related by the Saviour is no true story, but a parable or allegory; and that the servant represents one who has committed many grievous sins, and incurred a great debt towards Almighty God. Thou, O sinner, art the one of whom Christ speaks these words: "Thou knowest not that thou art wretched, and miserable, and poor, and blind, and naked." (Apoc. iii. 17.) Thou hast no idea of the amount of the debt with which thou art burdened. How wilt thou with thy good works pay ten thousand talents, when as long as thou livest thou canst not earn one single talent? So great is the punishment incurred by one mortal sin that by thy own strength thou couldst not compensate for it to all eternity. Yet there is a means whereby thy heavy debt may be cancelled. With the servant in the Gospel, fall at the feet of thy God and Lord, beseech Him, saying: "Lord, have patience with me; give me time to do penance, and I will discharge my debts to the full. If it is beyond my power to have Mass said for me, I will hear Mass as often and as attentively as I can, and offer it to Thee in payment of my heavy debt."

The learned Sanchez gives the same counsel: "When thou hearest Mass, think to thyself that it is thine own, given to thee by God the Father as well as by God the Son." "That this is so the priest declares when, turning to the people, he says: "Brethren, pray that my sacrifice and yours may be acceptable to God the Father Almighty." To all present he announces that this sacrifice is not his alone, but theirs; consequently it is thine also. Considering this, say to God: "Lord, how much do I owe Thee? A hundred, a thousand, or perhaps ten thousand talents? I acknowledge, Lord, my deep indebtedness. I am ready to discharge my obligations. I cannot, indeed, do this with my own merits, but I can with the abundant merits of Thy Son, present upon this altar, and given to me. I place this casket before Thee; take out of it as much as will defray my debt." Meditate thus with lively faith, and it will bring thee much comfort to know that in holy Mass we have a sufficient and unfailing fund from which our debts may be defrayed.

Now let us see how great the power of holy Mass is in order that we may place our trust in it. Theologians teach us that the Mass, as well in respect to him who celebrates it as to those who have it said for their intention and those who merely assist at it, never fails to effect the remission of the temporal penalty of sin, *ex opere operato;* that is to say, the potency and efficacy of the holy sacrifice of the Mass cannot be augmented by the piety of the celebrant, nor diminished by his sinfulness; but whenever it is rightfully and validly offered it is in itself, through its own inherent power, of infinite value and marvellous efficacy. Of itself, and not through our cooperation or that of the priest, does it avail for the remission of the temporal penalty of sin.

All poor sinners may take courage from this truth, since we are thereby assured that if they assist at Mass with contrition of heart they cannot fail to obtain remission of a part of the temporal punishment due to sin through the merits of Christ, which are applied to us in the Mass. Marchantius speaks of holy Mass as an effectual appropriation of the merits of Christ, the unlocking of His treasury, so that out of it we may take heavenly riches, and amply pay all that we owe. This is so vast and so full that if Christ were to give every sinner, past, present, and future, sufficient to cancel the penalty of his sins, there would still remain enough for countless worlds. Christ frequently gives us of this treasure: at our Baptism, when we awaken true contrition, when we go to confession and communion, when we perform good works; but never does He bestow it with such liberality as at the time of Mass. This the Church teaches in these words: "The fruits of that bloody oblation are received most plentifully in this unbloody one." (Sess. xxii. ch. 2.) This is so because the Mass is the noblest sacrificial act, the one most pleasing to God, most salutary to mankind; because in it Christ is at once the high priest and the victim. It is in order that the faithful may take delight in holy Mass that Christ then bestows His gifts with so lavish a hand.

This distribution of the riches of Christ's treasury is almost as if our divine Redeemer were to descend from the altar during Mass, and, passing from one to another of the persons present, were to place in the hand of each a piece of gold as the reward of his attendance there. No one is excluded from this bestowal of gifts, unless he be in mortal sin, or hear Mass with voluntary distractions. All others participate in this donation, but it varies in amount, according to the dispositions of the recipient. In what manner are these celestial coins to be expended? They may and ought to be presented to God the Father to discharge our debts, increase our measure of grace, and heighten our future felicity. Would that every sinner would lay this to heart, and, if he should fall into sin, hasten to church, hear Mass piously, and offer it to God to obtain forgiveness of sin, remission of its penalty, and amendment of life. This is the best and surest way to obtain these graces, and be preserved from the sin of relapse.

THE AMOUNT OF TEMPORAL PUNISHMENT THAT CAN BE CANCELLED BY ONE MASS.

The reader who perceives, from what has been said, that the temporal punishment of sin may be cancelled by holy Mass will perhaps be desirous to know to what extent the Mass avails for this purpose. Before answering this inquiry it is necessary first to expound the great excellence of holy Mass. The learned Father Lancicius says: "The value of the Mass is infinite. When celebrated by the priest it has, on account of the divine nature of the victim and the oblation, a value no less great than it had when offered by Christ Himself in the Last Supper. It was then an act of infinite value, as were all the works He performed when on earth, because of the infinite dignity of His divine person. Consequently the sacrifice of the Mass is of infinite value."

The same writer proceeds to explain at length that although the value of the Mass is unlimited, the measure of benefit each one derives from it is limited. Otherwise with one single Mass a man might expiate all his guilt and acquit himself of his huge debt, an idea quite at variance with the teaching of the Church. Yet it is certain that the infinite value of the Mass renders it a means of compensating for a great number of offences; in fact, were any one to hear Mass with perfect devotion, that one Mass would be sufficient to cancel his guilt and its penalty. What fervent thanks we owe to Our Lord for having, in this precious oblation, placed within our reach so easy a means of discharging our heavy debt! Since the Mass is of such infinite excellence, we do more by hearing it than by performing hard works of penance.

St. Laurence Justinian confirms this assertion when he says: "Take a pair of scales, and place in one scale all manner of good works: prayers, fasts, vigils, mortifications, pilgrimages, and what not; in the other scale place one single Mass. Hold up your scales, and you will see how entirely the latter outweighs the former; for in the Mass He is offered in Whom dwelleth all the fulness of the Godhead corporally, as St. Paul says [Col. ii. 9], Who in His person possesses an incomparable treasure of merits, and Whose intercession is alone omnipotent." This is as much as to say: If thou hadst performed all those works of penance, and piously offered them to God, thou wouldst only have offered human works, which are nothing in comparison to the infinite majesty of God. But when thou hearest Mass thou offerest divine gifts, the merits of Christ, the wounds of Christ, the body of Christ, the blood of Christ, the passion of Christ, the virtues of Christ, and thereby thou renderest to God infinite honor, infinite praise, infinite service, infinite satisfaction. Hence we may conclude how much of the punishment due to sin may be cancelled by one Mass, since in the balance of divine justice it so far outweighs all our works of penance. And since these penances, performed in a state of grace, suffice for the remission of the temporal penalty of one mortal sin, a Mass heard devoutly will surely atone for several.

And if any one should inquire further what is the exact amount of the pains of purgatory remitted or alleviated by one Mass, we reply that God has not revealed to His Church the severity or duration of the punishment to be undergone for mortal or venial sin.

It may, however, be asked: "If by hearing Mass we obtain exemption from so much of the penalty of sin, what may we not hope to escape by having Mass said?" I answer: A man gains much more by having Mass said for himself in his lifetime than by simply hearing Mass, for then the whole satisfaction or merit of the Mass belongs to him, and will be applied to him by the priest and by God. In this no one shares but he for whom the Mass is said. The amount of the temporal punishment thereby remitted is not revealed by God, but we may be sure that the satisfaction is of great value and efficacy. This efficacy is increased if the individual for whom the Mass is said is present at it. The learned Marchantius teaches this: "Holy Mass is of greater profit to the person for whom it is said if he be present at it than if he be absent. For although in his absence he receives all the benefit which the priest assigns to him, yet he does not derive from it the merit to which his presence would entitle him."

Here it may be well to mention a fact which is not generally known: When any one has Mass said in honor of some saint, or to obtain some petition, or to avert some dreaded calamity, he asks for the Mass for the special intention which he has in his mind, but does not think to appropriate to himself or to another person the satisfaction or merit of that Mass. If the priest also omits to do this, and the satisfaction of the holy Mass is not applied to any one in particular, it will probably go to the treasury of the Church, unless God, in His goodness, applies it to those who, through ignorance, have neglected to appropriate it to themselves. When, therefore, pious reader, thou dost have Mass said in honor of a saint, or for thine own intention, see that thou reserve for thyself the satisfaction or merit of the Mass. In this way thou wilt derive a twofold benefit from it: thou wilt honor the saint, and thou wilt discharge some of the debt yet due on account of thy sins. And if thou dost have Mass said to obtain some favor thy request will be heard if it be for the welfare of thy soul, and thou wilt obtain remission of a part of the temporal penalty awaiting thee. Remember this when thou hast Mass said, for it is of no slight importance.

All these considerations ought to inspire us with fresh zeal, and make us anxious to hear Mass daily, and on Sundays and festivals, if possible, to hear more than one Mass, and thus discharge in this world the penalty of our sins. The following example will show how profitable this practice is to us and how well-pleasing to God.

In his *History of Spain* Mariana speaks of a Spanish warrior named Pascal Vives who had a great devotion to holy Mass and assisted daily at one or more. It happened while he was serving under the standard of the Count of Castile that a large body of Moors, who at that time had conquered the greater part of Spain, laid siege to the castle of the count. The garrison, being totally unprepared to stand a siege, were reduced to dire distress, and the count resolved to make a sally with all his men, and risk their lives in a desperate attempt to drive back the Moors.

The next morning he heard Mass with all his soldiers, and, trusting in the divine assistance, sallied forth against his enemies. But Pascal Vives remained in the church and heard eight Masses, one after another, praying fervently that victory might be on the count's side. While he thus prayed and his comrades fought, behold! the latter saw Pascal Vives mounted on his charger making a gallant onslaught upon the Moors, hewing them down on every side. Calling to the soldiers to follow him fearlessly, he broke the ranks of the enemy, carried off their colors, and wrought great havoc amongst them. The contest lasted nearly four hours, only ceasing at the time when the eighth Mass, at which Pascal had assisted, was ended. The Moors were completely routed. The victory was universally ascribed to Pascal's heroic bravery, and the count gave orders that he should have all the honor of it. But when all was over Pascal had disappeared. He was sought for all over the battlefield, but nowhere was he to be found. The fact was he had stayed in the church, and there he remained almost all day, for he was ashamed to leave it, fearing lest the soldiers should mock at him for a coward, and the count dismiss him from his service. No tidings of the battle had reached him, and he did not know which side had gained the day. Presently the count, thinking it very likely that Pascal had gone to the church to give thanks to Almighty God for the victory, bade his followers go there in search of him. Pascal was accordingly found and brought into the presence of the count and his officers. When they all began to compliment him on his prowess and say that the victory they had won was, under God, to be ascribed to him, he was perfectly astonished and knew not what to say. After a short space, interiorly enlightened by God, he confessed the truth, declaring that he had taken no part in the contest, but had during the whole time been in the church, where he had heard eight Masses. The soldiers would not believe what he said, persisting that they had seen him with their own eyes in the thick of the fray, and had heard him calling on them to fight valiantly.

Then Pascal answered: "If it really is as you say, the brave knight who bore my semblance must have been my guardian angel, for I assure you I have not been out of the church to-day. Praise God with me and give thanks to Him from your hearts for having sent you an angel, through whose assistance you were enabled to vanquish the foe. But learn from this how pleasing it is to God that we should assist at Mass, and how profitable it is to us, for I am convinced that had I not heard those Masses my angel would not have appeared to you and led you on to so signal a victory." In these and other words he exhorted the soldiers to be very fervent in hearing Mass.

It is to be hoped that this incident will have a like effect on those who read it and make them for the future more diligent in their attendance at Mass. Above all, great sinners who have done little penance should do this. We know that so strict is divine justice no sin will go unpunished; it must be expiated in this world or in the next. Far better is it for thee, O sinner, to atone for thy sins of thy own accord in this world than to leave it to the just Judge to chastise thee for them in the next. And if thou canst not undertake difficult penances, choose the easy one of hearing Mass, whereby thou canst pay off all thy debts.

CHAPTER XVII.

THE HOLY MASS IS THE MOST SUBLIME WORK OF THE HOLY GHOST.

IN almost all the previous chapters of this book much has been said of God the Father and God the Son, and but little of God the Holy Ghost. In order that it may be seen to how great an extent the third person of the Holy Trinity cooperates in holy Mass we shall devote the present chapter to a consideration of His action in this central act of worship. It would be impossible to estimate rightly, much more to express in words, the good that Christianity owes to the work of the Holy Spirit. He is the divine charity and mercy, and is ever occupied in conciliating divine justice, and saving sinners from perdition. The Holy Ghost formed the sacred humanity of Jesus Christ of the substance of the Virgin Mary; He created His human soul, and united it to the Divinity in one person in an incomprehensible manner. He it was who brought the work of man's redemption to a happy consummation on the day of Pentecost, when He descended upon the faithful in the form of fire, kindling them with divine love, and converting by His grace hardened sinners, who were untouched by Our Lord's miracles and by His passion. He dwells ever with the true believer; and although by many He is dishonored and offended, yet He does not altogether abandon them, but knocks at the door of their heart, and asks for readmission there.

All these are great, nay, divine, acts, so that we may justly say that holy Mass is the chief and sublimest work of the Holy Ghost, and for this reason: All theologians agree that the mystery of the incarnation is the greatest marvel the hand of God has wrought, because thereby the infinite Godhead was united to the Manhood of Christ in one person. This was accomplished through the operation of the Holy Ghost; as we say in the Creed: "Who was conceived by the Holy Ghost." Although this wonder is unspeakably great, yet the miracle worked in holy Mass seems still greater, because herein the omnipotent Godhead and the perfect humanity of Christ are so abased that they are present in the minutest particle of the sacred host.

That the Holy Ghost is the agent in this mystery we know from the liturgy of the apostle James. Immediately before the consecration we find this prayer: "Send down, O Lord, we beseech Thee, upon these proposed gifts Thy Holy Spirit, that, coming upon them with His holy and glorious presence, He may hallow them, and make this bread the holy body, and this cup the holy blood, of Thy Son Jesus Christ." Almost identical are the words employed in the liturgy of St. Clement, pope and martyr: "We beseech Thee, O Lord, to send down Thy Holy Spirit upon this oblation, that He may make this bread the body, this chalice the blood, of Thy Christ." Both these eminent saints, who were contemporaries, attribute the transubstantiation of the bread and wine, not to Christ, but to the Holy Ghost, and Him they invoke to complete the work. For as the Holy Ghost operated the incarnation of the Son of God, according to the testimony of the archangel Gabriel: "The Holy Ghost shall come upon thee, and the power of the Most High shall overshadow thee" (St. Luke i. 35), so in every Mass He accomplishes the renewal of this mystery.

This is also indicated by the action of the priest, who,

before making the first sign of the cross over the host and chalice, after they have been offered, elevates his eyes towards heaven, stretches out both his hands, and, joining them again, invokes the Holy Ghost in these words: "Come, O Sanctifier, almighty, eternal God, and bless this sacrifice, prepared to Thy holy name." This proves beyond a doubt that the Holy Ghost descends from heaven to bless and hallow the holy sacrifice. Even so St. Ambrose says in his liturgy: "Send down, O Lord, the invisible majesty of Thy Holy Spirit, as He descended of old upon the holocausts of the patriarchs."

We will now inquire in what manner the Holy Ghost accomplishes the transubstantiation. The Abbess Hildegarde says: "On one occasion when the priest, vested, went up to the altar I saw a brilliant light, coming from heaven, irradiate the whole altar. This light was not withdrawn until the celebrant left the sanctuary at the conclusion of the Mass. I noticed that when the priest got to the *Sanctus* and began the canon a flame of extraordinary brightness shot down from above upon the bread and wine, illuminating them with its light as the rays of the sun make glass to shine. Upon this stream of light the sacred elements rose to heaven, and when they descended they were transformed into true flesh and blood, though to the eye of man they yet appeared to be bread and wine. As I gazed upon this flesh and blood I saw the signs of the incarnation, the birth, the passion, of Our Saviour reflected in them as in a mirror, and just as we know these events to have been accomplished when the Son of God was on earth."

This vision of St. Hildegarde shows us in how wondrous a manner the transubstantiation of the bread and wine is effected by the penetrating power of the divine fire, as by the power of natural fire wood is transformed into glowing embers. That which this holy abbess was privileged to behold occurs at every Mass: a celestial radiance surrounds the altar from the beginning to the end of Mass, and at the time of the consecration a flame of dazzling brightness descends from heaven, and changes the species into the true body and blood of Christ.

Of this we have two beautiful types in the Old Testament. It is recorded that, the first time Aaron offered sacrifice, "The glory of the Lord appeared to all the multitude: And behold, a fire, coming forth from the Lord, devoured the holocaust, and the fat that was upon the altar; which when the multitude saw, they praised the Lord, falling on their faces." (Lev. ix. 23, 24). The same thing happened at the consecration of Solomon's temple: "When Solomon had made an end of his prayer, fire came down from heaven, and consumed the holocausts and the victims; and the majesty of the Lord filled the house. Moreover all the children of Israel saw the fire coming down, and the glory of the Lord upon the house; and falling down with their faces to the ground, they adored, and praised the Lord." (II. Paral. vii. 1, 3.)

In both these instances the holy sacrifice of the Mass was typified, in which the Holy Spirit, as fire, descends from heaven to change the elements into Christ's body and blood. And although we poor mortals have not the grace to behold this mysterious proceeding, yet it takes place none the less certainly, and has been actually seen by some. It is related of the holy bishop and martyr Clement that, being sent by the Emperor Diocletian to the island of Rhodes, where, at the request of the bishop, he said Mass, at the time of the consecration the sacred host was changed into the semblance of a live coal in the sight of all present. A multitude of angels were also seen hovering around the host in joyful and happy adoration. The miraculous coal glowed with a brilliance so dazzling that the congregation could not bear to look upon it, and fell upon their faces, remaining in this posture until after the communion. Not until Clement prepared, with great reverence, to consume the sacred host did it resume its former appearance.

Baronius tells us that the same miraculous change took place several times when St. Ignatius, the Patriarch of Constantinople, was celebrating Mass with special fervor and recollection. In the Greek Church it was the custom to make use of wheaten bread, not hosts, for the holy sacrifice. How amazed were all who were hearing his Mass to see the bread glowing with celestial effulgence, a sure sign of the presence and operation of the Holy Ghost! For the Holy Ghost is a burning fire, and as such He appeared to the disciples on the day of Pentecost, to indicate that He is the ardent charity that unites the Father and the Son.

Baronius also relates the following story, which bears evidence to the presence of the Holy Spirit in Mass. At Formello, near Rome, there was, in early times, a bishop who acquitted himself most conscientiously of all the duties appertaining to his office, and was most reverent in his manner of saying Mass. Notwithstanding this he was accused by some evil-minded persons to Pope Agapetus of having given scandal to his flock by using one of the sacred vessels at table. The Pope, believing the accusation, caused the bishop to be brought to Rome and put into prison. On the morning of the third day after his unjust incarceration, a Sunday, an angel appeared to the Pope in a dream, and said to him: "On this Sunday neither shalt thou nor any other prelate say Mass, but only the bishop whom thou hast placed in confinement." The Pontiff awoke, and, thinking over this dream, said to himself: "Shall I allow a prelate to say Mass who lies under so grave an accusation of sacrilege?"

Before answering his own question he fell asleep again, and again heard the same voice saying: "I told thee no one but the imprisoned bishop is to say Mass." While the Pope still hesitated whether he should comply with this injunction, the voice spoke for the third time: "Beware how thou permit any other than the bishop who is in prison to celebrate in thy presence to-day." Thereupon the Pope, in some alarm, sent for the bishop, and inquired of him what was his manner of life, and bade him give an account of his actions. The prelate answered only these words: "I am a sinner." Then the Pope asked: "Is it true that thou didst eat and drink out of the vessels consecrated to the service of the altar." The bishop replied as before: "I am a sinner." As no other answer could be elicited from him, the pontiff proceeded: "Thou wilt celebrate Mass in our presence to-day." And when the bishop, in his humility, begged to be excused, he only repeated the command: "Thou wilt officiate at a solemn High Mass to-day before ourselves and all the cardinals." Upon receiving this express order the good bishop expostulated no longer, but prepared to obey. Attended by many acolytes, he went to the altar, and commenced the Mass. When he got to the prayer which is said at the time of making the first sign of the cross over the host and chalice, "Come, O Sanctifier, almighty, eternal God, and bless this sacrifice prepared to Thy holy name," he repeated it four times, and then stopped. The people grew impatient; at length the Pope said: "Why dost thou delay, and repeat this prayer so often?" The bishop answered: "Pardon me, Holy Father; I repeated the prayer because I have not yet seen the Holy Ghost descend upon the altar. May I request your Holiness to bid the deacon leave my side? I cannot venture to do so myself." The Pope then told the deacon to move to a little distance; no sooner had he done so than both the Pope and the bishop beheld the Holy Ghost come down from heaven, while the celebrant, with the deacon and acolytes, was enveloped in a luminous cloud. This miracle convinced Pope Agapetus of the innocence and sanctity of the bishop, and he much regretted having put him into prison. He resolved for the future not to act so precipitately, and to investigate a charge carefully before giving credence to it.

These miraculous appearances are intended to strengthen our belief that the Holy Ghost always comes down upon the altar to bless the divine oblation. On this subject Father Mansi says: " The unbloody sacrifice of the Mass is so venerable and sublime that the Holy Ghost descends in person to hallow it, while hosts of angels stand by and look on with the greatest delight; as St. Peter tells us: 'The Holy Ghost being sent down from heaven, on Whom the angls desire to look.'" (1. Pet. i. 12.)

How unutterable must be the holiness of this adorable sacrifice, since the Author of all holiness, the Spirit of God, Himself descends to bless, sanctify, and hallow it! How strengthening to the soul, how pleasant to the taste, is this bread of heaven, prepared for our nourishment by the Holy Ghost! For the operation of the Holy Ghost is no less indispensable, nay, far more so, to the preparation of this celestial food than is that of natural fire to the manufacture of our daily bread. For the sacred host, by the agency of this divine fire, does not become our spiritual sustenance alone: it is above all a sacrifice which we can offer to God the Lord for His glory and our own good. What a precious, what an inestimable, treasure we have in it! How much the Holy Ghost accomplishes in this mystery for our temporal and eternal welfare! For, as St. Paul says: " The Spirit helpeth our infirmity;

for we know not what we should pray for as we ought, but the Spirit Himself asketh for us, with unspeakable groanings. And He that searcheth the hearts knoweth what the Spirit desireth, because He asketh for the saints according to God." (Rom. viii. 26, 27.)

The meaning of this passage from St. Paul is that one divine Person of the Holy Trinity pleads with the other, for in the Godhead all the three are one, and equally entitled to issue commands and bestow gifts; and because, for the sake of distinguishing the Persons, we attribute principally to God the Father justice, to God the Son wisdom, to God the Holy Ghost goodness and mercy, St. Paul represents divine mercy entreating divine justice not to condemn sinners on account of their transgressions, but to save them by grace. We are sure that the Holy Spirit pleads for us at all times, and no less sure are we that He pleads for us in a special manner during holy Mass.

We know this too because at that time the holy angels also pray for us, as St. Chrysostom says: " During holy Mass it is not mortals alone who cry to God in supplication; the angels also bend the knee, and archangels plead for us." And as the reason of this he adds: " This is their acceptable time; the holy sacrifice is at their disposal; they exhibit the body of Christ, and intercede for the human race." As the angels choose the time of Mass because it is a time of mercy, when the anger of God is appeased by this all-prevailing propitiatory sacrifice, we may conclude that the benign and holy Spirit selects the same moment, that in which Christ in His humanity pleads with the Father, to " ask for us with groanings unspeakable " (Rom. viii. 26) that the severity of divine justice may be tempered by divine mercy.

Learn hence how ineffable is the goodness of the Holy Ghost, Who interests Himself in our salvation, and not only prays for us, but intercedes for us with unspeakable groanings. Who could believe this were it not expressly stated in Holy Scripture? Who can now doubt that we have a true friend in the Holy Ghost? Let us love and trust in Him, Who is indeed our true and faithful friend. And since it is preeminently at Mass that He pleads for thee, thou wouldst do well to hear Mass sometimes for His special honor and delectation.

CHAPTER XVIII.

HOLY MASS AFFORDS THE SWEETEST JOY TO THE MOTHER OF GOD AND THE SAINTS.

NEVER in her whole life was there a prouder, a happier day for Queen Esther than that upon which King Assuerus chose her from among all the maidens of his kingdom, with his own hand placed a crown upon her head, and made her queen over his vast dominions. No less certain is it that Mary, the blessed Mother of God, had no greater glory and joy than on the day when her divine Son conducted her into the realm of celestial bliss, raised her above all the choirs of angels, and crowned her queen of heaven and earth. It is impossible to conceive joy and glory greater than this. Nevertheless we are not wrong in affirming that holy Mass affords the blessed Mother of God her sweetest joy.

This statement is supported by the words of Blessed Alanus, who says: "Even as Eternal Wisdom made choice of one virgin amongst all others, that of her might be born the Saviour of the world, so that same Redeemer appointed a priesthood to dispense for all time the treasures of His redemption, through the medium of the holy sacrifice of the Mass and the Adorable Sacrament of the Altar. This it is which constitutes the greatest joy of the Mother of God, the greatest felicity of the blessed; this is the surest help of the living, the chief solace of the departed."

In this passage Alanus, a zealous servant of Jesus and Mary, asserts in no doubtful terms the excellence of the Mass, and asserts that naught else gives so great joy to the Mother of God. In order to understand this aright we must remember that, as theologians tell us, the bliss enjoyed by our blessed Lady and the other glorified saints is of a twofold nature: it is essential and accidental. Essential happiness consists in the beatific vision, the knowledge and enjoyment of God, according to the degree of glory to which the saint is admitted on his entrance into heaven. This degree remains the same to all eternity; it is impossible for any one to rise to a higher or sink to a lower one. Accidental happiness, on the contrary, consists in some particular honor or joy which some saint experiences when a favor is shown him by God, when special veneration, or some acceptable service, is rendered to him on earth. For instance, the feast of a saint may be kept with great ceremony, and many prayers offered to him. This accidental happiness, as it is called, the sacred humanity of Christ and all angels and saints are capable of receiving, as we know from the words of St. Luke: "I say to you that even so there shall be joy in heaven upon one sinner that doth penance." (St. Luke xv. 7.) The joy here spoken of is not essential, but accidental; it is renewed whenever a sinner is converted, and lost should the sinner revert to his evil ways.

From this explanation we see that Blessed Alanus in stating that the Mother of God derives the principal part of her happiness from holy Mass refers to her accidental, not her essential, joy. For although there are many ways whereby we may do honor to Our Lady and afford her pleasure, yet none of the accidental joys we thus procure her equals that which we can give her by hearing Mass. And why is it that we cannot, by reciting rosaries, the Little Office, litanies, psalms, and other prayers with the intention of showing her honor and increasing her joy, do half as much as we can do by piously hearing Mass in her honor, and offering to God her beloved Son, present upon the altar? It is because in the latter case we perform in her honor the highest act of Christian worship, and do God far better service than by the recital of psalms and prayers.

Besides this, we give her another and a most acceptable pleasure by hearing Mass. For since the glory of God and the salvation of sinners are what she above all things loves and desires, it causes her inexpressible joy to see us, by piously hearing Mass, offering to the Holy Trinity the worthiest service: praising, venerating, invoking, rejoicing the Most High, presenting to Him the most precious of all gifts. She sees us, moreover, worshipping her beloved Son with steadfast faith, humbling ourselves before Him in lowly adoration; with penitent hearts striking our breasts, earnestly imploring forgiveness of our sins; reminding God the Father of the pains that divine Son suffered, offering His blood for our cleansing, and assisting at the holy sacrifice with fervor and recollection. What could be more desirable, more delightful, more gratifying to the heart of Mary?

The following anecdote, related by the famous historian Baronius, will serve to show the joy one can give the Mother of God by hearing Mass in her honor, and how gladly she grants the petitions of those who assist at the holy sacrifice for that object.

In the year 998 Robert, the King of France, at the head of a large army, laid siege to the Castle of St. Germain, not far from Anjou. The besieged made a valiant defence, and succeeded in harassing the enemy so much that on the sixth day of the siege the king, exasperated at their resistance, resolved to take the fortress by storm. On hearing this the garrison were sadly cast down; in their distress they appealed for help and counsel to a pious Benedictine monk named Father Gislebert. He exhorted them to put their trust in Mary, and hear a Mass in her honor. This Mass he himself said at Our Lady's altar in the principal church, all the people devoutly assisting. The blessed Mother of God was not slow to make known the power of a Mass said in her honor. While it was being celebrated, a dense fog closed round the fortress, completely shutting it out from the sight of the besiegers, so that their gunners could not take aim. The besieged, however, saw the enemy as distinctly as ever, and did deadly work with their arrows. At length the king, seeing his men falling on every side, and fearing lest, if the combat were prolonged, his whole army would be cut off, sounded a retreat, and withdrew in high dudgeon.

Although miracles of this description are of rare occurrence, yet we may be sure that never is Mary invoked in vain. An appeal to her is always rewarded, and is far more efficacious than an appeal to any other saint. This was revealed to a Dominican saint by the Mother of God herself; he has left it in writing for our benefit:

1. " What Mary asks of God she invariably obtains.

2. " God withholds His mercy from no one for whom Mary prays.

3. " The world would long since have been destroyed had not Mary upheld it by her intercession.

4. "The love of Mary for sinners is greater than that of any one human being for another.

5. "Such is the love of Mary for sinners that, did God permit, she would be willing to make atonement for each one by daily bearing all the sufferings of the world.

6. "The least service shown to Mary, were it merely the recital of the Angelic Salutation, is worth more than an act a thousandfold greater performed in honor of one of the other saints.

7. "A single *Ave Maria* is of more value than any temporal gift of body or soul, of life or death.

8. "As the firmament of heaven surpasses all the stars in magnitude, so does the loving-kindness of Mary surpass that of all the saints.

9. "As the sun exceeds in its beneficent action all the other orbs, so does the assistance Mary renders us exceed that of all the other saints.

10. "The veneration shown to Mary rejoices all the blessed.

11. "The veneration paid to the saints may be compared to silver; that which is paid to Mary may be compared to gold; that which is paid to Christ, to precious gems; while that which is paid to the Holy Trinity is like the stars in splendor.

12. "Never does a day pass without some souls being rescued from purgatory by Mary."

These twelve privileges or graces are the crown of twelve stars which St. John saw encircling Our Lady's head. He who ponders them well cannot fail to feel himself irresistibly drawn to the service and veneration of Mary. Who would not gladly say a Hail Mary in her honor when he hears that she herself declares this short prayer to be worth more than any gift of body or soul? Who would not rejoice to enroll himself in her service when he is told that what he does for her is of far greater value than what is done for any other saint? Let us serve her, then, with zeal and fervor, especially by hearing Mass, and offering to her the sacrifice of her dear Son. For every time Mass is said Jesus is born anew in a mystic manner, and Mary's high dignity as His Mother is renewed. This Blessed Alanus tells us: "Whenever a priest neglects to say Mass, he robs the holy Mother of God of a portion of her maternal glory." Hence, whenever a priest says Mass, he renews the honor due to Mary as Mother of God, because she then, as it were, gives birth to her Son anew, and feels again the rupture she felt at that auspicious moment.

HOW HOLY MASS IS THE SWEETEST JOY OF THE SAINTS.

It will be both profitable and consoling for us to know to what extent and in what manner holy Mass can benefit the saints, and how it can be heard and celebrated on their festivals to their greater glory. We have already seen, in this chapter, how their accidental joy may be increased; it will be well to remind ourselves that it is our bounden duty to honor the saints. God Himself desires that we should glorify His faithful servants. He says: "Whosoever shall glorify Me, him will I glorify." (1. Kings ii. 30.) Moreover, the saints merit our veneration, because upon earth they shunned honors, they humbled themselves and deemed themselves worthy of scorn; they were, too, unjustly despised, mocked, and persecuted by the wicked; and on this account God wills that their innocence should be made clear as the day, and they should be praised and honored throughout all Christendom.

Of this we have an instance in Mardochai, who, although he was a pious servant of God, was persecuted by the proud Aman and condemned to death. But

God defeated the evil man's designs, and so directed the course of events as to cause them to conduce to the public exaltation of His faithful servant. For when King Assuerus said to Aman: " What ought to be done to the man whom the king is desirous to honor? Aman answered: The man whom the king desireth to honor ought to be clothed with the king's apparel, and to be set upon the horse that the king rideth upon, and to have the royal crown upon his head; and let the first of the king's princes and nobles hold his horse, and going through the street of the city, proclaim before him: Thus shall he be honored whom the king hath a mind to honor. And the king said to him, Make haste and take the robe and the horse, and do as thou hast spoken to Mardochai the Jew." (Esther vi. 6–10.)

Now if this heathen monarch caused such great honor to be paid to Mardochai on account of his fidelity, what, think you, will be the glory which our infinitely grateful God will show, and will command all the company of heaven to show, to His faithful servants for the services they have rendered Him, both on the day of their triumphant entry into the celestial courts, and also when the Church throughout all the world celebrates their feasts? For by the inspiration of the Holy Ghost He taught the Church, on the day set apart for the commemoration of His eminent servants and chosen saints, to honor and glorify them by prayers, devotions, panegyrics, pilgrimages, and processions; above all, by the holy sacrifice of the Mass. For thus shall those be honored whom the heavenly King desireth to honor.

The best means of honoring the saints is by offering the holy sacrifice of the Mass to God for their glory. Although the Mass is a representation of Christ's passion, and is offered up to Almighty God alone, yet the saints derive joy and glory from it, because it is celebrated in their honor, and fills all heaven with joy.

And if special mention is made of them by name their joy and glory are still further enhanced, and the Mass is still more delightful to them, according to the testimony of St. Chrysostom: "When a public ovation is offered to a king, the officers who have shared with him the perils of the war, and have borne themselves valiantly, are also mentioned by name, that they may likewise share in the glory of his triumph. So it is with the saints. They are honored and glorified in the presence of their Lord when His passion and death are triumphantly represented in holy Mass, and they too receive special mention, and the heroic deeds they achieved against their hellish foe are lauded and magnified. Then glory is given to God Almighty, for the might wherewith He fortified them in the strife, for the grace by means of which He secured them the victory." "One can give no greater satisfaction to the saints"—we quote the words of Molina—"than by offering the holy Mass to God in their name, thanking Him for the gifts He bestowed on them, commemorating their meritorious deeds, and offering these to the Holy Trinity in union with the sacrifice of the Mass."

On this subject we read in the revelations of St. Gertrude that "On the feast of St. Michael, while present at Mass, she offered the adorable body and blood of Christ to God, saying: To the honor of this great prince I presented to Thee, O dearest Lord, this most holy sacrament, to the eternal praise of all the angelic host, and the increase of their joy, their glory, and their felicity. She was then permitted to see in how wondrous a manner the Godhead received the sacrifice thus offered, and how the angelic spirits rejoiced with a joy so unspeakable that, had they not already been in possession of supreme happiness, it would have sufficed to make them happy to all eternity. For this the angels came, according to their order of rank, and reverently gave thanks to the saint." This passage has been examined and approved by learned monks and theologians, so that the statement contained in it cannot be contested. It is not said, be it observed, that St. Gertrude offered the Adorable Sacrament to the angels, but to God the Father, Who made it one with the Godhead, while the satisfaction thus afforded to Him was so great that of its infinite abundance the angels received an accession of celestial joy. The same thing occurs whenever thou dost offer the holy sacrifice to God the Father in honor of some saint.

In confirmation of the above we will quote a similar instance from the same source. Shortly after the death of one of the nuns of St. Gertrude's convent at Helpede in Saxony, in the odor of sanctity, another religious of the same house, hearing Mass for the deceased, said to God at the time of the elevation: "I offer to Thee, heavenly Father, this sacred host, the body and blood of Jesus, on behalf of our deceased sister; and with it I offer to Thee the love of His sacred Heart, which ever throbbed for Thee." Thereupon the spiritual vision of the nun was enlightened; she beheld her sister in religion, who was already in heaven, and who appeared now to be invested with a higher dignity, vested in more glorious apparel, surrounded with more splendid attendants. And the same took place whenever that religious made the same offering for the deceased.

Richly, indeed, was that offering rewarded! Who would believe that the accidental joy of the blessed could be thus augmented did we not receive the assurance on trustworthy authority? The revelations do not state that the soul was raised to a higher place, but that it appeared as if she were raised to a higher degree of glory. For a higher degree of glory belongs to the essential joy of the blessed, and, as we have said, that admits of no augmentation. Nevertheless the soul in question experienced a wonderful increase of accidental joy in consequence of the Mass being offered on her behalf.

Hence we may conclude that by offering one single Mass we can honor the saints in a manner most acceptable to God, and which enhances the felicity they enjoy. If, therefore, thou art desirous to glorify any particular saint, thy patron saint, for example, hear Mass in his honor; and at the elevation of the host offer the Son of God to His eternal Father for the greater glory and joy of thy patron. Look in the calendar every morning, and at Mass say to the saint who is commemorated that day that thou wilt hear the Mass in his honor; and at the elevation offer the holy sacrifice to God with that intention. At the hour of death thou wilt know how much merit thou hast gained by this practice.

CHAPTER XIX.

HOLY MASS IS OF THE GREATEST BENEFIT TO THE FAITHFUL.

IN speaking of the profit to be derived from holy Mass it is difficult to know where to begin or where to end. The holy fathers and doctors of the Church cannot say enough when they enlarge on the benefits holy Mass brings to the faithful. St. Laurence Justinian says: "Assuredly no human tongue is capable of telling how abundant are the fruits to be derived from the holy sacrifice of the Mass, how great the gifts and graces that flow from it." He then proceeds to enumerate a few of the most striking of these: "Through the sacrifice of the Mass the sinner is reconciled with God, the just is confirmed in his justice. Transgressions are forgiven, vices exterminated, virtues multiplied, merits augmented, temptations overcome." These are, indeed, fruits well worth having.

Father Anthony Molina, in his work on the dignity of the priesthood, has many beautiful and forcible passages relating to holy Mass that must awaken love and esteem for it in every Christian heart. "There is nothing," he says, "so profitable to mankind, so efficacious for the relief of the suffering souls, nothing so helpful for the attainment of spiritual riches, as the most holy sacrifice of the Mass. In fact in comparison with it all the good works which we perform by day or night, from the most virtuous motives, are of little or no account." These words almost surpass belief, yet what consolation they convey to us! The holy sacrifice of the Mass, if rightly offered, is said to outweigh in value all other works, even those practices of piety which are performed with real devotion, recollection of heart, profound humility, fervent charity, and purity of intention. The previous portion of this book, if read attentively, will have prepared our minds for the acceptance of this truth; yet for its further confirmation a few more witnesses may be brought forward.

Bishop Fornerus, commenting on the psalm *Miserere*, says: "He who, not being in a state of mortal sin, hears Mass devoutly gains more than he who performs some arduous work for the love of God, or goes on a distant pilgrimage. And no wonder, for the most virtuous of good works derive their worth and importance from their object, that is, from that which is done by means of them. Now what is nobler, more precious, more divine, than the sacrifice of the Mass!" Let all who seek to acquire celestial riches, who desire to do God acceptable service, lay to heart this noteworthy and consoling thought. Who will not rejoice to hear Mass if he knows that he can do nothing better, more meritorious, more acceptable to God?

Marchantius, writing on the same subject, says: "The Catholic Church can do nothing better, more holy, nothing more worthy of the most high God, more pleasing to Jesus and Mary, more gratifying to the angels and saints, more profitable for both the just and sinners, more advantageous to the souls in purgatory, than offer for them the sacrifice of the Mass." All theologians declare the same, and concur in placing holy Mass far above all other good works. Do thou let thy practice be in accordance with their teaching. We have, however, more to say on this subject.

In the preface to an old missal bearing the date 1634 we find an exhortation addressed to priests bidding them entertain a very high opinion of the excellence of the holy sacrifice, and never doubt that every time they celebrate it they render God more acceptable service than by the exercise of the loftiest virtues, or by suffering all conceivable tortures for His sake. Dost thou ask how can this be? It is because Christ exercises every virtue in the Mass, and at the same time offers to God His passion and death. All the praise, the love, the veneration, the worship, the thanksgiving, which Christ presents to the ever-blessed Trinity in every Mass far transcends all the praise of the angels, the adoration of the saints, so far, indeed, that were all the penances, the prayers, the good works of apostles, martyrs, confessors, virgins, and all saints offered to the Holy Trinity they would be less pleasing to the Divine Majesty than one single Mass.

The most important testimony of all to the profit which the faithful derive from holy Mass, the authoritative utterances of holy Church in the Council of Trent, has yet to be given: "We must needs confess that no other work can be performed by the faithful so holy and divine as this tremendous mystery itself, wherein that life-giving victim, by which we were reconciled to the Father, is daily immolated on the altar by priests." (Sess. xxii.) Had we no other testimony to or proof of the profitableness of holy Mass, this alone ought to be sufficient to induce pious souls to hear Mass daily.

Ponder well, O Christian, what the holy Catholic Church, infallible in matters of faith, declares to us in the aforegoing words. She expressly states, and imposes on our belief, that no other work can be performed by the faithful so holy and divine as the tremendous mystery of the Mass. This does not only refer to priests, but to the faithful in general. Priests can indeed do nothing more holy and divine than celebrate Mass; the laity can do nothing more holy and divine than hear Mass, serve Mass, join in offering Mass, have Mass said for their intentions, follow the prayers and unite in spirit with the celebrant. Since to do this is of all works the most holy and divine, it stands to reason that it should also be the most profitable and meritorious.

Accept, therefore, with thy whole heart, O Christian, the wholesome doctrine taught thee by thy mother, the Church. Thou canst perform many good works to the greater glory of God, in honor of the saints, for thine own spiritual profit and salvation, but none so divine, so exalted, so pleasing to God and the saints, none so profitable, so salutary, so meritorious, as pious assistance at holy Mass. For the Church herself declares that this surpasses all other works, as far as the sun surpasses the planets in power and splendor, as far as it exceeds all the stars of the firmament in its beneficent action upon the earth. How much thou wilt have to answer for the times when thou hast heard Mass indevoutly, or when thou hast for some temporal advantage neglected it altogether!

St. Francis de Sales thought so highly of Mass that he preferred it to mental prayer, although this is universally acknowledged to hold the first place among spiritual exercises. Writing to one of the nuns of the Order he had founded, soon after her departure to establish a monastery elsewhere, he said: "I beg you, my dear daughter, to arrange a chapel before all things, so that you may be able to hear Mass daily. If you cannot do this in your own house, then go every day to the nearest church, since the soul receives strength for the whole day if at its commencement she has been brought so near to Our Lord, present in the holy sacrifice." The nun, who was no other than St. Jane Frances de Chantal, wrote in reply: "Do you wish me to interrupt or even omit my meditation in order to hear Mass, or shall I leave the Mass on week-days in order to make my meditation?" The saint answered: "You will find it much more useful to hear Mass than to omit it under the plea of making your meditation at home; for the corporal presence of the sacred humanity of Our Lord, which we have in holy Mass, is of far more value than His fancied presence to our mind, especially as it is the wish of the Church that her children should hear Mass every day."

Thus St. Francis de Sales teaches us that to hear Mass is better and more profitable than mental prayer. Bishop Fornerus says the same: "The prayer of one who hears Mass piously, and offers it to God for the good of his soul, is worth infinitely more than other prayers, however long and fervent, even the prayer of contemplation." And to account for this he adds: "Because of the merits of Christ's passion, which make their power felt by a wondrous outpouring of grace and a plenitude of heavenly gifts." Consider what is here said, O pious soul, and thou wilt find that they are inspired from above, and contain most salutary teaching.

If thou desirest to meditate upon the life and passion of Christ, thou canst do this at no more suitable time than during the Mass, when all the mysteries of His life and passion are renewed in thy sight. Or if thou dost desire to place thyself in the presence of Christ, to hold converse with Him, there thou hast Him present in person, both in His humanity and His divinity. Nor will the ceremonies of the Mass distract thy attention; on the contrary, they will serve to increase thy recollection, if thou dost follow the action of the priest and consider the significance of the ceremonies.

Before concluding this chapter we will give a memorable instance, which is mentioned by several writers, of the profit to be derived from holy Mass.

There was once a poor workingman whose devotion to Mass was so great that he endeavored to hear it every day. One morning he had risen early and gone to the market-place to look out, with some other men, for employment, when he heard the bell of a neighboring church ring for Mass. He directly left the other men and betook himself to the church, where he heard Mass very attentively, and implored God to give him that day his daily bread. But on returning to the market-place he found all the other men had got work, and although he waited for some time, no one would give him a job. Presently he went back to his home with a heavy heart, for he could not help regretting that he had lost a day's work through going to Mass. On his way back he was accosted by a rich gentleman, who asked him why he was looking so sorrowful. The man told him that he had been to Mass and thus lost a day's wages. "Never mind," the stranger rejoined, "go and hear a Mass for me, and I will give you what you would have earned in the meantime." The poor man went back to the church and heard a Mass, and yet another. Then he went to the rich man's house, where a good meal was given him, besides a loaf and a shilling. For this he returned many thanks, and set out once more for his own home quite joyfully. He had not gone far before he met a gentleman of stately appearance, who asked him what made him look so happy. The man related what had occurred, and expressed his sense of obligation to the rich stranger. But his interlocutor said: "You had not nearly enough given you for the Masses you heard; go back to the rich man, and tell him he must give you more, or it will go ill with him." The poor man therefore returned to his benefactor, and delivered the message, at the same time describing the fine appearance and distinguished manners of his new friend. The rich man, thinking that it was some saint who had spoken to the workingman, gave him a sovereign and bade him say some prayers for him. The poor fellow was hastening home to tell his wife and children of his good luck, when he was again stopped by the same gentleman, who asked him how much had been given to him this time. He informed him of the amount he had received, and was enlarging on the generosity of his benefactor, when the other said: "Go back once more, and say to him that if he does not give you five pounds he will not be alive to-morrow." The man at first refused to make such a demand, but the order was repeated in so peremptory a manner that he yielded, and, returning reluctantly to his rich friend, related to him what he had been told to say. The message alarmed the rich man very much, for he had sinned grievously, and had not made a clean breast in confession, and rather than take the risk of a sudden and unprepared death he gave the five pounds that were required of him. That same night, while he was asleep, Christ appeared to him and said: "I am He who sent that poor man to you; I will tell you why I did so: The devil appealed to My strict justice to punish you, and called upon Me to pass sentence on you, and deliver you into his power, on account of your crimes, unconfessed and unrepented of. Fortunately for you that poor workingman came between you and your doom; by piously hearing Mass, and praying so fervently for you, he induced Me to revoke My verdict, and give you time to do penance. Wherefore confess your sins, amend your life, and be liberal in alms-giving." The rich man did all this, and was assiduous in hearing Mass besides.. Thus holy Mass was more profitable to him than all his wealth, since by it he was preserved from death, both temporal and eternal, and became a changed man.

This story may suggest the inquiry whether the holy Mass can be bought and sold. I answer, Certainly not; it would be a transaction like that of which Judas was guilty when he sold Our Lord for thirty pieces of silver. Yet, it may be said, priests take money for saying Mass. They do so, it is true; but the apostle Paul says: "They that serve the altar, partake with the altar." (1. Cor. ix. 13.) The priest takes the money as payment for his trouble, not in the least as the price of the merit of spiritual profit which he obtains for him who desires the Mass to be said; for it would be simony, and a great sin, to think spiritual things could be purchased with money.

Yet if a poor woman were to say to some rich lady: "If you will give me something to buy food, I will hear Mass for you to-day or to-morrow," this would be quite right and proper, for it would be equivalent to saying: I will part with the merit I obtain by hearing Mass, and will bestow it upon you. And in this way the poor woman would give the lady ten times more than she received, even though the sum was a large one. For every one who hears Mass may gain for himself no small share in the merits of Christ, by means of which he may pay off a considerable part of the debt due for sin, and purchase celestial riches. And if a poor man, of his own free will, gives thee this treasure for a trifling temporal recompense, Thou hast indeed made a good exchange, nay, the very best possible. Wherefore do thou often let a poor man hear Mass for thee, and by this simple means expiate thy past errors and increase the glory in store for thee in heaven.

CHAPTER XX.

HOLY MASS PROCURES FOR US AN INCREASE OF GRACE HERE AND OF GLORY HEREAFTER.

IN towns of any size and importance there is a market where on certain days all kinds of provisions and useful goods are offered for sale. The Church, nay, heaven itself, holds a market daily, and offers merchandise of the most valuable description to the purchaser —nothing less, in fact, than divine grace and celestial glory. But here the reader will ask: These things are above all precious and costly; how can one find sufficient money to purchase them? Thou needest not be anxious on that point; valuable as that merchandise is, it may yet be bought most cheaply, even without any money at all. Hear what the prophet Isaias says: " You that have no money, make haste, come ye and buy, without money and without any price." (Is. lv. 1.) The psalmist also tells us that these goods can be obtained gratis, for he says: "The Lord will give grace and glory." (Ps. lxxxiii. 12.) He gives us these at all times, but seldom with such liberality as at the time of holy Mass. But before we enter upon this subject it will be well to explain what grace is.

Grace is a supernatural gift by which man is made just, pleasing in the sight of God, and worthy of everlasting life. This grace is infused into the soul at Baptism, and never leaves it, unless it is obliterated by mortal sin. This grace is twofold: there is sanctifying grace and actual grace. By means of the first we are brought out of a state of mortal sin into a state of grace; from sinners we become just, from children of wrath we are made children of God and heirs of heaven. By means of the second man grows in grace by good works.

How precious grace is St. Thomas of Aquin tells us: "One single grace," he says, "is a greater good than all the good things of the whole world." If an angel had to state the true value of God's grace, he would be compelled to acknowledge that the least drop of grace outweighs all the gold, the silver, the jewels, all the wealth of the whole wide world. It is difficult to believe this, still more to comprehend it, yet it is undoubtedly true. For whosoever possesses the smallest degree of God's grace is the friend of God; and if he dies in this grace, for the sake of it God will give Himself to him as his reward, as He spoke to Abram: "I am thy protector, and thy reward exceeding great." (Gen. xv. 1.) Therefore, since in God are all the treasures of heaven and earth, nay, treasures far surpassing all that are in heaven and earth, it follows of necessity that if man, by faithfully cooperating with grace, receives God Himself as his reward, he obtains a hundred thousand times more than he would have had if the world with all its riches had been given him for his possession.

Furthermore, be it known that a pious Christian, by every good work he performs, increases God's grace within him, and this not merely by great works, but by every good work however insignificant, even by every holy thought and pious aspiration. All such thoughts, words, and works increase God's grace in the soul, and each one merits an accession of grace now and a greater reward hereafter, according to Our Lord's own words: " Whoever shall give to drink to one of these little ones a cup of cold water only, amen, I say to you, he shall not lose his reward." (St. Matt. x. 42.) That is to say, he will receive greater joy and glory in heaven, God will give Himself to him in more plenteous measure. He will grant him to know Him more clearly, to love Him more dearly, to enjoy Him more nearly. Now seeing that God's grace is earned so easily, and that he who corresponds to it obtains so great a reward, who will not strive to do what is good, and serve God with all his heart?

Consider what wonders grace works in the soul. In the first place it invests her with surpassing loveliness, rendering her so fair and attractive that the beauty of the sun, the stars, the flowers, of man himself, cannot compare with hers. Could we but see a soul in the state of grace we should be forced to admit that in comparison with it nothing fair in nature is of any account. God Himself takes pleasure in it, and would rather that heaven and earth should pass away than that the beauty of such a soul should be marred or destroyed by mortal sin. Even the least degree of grace is productive of this beauty, but it is enhanced and increased by each added grace.

Thus grace gains for the soul the favor of God, and causes it to be united to God in a close, tender, and familiar friendship. The soul, when beautified by grace, is indeed so dear to God that He is pleased to dwell with it rather than in heaven itself, provided it makes a due return for His love. And even if the soul does not do its part, He does not withdraw from it until it separates itself forcibly from Him by mortal sin. Then He forsakes it reluctantly, and feels this infidelity more deeply than men or angels can conceive. Nor does He yet altogether abandon the soul, but stands at the door, knocking from time to time, as if asking for readmission, as He Himself says: "Behold I stand at the gate and knock. If any man shall open to Me the door, I will come in to him." (Apoc. iii. 20.)

Since this friendship exists between God and the soul, no wonder that of His great liberality He makes it a participator in the abundance of His riches. He bestows on it virtue, piety, consolations, good desires, and interior joys. He protects and strengthens, governs and guides it, nay, He gives Himself to the soul, makes it one with Him, as Holy Scripture says: "He hath given us most great and precious promises, that by these you may be made partakers of the divine nature." (II. Pet. i. 4.) Are not the things of which we have spoken precious promises indeed, and glorious gifts? If the favor and grace of princes is eagerly sought after and highly prized, how much the more earnestly ought we to covet and strive to obtain the favor and grace of God?

Finally, the soul is ennobled by the grace of God to such an extent that it is made not His friend only, but actually His child. If an emperor were to adopt the son of a pauper, what an immense honor it would be for the child! But a thousand times greater is the honor conferred upon the soul whom Almighty God adopts as His child! In amazement at this condescension, St. John exclaims: "Behold what manner of charity the Father hath bestowed upon us that we should be called, and should be, the sons of God." (1. St. John iii. 1.) And St. Paul adds: "And if sons, heirs also." (Rom. viii. 17.) Oh, what a rich inheritance to be the heirs of God! As it surpasses our power to conceive the infinite greatness of God, so does it surpass our power to comprehend what an extraordinary honor and grace it is to be the child, the heir of God.

This brief explanation will enable us to understand in some measure how noble and how precious a thing divine grace is, how well it merits that we should use every exertion to obtain it. Sanctifying grace is to be acquired by contrition; actual grace, the increase of grace, is the reward of every good work which we perform in a state of grace. The more excellent that work is and the more perfectly it is performed the more and the greater graces does it merit. Hence we may infer that great graces may be obtained by hearing Mass devoutly, since that is one of the very best of all good works, as we have already seen. Moreover, all theologians teach that holy Mass operates an increase of divine grace and of celestial glory.

Furthermore, they teach that "not the priest alone, but those of the laity who have Mass said, or merely assist at Mass, can, each in his degree, merit an increase of sanctifying grace and of heavenly glory, but this depends entirely upon their cooperation." Hence we may conclude, first, that the priest merits an increase of grace and of glory by every Mass he celebrates. From the minuteness of the ceremonial he is bound to observe it may be gathered that the merit thus earned is of no trifling nature. It is, moreover, increased by the fact that the priest does all out of obedience, and the carefulness and accuracy wherewith he performs all that is prescribed also contribute to augment it.

Secondly, whosoever has Mass said, either for himself or for some other person, merits a large increase of grace and of glory, for, since he is the occasion of that Mass being said, he participates in the effect of it, and if he is in a state of grace he obtains an increase of grace.

Thirdly, all who hear Mass piously earn for themselves a great increase of grace, not only on account of the devotion they manifest, but rather for the sake of the various virtues which they exercise. First of all they awaken compunction and sorrow when they strike their breast, nor must they do this superficially, but from their heart. Furthermore, they exercise the sublime virtue of faith, sor they firmly believe that Christ is truly present in the sacred host, and that He offers Himself to His Father upon the altar on behalf of sinners. This faith transcends human reason, and consequently its exercise is the more meritorious. As often, therefore, as thou dost lift thine eyes to the sacred host, or, supposing thou canst not see it, as often as thou dost represent to thyself the presence of thy Lord upon the altar, thou dost practise a lofty virtue, meriting a great increase of grace in life, and after thy death a higher place in heaven.

Besides this exercise of faith, we perform an act of worship as often as we bow down and render to God external or interior reverence. Although this is our bounden duty, yet it is pleasing to Christ, and He rewards it with the gift of new graces. If, at the time of the elevation, we lift our eyes to the sacred host, we make an act of adoration most excellent and meritorious; and if we offer the sacred body and precious blood of Christ we pay Him the highest honor, the greatest service. For this gift is of such magnitude that God is thereby laid under an obligation to man. As often as we say during Mass: " My God, I present to Thee Thy beloved Son, I present to Thee His bitter passion, His cruel death," so often do we practise the virtue of generosity towards God, and our oblation merits a fresh grace as its recompense. Again, if we say: "I offer to Thee, O Lord, this holy sacrifice for all persons living or dead, especially for those for whom I ought to pray," this is an act of charity towards our neighbor which will be well rewarded. When we make a spiritual communion, that is, when we desire to receive the body and blood of Christ at the communion of the priest, we merit a special grace, and our souls will be nourished and refreshed. Above all, let us remember the words of the Church quoted above: "We must needs confess that no other work can be performed by the faithful so holy and divine as this tremendous mystery of the Mass," nor doubt that, since to hear Mass devoutly is of all good works the most excellent, the most meritorious, the most divine, we gain thereby a special increase of grace and of glory. Moreover, by hearing Mass we make reparation to God for the contumely wherewith heretics treat Him when they blaspheme the holy sacrifice.

The fathers of the Church state expressly that God rewards with special graces those who hear Mass. St. Cyril says: "Spiritual gifts are freely given to those who assist at Mass reverently." St. Cyprian: "This supernatural bread and this consecrated chalice are for the health and salvation of mankind." Pope Innocent III. says: "Through the power of the holy sacrifice of the Mass all virtues are increased in us, and we obtain a plenteous share of the fruits of grace." "Christians should never neglect holy Mass," says St. Maximus, "because of the grace of the Holy Ghost, of which all who are present are made partakers." Fornerus declares positively: "The potency of the merits of Christ's passion is most forcibly felt in holy Mass, in procuring for us graces and celestial riches in marvellous abundance."

Thus the fathers of the Church bear unequivocal testimony to the fact that divine grace is poured out richly, copiously, on all who assist at holy Mass.

To these witnesses another may yet be added Osorius writes: " If a father were to give his son the sum of 10,000 talents that he might trade with them, might not that son, with a little industry, make large profits? Undoubtedly he would soon become a wealthy man. Now consider what vast riches thy heavenly Father bestows on thee in holy Mass, that thou mayst be like a merchant, seeking good pearls and finding them. God the Father gives thee His only-begotten Son, ' in Whom are hid all the treasures of wisdom and knowledge ' (Col. ii. 3), and ' He that spared not even His own Son, but delivered Him up for us all, how hath He not, with Him, given us all things ? ' (Rom. viii. 32.) Thus, in giving thee His Son in holy Mass God the Father gives thee at the same time all His merits and the satisfaction He made for sin. He gives thee His flesh and blood, His body and soul, and all the treasures which He has earned. Behold what excellent gifts are daily conferred on thee, and how easily thou mightest become rich with a little industry; that is to say, if thou offerest the Son of God, with all His merits, to the Father in holy Mass. For as often as thou dost thus present the body and blood, the merits and riches, of Christ to the Eternal Father, thou countest out to Him, so to speak, the coins wherewith thou dost purchase heavenly treasures, and no inconsiderable increase of divine grace."

To those just mentioned let the reader add the seventy-seven graces and fruits of holy Mass enumerated in the third chapter of this book, and he will not hesitate to acknowledge that there is no good work of any kind whereby so much grace and merit may be acquired as by devout assistance at holy Mass.

HOLY MASS INCREASES THE CELESTIAL GLORY WHICH IS TO BE OUR PORTION.

Oh, how inconceivably great is the celestial glory for the enjoyment of which we are created, which we so earnestly desire, for which we long and sigh ! How can I find language to describe the increase of that glory when even the least degree of it is so sweet, so sublime, that, as St .Paul says: "Eye hath not seen, nor ear heard it, neither hath it entered into the heart of man." (i. Cor. ii. 9.) The Catholic Church does indeed teach us that "all the good works of one that is justified merit increase of grace and of glory" (Counc. Trent, Sess. vi. c. 24), but she does not say, she is unable to say, what amount of grace and glory they merit. "Every man increases and lays up merit for eternal life as often as he takes pains to hear Mass devoutly." Such were the words of Our Lord Himself to a saint, and observe, He does not speak of those who are devout, but of those who desire and endeavor to hear Mass devoutly, for they too will receive a rich recompense of heavenly glory. The reward will not be poor and insignificant, but rich and plenteous; as Christ says in the Gospel: "Good measure, and pressed down, and shaken together, and running over, shall they give into your bosom." (St. Luke vi. 38.)

Thus it may be confidently affirmed that by every Mass heard with a certain amount of devotion one may gain for one's self a higher degree of glory in heaven. Just as when we climb an eminence we reach a greater elevation at every step, so each time we hear Mass we rise to a higher place in heaven, and the height which we attain is greater or less in proportion to the fervor of our devotion. The higher our place in heaven the nearer we are to God, the clearer will be our knowledge of Him, the more ardent our love for Him, the more unbounded our enjoyment of

Him. Each degree we rise will increase our beauty, our brilliance, our nobility, our riches, our glory, and the esteem in which the saints hold us. This glory is only lost by mortal sin; and if lost it can be recovered by contrition and compunction. Hadst thou heard Mass every day of thy life, at what a height of glory would be the place destined for thee! What riches, what felicity, would be thine to enjoy! And if perchance thou hadst occasionally heard two or three Masses on one day, each one would increase thy glory in just the same degree.

Hear in what rapturous language St. Paul speaks of this in his Epistle to the Corinthians: "That which is at present momentary and light of our tribulation, worketh for us above measure exceedingly an eternal weight of glory." (II. Cor. iv. 17.) Weigh well the meaning of these words. It seems almost incredible that a light and momentary tribulation should earn for us a superabundant, eternal, immeasurable weight of glory. May one not reasonably hope that, since St. Paul holds it out as the reward of a trial which is light and transient, we shall receive the same for pious attendance at Mass? Wherefore if the way to Mass is long and toilsome; if in winter thou shiverest with cold; if thou art obliged to rise earlier to hear Mass; if the time of Mass sometimes seems long; if thou musput aside some necessary occupation in order to go to Mass, or if thou losest some temporal advantage on account of it; if occasionally thou feelest little or no devotion while present at Mass—these and similar disagreeables are slight and momentary afflictions, which thou must endure for the sake of performing a most excellent work. And we may justly draw the conclusion that this, that is momentary and light, will work for us an exceedingly great and eternal weight of glory in heaven, and each time raise us to a higher degree of glory.

The following story, related by a Franciscan father, will serve to illustrate what has been said on this subject. It tells us of a worthy farmer who all his life-long had so great a love for holy Mass that whenever he heard the bell ring for Mass he straightway left his work on his farm or in the woods and repaired to the church. It had been his habit to do this ever since he was a boy, but at length he began to feel the burden of years, and one day, when the way to the church seemed very long and tiring, he said to himself: "I am an old man now, I cannot walk as I did when I was young; I do not think it can be displeasing to God if I no longer go all this distance across the fields to the church. When I am at home I will obey the summons and go to Mass, but when I am out at work I shall quietly go on with what I am about." Just as he formed this resolution he heard footsteps behind him, and, turning round, he saw an angel with a lapful of lovely roses. This heavenly visitant was so beautiful to look upon that the good countryman thought it was the Lord God Himself. Falling on his knees, he cried: "O my God, whence is this that Thou shouldst come to me!" The angel replied: "I am not thy God, but thy guardian angel." "O kind angel," the man rejoined, "for what reason am I allowed the privilege of beholding thee?" "I am commanded by God to follow in thy path," the angel said; "I always do so whenever thou dost leave thy work to go to Mass." The man asked the reason of this, and the angel answered: "For every step thou dost take a rose springs up on thy way; I gather these roses, and carry them up to heaven. Look," he pursued, showing him the blossoms, "I have gathered all these on thy footsteps to-day, so do not do as thou proposest, but continue going to church as thou hast been accustomed to do from thy youth up, If thou dost persist in this laudable practice until thy life's end, at thy death I will crown thee with roses, and thy throne in heaven shall be decked with roses to thy eternal honor and glory." Thereupon the angel vanished; the man, his eyes full of tears, kissed the spot on which he had stood, and thanked God for this joyful apparition. Thenceforth it was always present to his mind; the beauty of the angel, the delicious fragrance of the flowers, created in him so keen a desire for heavenly things that the things of earth were distasteful to him. He lived but a short time afterwards, his death being due more to his ardent longing for heaven than to any mortal disease.

Hear how all the steps that this pious peasant took on his way to Mass were counted and rewarded by unfading flowers springing up upon his path. If his attendance at Mass was so richly recompensed, thinkest thou it will not be the same with thee? This we shall know, we may venture to hope, one day in heaven, when we shall with him enter upon the enjoyment of our eternal reward.

SPIRITUAL COMMUNION.

Divine grace and celestial glory may also be greatly increased by spiritual communion, if it be rightly and piously made. Spiritual communion is nothing else but a fervent desire to receive Our Lord and be united to Him. We may thus receive Him and enjoy His presence in a spiritual manner without actually communicating, to the great advantage and welfare of the soul. For even as Christ when on earth both healed many sick persons by laying upon them His sacred hands, and also restored many to health at a distance, as, for instance, the daughter of the woman of Canaan, the ruler's son, and the centurion's servant, so, while He imparts great graces to those who receive Him worthily in the Adorable Sacrament of the Altar, He is none the less generous towards those who only receive Him in desire. To this manner of communicating He refers in the words: "I am the bread of life: he that cometh to Me shall not hunger, and he that believeth in Me shall never thirst." (St. John vi. 35.) What is it to go to Christ but to believe in Him, to hope in Him, to love Him? He who does this, or desires to do this, communicates spiritually, and will not thirst to all eternity. Christ can bestow His grace upon the soul without the medium of the sacraments, and some persons receive more grace in spiritual than do others in sacramental communion, if the former are actuated by a stronger desire for union with Him than the latter. For the more ardent our desires the more ample is the grace imparted to us in spiritual communion.

How is this spiritual communion to be made? Bishop Fornerus answers this question: "All those who assist at holy Mass, and prepare themselves carefully, are fed with the body of Christ in a spiritual manner at the communion of the priest; for the potency of the Mass is so great that all who unite their intention to the intention of the celebrant, and desire to participate in the holy sacrifice, will, together with the priest, consume the sacred victim, and enjoy the fruits of this spiritual sustenance." This is a most consoling doctrine for all, especially for those who would gladly make a spiritual communion if they knew how. The bishop teaches them in these words that it is enough to unite their intention to that of the priest, and desire to communicate with him and partake in the graces of the holy sacrifice. That those who do this communicate spiritually, when the priest communicates actually, he proceeds to show by the following comparison:

"Just as the different members of the body are nourished equally with the mouth, although it alone receives the food, so at holy Mass the faithful, although they do not communicate sacramentally, are yet spiritually fed with the sacred aliment the priest receives. For it is meet that those who serve in spirit with the priest at the table of the Lord should also eat with him in spirit. Would it not be thought unseemly if the servants who waited at the king's table were allowed to go hungry away? Even so it cannot be imagined that those who assist devoutly at holy Mass would be permitted to depart without refreshment." This comparison affords a good argument to prove that those who assist piously at Mass communicate in a spiritual manner. The same writer continues:

"Just as when a grand banquet is given no member of the household is left to suffer hunger, so it is at the holy Mass, that great supper at which there is no one present who does not receive something, unless, indeed, he wilfully closes his mouth when Christ holds out to him the spiritual food." Again: "As in a cellar wherein new wine is stored the very air is so laden with the fumes of the wine that it is sufficient to intoxicate one, even so graces abound to such an extent in the Mass that they not only dissipate all evil in those who are present, but fill them with heavenly sweetness." These comparisons show in what manner all who assist at holy Mass may receive refreshment from spiritual communion.

In illustration of what has been said we will give an incident which is recorded of another pious peasant who was most exemplary in his devout attendance at Mass. He used to follow attentively all that the priest did at the altar, and in his own simple fashion meditated upon the passion of Our Lord. When the time came for the priest to consume the sacred host, he felt an overpowering desire to receive communion also. But as it was not customary at that time for the laity to communicate more than twice a year, the good peasant said to himself: "Alas! unhappy man that I am, I am not allowed to receive my God, I am deprived of the precious fruits of this divine sacrament. Thou alone knowest, O sweet Jesus, how I long to receive Thee, and be made one with Thee. But since the happiness of receiving Thee sacramentally is denied me, I beseech Thee, of Thine infinite condescension, to feed me spiritually with this celestial bread." Thus he breathed forth the desire of his heart, and at the communion of the priest he closed his eyes and opened his mouth, as if he were about to communicate. And one day when he did thus, and imagined himself to be kneeling at the holy table, he felt a particle of the host upon his tongue. He swallowed it reverently, his heart filled with ineffable consolation. From that time forth he longed more and more for holy communion, and whenever he was at Mass, at the communion of the priest, a particle detached itself from the sacred host and entered his lips. Thus we see God reward by a miracle the earnest desire for holy communion, and teaching us at the same time how pleasing to Him is spiritual communion, and how profitable to our souls.

The Church also teaches us how good and how salutary is this desire for holy communion, when she says: "Those who, eating in desire that heavenly bread which is set before them, are, by a lively faith which worketh by charity, made sensible of the fruit and usefulness thereof." (Counc. Trent, Sess. xiii. ch. 8.) This is as much as to say that those who earnestly desire to eat that supersubstantial bread are as truly nourished by it as if they actually partook of that sacred food.

CHAPTER XXI.

HOLY MASS IS THE MOST SURE HOPE OF THE DYING.

HOW bitter death is none can know but those who have experienced its terrors, yet when we watch by the dying we see how hard a thing it is to die. Well may we say with Aristotle: "Of all awful things nothing is more awful than death"; and this not only because of the separation of soul and body, but rather because it is the gate of eternity, a summons to appear before the tribunal of God's justice. The vivid representation of these and other terrors strikes the dying man with such anguish and alarm that his heart quakes within him, and a cold sweat bedews his body.

What wouldst thou advise him to do in this supreme moment? Whence shall the dying man take comfort, lest his courage fail him? Where shall he find support, lest the devil precipitate him into the abyss of despair? The counsel ordinarily given is to cling to the infinite mercy of God, to trust and steadfastly confide in that. But, as St. Gregory tells us: "Let him who has done all that in him lies trust to God's mercy, it will not fail him. But let not him who has not done all that in him lies cherish this same confidence, for he is only deceiving himself." Where is the man to be found who has done all that in him lies? He is truly one among thousands. For of whom can it be said that he does all the good that lies in his power?

If I were asked upon what a dying man might most surely place his trust, I should answer that nowhere could he find more sure ground for confidence than in holy Mass, provided that during his lifetime he had loved it dearly, heard it devoutly, offered it with a pure intention, and assisted at it with regularity. This I can assert from the authority of Holy Scripture, for David says: " Offer up the sacrifice of justice, and trust in the Lord." (Ps. iv. 6.) The sacrifice of justice is none other than the holy sacrifice of the Mass, which satisfies the demands of divine justice by paying the penalty due to sin, and expiating the outrage offered to Almighty God by man's transgressions. The sacrifices of the Old Testament could not do that; consequently they cannot be designated sacrifices of justice.

Therefore when David says: "Offer up the sacrifice of justice, and trust in the Lord," he addresses us Christians in the spirit of prophecy; admonishing us, and especially priests, to offer the holy Mass, the sacrifice of justice, as frequently as possible, and then place their steadfast hope in God, since they have thereby appeased His wrath, and made atonement for sin according to justice. We gather this from the context, in which he says: "By the fruit of their corn, their wine, their oil, they are multiplied." (*Ibid.* 8.) This evidently refers to priests, who are anointed with holy oil at their ordination, and offer in the sacrifice of the Mass the fruit of corn and wine, which by transubstantiation they render an acceptable oblation, pleasing to God Almighty, while they themselves are thereby enriched in virtue and merit. In conclusion David adds: "In peace in the self-same I will sleep, and I will rest; for thou, O Lord, hast singularly settled me in hope." (*Ibid.* 10.)

These words he places on the lips of the expiring Christian, thereby indicating to us what is the chief ground of reliance in the hour of death. The Church proves this to be so, by adopting these words as her own when she says of the dead, "May they rest in peace." David says: "I will sleep in peace"; the Church says: "Grant, O Lord, that they may rest in peace." Wherefore let him who in his lifetime has followed David's counsel, and frequently, even daily, in union with the priest, offered to God the sacrifice of justice, rely confidently upon the mercy of God, and when his last hour comes say with the psalmist: I will sleep the sleep of death in peace, trusting to the holy sacrifice of the Mass; and I will rest in my grave until the final judgment. I will not fear eternal death, for Thou, Lord, hast singularly settled me in hope. I do not believe that I shall be lost forever, because I have so many times offered to Thee the acceptable sacrifice of justice, thereby causing Thee infinite satisfaction, infinite honor, infinite service, infinite delight, infinite reparation for the offences my sins have been to Thee. In virtue of this Thou hast settled me in hope of eternal life. In this steadfast hope I shall fall asleep in the Lord; I shall rest in peace; I shall appear before the judgment-seat of Thy justice.

In this wise may each one prepare comfort for himself at the hour of death, and arm himself against pusillanimity and despair. He will not find that his confidence was misplaced. On the contrary, his experience will resemble that of a certain pious man of whom we are told that, having had all his life long a great devotion to holy Mass, and as far as possible assisted at it every day, when death came to him he placed all his trust in the holy sacrifice, and with this confidence fell asleep in peace. His parish priest, to whom he had greatly endeared himself by his piety, felt his loss acutely, and offered many prayers for his soul. One day a disembodied spirit, resplendent with glory, appeared to the good priest, and on his asking who it might be, it answered: "I am the soul of your late parishioner, for whom you are praying." The priest asked how it was with him in the world whither he had gone. "By the grace of God," was the reply, "I am an heir of eternal felicity. Although I do not need your prayers, I thank you very much for your charity in praying for me." "What good work did you perform in your lifetime," the priest inquired further, "by which you specially merited God's grace and favor?" "The principal good work that I did," he rejoined, "was my daily and devout attendance at holy Mass. It was that which obtained for me a happy death and a merciful sentence after death." "In what manner did you hear Mass?" asked the priest. "On leaving my house," the soul replied, "I made the sign of the cross, and on my way to the church I said a *Pater* for grace to hear Mass with right dispositions. When I entered the church, I knelt down before the crucifix, and recited five *Paters* and five *Aves* in honor of the five wounds of Christ. Furthermore, during the whole of the Mass I imagined myself on Calvary, with my crucified Redeemer before my eyes. At the elevation I humbly adored the sacred host, and offered myself body and soul to my God. Such was my daily practice, for which I now, through the merits of Christ's blood and wounds, receive an unspeakably great reward." Having said this, the soul disappeared from sight, leaving the good priest greatly edified and consoled.

This beautiful story is well adapted to encourage the pusillanimous, and strengthen their hope of eternal bliss. For there is nothing so sure and certain on which we can rely in the hour of death as daily and devout assistance at holy Mass, and I will explain why this is so. Our religion teaches us that there is nothing wherein we can hope more firmly or trust more fully than in the merits of Christ's death and passion. These are truly present in holy Mass; they are witnessed by all who stand around the altar; they are invoked, adored, offered by all who hear Mass aright. Nay, more, they are actually and freely applied to the souls of all; and every one in the congregation, unless he be in mortal sin, may claim them as his own. Thus he who trusts in holy Mass trusts in the merits of Christ, in His sacred passion and precious blood.

But, it may be urged, in confession and communion the merits of Christ are applied to the soul; consequently we may put our trust in the sacraments as well as in the holy sacrifice. To this I answer: There is a great difference between approaching the sacraments and offering the sacrifice of the Mass. The former must be received worthily; that is to say, real contrition is required for confession, true devotion for communion. He who approaches the sacraments without these dispositions, far from partaking of the merits of Christ, only burdens his soul with a fresh sin. And since only by a divine revelation can a man know whether he has received the sacraments worthily, no one can place his confidence in them; far from it; we must always tremble lest we should have received them unworthily, and thus be guilty of mortal sin. But in order to hear Mass one need not be in a state of grace, for, as we have already shown, if a man hears Mass in a state of mortal sin, he does not commit another sin; on the contrary, he receives the grace of conversion if he open his heart to divine influences. In fact, he is not wrong in hoping that, in virtue of the precious victim that is offered, God will, of His pure bounty, show him mercy. And he who, not being in a state of mortal sin, hears Mass, though with no great fervor, not only commits no sin, but is warranted in trusting confidently that, through the sacrifice of the body and blood of Christ, he will obtain an increase of grace and remission of a part of the penalty due to his sins.

An objection may, however, here be made by the reader: It is true that every man must, at his death, firmly trust in the sufferings and death of Christ, since Christ died for this end, namely, that He might blot out our sins and preserve us from eternal perdition. It is, therefore, upon His sufferings and death, rather than upon holy Mass, that we should place our confidence. I answer: Most assuredly all our hope is in Christ's passion and death, provided the fruits and merits of His sufferings are applied to our souls; if not, it is in vain that we trust in them. What does it profit the reprobate sinner that Christ suffered and died for him if in spite of this he is damned? And why is he damned? Because the merits of Christ's passion have not been applied to him; and the reason why they have not been applied to him, is because he was not worthy of it. How, then, can we make ourselves worthy? By true compunction, by a right reception of the holy sacraments, by good works, above all, by piously saying or hearing Mass. For holy Church bids us know that "the fruits indeed of that bloody oblation, the sacrifice of the cross, are received most plentifully through that unbloody one, the sacrifice of the Mass." (Counc. Trent, Sess. xxii. ch. 2.) And in the preceding chapter she states that the holy Mass was instituted in order "that the salutary virtue of the sacrifice upon the cross might be applied to the remission of those sins which we daily commit." Therefore, seeing that the merits of Christ are liberally imparted and appropriated to us in holy Mass, it stands to reason that upon it we should build our hope.

Thus every one whose habit it has been to assist frequently, gladly, reverently at holy Mass may take comfort to himself at his death from the consciousness that by offering to God so many Masses he has rendered Him excellent and acceptable service and an oblation of great price; that he has daily in all humility implored pardon, and offered the abundant merits of the Saviour in atonement for his sins; nay, more, the Son of God has pleaded with him and for him in every Mass, giving His precious blood for his redemption.

He whose hope rests on these grounds does not trust in himself, or in his own merits, but in Christ, in whose intercession and satisfaction it is granted him to participate in holy Mass. He trusts, therefore, in the passion of Christ, renewed in holy Mass; in the blood of Christ, mystically sprinkled upon his soul in holy Mass; in the merits of Christ, imparted to him, won by him, in holy Mass. He trusts in the great oblation offered by the hands of the priest, gratefully accepted by the Divine Goodness; he trusts in the prayers offered by the priest, by Christ Himself, to God the Father for his salvation. On such stable foundations as these we may, we will, rest our hope.

This hope is so certain that the learned Sanchez is warranted in saying: "We derive from holy Mass so steadfast a hope of the future life that supernatural faith is required in order to believe it at all." In other words, he who fully recognizes the tremendous power of the holy Mass, and the firm hope of salvation it affords us, is so overwhelmed with astonishment that he could not believe it were it not that God enlightens his mind by the light of the Catholic faith. This was acknowledged by the holy fathers, who, on the approach of death, regarded the devout celebration of Mass as their best preparation for encountering the last enemy.

Baronius relates of St. Theodore Studita, a valiant champion of the faith, who lived about 826 A.D., that before his death he was so worn by sickness that he resembled a corpse more than a living man. When the hand of death was already laid upon him, he implored of

God one last favor, that his life might be so far prolonged as to allow of his saying Mass once more, as a preparation for the final conflict. His prayer was granted; he rallied and recovered strength sufficiently to rise from his bed, and, to the amazement of all about him, walk unaided to the church. He said Mass with the utmost devotion, all present being moved to tears. This was his viaticum, for when, at the conclusion of the Mass, he returned to his chamber and laid down once more, he gently fell asleep in the Lord.

Baronius also mentions, in speaking of Tarasius, Patriarch of· Constantinople, that even when prostrated by severe illness he could not be kept from saying Mass every day. Inflamed by divine charity, he forced himself to disregard acute suffering, and to the last day of his life he continued to stand at the altar, thereby meriting a holy death and a happy eternity.

Many priests bear this in mind when they offer the holy sacrifice day by day, that they are making the best preparation to meet death. Well is it for them if they persevere unto the end in this holy practice; for the supernatural power of the Mass will fortify them mightily against the assaults of the evil enemy and will preserve them from eternal perdition. St. Gregory (Pope) gives them this assurance: " The holy sacrifice of the Mass is a safeguard from eternal damnation. If, moreover, the archangel Raphael could say: 'Alms delivereth from death, and the same is that which purgeth away sins and maketh to find mercy and life everlasting' (Tob. xii. 9), how much more can it be said of the all-prevailing sacrifice of the Mass that it rescues the departing soul from the powers of evil, cleanses it from sin, obtains for it mercy, and gives it a portion in life eternal."

Finally, listen to the magnificent promise made to all whose aim it is to hear Mass as often as possible; Christ

Himself is speaking to one of His saints: "I declare to thee that I will be to him who has assisted at Mass diligently and devoutly comfort and protection in the hour of death; and whatever the number of Masses he has heard with devotion on earth, such shall be the number of blessed spirits whom I will send to attend upon his departing soul." Oh, what consolation does this promise convey to us! Who would not under such conditions gladly assist at Mass? We are not, it is true, required to believe these words as an article of faith, but the revelations from which they are taken have been approved by the Church and believed in by the faithful for six hundred years.

PRAYER.

O Lord Jesus, if the promise Thou madest to Thy saints is to be fulfilled in my case, I shall when my last hour comes say with David: "The Lord is my light and my salvation, whom shall I fear? The Lord is the protector of my life, of whom shall I be afraid?" (Ps. xxvi. 1.) For if, according to Thy word, Thou sendest me at my death as many saints to befriend and protect me against my hellish foe as I have heard Masses with devotion, I need not fear the hosts of hell, for one single saint is able to put to flight an army of demons. Wherefore, I beseech Thee, most bountiful Jesus, do as Thou hast said and let not my hope be put to confusion. In order to render myself deserving of what Thou dost promise, I pledge myself to hear Mass devoutly every day, if possible, and offer it by the hands of the priest for Thy greater honor and glory.

Thus may the soul in hope and confidence in the efficacy of holy Mass depart out of this world and stand without fear before the judgment-seat of Christ. What, thinkest thou, will befall her there?

St. Boniface, Archbishop of Mayence, tells us something of this in a letter which he wrote to his sister. A certain brother in one of the monasteries then existing came to life again after his death, and related to St. Boniface what had happened to him after leaving this world: "When I was brought before the tribunal of God, all the sins of which I had been guilty rose up before me in hideous shape and made themselves known to me one after the other: I am the vainglory wherewith thou didst exalt thyself before thy fellows. Another said: I am the spirit of lying which often made thee fall. A third: I represent the idle words which thou didst often utter. In me, said a fourth, behold the foolish thoughts in which thou didst indulge both at church and elsewhere. And thus there passed before me in succession all the sins which through negligence, forgetfulness, or ignorance I had omitted in confession, accusing me vehemently, crying out against me with harsh and threatening tones. The devils who were present likewise bore witness against me, reminding me of the place and of the time of each and every sin. Afterwards the few good works I had done came up in their turn, one saying: I am the obedience which thou didst render to thy superiors. Another: I personate the fasting wherewith thou didst mortify thy flesh. The next: I represent the prayers which thou didst send up to heaven. In this manner one good work after another appeared for my consolation, the angels testifying to each one and extolling each one with words of praise."

That which happened to this pious brother, of whom St. Boniface gives a long account, will surely happen to thee, O reader, to me, and to all men on their exit from this world. The sins thou hast committed will rise up before thine eyes in appalling array; the good works thou hast performed will also appear to console and encourage thee. But if thou hast been diligent and devout in hearing Mass thou wilt behold a band of fair spirits advance towards thee, who will dispel thy fears and reassure thy heart, saying: " Recognize in us the Masses thou didst hear on earth; we will go with thee into the dread presence of thy Judge; we will speak in thy defence; we will show how deep was thy devotion, how many the sins thou didst expiate and the penalties thou didst cancel. Be of good courage; we will appease the wrath of thy Judge and implore mercy on thy behalf." Oh, what a relief to the poor, afflicted soul to meet with such friends to intercede for him with the strict Judge!

Furthermore, let us hope that thy experience will be similar to that recorded of the Blessed Nancker, Bishop of Breslau in the thirteenth century. This prelate was distinguished by his great love for holy Mass, which induced him to be present, if possible, at all the Masses said every day in his cathedral. Just at the time when he lay dying a pious matron of the city heard the voices of angels singing in such sweet and melodious strains that she thought herself transported to paradise. While she was wondering within herself what was the cause of this rejoicing, a voice said to her: " The soul of Bishop Nancker has left the body and is being carried by the angels to heaven." The good woman then asked in what way the bishop had merited this great honor and privilege. And the same voice replied: " Through the great affection and veneration he had for holy Mass." An example such as this ought certainly to encourage us in going to Mass. The pious bishop was taken up to heaven without passing through purgatory; nay, more, he was carried up by the angels in triumph with glad and jubilant songs. And why? Chiefly because of his great devotion to holy Mass; he had thereby paid all he owed to divine justice and merited a glorious entry into the courts of heaven. If thou wouldst escape the purgatorial fire and obtain a high place in heaven, imitate his example and be zealous in hearing Mass. And if it is not possible for thee to hear many Masses, as he did, at least do so in desire, and God will accept thy good intention and grant thee a happy end.

CHAPTER XXII.

HOLY MASS IS THE UNFAILING SUCCOR OF THE DEPARTED.

IT is quite impossible for us to imagine the cruel torments endured by the souls in purgatory. The fathers of the Church tell us that they are terrible in the extreme. St. Augustine says that the fire which purifies the elect is of the same nature as that which torments the damned. This fire is fiercer than any we have seen, or can conjecture, on earth. If we had no other testimony than this to the terrible character of the purgatorial fire, it would suffice to make us believe in its awful agony, and tremble at the thought of it. St. Augustine proceeds to describe it further: "Although this fire," he says, "is not eternal, it is marvellously intense, and inflicts worse pain than any ever suffered in this world. No physical suffering can equal it, not even the fearful tortures the martyrs endured." Now if, after hearing this, we read in the lives of the saints of the cruel tortures they underwent, we may form some faint conception of the awful nature of the pains of purgatory.

According to St. Cyril, Patriarch of Alexandria, it would be preferable to suffer all imaginable anguish to the end of time than to pass one day in purgatory. My God, how intolerable those pains must be if an unhappy soul suffers more in one day than a man could suffer from now until the day of judgment! St. Thomas of Aquin declares that a single spark from the flames of purgatory is worse than all the most dreadful tortures of this life. Terrible words, almost surpassing our powers of belief! Alas, what is to become of us, wretched sinners, if after our death we are plunged into those scorching flames? What intense suffering, my God, is in store for us then! And yet not the slightest doubt can be entertained that, unless we endure these torments, we cannot enter heaven; for we are not holy and perfect: far from it, we are full of evil desires, and are soiled with the stains of sin.

Many more passages from the fathers might be quoted concerning the pains of purgatory, but we will content ourselves with the words of St. Bernadin, who says: "There is as much difference between our material fire and the fire of purgatory as between a painted fire and a real fire." St. Magdalen of Pazzi, who several times had a vision of purgatory, and even descried her own brother there, said that a large fire on earth appeared like pleasure-grounds in comparison to the fires of purgatory. This forcible comparison is enough to give us some idea of the agony suffered in purgatory, and to urge us to make atonement for our sins now, that we may not have to expiate them hereafter in the torturing flames. It ought also to awaken within us heartfelt compassion for the holy souls who at the present time are enduring the terrible torture of that fiery prison, and on that account deserve our deepest commiseration.

There are many different ways of helping the suffering souls and delivering them from purgatory; but none of those is so sure and so effectual as the holy sacrifice of the Mass. The Church, speaking by the Council of Trent, declares this to be the case: "This Œcumenical Synod teaches that the souls detained in purgatory are helped by the suffrages of the faithful, but principally by the acceptable sacrifice of the altar." (Sess. xxv.) This is laid down as an article of faith, which no man can gainsay. The same was asserted two centuries previously by the angelic doctor St. Thomas: "By no other oblation can thè souls in purgatory be more speedily released than by the sacrifice of the Mass."

The reason of it is this: In the Mass not only do the priest and the congregation pray fervently for the deliverance of the holy souls, but at the same time they offer to God the full amount of the debt yet owing to divine justice, and thus appease His just anger. Everybody will understand that if any one does not merely ask that a debtor may be released from prison, but also pays what he owes, the prisoner will at once be set free. The holy souls are in the grace of God; they have made their peace with Him in the Sacrament of Penance. They are still captives in that awful, fiery prison on account of the punishment due to their sins, and the stains which still cleave to them. If, moved by compassion, thou dost plead for them, and bestow on them the merit of thy prayers, thou wilt, it is true, discharge a part of their debt, but not sufficient to effect their release. The Judge Himself has passed on them this terrible sentence: "Amen, I say to thee, thou shalt not go out from thence till thou repay the last farthing." (St. Matt. v. 26.) Learn from these words the pitiless severity of Our Lord, since He declares He will not forgive one miserable farthing to the debtor who owed Him a thousand talents, and who has paid off the whole amount with the exception of that one last farthing. But if thou hearest Mass for one poor soul, and offerest it to divine justice with that intention, rest assured that thou wilt pay at any rate a considerable portion of his debt.

From what amount of punishment the soul is freed by one Mass is uncertain, for God has not made it known, and opinions are divided about it. One thing, however, admits of no doubt, namely, that a Mass said or heard in one's lifetime has much more satisfactory value than one said after death. According to St. Anselm, a single Mass in one's lifetime is equivalent to many after one's death. How are we to account for this?

(1) Every Mass which a man says or hears obtains for him an increase of glory in heaven; this is not the case when Mass, or even hundreds of Masses, are offered for him after his death.

(2) If thou hearest Mass, or hast Mass said for thee, when in a state of wrath, God will perchance for the sake of that Mass bring thee to a knowledge of sin, and grant thee the grace of contrition, and thus thou mayst return to a state of grace; this would be impossible after death. For if, neglecting Mass, thou wert to die in mortal sin, no number of Masses offered for thee could procure thy return to a state of grace.

(3) All the Masses which thou hearest, or which are said for thee, will await thee at thy death: they will go with thee to the judgment-seat, they will plead for mercy for thee, and if they do not preserve thee altogether from the cleansing flames they will at any rate shorten the time of thy detention. But if the Masses are not to be said until after thy death, thou wilt have to await in anguish the alleviation they will bring.

(4) If in thy lifetime thou dost give an alms to have Mass said for thee, the money comes out of thy own pocket, and involves some sacrifice on thy part, freely made to thy God. But the dead do not spend their own money: it belongs to them no longer, but to their

heirs. Wherefore it is to be feared that the Masses for which money is bequeathed are but of little value to him for whom they are said.

(5) Finally, one Mass said in thy lifetime will do more to free the soul from the punishment of sin than many Masses after death. For our sojourn in this world is a time of grace, afterwards comes the time of just retribution; now it will be far easier for us to make our peace with our Judge than it will be hereafter. A slight penance voluntarily performed in this world has more value in the sight of God than compulsory penance of much greater severity in the world to come; just as we value a small piece of gold more than a large lump of lead.

The following examples testify to the immense efficacy of holy Mass in mitigating or remitting altogether the pains of purgatory.

Breidenbach speaks of a certain citizen who shortly after his death appeared to one of his servants, wrapped in flames, and, telling her that he was suffering unutterable torments, begged her to bid his son have some Masses said for him. The son had three Masses said directly, and the servant, who assisted at them, beheld the spirit of her deceased master present on his knees. At the conclusion of the three Masses he appeared to her again, and desired her to thank his son in his name, and inform him that he had been sentenced to five years in purgatory. In consequence, however, of the three Masses and the suffrages of the faithful which were offered for him four years and four days of punishment had been remitted to him.

In the annals of the Cistercian Order it is recorded that in the time of St. Bernard of Clairvaux a lay brother who had died appeared to one of the fathers in the night after his demise, saying: " Come with me, and see the dreadful torments which by divine justice I am condemned to suffer." He then led him to the edge of a deep, fiery abyss, and told him that he was constantly thrown into that abyss by the devils, who treated him with such barbarity that he would rather be ill-treated a hundred times over by men than once by the devils. The next morning the pious father who had witnessed this related it to St. Bernard. He immediately called all the monks together, depicted to them the unhappy condition of their deceased brother, and bade them do their utmost by their prayers and Masses to appease the anger of God, and rescue the soul of their brother from the power of the demons. The monks did so, and a few days later the soul of the departed brother appeared again to the same father, this time with a joyous countenance. On being asked how it now was with him, he replied: "Thanks be to God, I am now free from pain." The father inquired by what means he had been delivered: "Come and see," his visitant answered. Then conducting him into the monastery chapel, where several priests were offering the holy sacrifice with great devotion, he uttered these remarkable words: "Behold the weapons of God's grace, whereby my deliverance was effected. This is the citadel of divine mercy, the power of which cannot be overcome. Behold the wondrous victim, Who takes away the sins of the world. I tell you of a truth nothing can resist the weapons of divine grace, the omnipotence of divine mercy, the efficacy of the salutary victim, but the hardened heart of the unrepentant sinner." Thereupon the apparition vanished. The good father told the rest of the community about the release of their suffering brother and the great potency of the holy sacrifice, inspiring them all with more fervent appreciation and love of holy Mass.

These examples should teach us to be diligent in

prayer for our departed friends; for it is not as easy for them to gain an entrance into heaven as we imagine. If we cannot have Mass said for them, we may at any rate hear Mass as often as possible for them, and ask others to do the same in their behalf. A good man once told a poor widow who complained to him that she was unable through poverty to have Mass said for her deceased husband: "Go to church and hear several Masses, and offer them to God for your husband; very probably this may do more to help him than if a Mass was said for the repose of his soul." This is good advice to give to the poor who cannot afford to have Mass said. For although it is undeniably more to have Mass said than merely to hear it, yet each time we hear Mass for some suffering soul its pains are mitigated, and it is sprinkled with the blood of Christ in virtue of the oblation offered to God.

Of this we have a type given us in the Old Testament, inasmuch as God says: "I have given you the blood, that you may make atonement with it upon the altar for your souls, and the blood may be for an expiation of the soul." (Lev. xvii. 11.) St. Thomas, commenting on this passage, says: "In these words it is foretold that the sacrifice of the body and blood of Christ is of avail for the souls in purgatory." For if under the Jewish law the blood of the holocaust was for the cleansing of the soul, how much more will the precious blood of Christ, offered upon our altars, purify our souls, and the suffering souls besides, from every stain, and deliver the captives from their fiery prison.

At the time when this precious blood was shed upon the cross all the souls detained in purgatory were set free, according to the words of the prophet Zacharias, which he addresses to the Saviour: "Thou also by the blood of Thy testament hast sent forth Thy prisoners out of the pit, wherein is no water." (Zach. ix. 11.) In this passage the prophet declares that the general redemption of the souls in limbo was to be ascribed to the blood of Christ shed for them. In what terms shall we speak of the power of holy Mass, wherein the blood of the new and eternal testament, the same precious blood, is continually shed for the remission of sins? Who can doubt that it is all-prevailing to refresh, to cleanse, to release the holy souls? Never was a cooling draught so grateful to the parched lips of the fever patient as the precious blood of Christ is to the souls in purgatory, when shed for them and mystically sprinkled upon them in holy Mass, in its power to cool, refresh, cleanse, and ransom them.

An incident from the life of Blessed Henry Suso of the Order of St. Dominic may aptly be introduced here. It is related of him that when making his studies at Cologne he entered into an agreement with a priest of his Order that whichever should outlive the other should say a certain number of Masses for the repose of his friend's soul. After his studies were ended Father Suso remained at Cologne, while his friend was sent into Swabia, where a few years later he died. On the news of his death reaching Father Suso he remembered his promise, but was unable immediately to fulfil it. However, he prayed very earnestly for his friend, fasted, and took the discipline in his behalf. Before many days had passed the deceased appeared to him in great affliction and said: "False friend that thou art, why hast thou not accomplished the promise thou madest to me?" Blessed Suso, startled and alarmed, replied: "Do not be angry with me, O my friend; I have really been prevented from saying the Masses as yet, but I have offered many prayers; I have fasted and chastised my body for thee." The apparition answered: "Thy prayers are not powerful enough to deliver me out of the torments I endure. The blood of Jesus Christ, consecrated and offered up in holy Mass, alone avails to set me free. If thou hadst said the promised Masses, by this time I should be released from my prison; it is entirely thy fault that I am still a prey to the devouring flames." This and yet more in the same strain did the unhappy soul say to Father Suso; then he left him, overwhelmed with grief and sorrow. As soon as he had recovered himself a little he hastened to his superior, narrated to him what had occurred, and begged permission to set aside the Masses prescribed for him to say in order that he might fulfil his promise to his friend. When this had been done, the soul appeared to him once more and intimated to him that he was then at rest and would pray for him in heaven.

This story teaches us the immense power of Christ's blood, consecrated in the Mass, and the welcome relief it affords to the holy souls when it is offered up for them. St. Gregory says authoritatively: "When the holy sacrifice is offered and special intercession made by the priest for the souls of the departed, they are released from their pains."

The suffering souls also experience a great alleviation when the graves are incensed and sprinkled with holy water. The holy water does indeed only materially moisten the earth, but in its beneficent virtue it refreshes the souls in purgatory, just as the waters of Baptism falling on the head of the infant have power to cleanse his soul. Wherefore see that thou frequently sprinkle the last resting-place of thy friends with holy water, for thereby thou wilt allay the heat of the flames that torture them.

CHAPTER XXIII.

THE MANNER AND MEASURE IN WHICH THE PRIEST AND THE ANGELS PRAY FOR THOSE WHO ARE PRESENT AT HOLY MASS.

PIOUS persons are often heard to complain that they feel no devotion and are much troubled by distraction in prayer. No better counsel can be given to them than to go diligently to Mass, and unite their prayers to the prayer of Christ and of the priest; thus their imperfect petitions will be made perfect, as a copper coin is gilded by being immersed in molten gold. Prayer that is offered in union with the holy sacrifice, as Fornerus says, far surpasses in value all other prayers, however long, however fervent. The reason of this shall be expounded in the present chapter for the encouragement of the reader.

The priest is bound to pray for the people, and offer the Mass to Almighty God for their salvation. Supplications for those who are present form a part of the Ordinary of the Mass, and must not be omitted. Moreover, all the collects, the secret prayers, and the concluding prayers, and all others which are written in the plural, are said in the name of the congregation and for their benefit. Each one who is present at Mass may be assured that those prayers are offered for him, and will profit him as much as if there was no one else in the church but the priest and himself. But in order that every one may know what and how many are the petitions offered on his behalf they shall be mentioned singly here.

First of all the clerk, in the name of the people, says the *Confiteor*, or general confession, and the priest gives the absolution to all present: "May Almighty God have mercy upon you, forgive you your sins, and bring you to life everlasting. Amen." "May the almighty and merciful Lord grant us pardon, absolution, and remission of all our sins. Amen." When the priest goes up to the altar, he prays for himself and the people, saying: "Take away from us, we beseech thee, O Lord, our iniquities, that we may be worthy to enter with pure minds into the holy of holies, through Christ, Our Lord. Amen."

The *Kyrie eleison*, the *Gloria in excelsis*, as well as all the collects, are likewise recited by the priest for himself and for the congregation. He often turns to the people, saying: "*Dominus vobiscum*" ("The Lord be with you"). In this salutation, which is repeated eight times, he wishes for them spiritual welfare and salvation. For if God is with us, we have His grace, His blessing, His assistance, His mercy. In the Creed the priest makes public profession for himself and for us all of the faith that is in us, the faith in which we desire to live and hope to die.

At the offering of the host he says: "Accept, O holy Father, almighty, eternal God, this immaculate host, which I, Thy unworthy servant, offer unto Thee, my living and true God, for my innumerable sins, offences, and negligences, and for all here present; as also for all faithful Christians, both living and dead, that it may be profitable for my own and for their salvation, unto life eternal. Amen." At the pouring of the wine and water into the chalice he says: "O God, Who, in creating human nature, didst wonderfully dignify it, and hast still more wonderfully renewed it, grant that, by the mystery of this water and wine, we may be made partakers of His divinity Who vouchsafed to become partaker of our humanity, Jesus Christ, Thy Son, Our Lord," etc.

At the offering of the chalice he says: "We offer to Thee, O Lord, the chalice of salvation, beseeching Thy clemency that, in the sight of Thy divine majesty, it may ascend with the odor of sweetness for our salvation, and for that of the whole world. Amen."

After the washing of hands he says: ".Receive, O Holy Trinity, this oblation, which we make to Thee in memory of the passion, resurrection, and ascension of Our Lord Jesus Christ, and in honor of the Blessed Mary, ever virgin, of blessed John the Baptist, of the holy apostles Peter and Paul, of these and of all the saints, that it may be available to their honor and our salvation, and may they vouchsafe to intercede for us in heaven whose memory we celebrate on earth. Amen."

After this follow the secret prayers, which are full of meaning, and are recited in a low voice for the salvation of the priest and the people. They are generally three in number, sometimes five; on great feasts there is only one. In the preface the priest, raising his voice, praises God in his own name and that of the faithful, and calls upon all who are present to magnify God, saying: "The Lord be with you. Lift up your hearts. Let us give thanks to the Lord our God. For it is meet and just, right and salutary, that we should always, and in all places, give thanks to Thee, O holy Lord, Father Almighty, Eternal God. Through Christ Our Lord, through Whom the angels praise Thy majesty, the dominations adore, the powers do hold in awe, the heavens and the virtues of the heavens, and the blessed seraphim do celebrate with united joy. In union with whom we beseech Thee that Thou wouldst command our voices also to be admitted with suppliant confession, saying: Holy, holy, holy, Lord God of Sabaoth. Heaven and earth are full of Thy glory. Hosanna in the highest. Blessed is he that cometh in the name of the Lord. Hosanna in the highest!"

After the preface follows the canon of the Mass, which is read in a low voice; from this only a few prayers, intended for the congregation, shall be taken. At the *Memento* the priest says: "Be mindful, O Lord, of Thy servants, men and women, N. and N." He then prays silently for those for whom he intends to offer up that Mass, or who have been particularly commended to his prayers. Afterwards he proceeds: "Be mindful, also, O Lord, of all here present, whose faith and devotion are known unto Thee, for whom we offer to Thee this sacrifice of praise, or who offer it up for themselves, for their families and friends, for the redemption of their souls, for the hope of their safety and salvation, and who pay their vows to Thee, the eternal, living, and true God."

These words have been commented upon in the following manner: "Learn from this, O Christian, that thou needest not distress thyself if on account of thy poverty thou canst not have Mass said for thyself, or for thy friends, whether living or dead. For the Mass which thou dost hear is offered by the priest for thy intention; and he prays God to give to thee and those for whom thou dost ask the merits of this holy sacrifice according to thy devotion and thy desire."

After the *Memento* a solemn commemoration is made of the glorious and ever-virgin Mary, Mother of our Lord and God, Jesus Christ; of the apostles, martyrs, and saints, to honor their memory and entreat that by their merits and prayers we may be defended by the help of the divine protection. Then, spreading his hands over the oblation, the priest says: "We therefore beseech Thee, O Lord, graciously to accept this oblation of our service, as also of Thy whole family; dispose our days in Thy peace, command us to be delivered from eternal damnation, and to be numbered in the flock of Thy elect, through Christ, Our Lord. Amen."

After the elevation of the chalice he says: "Wherefore, O Lord, we, Thy servants, as also Thy holy people, calling to mind the blessed passion of the same Christ, Thy Son, Our Lord, His resurrection from hell and glorious ascension into heaven, offer unto Thy most excellent majesty, of thy gifts and presents, a pure host, a holy host, an immaculate host, the holy bread of eternal life, and the chalice of everlasting salvation.

"Upon which vouchsafe to look with a propitious and serene countenance, and to accept them as Thou wert graciously pleased to accept the gifts of Thy just servant Abel, and the sacrifice of our patriarch Abraham, and that which Thy high priest Melchisedech offered to Thee, a holy sacrifice, an immaculate host."

Bowing down profoundly, he proceeds: "We most humbly beseech Thee, Almighty God, command these things to be carried by the hands of Thy holy angel to Thy altar on high, in the sight of Thy divine majesty, that as many of us as, by participation at this altar, shall receive the most sacred body and blood of Thy Son may be filled with all heavenly benediction and grace. Through the same," etc.

After this comes the commemoration of the dead, when the priest offers the holy Mass for the souls for whom it is said, or those for whom he intends to pray. He then proceeds: "And to us sinners, Thy servants, hoping in the multitude of Thy mercies, vouchsafe to grant some part and fellowship with Thy holy apostles and martyrs, into whose company we beseech Thee to admit us, not considering our merits, but freely pardoning our offences."

He next recites the *Pater noster* for himself and all the faithful, and at the conclusion of it he prays that we may be delivered from all evils, past, present, and to come, and through the intercession of the blessed and glorious

Mary, ever virgin, Mother of God, together with the blessed apostles Peter and Paul, and Andrew and all the saints, by the assistance of divine mercy we may be always free from sin and secure from all disturbance.

The *Agnus Dei* is repeated three times: " Lamb of God, Who takest away the sins of the world, have mercy upon us." The short prayers which immediately follow are said by the priest for himself alone, but the last collects, or post-communion, are said for the congregation as well. The concluding prayer runs thus: "O Holy Trinity, let the performance of my homage be pleasing to Thee; and grant that the sacrifice which I, unworthy, have offered up in the sight of Thy majesty may be acceptable to Thee, and through Thy mercy be a propitiation for me and all those for whom I have offered it. Through Christ," etc. Finally, the priest gives the sacerdotal blessing to the people in the name of Christ and the authority of the Church, and reads the last gospel.

Here the reader will see all the prayers which the priest says on his behalf, when he assists at holy Mass. The cogency of these prayers cannot be doubted, for they were composed by St. Peter and other holy popes, under the inspiration of the Holy Ghost, to Whose operation they also owe their sacred character and their unfailing efficacy. The priest does not indeed pronounce them as coming from himself; he speaks in the name of Christ, in the name of all Christendom, whose envoy he is, for the Catholic Church, that is, the great body, of the faithful, depute the priest, as their chosen ambassador, to ascend for them the steps of the altar; they commission him to present their petitions to God whilst celebrating the great act of worship; to negotiate with Him the all-important business of their welfare in time and in eternity. With what forms and with what words he is to hold communication with God is prescribed by the Church, and embodied in the ritual and prayers of the missal.

Now when the priest, placing himself in the presence of God, goes up to the altar, God the Father does not regard him as a sinful man, but as an ambassador, fully empowered by His Church to treat with Him. He therefore listens to what he has to say, He refuses no reasonable request that he puts forward. Nay, more, He esteems him as the representative of His only-begotten Son, for the priest personates that Son at the altar; he wears the garments of His passion; he utters in His name the words of consecration: "This is My body. This is the chalice of My blood." And since the priest is thus Christ's representative, his supplications have the more weight with God; in fact Christ Himself presents them to His heavenly Father. Moreover, because the priest at the altar does not merely offer prayers, but an oblation of infinite value, nothing less than the consecrated body and blood of Christ, God the Father cannot refuse to accept his offering. He cannot reject his prayer. Wherefore do thou unite thy feeble, imperfect petition to the prayer of the priest, and, together with that prayer, it will be carried up to heaven, transformed and ennobled. In this wise does the priest help thee to pray, and what thou lackest in devotion will be amply supplied by the potency of his intercession.

WHETHER ALL MASSES ARE OF EQUAL VALUE.

Here it is necessary to distinguish between the victim and the sacrificial act. The victim is the same in all Masses, none other than Jesus Christ Himself, and so far all Masses are equally good, equally precious. With regard to the sacrificial act, the offering of the victim, the more devoutly the priest says the Mass the more acceptable to God is the sacrifice he offers, and the more abundant are the graces it brings down from above, both upon the priest who celebrates the Mass and the individual for whom he offers it.

We find a confirmation of this in the writings of St. Bonaventure, who says: "All Masses are equally good, as far as Christ is concerned; but as far as the priest is concerned, one may be better than another. Therefore it is more profitable to hear the Mass of a good priest than of an indifferent one." Cardinal Bona also corroborates this opinion: "The more holy and pleasing to God," he says, "a priest is the more acceptable are his prayers and oblations; and the greater his devotion the greater the benefit derived from his Mass. For just as other good works performed by a pious man gain merit in proportion to the zeal and devotion wherewith they are performed, so holy Mass is more or less profitable both to the priest who says it and to the persons for whom it is said according as it is celebrated with more or less fervor." This is the reason why in the Mass the priest frequently beseeches God graciously to accept his oblation, and to vouchsafe that it may be conducive to his own salvation and that of the people.

HOW THE ANGELS PRAY FOR US IN THE TIME OF HOLY MASS.

It is impossible to deny or doubt that the angels are present at holy Mass. The Catholic Church teaches it, and the psalmist does the same when he says: "He hath given His angels charge over thee, to keep thee in all thy ways." (Ps. xc. 11.) From this we know that they go about with us everywhere, that they are to us ministering spirits, as St. Paul says (Heb. i. 14), ever ready to help us. Oh, how delighted they are to accompany us to holy Mass! How eagerly they do all they can to keep us from inattention or irreverence! We know at least that there are as many angels in the church as there are people, because every one has his guardian angel at his side to aid him in his prayers and to adore with him Christ present upon the altar. Wherefore see that thou ask thy guardian angel to hear Mass with thee and for thee, and in thy name to worship the divine victim, to offer Him to God, to implore His grace. Thus what is wanting on thy part will be made good by him, and the holy sacrifice will be more acceptable to God Almighty.

Besides the angels guardian, thousands of celestial spirits from the higher choirs of angels assist at Mass, reverently worshipping their Lord and God in this sublime mystery. It was revealed to St. Mechtilde that three thousand angels from the seventh choir, the thrones, are ever in devout attendance around every tabernacle where the Blessed Sacrament is reserved. Doubtless a much greater number are present at holy Mass, which is not merely a sacrament, but also a sacrifice.

St. Paul, in his Epistle to the Hebrews, gives us to understand that the angels assist at holy Mass. He says: "You are come to the company of many thousands of angels, and to Jesus the mediator of the New Testament." (Heb. xii. 22, 24.) This text is most applicable to holy Mass, where Christ is present, exercising the office of a faithful mediator, and with Him many thousand angels. When at Mass, therefore, we can take David's words upon our lips, and say: "I will sing praise to Thee, O Lord, in the sight of the angels: I will worship towards Thy holy temple, and I will give glory to Thy name." (Ps. cxxxvii. 1, 2.) For then we are kneeling in the midst of angels, surrounded by thousands of bright spirits, who are hearing Mass with us, and praying earnestly for us. And knowing this, we shall do well to recall the admonition of St. Chrysostom:

"Forget not, O man, in what company thou art at the time of this solemn sacrifice. Thou standest amid cherubim and seraphim and other exalted spirits of high rank." Let us beware, then, lest we grieve these celestial powers by our want of devotion.

That the angels pray for us St. Chrysostom states in the most explicit manner: "When the priest at the altar offers the stupendous and sublime sacrifice, the angels stand beside him, and all around the altar are ranged choirs of heavenly spirits, who raise their voices in honor of the victim Who is immolated. Thus it is not lowly mortals alone who call upon God: the angels kneel before Him, the archangels plead on behalf of men. It is their most accepted time; the sacred victim may be said to be at their disposal. Through Him they urge their petitions. We may imagine them speaking in this wise: 'We pray, O Lord God, for those whom Thy Son loved so tenderly that for them He suffered death; we plead for those on whose behalf He shed His precious blood; we implore grace for those for the sake of whom He offered His sacred body upon the cross." How cheering for us to know that the holy angels pray so earnestly during Mass for all who are present, that they implore mercy for us poor sinners. For the supplications the angels proffer are much more potent than those which we mortals send up to heaven, for the angels are inflamed with the love of God, they behold Him face to face, they speak with all the devotion of their pure hearts. Consequently they obtain what they ask of God more readily than we do, with our cold, careless petitions, so full of distractions. Wherefore if thou dost unite thy prayers during Mass to those of the angels they will together with them pierce the clouds, and will obtain a favorable hearing more certainly than if thou didst offer them at home and alone.

Not only are the angels present at the holy sacrifice, they offer it with our prayers to Almighty God. St. John tells us this in the Apocalypse: "An angel came and stood before the altar, having a golden censer; and there was given to him much incense, that he should offer of the prayers of all saints upon the golden altar, which is before the throne of God. And the smoke of the incense of the prayers of the saints ascended up before God from the hand of the angel." (Apoc. viii. 3, 4.) These words tell us plainly that the angels hover around us in the church, receiving from the lips of the faithful their pious prayers and delivering them to one of the most exalted of their number, that he may carry them to heaven and present them like fragrant incense upon the golden altar which stands before the throne of God. Kindled by him, they rise up as a sweet and agreeable odor in the presence of the Most High.

That this offering of our petitions is chiefly made during holy Mass is sufficiently indicated by the words: "The angel stood before the altar"; for why should the angel stand before the altar unless the holy sacrifice was offered upon it? And why should he place the sweet incense of the prayers of the saints upon it if he did not at the same time with the incense bear upwards the sacred victim? For to that and no other altar does the sacrificial victim rightly belong, and there it is daily placed, according to the prayer the priest recites at the consecration: "We most humbly beseech Thee, Almighty God, command these things to be carried by the hands of Thy holy angel to Thy altar on high, in the sight of Thy divine majesty."

All this proves that the holy angels with joy bear on high the sublime mysteries, together with the prayers offered during the time of their celebration, and offer them to the ever-blessed Trinity as an odor of sweetness. It is evident, then, that the prayers we send up at the time of Mass, when we pray with the holy angels, surrounded by thousands of angels, are of far more efficacy than those which, with equal devotion, we utter at home. Wherefore let us do what in us lies to hear Mass daily, that our prayers may be carried up to heaven in the angels' pure hands, and we may beseech the Most High to receive them graciously, and pardon our indevotion for the sake of the devotion of the celestial spirits to whom we associate ourselves.

CHAPTER XXIV.

HOLY MASS DOES NOT HINDER OUR WORK, BUT HELPS US IN IT.

THE principal excuse which Christians allege for not hearing Mass is their work. All the time that they are not at work they consider lost time, and more especially the time they spend in assisting at Mass, or some other divine service. In this they are mistaken, and sorely deceived by the devil, as I will now proceed to explain. If, on his way to work, a man meets a friend who has got a great deal to tell him, he might easily waste half an hour listening to the news, forgetting all about his work. But if any one proposed to that man to hear a Mass, he would answer that he must be off and away to his business. So if a man had a drink offered him when on the way to his work, he would surely stop and spend half an hour in the tavern, and not think himself the loser by it, whereas if he had had to go to an early Mass before starting, he would have regretted the loss of so much time.

Thus does Satan shamefully strive to blind us, and by all manner of means to deter us from the salutary practice of hearing Mass. Wherefore I intend to demonstrate in this chapter that, far from being a loss of time for persons who have to work for their living, it brings them no small profit, and instead of hindering helps them in their daily toil.

In support of this assertion the highest of all authority can be quoted, the divine Saviour Himself, Who, when blaming excessive solicitude in providing for our temporal needs, said in conclusion: "Seek ye therefore first the kingdom of God and His justice, and all these things shall be added unto you." (St. Matt. vi. 33.) Commentators explain this passage as alluding to hearing Mass; as if Our Lord had said: " Be not over-solicitous about your bodily sustenance, but in the first place pay God homage by hearing Mass before beginning the day's labors, and He will requite this service by providing what is necessary for the body." Supposing any one were to render a great and most acceptable service to some man of high rank, noted for his kindness, dost thou imagine that he would leave that service unrewarded? Certainly not; he would recompense it liberally. Now when thou hearest Mass devoutly, and offerest it to thy God, thou dost render Him an infinite service, infinite honor, infinite satisfaction; thou dost present to Him a gift so costly that all the treasures of heaven cannot outweigh it. Can it be supposed that God will let Himself be outdone in gratitude by man, that He will allow this good service, this precious gift, to be unrewarded, or, what is more, that He will permit thee to be a loser by it? By no means. We know God to be a rewarder of all that is good, and therefore He cannot fail to reward that highest of all services, or else thou couldst reproach Him with it before angels and men at the judgment-day, and that is a thing He would never permit. I will now give an instance of the manner in which God sometimes visibly rewards devout attendance at Mass.

In the life of St. John the Almoner we read a story of two shoemakers who lived in Alexandria. One of these men had a wife and a large family to support, yet he went to Mass every day; and God so blessed his industry that although he was very poor at first he soon had a flourishing business. The other was married, but had no children; he worked early and late, never going to Mass except on Sundays, and yet he could scarcely earn a living. Unable to understand how it was that his neighbor got on so much better than he did, he one day went to him and asked how it was that he, who had a wife and a number of children, was so well off, whilst he himself, who worked more hours a day, and had no family, found it more and more difficult to keep the wolf from the door. The other man replied: "I have discovered a hidden treasure, and every day I go to draw something from it. That is why I get richer day by day." "My good fellow," his neighbor rejoined, "do show me where the treasure is, and let me, too, fill my pockets from it." "Very well," the pious cobbler said, "come to me early to-morrow morning and I will show you the place where lies hid so great a treasure that it is enough to enrich the whole town." The next morning the poor man made his appearance betimes, delighted at the idea of having the secret disclosed to him. But his neighbor only took him to Mass with him; the following day he did the same, and also the day after. At last the poor man lost his temper, and said: "I know the way to church without your guidance, and I have been to Mass ever since I was a child; if you do not intend to show me the treasure you spoke of, at any rate you need not make a fool of me." The other answered gently: "Do not be angry with me, neighbor; I have not been making a fool of you, for I have really shown you the place where I find my riches. It is none other than the church, and the treasure itself is holy Mass; hence come my gains, this is why we never know what it is to want bread. Do as I do, and doubtless God will do the same for you. Remember the words of our divine Lord: 'Seek ye first the kingdom of God and His justice, and all these things shall be added unto you.' From the time of my marriage I have sought the kingdom of God by hearing Mass daily; and I can truly say that all these things, that is, the supply of my temporal needs, have been given to me by God. You, on the contrary, have neglected Our Lord's salutary counsel, and have preferred your work to the service of God; consequently your temporal wants have not been supplied, and you have been left in poverty." These words had the desired effect; the other shoemaker saw that he had been negligent in serving God; from that day forth he made it his habit to go to Mass, and found that the divine blessing was no longer withheld from him.

The pious cobbler was right in calling holy Mass a treasure; it is indeed a treasure, one of which it may be said: "It is an infinite treasure to men, which they that use become the friends of God." (Wis. vii. 14.) It is a mine of gold out of which riches may be dug for time and for eternity. For he who hears Mass in a state of grace will share in the merits of Christ, and these are truly nuggets of celestial gold. He also receives the blessing of his heavenly Father, a far better one than the blessing Isaac gave to his son Jacob when he said: "God give thee of the dew of heaven, and of the fatness of the earth, abundance of corn and wine." (Gen. xxvii. 28) For this benediction was confined to earthly things alone, whereas the benediction we receive in the Mass relates to supernatural things as well; for after the consecration the priest prays that "as many of us as, by participation at this altar, shall receive the most sacred body and blood of Thy Son may be filled with all heavenly benediction and grace." In virtue of this fervent petition, and by the operation of the holy sacrifice, thou shalt experience the blessing of God in body and soul, in thy work and occupations, in matters temporal and spiritual. The benediction of ancient times shall find its fulfilment in thee: "Blessed shalt thou be coming in and going out. Blessed shalt thou be in the city and in the field. The Lord will send forth a blessing upon all the works of thy hands." (Deut. xxviii. 6, 3, 8.)

Those who work with their hands, whether in the workshop or in the fields, will experience the truth of the saying: "Without God's aid no progress is made." For let them toil as they may, unless the divine blessing rests upon their labors they will meet with no success. Now there is no better means of obtaining an abundant blessing from God than holy Mass. For in the Mass Christ Himself gives us His divine benediction; in fact St. Bridget was privileged to behold Him, at the moment of the elevation of the sacred host, raising His august right hand to make the sign of the cross upon the prostrate worshippers, while He said: "My blessing be upon all you who believe in Me." Our Lord bestows this benediction upon all who go to Mass, He blesses their work and all they do. If thou dost absent thyself from Mass because of thy work, thou dost lose the blessing of God, and thy work will not profit thee for time or for eternity, as it would if thou soughtest God's blessing to begin and to accomplish it.

Those who neglect Mass ought not, if they are in want, to wonder what is the cause of their impoverished circumstances, for if we give grudgingly to God He will give grudgingly to us. If merely from indifference and carelessness thou dost withhold from Him the worship that is His due, the satisfaction which thou couldst render to Him by hearing Mass, He will withhold from thee thy daily bread, and His blessing will not be upon thy work.

Beware of saying: What use is it to hear Mass? I am none the richer, none the happier, for it; it makes no difference to me whether I have or have not heard Mass. This is the way in which foolish and ungodly persons speak, who have no just idea of what holy Mass really is. Any one who has read this book will have learnt enough of the virtue and excellence of the Mass to make him rejoice in it. Hearing Mass is not only useful for the soul, but for the body as well; the benefit we derive from it is material as well as spiritual. As Fornerus says: "The very food thou dost eat on the day thou hast been to Mass nourishes thee better; thy work succeeds better; any troubles that weigh on thee appear less heavy." Again another pious writer says: "He who begins the day by going to Mass will be attended by better fortune in his work, in his business, in whatever his hand finds to do, or wherever his feet carry him. And when thou hast heard Mass in the morning, if, later in the day, thou shouldst be suddenly overtaken by death, be assured that Christ will be present with thee in thy last moments, as thou wert present with Him at holy Mass." Let words such as these, setting forth the great utility of the holy sacrifice, incite us to assist at it as frequently as possible.

We may go farther, and say, not only does holy Mass not hinder our work: it does more, it furthers it, as experience has often proved. It is related of St. Isidore, a Spanish saint of comparatively humble birth, that he was engaged by a wealthy nobleman of Madrid to cultivate his lands for a fixed annual salary. He fulfilled his duty with exemplary industry, but without discontinuing any of his religious exercises; every morning he heard Mass in more than one church, and spent some hours in prayer. His piety was so pleasing to God that an angel was sent to help him in his work on the farm lest anything should suffer through his absence. However, the owners of the adjoining land, actuated by jealousy, accused him to his employer of neglecting the field-work to hear Mass, to the injury of the crops. The nobleman, greatly enraged at hearing this, went to the farm at once, and rebuked his steward in no measured terms for his dishonest conduct. The saint replied quietly: "I know, sir, that I am your servant, but I have another master, the King of kings, to Whom I also owe obedience. If, however, you think that your interests suffer through my coming late to work, when harvest time comes, you can deduct whatever you think proper from my share of the produce." Pacified by this answer, the proprietor said no more, and left the pious farmer to go to Mass as he pleased. Meanwhile he was desirous to know really how much time was taken from agriculture, so one morning he went very early to his fields, and concealed himself behind a rock. Finding that Isidore did certainly begin to plough at a very late hour, he went towards him, intending to take him severely to task. What was his astonishment when he descried two strangers, with a team of white oxen, ploughing one on each side of his steward. For a while he stood riveted to the spot, contemplating this extraordinary apparition. Then he advanced nearer, stepping over the newly-made furrows, but when he was almost close up to them they vanished out of sight, the unknown husbandmen, the snow-white oxen, and the plough they were driving. Overwhelmed with astonishment, he called out to Isidore: "My good man, for God's sake tell me who those men are who are ploughing this field with you." The saint looked up with a smile, but answered nothing, for indeed he did not know what to say. His master continued: "I am positive that I saw two men at work with you, but as soon as I came near they both disappeared." "I declare before God," Isidore replied, "that I have not seen any one helping me; I have not even asked assistance from any one, except God, Whom I implore every day to come to my aid." Then the proprietor of the estate knew that the laborers he had seen were angels, and congratulated himself on having so saintly a man in his service.

This story forcibly illustrates what has been said above, that hearing Mass is a help, not a hindrance, to our work, for God ordains that, for the service we render Him, we should do our work more easily and succeed better in it. The time we take from our daily avocations to spend in the service of God is not wasted; on the contrary, it is very well employed, and earns for us from God a temporal and an eternal reward. Has He not told us, with His own divine lips: "Seek ye first the kingdom of God and His justice, and all these things shall be added unto you?" (St. Matt. vi. 33.) This is tantamount to saying: Hear Mass in the morning, and thou shalt have an abundant blessing on all thou doest in the day.

CHAPTER XXV.

GREAT MERIT IS GAINED BY OFFERING HOLY MASS IN A RIGHT MANNER.

LET me counsel thee, pious reader, to read the following chapter attentively, and impress well upon thy memory the truths it contains; for they are of great importance, and will, if duly carried out, be of no slight profit to thy soul. Bear in mind that holy Mass is the true and supreme sacrifice of the Christian religion, and that all those who would assist at it aright should join in offering it to the most high God. The Mass is not to the Christian merely a form of prayer, it is an act of worship and a sacrifice; for all who hear Mass offer the divine oblation together with the priest. First of all there is the great high priest, the chief sacrificer, Christ, Who Himself offers every Mass that is said to His heavenly Father. Then there is the officiating priest, who immolates the divine victim. Thirdly, there are the faithful, who, present at the holy sacrifice, have also the power of offering it, and in fact sometimes do so with greater profit than the priest himself. Fourthly, there are those who either pay for the Mass, or provide something necessary for celebrating it, such as the chalice or the vestment. Lastly those too must be included who, unable to assist in person, unite themselves in spirit to the priest, and join with him in his sacrificial act whilst remaining in their own homes. They also, since they participate in a certain measure in offering the holy sacrifice, participate in its fruits, and may, if they so will, assign to others the benefit of those fruits. Ponder well these truths, for they contain valuable instruction and comfort.

One of the greatest graces which are granted to the children of the Church is that the privilege of offering to the Divine Majesty the sacred and sublime sacrifice of the Mass is not the prerogative of priests alone, but belongs to the laity as well, to men, women, and children. This favor was not shown to the Jews; no one but the priest was permitted to offer the holocaust, or to kindle the incense in the temple. Any man presuming to do so would have been guilty of sacrilege. We read in Holy Scripture that when King Ozias desired to burn incense upon the altar of incense the priests withstood him, and said: "It doth not belong to thee, Ozias, to burn incense to the Lord, but to the priests, who are consecrated for this ministry; go out of the sanctuary, do not despise: for this thing shall not be accounted to thy glory by the Lord God." (II. Par. xxvi. 18.) Ozias was very angry at this, and, still holding the censer in his hand, threatened to revenge himself on the priests. And presently the Lord smote him with leprosy in his forehead, which when the priests saw they hastened to thrust him out. The king remained a leper to the day of his death. Such was the terrible chastisement inflicted on him for his presumption in wishing to burn and offer incense to the Lord in the temple.

In the New Testament the case is very different; under this dispensation it is graciously permitted to ordinary people to offer, not incense only, but the precious blood of Christ in the holy Mass. St. Peter lays stress on this prerogative of the Christian in contradistinction to the Jew when he says to believers in general: "You are a chosen generation, a kingly priesthood, a holy nation, a purchased people. Be you also as living stones built up, a holy priesthood, to offer up spiritual sacrifices, acceptable to God by Jesus Christ." (I. Pet. ii. 9, 5.)

In these words the apostle designs to teach us that all the faithful of either sex are members of a spiritual priesthood, and have received from God the power to offer spiritual sacrifices. But when they offer the Mass by the hands of the priest they do more, they offer what is better than a spiritual oblation, namely, a visible one, even the self-same victim Whom the priest holds in his hands. Happy indeed are the laity in being thus privileged, through the divine bounty, to purchase the inestimable treasure of the body and blood of Christ, and with a few words to offer it to God for their own immeasurable profit! Make frequent use, O pious Christian, of this thy glorious prerogative; it is the easiest way of acquiring eternal riches. This sacrificial act is the chief, the most important, part of hearing Mass, for without it thou wilt neither gain much profit to thyself nor give pleasure to God.

"Hearing Mass," says a spiritual writer, "does not merely consist in being present in person when it is celebrated, but in offering it to God conjointly with the priest." Remember this and act upon it if thou desirest to hear Mass well, and with profit to thy soul. "All the faithful are able to offer the holy sacrifice, not, indeed, of themselves, but through the instrumentality of the priest. In order that a layman or any secular person should offer the Mass he must either pay for it, serve it, or at any rate hear it. The faithful who are absent cannot be said, in virtue of being members of the Church, to partake in the oblation unless they cooperate with the priest in one of the ways above mentioned."

All this is undeniably true. It is not enough to be present at Mass in order to share in the fruits of the Mass: we must make a definite offering of it to God in union with the officiating priest. The Mass is a sacrifice, and it appertains to the nature of a sacrifice that it should be offered to the Deity. Therefore those persons who fail to do this, either with their lips or in their heart, do not derive half the benefit from the Mass that others do, although they fulfil the precept of the Church, whilst piously reciting other prayers that have nothing of the character of an offering.

To take an illustration: Suppose some one recites the Rosary several times with devotion, offering it up to God and His blessed Mother, he presents an acceptable gift, which will obtain a rich reward. But if, on the other hand, some other individual were to hear one single Mass, and fervently offer it to Almighty God, which of the two would present the nobler oblation and receive the greater recompense? The latter, undoubtedly; for the Rosary, although a most excellent form of prayer, consisting mainly of petitions sanctioned by God Himself, is at the best an earthly, imperfect oblation. Whereas holy Mass is purely supernatural; the most perfect, the noblest, the most divine oblation, for in it are offered the blood, the wounds, the tears, the death, and the merits of Christ. What other oblation is there as sacred, as perfect, as acceptable to God the Father?

It may, however, be said that whosoever offers the Rosary or other devotions offers something that is his very own, and has cost him some amount of trouble; while he who offers a Mass, or the merits of Christ, presents gifts not his own, but belonging to another, even to Christ, Who suffered for him. On the other hand, however, we may answer, he who offers the holy sacrifice, or the merits Christ earned by that sacrifice, presents no alien gift, but one that is essentially his own, because in the Mass Our Lord's merits are bestowed upon us, and given us for our own. "All that Christ merited by

His passion, His death, the shedding of His blood, we appropriate to ourselves in the unbloody sacrifice of the Mass," says a pious divine. The Church lends her authority to this consoling doctrine when she says: "The fruits of that oblation, of that bloody one, to wit, are received most plentifully through this unbloody one." (Coun. Trent, Sess. xxii. ch. 2.) In this decree the Church distinctly teaches that by hearing Mass the merits of Christ, the fruits of His passion, are freely communicated to and bestowed upon us. Wherefore, since what we receive as a gift is as completely our own as what we earn ourselves, we are able at the time of Mass to present the merits of Christ to God the Father as our own oblation, and thereby give infinite satisfaction to His divine majesty.

Ponder well the immense favor Christ bestows on thee in making thee a mystical priest, and empowering thee to offer the holy sacrifice of the Mass, not for thyself alone, but also for others. Bishop Fornerus tells us: "It is not the priest alone who offers the Mass for himself and for others: every Christian who is present may do the same, for his own needs and those of his friends." This is expressed in the prayer following after the *Sanctus:* "Be mindful, O Lord, of thy servants N. and N.; and of all present, whose faith and devotion are known, for whom we offer, or who offer, up to Thee this sacrifice for themselves, their families and friends." The meaning of these words is too obvious to be mistaken.

Moreover, when the priest says the *Orate fratres*, he turns towards the people and invites them to help him in offering the holy sacrifice: "Brethren, pray that my sacrifice and yours may be acceptable to God the Father Almighty." As if he would say: I am about to perform a work of great importance, to offer an oblation which in my own strength I cannot do; I ask you to pray for me and assist me with your cooperation, for it concerns you nearly, the sacrifice is yours as well as mine, and for this reason you are bound to help me. After the elevation of the chalice he says: "O Lord, we Thy servants, as also Thy holy people, offer unto Thy most excellent majesty, of Thy gifts and grants, a pure host," etc. Here the priest says in so many words that not he alone, but all the holy people of God with him, offer this pure holocaust. If the congregation do not respond to this appeal on the part of the priest either by word or in thought, they defraud him, but they injure themselves far more, for they lose a great merit. "Think, O fools," says Fornerus, "of how great a good you deprive yourselves by going to Mass so seldom, or by neglecting when you do go to offer it up for yourselves and for your friends."

We shall all do well to lay this to heart, for not only those who absent themselves from Mass through indifference, but also those who hear it in a superficial manner, occupying themselves meanwhile with their daily prayers, lose a great deal that they might gain. We can do nothing better during Mass-time than make an act of oblation; the more frequently and the more fervently we do this the more we please God, the more satisfaction we make for our sins, the more reward we lay up in heaven. As often as we make this oblation to God it is as if we said to Him: I pay Thee this price for the remission of the temporal punishment due to my sins, for the purchase of celestial treasures, for the relief of the suffering souls in purgatory.

It is indeed at any time highly profitable for us to say: "My God, I offer Thee Thy beloved Son; I offer Thee His passion and death; I offer Thee His virtues and His merits." But this act has a twofold value when it is uttered during the celebration of holy Mass. For at other times this oblation is only one of the lips and of the heart: during holy Mass the oblation is a real and actual one; for then Christ Himself is present in person with all His merits and virtues. On the altar He is mystically immolated, His passion and death are renewed. In holy Mass His merits are abundantly communicated to us; nay, He gives us Himself that we may present Him to His Father. If these words of oblation, uttered apart from the Mass, are so powerful, as we learn from these words of Christ spoken to a saint: " There is no sinner, however great, who may not hope to obtain forgiveness if he offers to God My undeserved sufferings," what will not the effect be of the actual oblation of His passion in holy Mass when it is renewed upon the altar and participated in by all who are present at the time?

It is said that Our Lord said one day to St. Mechtilde: " Behold, I give thee My charity, My prayers, My bitter sufferings; I make them Mine that thou mayst give them back to Me. To each one who does this I return his gift in twofold measure; and as often as it is presented to me I will restore it thus increased. This is the hundredfold which is promised to men in this world and eternal life hereafter." From this we learn that not to one privileged soul alone does Our Lord communicate His merits in holy Mass, but to all faithful Christians; and we also learn that we may offer Him His own gifts to our own incalculable profit.

THE INFINITE VALUE OF THE VICTIM OFFERED TO GOD IN HOLY MASS.

According to the learned Father Sanchez, there is no part of the Mass which imparts to us greater consolation and spiritual joy than the prayer said by the priest immediately after the elevation of the chalice, when he offers to God the spotless Lamb, Who takes away the sins of the world: "We Thy servants, as also Thy holy people, offer unto Thy most excellent majesty a pure host," etc. He speaks of the people as holy because they are sanctified by the holy sacrifice, conformably to Christ's own words: "For them do I sanctify Myself, that they also may be sanctified in truth." (St. John xvii. 19.) Those who are present are also sanctified by the sprinkling of His precious blood, shed upon them at the time of the elevation of the chalice, as St. Paul says: "That He might sanctify the people by His own blood." (Heb. xiii. 12.)

Observe how impressive are the words wherewith the priest offers the holy sacrifice to God in the name of the congregation: "O Lord, we Thy servants, as also Thy holy people, offer unto Thy most excellent majesty a pure host, a holy host, an immaculate host," etc. It is indeed a precious victim which the priest and all present with him offer unto the Divine Majesty; one in which Almighty God will rejoice and the company of heaven will exult. This pure, holy, immaculate sacrifice is none other than the most pure body, the most holy soul, the immaculate blood of Jesus, Who is slain upon the altar, not by an actual and painful, but by a supernatural and mystical, immolation. The sacred humanity of Christ is the true holocaust, which He in His divine nature offers at the same time as the priest, and each one of the faithful who, with his lips or in his heart, says: "My God, I offer Thee Thy beloved Son, by the hands of the minister, under the form in which He now lies upon the altar."

If it be asked what it is that the priest, and the people with him, offer up when the above-named words are uttered, I reply: They present to God Almighty a gift so precious that it exceeds in value the wide world with all its treasures; so much so that were the whole earth ours to give it would be a gift far inferior to that which we offer to God in the person of His Son. Again be it asked: What is it we present to God when we offer Him the holy Mass? We present to Him a treasure so costly that it outweighs the vast heavens and all their infinite riches. Nor need we stop here; once more be it asked: What do we give to our God when we offer to Him Jesus Christ in the holy sacrifice of the Mass? We offer Him a gift of such unspeakable worth that nothing short of the almighty, infinite Deity and His boundless perfection and majesty can equal it. More cannot be said than this, for in the whole universe nothing exists, nothing can be conceived, greater than God Himself. Now reflect within thyself how priceless a treasure thou dost offer to the Most Holy Trinity in presenting the divinized humanity of Christ for its acceptance. How great is the honor done to God, how great the gratitude (if we may so speak) He owes thee for this precious jewel, will be made more evident by the following comparison.

Suppose the inhabitants of a vast realm were to unite together to have a costly and beautiful goblet fashioned out of the purest gold, exceeding in elegance and skilful workmanship anything that had ever been seen or designed, and were to send this goblet by the hand of a brilliant embassy to their ruler as a token of their loyal and affectionate fidelity, how great would be the gratification of the monarch on receiving this gift from his subjects, and how graciously he would thank them for it. But if they were to set in the gold of the goblet a diamond of such value that the whole wealth of the kingdom could not purchase it, what would not the country expect from its ruler in return for such a present?

Let us apply this to holy Mass. In it we present to the most high God the humanity of Christ, which is so noble, so sacred, that nothing equal to it has ever been, or ever will be, created by the hand of God. Every worshipper present at Mass offers this sacred humanity, this precious and beautiful goblet, if after the consecration he raises his heart to God and says: "My God, I offer Thee Thy beloved Son, here present upon the altar." And with this costly vessel we offer a priceless jewel, comparable only to the Godhead itself, the divinity of Jesus Christ. For it is in the sacred humanity that His divine nature dwells, as St. Paul says: "In Him dwelleth all the fulness of the Godhead corporally." (Col. ii. 9.) The humanity and the divinity of Jesus Christ are both offered to God in holy Mass, for they are inseparably united. When, therefore, thou dost offer to God the costly jewel of Our Lord's divinity, set in the pure gold of His sacred humanity, a gift surpassing in value all that is in heaven and on earth, dost thou not cause infinite gratification to thy heavenly Father? Thou presentest to Him the Son of Whom He said: "This is My beloved Son, in Whom I am well pleased." (St. Matt. iii. 17.) For this thou wilt be richly rewarded, for He Whom thou honorest by this gift cannot be surpassed in liberality and in gratitude. By this means thou wilt cancel many a debt, since what thou givest is infinitely more than what thou owest; and it is not the property of another, it is thy very own, given to thee by Christ, as we have already seen. If Christ is ours, all that He has is ours also; how rich, therefore, we may be made by one single Mass, provided we hear it in the right manner!—richer than anything upon God's earth could make us. Take heed, therefore, to offer God the Son to His heavenly Father frequently in holy Mass; the more often thou dost make this offering the richer wilt thou be.

Make it thy habit always to offer thy oblation by the hands of the priest, saying: "My God, I offer Thee Thy well-beloved Son by the hands of the priest." As much as to say: "My God, I am not worthy to ascend to Thy altar, and take the divine victim in my unconsecrated hands; therefore I do this in spirit; I place my hand in intention under the arm of the priest, and thus join with him in elevating the sacred host and the chalice." It is recorded of Henry I., King of England, that he heard three Masses every day, kneeling on the altar steps. When the officiating priest elevated the sacred elements, he loved to place his hand under the priest's arm, assisting him in the action. Thou canst not do the same except in intention; but God, Who reads the heart, will accept the will for the deed.

The precious blood of Christ must be offered to God as well as the sacred host; this is a meritorious work, about which too much cannot be said. We read in the life of St. Magdalen of Pazzi that she was supernaturally taught that the oblation of Christ's blood was most efficacious in turning away the divine anger, provoked by the transgressions of mankind. In fact, God complained to her of the little done by man to appease His wrath, and exhorted her to do her utmost with this aim. She therefore was accustomed many times—no less than fifty times a day—to offer the sacred blood of Christ for the living and the dead. And repeatedly it was granted her to see souls whom she had been instrumental in converting, or of releasing from purgatory, by this oblation of the precious blood.

She used also to say that it was much to be feared that the impenitence of sinners is to be attributed to our apathy. For if we were more zealous in offering the blood of Christ to God on their behalf, He would doubtless, moved by our prayers, have preserved them from eternal reprobation; and she admonished all Christians constantly to make this oblation of Our Lord's passion and His precious blood for the erring and the sinful. Let us remember this, for it places within our reach an easy means of appeasing the wrath of God, of converting sinners, relieving the suffering souls, expiating our own wrong-doing. At no time, as we have already said, can this oblation of the precious blood be made so opportunely, so effectually, as during the celebration of holy Mass. It is then offered not only by word, but in deed, for the sacred blood is truly and actually there in the chalice and is offered up by the priest not only in his own name, but in that of the whole Church, and more especially of those who are present. Each one, therefore, who says: "O Lord, I offer Thee this sacred blood by the hands of the priest," offers that which the priest elevates in the chalice, and merits far more than if he uttered the same words at some other time.

St. Magdalen of Pazzi also speaks of the incalculable value of such an oblation. "When the Christian," she says, "offers this precious blood to God the Father, he offers a gift beyond all recompense. It is a gift of such infinite worth that by it the Creator is laid under an obligation to His creature." This sounds like an exaggeration, but it is not so, for what is there in heaven or on earth to compare with the precious blood of Christ? One single drop is worth more than oceans of the blood of martyrs. St. Thomas of Aquin tells us that one single drop would have been enough to redeem the whole world. Hence it follows that if, for this oblation, God were to grant thee the remission of thy sins, it would be no adequate recompense, since by one drop the guilt of all the sinners on earth can be cleansed away, and even if for the sake of it He were to give thee heaven itself, this would still be no equivalent, since this sacred blood is able to purchase the eternal salvation of all mankind. Thus God would remain thy debtor.

If thou hadst been present upon Mount Calvary, and hadst caught some drops of the blood that flowed from the Saviour's wounds, and offered them to God the Father with steadfast faith, fervent love, and heartfelt contrition, wouldst thou not have felt confident that thy sins would be forgiven, and the penalty due to them remitted? Well, that which took place on Calvary is enacted mystically in holy Mass; Christ exhibits Himself to His Father as He hung upon the cross, and the blood from His sacred wounds flows into the chalice. Do thou in spirit take this same blood in thy hand, and present it to God with the like fervor as thou wouldst have done on Calvary, and be assured thou wilt gain nothing less than thou wouldst then have gained. For what sin is so heinous that it cannot be forgiven, what stain so dark that it cannot be purged away, what debt so heavy but it cannot be remitted, for the sake and by the power of that precious blood? It is more than sufficient to blot out, to expiate, to cancel the iniquities, the debts of all mankind. Put thy trust, therefore, in this sacred blood, and offer it to thy God in holy Mass with all the fervor of thy heart. Call the holy angels to thy aid, and implore them to offer it on thy behalf before the throne of God, and obtain for thee the remission of thy sins.

CHAPTER XXVI.

SOME PRACTICAL HINTS CONCERNING THE WAY OF HEARING SEVERAL MASSES AT ONE AND THE SAME TIME.

MANY persons are of opinion that nothing more is gained by hearing two or more Masses at one and the same time than if one alone is heard. In this they are much mistaken, as I will now proceed to show. I do not intend to say that if one has promised to hear two or more Masses for some definite intention, or if they have been enjoined on one as a penance, more than one can be heard at once; what I do say is that two or more Masses, heard of one's own free will, may be heard simultaneously with as much profit and advantage as if they were heard consecutively.

It may here be well to recall what was said in the twenty-second chapter, that every priest is bound to pray in the Mass for all who are present, and to offer the holy sacrifice for them. If only one priest stands at the altar, he alone prays for thee; whereas if there are other priests celebrating Mass at the different altars, they also pray for thee, and thus thou hast the benefit of more prayers than if thou heardst but one Mass.

Moreover, in the same twenty-second chapter it was said that the holy angels, who are always present at Mass, pray earnestly for the congregation. The more Masses that are said the greater the number of angels who are present, and consequently the greater number of intercessors who pray for thee.

Furthermore, it was stated that Christ, as the great high priest, intercedes in every Mass that is celebrated for His Church, and especially for all who assist at the Mass, for each of whom He offers the sacrifice of Himself. Yes, He makes Himself the advocate of each one individually. He lays the needs of each one in particular before God, and for each one He offers His sacred body and blood. As He suffered for all mankind in general, so He suffered for each individual; as St. Paul says: "The Son of God loved me and delivered Himself for me." (Gal. ii. 20.) Every Christian may take upon his lips these words of the Apostle: each one is warranted in saying that Christ died as much for him alone as for the whole human race. As it was in the sacrifice of the cross, so it is in the sacrifice of the altar, wherein Christ intercedes for all in general and for each one in particular.

Wherefore, if thou dost assist at one Mass, in that Mass Christ certainly pleads for thee. If, however, two or more are said at one and the same time, in each of these He pleads for thee, He grants thee a share in His merits, He nourishes thee spiritually with His sacred body and blood, He bestows on thee a greater degree of grace here and of glory hereafter, He gives thee His heavenly benediction. In all these and other spiritual favors thou art made partaker in every Mass thou hearest, if thou art in a state of grace; and the more Masses thou hearest the more those favors are multiplied. Consequently it is most advantageous to thee to hear several at once, and thou shouldst rejoice whenever it is within thy power to do so.

The reader may now ask what it behooves him to do in order to participate in many Masses at the same time. Let him observe that it does not suffice to be present while several Masses are being said unless he unites his intention to each one; that is to say, he must adore Christ on each altar, and offer Him to God the Father with the desire to hear each Mass severally. When, therefore, thou seest the priest go up to the altar, say in thy heart: "I will hear this Mass and offer it as an oblation to God"; and repeat this whenever another Mass is begun. And if, when thou enterest the church, several Masses are going on, make a general intention to assist at them all.

At the commencement of the Mass one's daily prayers, the Rosary, or confraternity prayers may be said up to the time of the consecration. Then it is well to leave those orisons, and make an act of faith in the presence of Christ upon the altar, to adore Him in all humility when the priest genuflects, to implore His mercy at the elevation, and during the consecration of the chalice devoutly offer to God the sacrifice of His Son. The same may be done at the elevation of the chalice. After that we may proceed with our private devotions till another priest comes to the consecration; they should then be again broken off, to give place to acts of adoration and oblation. This should be done whenever the sacred elements are consecrated and elevated at any of the altars; for our bounden duty requires that we should adore our God present on the altar, and our own interest demands that we should offer to God the Father this precious gift, for which a rich recompense awaits us.

It may perhaps be urged that if we are in the church while several Masses are being said, and we stop our ordinary prayers whenever we hear the bell ring for the consecration, we shall never get them done. I answer that nothing will be lost by this if meanwhile we hear several Masses; on the contrary, we shall be the gainers, as will be seen from the following parable: A vine-dresser who was digging up his vineyard found to his surprise a treasure hidden in the ground. He carried it home without saying a word about it; then he returned to his work. Presently he discovered another, and, once more laying down his spade, he carried it to his house. Again he went back, and resumed his labor; and again, before he had been at work many minutes, he found some more coins. Away he went at once to his house, highly elated, eager to acquaint his wife with his good fortune. But she said: "I do not see any cause for rejoicing, for if you go on in this way our vineyard will never be dug, and we shall have no grapes next season." "On the contrary," her husband replied, "would to God I could find nothing but these treasures; then I should not trouble myself about the vineyard any more, for they would bring me in ten times more than my vineyard at its best." Whoso considers this parable will be convinced that by repeatedly offering Our Lord at the consecration we shall profit incomparably more than by reciting our ordinary prayers, and that it is better to omit them rather than the oblation of one single Mass, if we have not time for both.

Furthermore, let it be observed that if, on entering the church, we find that the priest has already got to the *Pater noster*, or the *Agnus Dei*, or perhaps to the communion, it is well to kneel down at once and say the prayers thou dost usually say at the consecration, until the priest takes the ablutions, for thus thou shalt to a great extent share in the fruits of the Mass. And if two priests should reach the consecration at the same time, recite thy accustomed prayer with the intention of adoring Christ present on both altars at the same moment. And if thou art where thou canst not see the priest, thou canst hear his Mass equally well, provided thou dost notice when the bell is rung for the consecration, and dost make an act of adoration and of oblation. And even if thou canst not hear the bell, it is yet possible to participate in the Mass, if it be thy intention to hear all the Masses that are said at the time. Furthermore, if, when about to leave the church, thou shouldst notice that one of the priests has just got to the consecration, wait until after the elevation, in order to worship the sacred body and blood of Christ, and offer them to God the Father. Thus thou wilt gain a spiritual treasure, which, unless thou shouldst die in mortal sin, will be thine to enjoy to all eternity.

In illustration of this subject a story shall be given from the legend of St. Elizabeth, Queen of Portugal. This royal lady had a favorite page, whose father had, when dying, enjoined upon him these two things: to hear Mass daily, and serve the king faithfully. The youth had observed his father's precepts, and endeared himself to the queen by his piety, so that she often gave him wise counsel, and sent him to distribute alms to the poor of Lisbon. The manner in which she preferred him to the other pages attached to the court, whose dissolute manners she abhorred, awoke their jealousy, and led them to slander him to the king most shamefully. The king believed these calumnies, and thought of a plan for getting rid of the young man secretly. One day he rode out to a chalk-pit at a little distance from the town, and calling to the chalk-burner, told him that if, early the next morning, some one came to him, and asked him if he had fulfilled the king's behest, he was immediately to throw him into the flaming kiln. "And if," the king added, "you dare to disobey, I will have you cast into the fire instead of him." The chalk-burner promised to comply with the orders given him, and his royal visitor departed. The next morning, at a very early hour, the king summoned the page in question to his presence, and bade him go with all speed to the chalk-kiln outside the city gates, and ask whether the orders given by the king on the preceding day had been executed. On receiving the answer he was to return to the palace without delay. The page hastened on his way, regretting sorely, as he passed out of the gates, that he had not, as was his habit, heard Mass that day, for he feared that he would not have the opportunity of doing so. However, his road led him past several churches, each of which he entered, and thus heard portions at least of several Masses. Meanwhile the king was anxious to learn whether his messenger had met with the fate decreed for him. In order to ascertain this he despatched one of the other pages, a godless young fellow, to ask the chalk-burner whether his commands had been carried out. Guessing what this errand signified, and exulting over it, the young scoundrel sped along so quickly that he reached the kiln before his pious comrade. Breathlessly he inquired of the chalk-burner whether the king's bidding was done. "Not yet," the man replied, "but I will do it now." So saying he seized the unhappy youth, bound him hand and foot, and, in spite of his struggles and expostulations, cast him into the kiln. Scarcely was the furnace-door closed when the other page arrived, and put the same question to the man. "If you had come ten minutes sooner," was the reply, "you would have seen your comrade in the flames, although he protested all along that you were the one for whom this fate was destined." The young man was horrified at hearing this, for he had not the slightest idea what he had done wrong. When he returned to the palace, his royal master, astonished at his reappearance, asked him if he had not been to the chalk-kiln. The page fell at his feet, and told him all that had occurred. The king, convinced of his innocence, went with him to the queen, who explained that the reason why she had admitted the young man to her private apartments was in order that she might commission him to distribute her alms in secret.

Imitate this pious youth in his desire to assist at the holy sacrifice, and pay due homage to the Saviour. We will now proceed to show how it is possible to hear, not one or two, but all the Masses that are being said all over Christendom while we are hearing one Mass, and derive profit from them all.

It is alleged by some that the mere desire to benefit by all the Masses that are said or will be said is sufficient to make us participate in them. Others, on the contrary, say that, although this intention is commendable and even meritorious, we cannot share in the fruits of a Mass unless we in some way share in the act. This latter opinion appears to be the correct one; for if it were possible to participate in all Masses merely by means of a pious intention, it would be quite superfluous to go to Mass except on days of obligation: we could enjoy the benefit of them in our own homes.

However, it is certain that if any one, whilst assisting at Mass, fervently desires that it were possible for him to hear all the Masses celebrated at that time, if he begs to have a share in them, adores Christ present at once on so many altars, and offers the sacred victim to God the Father, he will infallibly be permitted to participate in their fruits. For in so far as he can he joins in offering each and all, and would only too gladly do more if it lay within his power. Can it be doubted that God, Who accepts the good will for the deed when the latter is out of a man's reach, will reward him as he desires?

If this really is so, how great is the recompense of one who hears holy Mass in this manner! For whilst assisting at one Mass he assists in spirit at all the Masses that are being offered at that time throughout the whole world. How great are the riches to be thus gained! It is said that no less than 50,000 Masses are said simultaneously in one hour, and in every one of these we may obtain a share if we offer them in union with the one we are hearing.

It may prove a consolation to religious who have not the opportunity of hearing more than one Mass, as well as to persons living in the world who are prevented by their daily avocations or other circumstances from spending much time in the church, to know whilst hearing one Mass they may share in many thousands at which they cannot be present. Nay, more; those who find themselves altogether precluded from attendance at Mass may, if they devoutly read the prayers for Mass at home, and in spirit follow all that are being offered at that hour, adoring Christ immolated on so many altars, profit much by those Masses though they cannot actually assist at them. For in intention they unite with the priests in offering them, and in the prayers the priest says for the people they are included. May the remembrance of this afford solace to many sick persons, and prisoners, and others who are not in a position to hear Mass.

" Count thyself happy," says a pious writer, " when a priest promises thee a memento in his daily Mass. In fact, thou wouldst do well to ask this of every priest, for thus thou wouldst have many to offer for thee the holy sacrifice and unlock for thee the treasury of the merits of Christ. If thou dost earnestly desire to hear Mass, and yet art prevented, God accepts the will for the deed. And if thou wishest that thou couldst hear a Mass in Jerusalem or at Loreto, thou canst do this by assisting at one in spirit, and in intention drawing the waters of grace from that fountain. It may even be that by this means thou wilt obtain more grace than those who, though present in person in the holy place, do not raise their hearts to God. It is true Christ bestows His grace liberally on all who are present, but He gives a twofold measure to those who, absent through obedience, are present in spirit."

CHAPTER XXVII.

AN EXHORTATION TO HEAR HOLY MASS DAILY.

WE may venture to hope that an attentive perusal of this book and careful consideration of the truths it contains will have awakened in the breast of the reader a fervent love for holy Mass, so that no further arguments will be needed to induce him to hear it daily.

A few admonitions may, however, yet be added to kindle his zeal to a still hotter flame.

In the first place, let me tell thee, O Christian, that no hour of the whole day is so precious as that wherein thou dost hear Mass, and offer that Mass to the ever-blessed Trinity. It is indeed a golden hour, for all that thou dost in cooperation with the holy sacrifice is changed to gold. The other hours of the day, in comparison with it, may be likened to copper. It may be alleged that work is of greater importance than hearing Mass to those who earn their bread. To this I reply: Hearing Mass is more important than our work, because it contributes largely to our eternal welfare. I do not say that a man should neglect his work altogether, but that he should spare half an hour from it for the service of his God: his work will get on all the better for it, for God will bless it more abundantly. Those who absent themselves from Mass out of indifference or for the sake of some temporal advantage change the hour that might be golden into one of lead, and sustain a loss incalculably greater than any earthly loss, for in that hour they might have won a hundred times more than they could earn by a whole day's labor. Our Saviour teaches us this in those memorable words of His: "What doth it profit a man if he gain the whole world and suffer the loss of his own soul?" (St. Matt. xvi. 26.) By not going to Mass on week-days for the sake of temporal profit we do our soul an immeasurable injury for which no worldly wealth can compensate. Shall we, then, heedless of Our Lord's warning, throw away eternal riches for the things of time and sense?

If those who, being dependent on their own exertions, are accustomed to absent themselves from Mass on account of some paltry gain, or an employment that ill repays their toil, would carefully consider these truths, they would surely alter their conduct, and spare a short time from their work just to hear Mass. How very little can be earned by the labor of one's hands in one brief half hour? How short-sighted, then, is the man or woman who prefers to lose the treasures contained in holy Mass rather than deprive himself or herself of a few halfpence! By going to Mass they might earn treasures wherewith to purchase heaven; but they will renounce these if the least diminution of their wages is involved— not that I believe they would be the losers in the end, for God, of His divine bounty, would so prosper their work as to more than make up for the time they took from it.

To this another reason may be added to show the folly of these people. If money dropped down from the clouds, would not every one hasten out to pick it up? Those who stayed indoors and went on with their work would be the derision of their neighbors. Yet, of a truth, in every Mass, not earthly riches from the clouds, but celestial riches from heaven, are showered down on all who are present, and all are free to possess themselves of them. But what are the riches which drop down from above? An increase of divine grace; an increase of merit and virtue; an increase of eternal glory; celestial consolations; the divine blessing in temporal affairs; the pardon of venial sins; the remission of a great part of the debt due to divine justice; a share in the infinite merits of Christ. Grace and mercy, temporal welfare, and eternal salvation—such is the heavenly dew which distils from above. Are not these things more precious than refined gold? Wherefore, if, on account of the slight trouble it costs us, or the trifling pecuniary sacrifice it entails, we omit going to Mass on week-days when we might do so, we are guilty of greater folly than those who would stay indoors at their work if gold were rained down from the clouds.

Clingius says: "Holy Mass, as the central act of religion, takes precedence of all other devotions; if it be neglected, the fount of interior piety will run dry." Just as the sun surpasses all the planets, so the Mass surpasses all other forms of worship.

The light, the heat, the power of the sun are incomparably more useful to the earth than those of all the planets together. In like manner devout attendance at Mass is more pleasing to God, more profitable to thyself, more salutary for the living, more helpful to the dead, than all thy prayers and good works for the whole day. By these, it cannot be denied, thou dost indeed serve and please God; thou dost rejoice the angels and gain much merit for thyself; but by hearing Mass how much greater is the honor thou givest to God, the joy thou causest to the angels, the reward to which thou art entitled! And all this with far less trouble to thyself.

Supposing a man at work in the fields should find a treasure, and immediately leave off work, doing no more for the remainder of the day, would he not in the evening be a much richer man than his fellow-laborer who, though he toiled industriously all day long, only received his accustomed wages? Assuredly he would. So it is with thy good works; however piously they are performed they will not, comparatively speaking, be of great merit. Whereas, if thou hearest Mass, thou findest a treasure, nothing less than Christ's merits, which are communicated to us in holy Mass, and in which we receive more than our thoughts can compass. Holy Mass is a gold mine; those who work it earn far more than if they labored in a stone-quarry; and in like manner those who hear Mass piously derive from it very much more spiritual wealth than others do from the performance of works of penance. The Church recognizes the Mass as the greatest of good works when she says: "We must needs confess that no other work can be performed by the faithful so holy and divine as this tremendous mystery." (Counc. Trent, Sess. xxii.) Since holy Mass is the most holy and divine, it must needs be the most meritorious and profitable, means of obtaining heavenly riches. Let every one beware how he allows himself to be prevented from going daily to Mass, for where would the man be found who would stay away if he could earn eight or ten pounds by going? And what are ten pounds in comparison to the spiritual treasures which are the reward of those who hear Mass devoutly? Compared with the holy sacrifice of the Mass, earthly gold is but a handful of sand!

We therefore earnestly and humbly entreat the reader to be regular in going to Mass every day, in so far as this is possible. Let us not forget that we are created to serve God to the best of our ability, and by our service to glorify Him. We cannot do this better than by hearing Mass, which is the highest act of worship, the one whereby He is most honored. We are bound to render to our God the thanks that are His due for all the benefits He has conferred on us, both bodily and spiritually. This cannot be done better than by hearing Mass, for it is the noblest of all thank-offerings.

The object and end of our existence upon earth is to praise the Divine Majesty according to His great glory. This cannot be done better than by hearing Mass, for it is the most sublime sacrifice of praise. Our Lord has said: "Every tree that bringeth not forth good fruit shall be cut down, and shall be cast into the fire." (St. Matt. vii. 19.) We cannot bear fruit better than by hearing Mass in a state of grace, for it is the most perfect sacrifice of satisfaction. We daily stand exposed to the danger of falling into sin, of being overtaken by misfortune; we cannot guard against these perils better than by hearing Mass, for it is the most efficacious propitiatory sacrifice. Death and the devil constantly dog our footsteps and lay in wait for us, desirous to snatch us away and precipitate us into hell; we cannot shield ourselves against their arrows better than by hearing Mass, for it is the surest protection against the evils that threaten us. Finally, let us not forget that in the hour of death we shall be in some need of the Saviour's assistance; there is no better means of assuring ourselves of this than by hearing Mass devoutly, for have we not heard how Christ Himself gave to one of His servants the promise that he would send for his solace and support at his last moments as many blessed spirits as he had heard Masses with devotion during his lifetime? Reflect upon these truths, and resolve from henceforth to hear Mass, if possible, every day.

If it should be out of thy power to do this, have a Mass said for thy intention occasionally, in order thus to make amends for thine own shortcomings in God's service, and to cancel the punishment due to thy daily transgressions. If, perchance, thou lackest the means of doing this, give an alms, according to thy power, to some poor man, and let him hear Mass for thee. This he will do most readily, and make over to thee the amount of satisfaction for sins committed which he earns by hearing Mass. In this manner he obtains a special grace for thee from God, for thy welfare in time and in eternity.

If it be asked whether one can really hear Mass on behalf of another person, I answer: Most undoubtedly; and to do so is very preferable to going to communion for some one else. Holy communion is essentially a sacrament, and the food of our souls. It is impossible to benefit another by partaking of food in his stead, and it is certain that we cannot receive a sacrament for another, nor can we transfer to another the nourishment, the grace, our soul receives in holy communion. Is there nothing, then, that we can give to any one by going to communion for him? Yes; all good works discharge a part of the temporal penalty due to sin, and holy communion, being a most sacred and excellent act, has considerable power to do so. We are free to renounce this benefit for ourselves, and to bestow it upon, assign it to, another person. Besides, as after holy communion we are presumably in the grace of God, our prayers on behalf of another will be more fervent and more efficacious.

It is otherwise in regard to hearing Mass, for it is especially instituted for the benefit of many, not of one alone. We have seen that the priest, in the canon of the Mass, prays thus: "Be mindful, O Lord, of Thy servants N. and N., and of all here present, for whom we offer, or who offer, up to Thee this sacrifice of praise for themselves, their families, and their friends." These words clearly indicate that all who assist at holy Mass offer it for themselves and for those who are related to them, and obtain great graces for them in virtue of that sublime sacrifice. In addition to this each one is empowered, and indeed ought, to give to the individual for whom he hears Mass the share in the merits and satisfaction of Christ to which devout attendance at Mass entitles him.

THE EXAMPLE OF THE SAINTS IS AN INCENTIVE TO US TO HEAR MASS DAILY.

The proverb says: "Example is more powerful than precept." If all the arguments hitherto urged have not had the effect of inducing the reader to make a practice of assisting at Mass every day, the example, which shall now be brought forward, of saints who, although their time was engrossed with weighty affairs, never failed to do so may perhaps have some influence.

The ecclesiastical historian Baronius tells us that in the early ages of Christianity priests were at liberty to say as many Masses every day as they chose. The holy Pope Leo III. had recourse to the holy sacrifice in all his necessities, and was known, in times of affliction, to celebrate no less than nine Masses in one day, with great fervor and recollection.

The saintly Bishop Ulrich was accustomed to say three Masses every day, unless prevented by sickness or stress of business. Since 1073 the practice of saying more Masses than one has been abolished, Christmas Day alone being excepted.

St. Hedwige of Poland is said to have had a profound veneration for holy Mass. She always assisted at as many as she could; and if enough were not celebrated in the chapel attached to the palace to satisfy her devotion, she sent for other priests, recompensing them liberally for their trouble. Raynaldus records of St. Louis of France that he was in the habit of hearing two, three, sometimes even four Masses daily. His courtiers murmured at this, saying it was not right for the king to spend all the morning at prayer in the chapel instead of attending to state affairs and leaving Mass to the clergy. The king, hearing what they said, answered: "I wonder that you should complain of my hearing Mass, for not one of you would think me to blame if I spent twice as much time in hunting or playing dice." This was a very good answer, and it applies to many amongst ourselves as well as to the officials of King Louis' court. For in our blindness we imagine that it is a waste of time and loss of money to go to Mass on week-days. But if two or three hours are spent in idle conversation, at play, over our wine, or perhaps in sleep, we think that the time thus squandered has been most profitably employed. What an unfortunate delusion!

The same historian tells us that Henry I. of England was also accustomed to hear three Masses every day, even when engrossed with urgent affairs of state. It is said that once, when he was talking with the King of France, the conversation turned upon hearing Mass; and the French king remarked that one ought not always to go to Mass, but to hear sermons as well. Henry I. courteously replied: "It is a greater pleasure to me to see my friend frequently than to hear others speak in his praise." With this opinion I who write this book fully coincide; in fact, I have often told people who asked me whether it was better to go to Mass or to hear sermons that to assist at Mass was by far the best. One ought not, however, to eschew sermons altogether, for they are very useful, and even necessary, especially in the case of hardened sinners, to awaken in them a sense and an abhorrence of sin.

The Blessed Anthony of Stroncone delighted in hearing Mass above any other spiritual exercise. He assisted at the holy sacrifice, and served the Mass with such fervor and joy of heart that he forgot all about his meals. If Mass could have been celebrated all day long from early morn until night closed in, he would always have been present, without ever leaving the church. When he grew old, and his enfeebled limbs could hardly support him, he would still totter to the church in order to hear Mass, and this he did even when the hand of death was already upon him, for he rose from his bed to fill his accustomed place near the altar. Let us take example from this Franciscan brother, who was beatified in the year 1690, and be more zealous than ever in our attendance at holy Mass.

We read in Baronius that the Roman Emperor Lothaire used to hear three Masses every day, even when he had to take the field against the enemy. Surius tells us that Charles V. invariably heard Mass every morning; only once in his whole life did he omit to do so, in the campaign he made against Tunis. In the Roman breviary it is stated of St. Casimir that he was so carried out of himself during the time of Mass that he was thought to be in an ecstasy.

The legend of St. Wenceslas tells us that when the Emperor Otho summoned all the princes and nobles of the realm to attend an imperial diet at Regensburg at a very early hour, Wenceslas, instead of betaking himself to the house of Assembly, went to Mass, and did not leave until the priest quitted the altar. Meanwhile the emperor and the princes were waiting for him impatiently; at length, finding he did not come, the emperor said: "We will open the diet without Wenceslas; and when he comes let no one rise up or make room for him." Presently Wenceslas made his appearance, and the astonished monarch saw that he was accompanied by two angels. Rising from his throne, he hastened to meet him, and clasped him in his arms. The princes were angry when they saw the emperor receive Wenceslas in so very different a manner to that in which he had ordered them to receive him, but he answered their expostulations by telling them what he had seen, and that he felt compelled to show honor to one thus favored. In fact, he took the regal diadem from his own head, and then and there crowned Wenceslas first King of Bohemia.

When we hear of all these kings and potentates who, although they were burdened with all the business that in those days belonged to the ruler of a kingdom, made it their practice always to hear one, if not more than one, Mass every day, how shall we excuse ourselves before God for neglecting to assist at the holy sacrifice on account of our less weighty, often trivial, occupations? It is greatly to be feared that at the Last Judgment this awful sentence will be ours: "The unprofitable servant cast ye out into the exterior darkness. There shall be weeping and gnashing of teeth." (St. Matt. xxv. 30.)

But it may be asked: How could God condemn me for not hearing Mass, when there is no express command to hear it on week-days? I reply: He will not condemn thee for neglecting to hear Mass on days that are not of obligation, but because thou hast been slothful in His service, and not made use of the talent confided to thee, of His grace, that is, which would be communicated to thee in holy Mass.

Nor, when we neglect Mass, ought the loss to ourselves alone to be considered, but the loss to God and to the blessed in heaven. The injury done to them is thus expressed by the Venerable Bede: "If a priest, without committing mortal sin, neglects to celebrate Mass, he deprives the Most Holy Trinity of the honor which is Its due, he deprives the angels of a source of joy, the sinner of forgiveness, the just of assistance, the departed of relief, the whole Church of spiritual benefit, and himself of a salutary medicine. See how much harm results from the indifference of one priest; the loss occasioned is almost as great if a layman fails to assist at the divine mysteries when it is in his power to do so."

Many instances might be given in which neglect of Mass has met with condign punishment, but one incident must suffice. In the year 1570 in the depth of winter three merchants journeyed together from Eugubo to Cisterno for the annual fair. Trade was good; they made a great deal of money. At the close of the fair (it was a Saturday night) one of them said to the others before retiring to rest, for all three had taken up their quarters at the same inn: "We must start to-morrow morning long before daybreak in order to reach home before nightfall." One of his companions acceded to the proposal; the third negatived it, saying that as it would be Sunday they had much better hear Mass before setting out, and then go on their way with the blessing of God. But the others would not be persuaded; so he let them begin their journey without him. As soon as he had been to Mass, and taken a hasty breakfast, he mounted his horse and rode quickly after them. Now, when the two merchants had got about two miles on their way, they came to a wooden bridge which spanned a wide river. Just as they were crossing it the stream, much increased in volume by recent rains, carried away the supports of the bridge, and they were both precipitated into the water. The two horses swam to shore, but their riders, weighted by the bags of gold which they carried on their person, perished miserably. God grant that they did not lose their souls as well as their lives and their money. About an hour later the third merchant reached the spot, and was informed by the inhabitants of the fatality that had occurred. He was shocked to see the bodies of his two friends, which had been recovered by the peasantry, laid out on the bank of the river. It was impossible not to recognize in this event the just judgment of God, and he gave hearty thanks to Providence for having preserved him from a watery grave for the sake of the holy sacrifice at which he had assisted. He arrived in safety at home, and it was his painful duty to acquaint the families of the two other merchants with the sad tidings he brought. The terrible fate that overtook these men ought to be a useful lesson to us never to miss Mass on Sundays or holydays on account of any worldly advantage. Many men of business do this without the least scruple, but they are none the less guilty of mortal sin, since it is not permissible to allow ourselves to be deterred from hearing our Mass of obligation because of any temporal loss or inconvenience.

Children whose parents keep them from Mass on holydays without absolute necessity should imitate St. Genevieve, the patron saint of Paris. When quite a child, as she was in the act of going to church on a holyday of obligation, her mother ordered her to remain at home to take care of the house. She answered: "Mother, I cannot miss Mass with a clear conscience; I would rather displease you than offend against God." The woman, irritated by this speech, struck her daughter a hard blow on the cheek, and scolded her harshly for her undutiful conduct. Her punishment was not long delayed; the mother was struck with total blindness, and thus she remained for two years, until she acknowledged how wrong she had been, and in answer to Genevieve's constant prayers her sight was restored to her. Thus children who are kept from going to Mass when it is of precept should respectfully represent to their parents that they are bound to obey God rather than man.

It is the duty of masters and mistresses to exhort the members of their household to perform their religious duties and do what is right. If they neglect this, they are more to blame than they perhaps imagine, for St. Paul says: "If any man have not care of his own, and especially of those of his house, he hath denied the faith, and is worse than an infidel." (1. Tim. v. 8.) These words are forcible and may well alarm us, for St. Chrysostom expounds the word "care" as having reference to the spiritual, not the physical welfare of their dependents. And if the head of a household who neglects to provide his children and domestics with the food and clothing necessary for their bodies is to be counted as a heathen or unbeliever, how much more will he deserve to be regarded by Almighty God as one who denies the faith and worse than an infidel, if he is utterly indifferent to their spiritual needs.

CHAPTER XXVIII.

AN EXHORTATION TO HEAR MASS DEVOUTLY.

IT is greatly to be deplored that Christian people have so little devotion for holy Mass, and assist at it with indifference and carelessness. For the most part such persons are so distracted that they look at every one who comes in or goes out, they pray with the lips only, and even after the consecration are too idle to remain on their knees, as if they really did not believe in the holy sacrifice. Observing the conduct of these professing Christians, one cannot but feel grieved that miserable mortals should not show more respect to the Lord their God, Who works such wonders in their sight upon the altar.

The Church teaches us with what reverence we ought to assist at holy Mass, in the words which have already been quoted: "If we must needs confess that no other work can be performed by the faithful so holy and divine as this tremendous mystery, . . . it is also sufficiently clear that all industry and diligence is to be applied to this end, that it be performed with the greatest possible inward cleanness and purity of heart, and outward show of devotion and piety." (Counc. Trent, Sess. xxii. Decree concerning the celebration of Mass.) It is not necessary to have any sensible devotion, it is enough if one has a fervent desire to assist at this sacred oblation with due attention and profound reverence.

Let not the reader be over-anxious and troubled if he fail to experience the fervor and recollection he would fain have when present at holy Mass, but let him persevere in prayer, deeming himself unworthy of the grace of devotion. It is quite different if one has no devotion or even the wish for it, for in that case one loses a great deal and deprives one's self of the merit and consolation that might be his.

It is said that one day while St. Mechtilde was hearing Mass, she beheld Christ seated upon a lofty throne of crystal, from the base of which two streams of clear and sparkling water gushed forth. While she wondered within herself what these two rivulets could signify, it was revealed to her that one represented the forgiveness of sin, the other consolation and sensible devotion: graces communicated in a special manner through the virtue of Christ's bodily presence to all who were present at holy Mass, and obtained with far greater facility at that time than at any other. Consider well these words which indicate to us the privileges accruing to us in consequence of Our Lord's presence on our altars. St. Mechtilde proceeds to relate how, at the moment of the elevation of the host, she saw Christ rise up from the crystal throne and hold His sacred Heart aloft with both hands. This Heart was transparent, and appeared full of healing balm, which overflowed all around, without, however, suffering any diminution. The hearts of all the people who were present hovered below: some filled with oil and balm burnt brightly; others were empty and were kindled by no flame. The saint was told that the hearts that burnt thus brightly belonged to those who heard Mass gladly and piously; the others were the hearts of those who were cold and indifferent.

What, then, are we to do if sometimes we feel no devotion at holy Mass, and cannot awaken any within our hearts? We must follow the counsel Our Lord gave to St. Gertrude, concerning whom we read in her revelations that once when, despite all her efforts, she could not help frequent distractions arising from human frailty whilst in choir, she said to herself: What possible use can these indevout prayers be? It would be wiser not to say them at all. She was about to leave the choir, but at that moment Christ appeared to her, holding His Heart in both hands. "See," He said to her, "I place My loving Heart before thine eyes, that thou mayst commission it to accomplish all that thou canst not of thyself perform; then nothing will be wanting to it in My sight." At this the saint was much amazed; she thought it would he derogatory to the sacred Heart to supply her deficiencies. But Our Lord said to her: "If thou hadst a beautiful voice, and delightedst in singing, wouldst thou not be displeased if one whose voice was poor and weak would not allow thee to take her part? So My Heart earnestly desires that thou wouldst, by sign if not by word, make Me thy substitute, to do perfectly what thou canst do but imperfectly." What a happy and comforting doctrine is this! It is indeed an easy method of filling up what is lacking to our devotion. Wherefore, if we are distracted at Mass and feel but little devotion, we will say to Our Lord: O sweet Jesus, I grieve from the bottom of my heart that I am so distracted at my prayers; I beseech Thy sacred Heart to supply what is wanting to them.

In order to hear holy Mass devoutly, observe the following rules: When preparing to go to Mass, bethink thyself where thou art going, and what thou art about to do. Thou art not going up to the temple to pray like the Pharisee and the Publican, but with David, to offer sacrifices, as he says in the fifty-third Psalm," I will freely sacrifice to Thee "; and in the one hundred and fifteenth Psalm (7, 8), " O Lord, for I am Thy servant, I am Thy servant, I will sacrifice to Thee the sacrifice of praise, and will call upon the name of the Lord." "Hearing Mass is not so much a prayer as an act of worship and sacrifice, an offering of the divine oblation. For all who assist at holy Mass in the right manner ought to unite with the priest in his sacrificial act." The same writer whose words we quote proceeds to explain what is meant by the terms he employs. "To make or offer a sacrifice is the highest act or exercise of any of the moral virtues. For when we offer sacrifice, we intend to show by our oblation that God is the supreme Lord, to Whom infinite honor and glory belong, and that we are His subjects, of whom He can dispose according to His good pleasure. Consequently, sacrifice is of all meritorious works the one most pleasing to God and the most profitable to man."

Consider how excellent a work thou dost perform when thou offerest sacrifice, and make it thy aim to do this as perfectly as possible, since so much depends upon its being offered worthily. At the commencement of the Mass it is well to make a firm resolution to profit as much as possible by it. If there are any prayers which we have promised ourselves or others to recite, they may be said independently of the Mass until the consecration; then these private devotions should be suspended, in order that we may join with the priest in adoring Jesus Christ, and offering Him as an oblation to God the Father. By employing one's self in this manner after the consecration the greatest benefit will be derived from hearing Mass.

Some people say they have a scruple about omitting their daily prayers in order to follow the Mass. They ought rather to have scruples about neglecting the prayers of the Mass for their ordinary devotions, since the former are much more important than the latter. They may be compared respectively to gold and copper; besides, our daily prayers may be said at any time, while the prayers of the Mass only have their full value when said while the holy sacrifice is being offered. Even if the prayers we are accustomed to say every day were entirely omitted for once we should not be anything like as much the losers as if the acts of adoration and oblation were not made during Mass. For, as holy Mass surpasses all other devotions and spiritual exercises, so the prayers which include the act of oblation exceed in value all other forms of prayer.

At the Confiteor strike thy breast three times, and awaken contrition and sorrow for sin, as far as thou art able. Consider how Christ lay prostrate upon His face in the Garden of Olives, expiating thy sins with bitter tears and sweat of blood. Then continue thy ordinary prayers. At the Sanctus bow thyself down and adore the Most Holy Trinity in all humility: for the words of the Sanctus are most venerable, they are uttered as the prophet Isaias tells us (ch. vi. 3) by the seraphim in heaven, and when spoken by the priest, a bell is rung to warn the congregation to assume a posture of reverence. After the Sanctus comes the Canon. This portion of the Mass is read in a low voice, out of respect for the sacred mysteries. The apostle James teaches us in his liturgy, what our behavior should be at this solemn moment. "Let everyone," he says, "keep silence and tremble with awe, and withdraw his thoughts from earthly things, for the King of kings, the Lord of lords, is about to come, to be immolated upon the altar and given as food to the faithful. The choirs of angels go before Him in majesty and might, covering their faces and singing canticles of joy and exultation."

St. Bridget describes how on one occasion she heard, at the time of the consecration, the stars of the firmament and all the powers of heaven making sweet melody as they moved in their appointed courses. This harmony resounded far and wide; with it were mingled the voices of innumerable celestial spirits, chanting in tones of ineffable sweetness; the angelic choirs paid lowly reverence to the priest; the devils trembled with fear and fled in dismay.

Who can hear without astonishment the preparation made in the celestial spheres when the moment of consecration approaches in order that this wondrous miracle, this tremendous mystery, may be worthily celebrated! Yet we insignificant mortals assist at the divine mysteries with little or no reverence; we think little of their supernatural character, and regard the transubstantiation of the bread and wine as an ordinary, every-day occurrence. Were God to open our eyes as He opened the eyes of some of His saints, what marvels should we behold, what sublime proceedings should we witness! We should see the whole heaven engaged in preparing for the reenactment of the Saviour's life, His passion, and His death. We should see, to our joy and amazement, sun, moon, and stars lend their brilliance to the scene; the hosts of heaven, the choirs of angels with their entrancing melodies, add glory to the solemn drama. Could we see what is now invisible, we should, as St. James says, tremble and stand in awe, oblivious of this world and its fleeting joys.

Hitherto we have only spoken of what precedes the consecration; we will now speak of that sacred act itself. When the moment comes for this incomprehensible mystery to take place, the gates of heaven roll back, and the Son of God, clothed in majesty, descends in person to renew the work of our redemption. He has condescended, in His revelations to St. Mechtilde, to explain the manner in which He comes.

"In the first place, I come with such profound humility that there is no one so insignificant present at holy Mass to whom I will not stoop, to whom I will not go, if only he is desirous to receive Me. In the second place, I come with such untiring patience that there is no one, even be he My worst enemy, whose presence I do not tolerate; nay, whose offences I will not willingly forgive, provided he wishes to be reconciled to Me. Thirdly, I come with such abundant charity that there is no one, howsoever cold and hardened, whose heart, if he so crave, I will not kindle and soften with My love. Fourthly, I come with such kindness and generosity that I am ready to make the most destitute abound in riches. Fifthly, I bring with me food so sweet to the palate that all who hunger and thirst may be refreshed and satisfied. Sixthly, I come resplendent with light so brilliant that no heart can be so blind, so wrapped in darkness, as not to be enlightened and purified by My presence. Seventhly, I come with such plenitude of sanctity and graces that there is none so slothful, so listless, so indevout, whom I cannot arouse from his stupor."

Well were it for us carefully to consider in what a sweet and gentle manner our dear Lord comes down from heaven to us in holy Mass; how earnestly He longs to raise the abject, to make peace with the hostile, to soften the obdurate, to enrich the poor, to feed the hungry, to enlighten the ignorant, to encourage the faint hearted. In holy Mass He fulfils the words He spoke of Himself: "The Son of man is come to seek and to save that which was lost." (St. Luke xix. 10.) And again: "God sent not His Son into the world to judge the world, but that the world may be saved by Him." (St. John iii. 17.) He comes to us in holy Mass, not for the chastisement or condemnation of sinners, but to restore them to grace, to visit them with His mercy. There is no occasion for the sinner to feel apprehension about going to Mass: he will not meet his Judge there, but his Advocate. Far from adding sin to sin, if he hears

Mass while in mortal sin, he gives himself a chance thereby of returning to a state of grace, through the lovingkindness of our God. And if, through the frailty of our nature, we are distracted and inattentive at Mass, this is no great sin, especially if previously we made a resolution to be attentive at our devotions.

Now we must direct our thoughts to the consecration itself, and ask ourselves what the sacred humanity of Christ may be supposed to feel on beholding itself multiplied a hundredfold by virtue of the words of consecration, and hidden under the form of the host. Our Lord does not behold Himself as a man beholds himself in a mirror, for the man only contemplates his external lineaments, whereas Christ sees His personal presence multiplied, as it were another self, while He Himself remains the same. Nevertheless He beholds Himself in two places, nay, in many places, for He is present on thousands of altars at once, everywhere, in fact, where the act of transubstantiation takes place. Thus His joy doubtless is also increased. This is a mystery which no human intelligence can fathom, nor can a created nature appreciate its ineffable sweetness.

St. Bridget, who was permitted to witness in spirit what went on in the heights of heaven during the consecration, says that she saw the sacred host, under the appearance of a living lamb, enveloped in flames, surrounded by angels, countless in number as the motes in the sunbeam, adoring and serving Him, as did also an innumerable multitude of the blessed. What a glorious festival, O my God, must that have been at which thousands of angels and blessed spirits assisted. There was not one too many, not one unnecessary, not one unemployed. How were they occupied? In adoring and serving the Lamb.

Could we but see for once what passes upon our altars

at the time of the consecration, we should indeed tremble and stand in awe. Hear what St. Francis says about it: "Let man be struck dumb, let the whole world tremble, the heavens themselves be amazed, when the Son of the living God lies upon the altar under the hand of the priest. O wonder of wonders! The only-begotten Son of God, the Lord of all creation, abases Himself so deeply that for man's salvation He deigns to conceal Himself under the form of a morsel of bread!" We think little of this because we do not see it with our bodily eyes; the angels, who look upon it, adore with trembling, as is said in the preface. The devils fly in terror at the sight of this great mystery. Just as when Christ spoke the words: "I am He" (St. John xviii. 5), His enemies, who had come to arrest Him, went backward and fell to the ground, so when the words are uttered: "This is My body," the devils turn and flee, and cease for a time to assail the souls of those who offer the holy sacrifice.

From all that has been said it will be apparent how tremendous are the mysteries involved in the act of consecration; and as we have seen how the angels and saints exert themselves to the utmost in the service of their Lord, is it not incumbent on us to do all that in us lies, to strive with all the powers of body and soul, that the divine oblation may bear in us the richest fruits? Is it not reasonable that we Catholics should break off our ordinary prayers, that we should raise our eyes to the altar, make an act of lively faith, humbly adore the Lamb of God, offer Him from our hearts to His heavenly Father, and continue in such sentiments as long as He is present upon the altar?

And when the words of consecration have been spoken, let us imitate the priest: He genuflects immediately, adoring the God Whom he holds in his hands.

Do thou do the same; bend low thy head, remembering that thy God is present before thee under the veil of the host, and pay Him profound homage. This is thy bounden duty, and reason, too, requires of thee that thou showest the honor that is due to thy sovereign Lord and God. Several passages of Holy Scripture tell us this: First of all, when the evangelist St. Matthew says of the three kings: "Entering into the house, they found the child with Mary His Mother, and falling down, they adored Him." (St. Matt. ii. 11.) When the man who was born blind heard from the lips of Christ that He was the Son of God, "falling down, he adored Him." (St. John ix. 38.) When the eleven disciples saw Our Lord on the mountain in Galilee, we read that they adored Him. (St. Matt. xxviii. 17.) Let us do likewise when we see the priest genuflect in adoration; it is incumbent on us to do so, and if we fail in what is so evidently our duty, we shall incur the guilt of sin.

CHAPTER XXIX.

THE DEVOTIONS TO BE PRACTISED AT THE ELEVATION.

THE elevation is the central ceremony of holy Mass. It was appointed by the special inspiration of the Holy Ghost, and has been performed by the Church in all times with profound reverence, to the great edification of the faithful. How solemn and sublime a ceremony when the sacred host and the consecrated chalice are lifted up above the altar! Songs of joy resound in the courts of heaven; the earth is visited with salvation; the souls in purgatory experience a mitigation of their pains; hell trembles and is afraid. How glorious a gift, how excellent an oblation, does the priest present to the Most Holy Trinity when he elevates the sacred host, and sends it up to heaven by the hands of the angels! How gratifying is this sight to the most high God! How gladly does He contemplate the wondrous mage of His well-beloved Son!

What is it, then, which the priest places before God the Father at the elevation? It is the divinized humanity of His only-begotten Son. It is the perfect likeness of the ever-blessed Trinity. It is a jewel costly beyond all compare. Not in one shape alone, but in many, is this God made man placed by the priest before the eyes of the Eternal Father. He shows Him to His Father once more become incarnate, born anew into this world; He shows Him to His Father in His sweat of blood, torn by scourges, crowned with thorns, crucified and slain. He shows Him to His Father reconciling God and man, redeeming the human race, discharging the sinner's debt, pleading from the cross for transgressors. He shows to God the Father the unsullied purity, the profound humility, the unconquerable patience, the fervent charity, the perfect obedience, all the virtues which His divine Son practised upon earth, thereby rendering Him the most exalted service and giving Him the greatest satisfaction. With what joy does God the Father behold this solemn elevation, this vivid image, of His only-begotten Son!

But it is not the priest alone who performs this act: Christ places Himself before the eyes of God the Father, and offers Himself to Him in so sublime a manner that no created intelligence is capable of comprehending it. We read in the revelations of St. Gertrude that she was privileged to see this during the elevation of the sacred host: Christ standing before His Father, and making the oblation of Himself for the faithful in a manner past human comprehension.

St. Bonaventure places these words on the lips of both priest and people: " Behold, O Eternal Father, this Thy only-begotten Son, Whom all the world cannot contain, is now a prisoner in our hands. We will not surrender Him to Thee until for His sake Thou grant us what we earnestly request from Thee. We implore forgiveness of our sins, remission of our debts, an increase of grace, abundance of virtue, and the bliss of the world to come." And the priest may at the elevation speak thus in all justice to the people: " Behold, O Christians, here is your Saviour, your Redeemer, your Sanctifier. Contemplate Him with sincere faith, pour out your hearts to Him. ' Blessed are the eyes that see the things which you see.' (St. Luke x. 23.) Happy indeed are the eyes that gaze with reverence on this sacred host, and firmly believe that Jesus is hidden under this lowly form." Each of us can then say with the patriarch Jacob: " I have seen God face to face, and my soul has been saved." (Gen. xxxii. 30.) We have indeed a better right to employ these words than Jacob had, for he had only seen an angel sent from God, whilst we gaze upon the Saviour Himself, concealed under the appearance of bread. Believe firmly that it is in very truth thy Saviour, and pay Him the reverence due to Him, and it will be for thy salvation; thou canst then say with Jacob: " I have seen God face to face, and my soul has been saved."

At the elevation the faithful should raise their eyes to the altar and gaze reverently at the Adorable Sacrament. This is pleasing to God and profitable to one's own soul, as Christ condescended to reveal to one of His saints in these words: " As often as any one looks in devout adoration at the sacred host or, being unable, wishes that he could do so, his reward in heaven is increased, and he is entitled to a special degree of bliss in the enjoyment of the beatific vision." This is indeed a rich recompense for our devout contemplation of the sacred host; let us not lose it by our own neglect.

How much we may profit from thus fixing our devout gaze upon the sacred host may be gathered from one of the types of the Old Testament. In the twenty-first chapter of Numbers we read that when the people murmured against God and against Moses the Lord sent among them fiery serpents, which bit them and killed many of them. The people in their alarm came to Moses, asking his help, and he prayed for them. And the Lord said to him: "Make a brazen serpent, and set it up for a sign; whosoever being struck shall look on it shall live." In obedience to this command Moses made a brazen serpent, and set it up upon a high staff, and those who were bitten were healed by looking at it. We know this brazen serpent to have been a type of Christ, from His own words: "As Moses lifted up the serpent in the desert, so must the Son of man be lifted up." (St. John iii. 14.) Now, if looking upon that serpent of brass was efficacious to preserve from death the Jews who were bitten by the venomous serpents, how much more will the pious, looking at Christ Himself when He is lifted up in the holy Mass, heal souls suffering from the fatal poison of sin, console the afflicted, strengthen the faint-hearted !

When the sacred host is lifted up in our sight, it is above all things necessary to awaken a lively faith in the real, personal presence of our blessed Lord in the sacred host, as our Creator and our Redeemer, making the oblation of Himself to God the Father for us miserable sinners.

This exercise of faith is highly meritorious, because we believe that which is contrary to the evidence of our senses, above the grasp of our understanding. How much we merit by this act of faith Christ Himself tells us: "Blessed are they that have not seen, and have believed." (St. John xx. 29.) That is to say: Those who, though they are unable to see Me in the Adorable Sacrament, yet firmly believe Me to be present in it, exercise so excellent a virtue that by it they may earn eternal felicity. The more often we do this the greater will be our share of grace here and of glory hereafter.

The following incident taken from the life of the famous theologian Hugh of St. Victor bears the same testimony. It had long been the earnest desire of this pious priest to behold Our Lord in the consecrated host, and many were his prayers to obtain that favor. At last his prayer was granted and his desire fulfilled. One day, while he was saying Mass, he saw the divine Child reposing upon the corporal. His joy and the consolation he experienced were boundless, but presently the holy Child whispered to him: "Because thou hast thus seen Me with thy bodily eyes, O Hugh, thou hast lost all the merit of faith." Thereupon the Infant vanished from sight, leaving the priest as full of regret for the merit he had lost as he had been of delight at the visible presence of his Lord. Let this example serve to strengthen our faith, and at the same time encourage us by the assurance that we merit greatly in the sight of God when we look upon the sacred host and make an act of steadfast faith.

St. Louis of France was deeply impressed with the value of faith. One day, when a priest who was celebrating the holy sacrifice in the palace chapel elevated the sacred host, all who were present beheld in its place a lovely Infant. A servant went running to the king, who was not in the chapel at the time, begging him to hasten thither to see this wondrous sight. But Louis calmly replied: "Let unbelievers go to look upon the divine Child; I, for my part, am so firmly convinced of His personal presence in the sacred host that I do not care for further evidence." It cannot be supposed that this pious king did not feel a natural desire to see the beauteous Infant; he denied himself the gratification which the sight would have afforded him in order not to lose the merit of believing what he had not seen, and thus gaining a higher degree of glory. Imitate this good king, and however thou mayst desire to behold Christ in the sacred host, content thyself with believing, and comfort thyself with the thought that thou wilt see thy Lord in His glory all the more clearly hereafter.

After this act of faith and the adoration of the sacred host the act of oblation should follow. The oblation of the sacred host is the most real and most powerful atonement for the guilt of man. In other words: There is no more efficacious means of appeasing the anger of God than by offering to Him the body and blood of His Son in the consecrated host. Let sinners remember this, and immediately after the elevation offer the sacred host with all their heart for the remission of their sins. This applies to all who are present at Mass, whether guilty of mortal or venial sin.

After this oblation comes the elevation of the chalice, which has a special meaning and supernatural power. For in it the precious blood of Christ is shed anew in a mystical manner, and sprinkled upon all who are present. This is signified in the words of consecration: "This is the chalice of My blood, . . . which is shed for you and for many to the remission of sins." Thus, when thou dost assist at holy Mass, it is just as if thou didst stand upon Calvary beneath the cross, with contrition of heart, and wert sprinkled with the precious blood. And as thou wouldst then have been cleansed from all stain of sin, so now, no less surely, wilt thou be sprinkled with that same blood, and, if thou art repentant, be cleansed from thy guilt.

God commanded the Israelites: "The whole multitude of the children of Israel shall sacrifice a lamb. And they shall take of the blood thereof, and put it upon both the side-posts and on the upper-posts of the houses. And I shall see the blood and shall pass over you; and the plague shall not be upon you to destroy you, when I strike the land of Egypt." (Ex. xii. 6, 7, 13.) If the blood of the paschal lamb, sprinkled upon the door-posts, preserved the Israelites from the sword of the destroying angel, how much more will the precious blood of the spotless Lamb, shed for us upon the cross, and daily applied to our souls in holy Mass, avail to protect us from the rage of the evil spirit, "who goeth about as a roaring lion, seeking whom he may devour." (1. Pet. v. 8.)

And what are those to do who are not present in the church? For their benefit the custom of ringing the church bell at the elevation was introduced, as a signal to all who heard it that their Lord and God was lifted up in holy Mass. At the sound of this bell we ought to kneel down, look in the direction of the church, and adore our Lord God in the hands of the priest. This is a good and salutary practice.

WHAT OUR BEHAVIOR OUGHT TO BE AFTER THE CONSECRATION.

After the elevation of the sacred elements we can do nothing better than follow the example of the priest. As this sacrifice is ours as well as his, and it is incumbent on us as well as upon him to offer it, let us as far as possible imitate his actions. After he has replaced the chalice upon the corporal he says: "Wherefore, O Lord, we Thy servants, as also Thy holy people, offer unto Thy most excellent majesty, of Thy gifts and presents, a pure host, a holy host, an immaculate host, the holy bread of eternal life, and the chalice of everlasting salvation." There are no more consoling words in the whole Mass, according to Sanchez, than this prayer after the elevation, for neither priest nor people can do anything better than offer this holy sacrifice to God. To resume our own private devotions immediately after the elevation would therefore be to miss the oblation of the Mass, and to offer to God our miserable cold petitions in the place of the unspeakably precious sacrifice; by this we should indeed lose much.

What have we poor mortals, then, to offer to a God of infinite riches? Destitute though we are in virtue and in grace, yet we possess in holy Mass a treasure of inestimable value, wherewith heaven and earth may be enriched. To this St. Paul refers when he says: "He that spared not His own Son, but delivered Him up for us all, how hath He not also, with Him, given us all things?" (Rom. viii. 32.) Not only did God give us His Son in times long past: He delivers Him up for us again and again in holy Mass (as has already been abundantly proved in these pages), and with Him He bestows on us all His riches, so that we have wherewithal to pay our debt and purchase eternal treasures. Make good use, therefore, of this wealth that is in thy hands, and offer it to thy heavenly Father during the celebration of Mass with words such as these:

"I offer Thee, O heavenly Father, this holy sacrifice; I offer Thee Thy beloved Son, His incarnation, His birth, His passion; I offer Thee His sweat of blood, His scourging, His crowning with thorns, the carrying of the cross; I offer Thee the crucifixion, the cruel death He endured, the crimson stream that flowed from His wounds; I offer all that He did and suffered for me, which is now reenacted in this Mass. I offer it to Thee for Thy greater glory and for my own salvation. Amen."

This simple but useful prayer may be learnt by heart, and repeated after the consecration. We know how powerful this act of oblation is, and how much may be gained by it, from the words of Christ Himself, Who said that whoever should offer His passion and merits as if they were his own should receive them again in twofold measure. It is well, therefore, to make it our habit, every time that we hear Mass, to beseech Our Lord to make amends for our indevotion and the imperfection of our oblation, and for this end to offer the holy sacrifice to His Father in our stead. "Since I know not how to offer this holy Mass aright, do Thou, my dearest Lord, take my place, and present it for me, I pray Thee, to Thy Eternal Father."

Above all, make it thy endeavor to assist at Mass with the utmost reverence and attention. Be careful not to speak or laugh with others, or to rise from thy knees without urgent cause, from the time of the consecration until the communion; for it ill becomes us, in Christ's immediate presence, to study our own ease when He stoops so low for us. Any sin which is committed during the time of Mass is of greater moment, for it is a profanation of the highest act of worship, an insult to Christ, Who is present in person, renewing the great work of redemption. St. Chrysostom says that those who talk and joke at the time of Mass deserve to be struck with lightning there and then. He bids them remember, and those also who do not check or rebuke them, that they will have to answer for it at the judgment-seat of Christ.

CHAPTER XXX.

THE REVERENCE WHEREWITH WE OUGHT TO HEAR HOLY MASS.

HOLY Church, in the decrees of the Council of Trent, impresses on us the reverence with which holy Mass is to be heard: " If we must needs confess that no other work can be performed by the faithful so holy and divine as this tremendous mystery itself, wherein that life-giving victim is daily immolated upon the altar by priests, it is also sufficiently clear that all industry and diligence is to be applied to this end, that it be performed with the greatest possible inward cleanness and purity of heart, and outward show of devotion and piety." (Sess. xxii.) Both priests and people may learn from this—the former to say Mass with all possible devotion, the latter to assist at it with all piety and fervor.

The historian Josephus tells us that seven hundred priests and Levites served daily in the Jewish temple; they slaughtered the victims, cleansed them, cut them in pieces, and burnt them upon the altar, preserving meanwhile the utmost outward reverence, and silence so perfect that it might have been thought there was but one priest officiating.

With the early Christians it was the same. St. Chrysostom writes of them that, on entering the church, as they crossed the threshold they stooped and kissed the ground, and that during the celebration of the Mass the silence that prevailed could not have been more profound had the church been empty. We may here again remind the reader of the words of St. James' liturgy: "Let every

one keep silence and tremble with awe, let nothing
earthly occupy his thoughts, for the King of kings, the
Lord of lords is about to come, to be immolated upon the
altar, and to give Himself for the food of the faithful."
St. Martin never allowed himself to sit in church, but
remained kneeling or standing during the whole time,
praying with an awestruck expression of countenance.
When asked the reason of this, he replied: "How can I
do otherwise than fear when I stand in the presence of
my God and my Lord?" David expresses the same feeling when he says: "I will come into Thy house, I will
worship towards Thy holy temple in Thy fear."
(Ps. v. 8.)

The words God spoke to Moses out of the burning
bush may also be appositely quoted in this place:
"Put off the shoes from thy feet; for the place whereon
thou standest is holy ground." (Ex. iii. 5.) How much
more reverence is due to our churches, which have been
consecrated by the bishop, and where the holy sacrifice
is daily offered. David went with fear and trembling into
the tabernacle, where the ark of the covenant stood; how
much the more reason have we sinners to enter with holy
fear and profound respect into our churches, where the
Blessed Sacrament is present, where Mass is celebrated,
and assist with reverence at the greatest of all mysteries!
God Himself gives us the command: "Reverence My
sanctuary." (Lev. xxvi. 2.) This applies with more
justice to our churches than to the tabernacle of the
Israelites, just as Jacob's ladder and the altar at Bethel
are typical of the Christian Church rather than of Solomon's temple. Of our sanctuaries we may rightly say:
"How terrible is this place! this is no other but the
house of God, and the gate of heaven." (Gen. xxviii. 17.)

Hence it may be seen how much they are to be
blamed who regard the church with no more respect

and reverence than their own house, never thinking, apparently, that it is the house of God, the dwelling-place of the Son of the Most High. Some persons are so shameless as to stare about them, watch all who come in or go out, and even talk or laugh, while the holy sacrifice of the Mass, before which the angels fall prostrate upon their faces, is being offered. To these Christ might well address the words He spoke to those who bought and sold in the temple: "My house is the house of prayer, but you have made it a den of thieves." (Luke xix. 46.) Commenting on this passage, Cornelius à Lapide says: "The Christian church is in very truth the house of God, for Christ dwells therein in the Adorable Sacrament of the Altar. If He drove the Jews with scourges out of the temple, how much the more do Christians deserve a like treatment who profane His holy house with idle chatter, inquisitive glances, and rude staring at strangers."

In connection with looking about one in church at Mass-time, the Blessed Veronica of Binasko relates the following experience: "Once when, prompted by curiosity, I happened during the time of Mass to look at one of the sisters who was kneeling near the altar, the angel of God, who is constantly beside me, rebuked me with such severity that I almost fainted with terror. How threateningly he looked at me as he said: 'Why dost thou not keep watch over thy heart? Why dost thou gaze thus curiously at thy sister? Thou hast committed no slight offence against God.' Thus spoke the angel, and by Christ's command he enjoined on me a heavy penance for my fault, which for three days I bewailed with tears. Now, when I hear Mass, I never venture so much as to turn my head, for fear of incurring the displeasure of His divine majesty."

If it is sinful to look about one out of curiosity, how

very wrong it must be to talk in church and in the time of Mass. It is much easier to restrain one's tongue than one's eyes, and on that account it is more wrong to speak in church than to let one's eyes wander; besides, not only is it a greater offence against God, but it gives scandal and disturbs others at their prayers. In order to guard against this fault let us remember Our Lord's words: "I say unto you, that every idle word that men shall speak, they shall render an account for it in the day of judgment." (St. Matt. xii. 36.) If we shall have to give an account of every idle word that we speak, how severely will the just Judge punish the idle words spoken at Mass-time, whereby we have shown such want of respect for His service!

In order to show the full amount of reverence due to the holy sacrifice of the Mass it is well to remain on one's knees all the time. For if St. Paul says: " That in the name of Jesus every knee should bow, of those that are in heaven, on earth, and under the earth " (Phil. ii. 10.), how much more ought we to bow the knee when the divine Saviour is present in person upon the altar, and the work of our redemption is renewed. Some people are in the habit of standing throughout the Mass, only just kneeling down at the consecration, and rising to their feet immediately after, or even quietly sitting down, as if Our Lord were no longer present. This is most unseemly, and contrary to the usage of Christians. Those who cannot kneel the whole time should do so from the consecration until after the communion of the priest. Mothers ought to leave very young children at home, as they disturb not only those who bring them to church, but other people, and sometimes even the priest himself. But bigger children, who are old enough to be still, may be brought to Mass.

It is a most objectionable custom for women to come

to Mass very much dressed. The holy Pope Linus used to insist on the Apostle's injunction being observed, which required every woman to wear a veil when she went to church. St. Charles Borromeo was accustomed to say that women who were not thus veiled should be refused admittance into the church. According to St. Clement of Alexandria, the reason of this command was lest the beauty of the fair sex should distract the attention of men. Much harm is done by those who come to Mass splendidly and elaborately dressed, because they attract attention to themselves which ought to be given to the Mass, and thus lead others into sin. St. Ambrose says of such persons: "The more admiration they receive from men the more vile they are in the sight of God; the more they are praised by their fellow-creatures the more they are despised and hated by God."

Women thus bedizened should, when they look upon the crucifix, imagine that they hear the voice of Christ speaking to them thus: "Behold Me, O my daughter, hanging upon the cross naked, covered with blood and wounds, to atone for thy vanity. Despising My abjection thou dost deck thyself with rich apparel, and appear without shame before My sight at Mass, giving scandal by thy evil example. Take heed lest for all thy fine garments thou art not after death cast into hell-fire."

Let every one take warning by these words, and reflect that to be overdressed to any great extent is sinful, more so than one is apt to imagine, for it is a sin which is seldom repented of, confessed, and forsaken. Examine thy conscience as to how far thou hast erred in this respect by spending too much time and care on the adornment of thy person, causing scandal to some, leading others to follow thy example, or exciting envy in the minds of those who are too poor to dress as thou dost. By not giving a thought to all these sins, not confessing or bewailing them, thou wilt live and die in them, and incur no slight risk of eternal damnation.

CHAPTER XXXI.

THE CEREMONIES OF HOLY MASS, AND WHAT THEY SIGNIFY.

BEFORE proceeding to explain the ceremonies of the Mass we must ask the reader to observe that it consists of three principal parts—the offertory, the consecration, and the communion. These three parts were instituted by Christ Himself. The offertory is the giving of thanks and blessing of the bread and wine, whereby both are consecrated to the service of God. This was done at the Last Supper, when Our Lord took bread and wine, gave thanks to His heavenly Father, and blessed them. The consecration consists in the repetition of the words which Christ spoke on that memorable occasion: "This is My body; this is My blood." The consecration is the most important part of holy Mass, because by it Christ becomes present on our altars, and in it lies the essence of the sacrifice, as the reader will have seen from the earlier chapters of this book. The communion is the consumption of the sacred oblation. This was also done in the Last Supper, when Our Lord gave His flesh and blood to be eaten by the apostles under the form of bread and wine. All that precedes the offertory, the various psalms, prayers, and lections, was formerly called the Mass of the catechumens, because the catechumens, that is, those who were under instruction, but were not as yet baptized, might be present at it, while they had to withdraw before the Mass, properly so called, commenced with the offertory. This Mass of the catechumens may also be denominated as the prelude, or introduction to the Mass.

THE INTRODUCTION TO THE MASS, OR MASS OF THE CATECHUMENS.

Before the Mass the priest washes his hands, praying God meanwhile to grant him the grace to offer the holy sacrifice with clean hands and a pure heart. He then vests, repeating at the same time the prescribed prayers, takes the chalice with all that appertains to it, and goes to the altar accompanied by the acolytes, or servers. At the foot of the altar-steps he genuflects if the Blessed Sacrament is reserved in the tabernacle, or if not merely bows his head, before ascending the steps to the altar. After placing the chalice, covered with the veil, upon the corporal, which is spread upon the altar, he opens the missal, finds the places, and returns to the middle of the altar. Thence he goes down to the foot of the altar, again bows down, makes the sign of the cross, and recites with the clerk or server the psalm *Judica me*. This psalm expresses the feelings which ought to animate both priest and people at the moment of commencing this highest act of worship.

Then the priest, bowing down, says the *Confiteor*, or general confession, and the clerk does the same afterwards, in the name of all present. Both strike their breasts, with the contrite publican, as an outward manifestation of the compunction of their hearts. The priest, standing upright, gives the absolution, and prays God to grant to the people the remission of their sins in the *Misereatur* and *Indulgentiam*. He stands upright after bending down in a lowly posture, to signify that both priest and people are lifted up and comforted by the knowledge that they have received forgiveness of sin.

After the *Confiteor* and the succeeding versicles are ended the priest goes up to the altar and kisses it as a sign of respect for Christ, Who will come down to be the victim, and also to mark the bond of charity which unites us to the saints, whose relics rest beneath the altar-stone. If it is a High Mass, the altar is incensed as a token of profound reverence towards God. Let this remind us that our prayers ought to ascend to heaven as the clouds of incense rise in the air. The officiating priest is also incensed, out of respect for his sacred office, and also to show that his virtues, like the fragrant incense, ought to edify all the community.

The priest then goes to the missal, and, making the sign of the cross, reads the *Introit*, or entrance of the Mass. This is generally a verse taken from some part of Holy Scripture, with the first verse of one of the psalms, having some connection with the season of the ecclesiastical year or the festival of the day. It closes with the ascription of praise to the Most Holy Trinity: "Glory be to the Father," etc.

With a sense of complete dependence upon God, and the need both he and all the people have of the divine assistance, the priest says alternately with the server the *Kyrie eleison, Christe eleison, Kyrie eleison*, repeating each three times to the three Persons of the Holy Trinity. The words *Kyrie eleison* are Greek, and mean, Lord, have mercy upon us.

This calling for grace and mercy is followed by the *Gloria in excelsis*, an expression of thankfulness and joy at our redemption, which finds its renewal in every Mass. The beginning of this hymn of praise was sung by the angels at the birth of Christ; the remainder is an ascription of praise to God and an expression of our gratitude to Him. The *Gloria*, being a hymn of joy, is omitted in Masses for the dead and on the Sundays of Advent and

Lent, besides any other days on which joy is unsuitable.

After the *Gloria*, or when it is omitted immediately after the *Kyrie*, the priest kisses the altar, and, turning to the people, says: "*Dominus vobiscum*" ("The Lord be with you"); and the server answers for the people: "*Et cum spiritu tuo*" ("And with thy spirit"). These words express the wish of the priest for the faithful who are present that the Lord may be with them and help them to pray in spirit and in truth. For we need a special grace in order to pray aright. The people reciprocate the wish of the priest: May the Lord assist thee in thy prayer, and in offering the holy sacrifice. This versicle and response is repeated several times in the course of the Mass, to signify the intimate connection that exists between the priest and the people, and as a mutual support and encouragement to perseverance and fervor in prayer.

The priest then returns to the book, and after bowing his head in the direction of the crucifix invites the congregation to unite with him in his supplications, saying: "*Oremus*," ("Let us pray"). The prayers which follow are called collects, or collective prayers, because all the interests and needs of the Church and of those of her children who are present are summed up by the priest and laid before God. They conclude with the usual termination, "Through Jesus Christ Our Lord," on account of the promise given to us that the Father will grant all that we ask in the name of His Son. At the end the people respond: "Amen, so be it."

At the "*Dominus vobiscum*" and "*Oremus*" the priest extends his hands, raises them, and again folds them, to indicate that it is from above that he looks for the fulfilment of his petition. Folding the hands is a mark of humility, which acknowledges that we can do nothing in our own strength, that we put all our trust in the Lord. While reading the collects the priest stretches out his hands in memory of the Saviour Who, with arms extended upon the cross, interceded for the whole human race.

The collects being ended, the priest reads the lesson, a passage taken from the Old or New Testament. If from the latter, it is never a part of the Gospels, but of the Acts of the Apostles, the Epistles, or the Apocalypse. As for the most part these lections are taken from the epistles of the apostles, they are called the Epistle, the Latin word *epistola* meaning a letter. The epistle appointed to be read in the Mass always has reference to the ecclesiastical season or the festival of the day, and is intended to awaken in us sentiments in accordance with the season or the saint commemorated on the day. At the end the clerk gives thanks in the name of the people for the instruction thus received, saying: "*Deo gratias*" ("Thanks be to God").

Then follow some sentences of Scripture, called the *Gradual*, from the Latin *gradus*, a step, because they replace a psalm which used to be sung by the choir on the steps of the altar while the book was moved to the gospel side, and the deacon prepared to read the Gospel. During Paschal time the joyous *Alleluia* ("Praise the Lord") is substituted; while in Lent the *Tractus*, a long psalm, is solemnly chanted, without any pause being made. In the Mass for Easter Day, and Whit Sunday, and throughout the octave of both of these feasts, as well as on the festival of Corpus Christi, a hymn, or *Sequence*, follows, so called because it follows upon, or is to a certain extent a continuation of, the *Gradual*. In the Mass for the feast of the Seven Dolors of Our Lady the *Stabat Mater* is read as a sequence, and in Masses for the dead the *Dies iræ*.

The *Gospel* is of far more importance and dignity than the Epistle, for it contains the word of God, proceeding, not from human lips, but communicated to us by the only-begotten Son of God Himself. Accordingly from the earliest times the reading of the Gospel was attended with solemn ceremonies. Before reading it the priest stands for a few moments bowing down before the altar, reciting the *Munda cor meum*, wherein he begs God to cleanse his heart and his lips, that he may be worthy to proclaim those heavenly words. At High Mass this prayer is said by the deacon, kneeling before the altar; at its conclusion, taking the book, he kneels before the priest, asking and receiving his blessing. In order to read the Gospel the priest passes to the right side of the altar to represent the transition from the Old Law to the teaching of Christ. At solemn High Mass the deacon, whose office it is to read the Gospel, looks towards the north. According to St. Gregory the Great, the north is emblematic of the heathen world plunged in darkness; and it is to signify that the light of Christian doctrine and the example of Jesus Christ are to dispel that darkness that the deacon turns his face to the north whilst chanting the Gospel. The lighted candles held on each side of the missal have the same meaning, while the incensing of the book shows the respect we owe to the word of God. The reading or singing of the Gospel begins with the salutation: "*Dominus vobiscum*," etc., and the words: "*Sequentia sancti evangelii secundum Matthæum*"; that is to say, "What follows is taken from the holy Gospel of St. Matthew" (or whichever evangelist it may be). The acolytes answer: "*Gloria tibi, Domine*" ("Glory be to Thee, O Lord"), and both priest and people make the sign of the cross upon their forehead, mouth, and breast to signify that they pray God to enlighten their understanding, and open their hearts to receive His sacred teaching, and make them ever ready to profess it with their lips. The priest (or deacon) previously makes the sign of the cross on the book, in the place of the Gospel he is about to

Ceremonies of Holy Mass, and what they Signify. 359

read, to signify that it is the word of Jesus crucified, from whence proceed salvation and benediction. The people stand while the Gospel is read, to denote their reverence for God's Word, and their readiness to do whatsoever is commanded by it.

At the end of the Gospel the server gives thanks on behalf of the people for the heavenly doctrine, saying: "*Laus tibi, Christe*" ("Praise be to Thee, O Christ"). The priest then kisses the book out of reverence for the sacred words he has been reading, and to show that they are to us a message of grace and mercy. This is also indicated by the words he says: " May our sins be blotted out by the words of the Gospel." From the earliest times it has been customary on Sundays and festivals at this point to read the Gospel for the day from the altar, or to deliver an instruction from the pulpit, the sermon of our own time. At the close of this instruction the catechumens, in the first centuries of Christianity, used to leave the church. The introduction to the Mass ends with the reading of the Gospel.

With the reciting of the *Credo*, or Nicene Creed, we pass to the Mass properly so called. This confession of faith is the fruit of the Gospel that has been proclaimed. The cardinal clause of the Creed is that which expresses the incarnation of the Son of God ("*Et incarnatus est*"), at which the priest and all the people bend the knee. The *Credo* is said on all Sundays, the festivals of Our Lord and His blessed Mother, the feasts of apostles and doctors of the Church, and on many other days, besides the octaves of feasts. As this profession of faith follows upon the teaching we have received, so it prepares us for the celebration of the holy mysteries, for without a deep and lively faith we can neither appreciate them nor profit by them.

FIRST PART OF HOLY MASS: THE OFFERTORY.

After the *Credo* the priest turns to the people and says: "The Lord be with you," and with the words, "Let us pray," he incites them to follow the prayers attentively, and unite in the sacrificial act which is about to commence. The verse, called the offertory, that he reads is taken from Holy Scripture, and is appropriate to the day or season. The priest then uncovers the chalice, and, placing the host upon the paten, offers it up, praying God graciously to accept this immaculate host for the present needs and eternal salvation of all the faithful. The elevation of the bread signifies the complete surrender we make of it and of ourselves into the hands of God. The priest raises his eyes to heaven to show that the oblation is made to God; he drops them again in token of his own unworthiness. Then, making the sign of the cross with the paten, in memory of the sacrifice of the cross, about to be renewed in the Mass, he places the host upon the corporal, and, going to the epistle side of the altar, pours wine and water into the chalice. He blesses the water before it is mixed with the wine, praying that by the mystery of this water and wine we may be made partakers of His divinity, Jesus Christ, Who became partaker of our humanity. The wine is not blessed, because it represents Christ, the Eternal Son of the Father, the source of all benediction. The water represents our human nature, which stands in great need of blessing. The mixture of the wine and water is said by theologians to represent the union of the divine and human nature in Our Lord. Returning to the middle of the altar, the priest offers up the chalice, and, lifting up his eyes, he entreats the Father of heaven of His clemency to accept that chalice of salvation for the salvation of the whole world. He then makes the sign of the cross over the corporal with the chalice, places it upon the corporal, and covers it with the pall.

The reason why the priest designates the oblation as "this immaculate host" and "the chalice of salvation" is because it is destined to be changed into the body and blood of Christ. This offering of the oblation must be distinguished from the offering of the holy sacrifice itself; for this does not indeed consist in an oblation of bread and wine, but of the body and blood of Christ, and it cannot take place until the consecration.

Bowing down over the altar, the priest humbly prays God to accept the offering; he then blesses the elements, and invokes the Holy Ghost to descend and sanctify them. At High Mass the elements, the altar, and the celebrant are all incensed. The reader may see in the cloud of incense veiling the altar an emblem of the divine majesty, for the Lord is soon to come down from above, as He did once of old on the occasion of the dedication of the temple at Jerusalem, filling the whole house with a visible cloud. By this He manifested His approval of the place chosen for the offering of prayer and holocausts.

The offertory concluded, the priest goes to the epistle side of the altar, where he washes his fingers while he recites the twenty-fifth Psalm. This is to remind both priest and people of the cleanness and purity of soul and body with which we ought to appear before the Lord. Returning to the middle of the altar, and bowing down, with joined hands in all humility he entreats the Most Holy Trinity to vouchsafe graciously to receive this oblation. Then, kissing the altar, he turns to the people, and with the words: "*Orate fratres*" ("Brethren, pray," etc.), invites them to join with him in imploring the same grace.

Turning again to the altar, the priest begins the *Secreta*, or secret prayers, so called because they are said in a low voice. These prayers are different every day, and correspond in number and arrangement to the collects. The concluding words: "*Per omnia sæcula sæculorum*" ("World without end"), are said audibly, and are the beginning of the Preface.

The *Præfatio*, or preface, forms the introduction to the second part of the Mass, the consecration. After the *Dominus vobiscum*, to which the usual answer is given, the priest solemnly uplifts his hands to denote the elevation of his heart, saying: "*Sursum corda*" (" Lift up your hearts "), to which the people reply: "We have lifted them up to the Lord." With these words he calls upon all who are present to unite with him in giving thanks to the Father Almighty, the Eternal God, to the glory of Christ Our Lord. And since the praise of mortal lips is only too weak and imperfect, he expresses the desire that their voices may be permitted to join in the triumphant song of the angelic choirs, and with them he exclaims in holy exultation: "Holy, holy, holy, Lord God of Sabaoth: heaven and earth are full of Thy glory. Hosanna in the highest. Blessed is he that cometh in the name of the Lord. Hosanna in the highest."

SECOND PART OF THE HOLY MASS: THE CONSECRATION.

The prayers from the *Sanctus* to the *Pater noster* are called the canon of the Mass. This word means a fixed rule, the prayers being the same for every day in the year, whereas a large portion of the prayers and ceremonies in the other parts of the Mass vary according to the different ecclesiastical seasons, the festival of the day, or other circumstances. The prayers of the canon are read in a low voice, to indicate to the congregration the vast solemnity of this tremendous mystery. The words of consecration form the central point of the canon.

When the priest begins the canon, he raises his eyes and his hands to heaven. This is in imitation of Our Lord, Who, before performing His miracles, looked up to heaven. He then drops them again, kisses the altar, and recites the prayers with extended hands, like Moses when interceding for the people.

As in the offertory prayers, so in the prayers immediately preceding the consecration, we remark the twofold supplication, that God would mercifully accept the oblation, and would vouchsafe to grant us peace and salvation. This general petition is followed by more special ones, that for the sake of this unspotted victim He would protect and bless the holy Catholic Church, the Pope, the bishops, as also all orthodox believers. Furthermore, some persons are mentioned by name, whom God is entreated to remember in mercy; those who offer this sacrifice, or for whom it is offered, with their families and friends.

After thus praying for the members of the Church militant here upon earth the priest honors the memory of the blessed in heaven, the Church triumphant, beseeching God that by their merits and prayers we may be defended by the help of His protection. Foremost among the saints whose names are introduced here he mentions the ever-blessed Virgin Mary, Mother of the same Lord Jesus Christ Who is directly to appear as our victim upon the altar.

Under the Old Dispensation it was customary for the officiating priest, before immolating the sacrificial victims, to lay his hands upon the head of each, beseeching the Most High to grant forgiveness of sin, and to bestow upon him what was salutary and needful for soul and body. In imitation of this ancient ceremony the priest of the New Testament extends his hands over the oblation, before the mystic immolation of the victim of atonement, the Lamb of God, in his own name and that of the people, and prays that God, reconciled with him and with the congregation, would grant them peace in this life, deliver them from eternal damnation, and number them in the flock of His elect.

The scene now changes to the cenacle in Jerusalem, where Jesus on the night before He suffered instituted and celebrated the holy sacrifice of the Mass, and the priest, His representative, reenacts what He did then. After the transubstantiation of the bread into the sacred body, of the wine into the precious blood, of Christ the priest kneels and adores the sacred elements; then he elevates them, holding them on high to the veneration of the faithful. The bell is rung as a signal that the solemn moment has come, that Christ, God and Man, to Whom be glory and worship in all eternity, is actually present upon the altar. All present kneel, and, bending low in humble adoration, strike their breasts saying in their hearts: "Jesus, to Thee I live, to Thee I hope to die; in life and in death I am Thine."

Slain without shedding of blood, Christ now lies upon the altar in a state of mystic death. With profound humility and heartfelt fervor the priest beseeches Almighty God to look propitiously upon this sacred oblation, and, accepting it, to grant to the living heavenly benediction and grace, and also to all that rest in Christ a place of refreshment, light, and peace. Here, striking his breast, the priest breaks the solemn stillness by saying: "*Nobis quoque peccatoribus*" ("And to us sinners"), continuing again in a low voice: "to Thy servants, hoping in the multitude of Thy mercies vouchsafe to grant part and fellowship with Thy holy apostles and martyrs."

This prayer closes with the words: "Through Christ Our Lord," and is connected with what follows by this ascription of blessing, honor, and glory: "By Whom, O Lord, Thou dost always create, quicken, sanctify, bless, and give us all these good things. Through Him, and with Him, and in Him, is to Thee, God the Father Almighty, in the unity of the Holy Ghost, all honor and glory. Amen." While this is said, the sacred host is held over the chalice, and both are slightly elevated, that the act of veneration may accompany the spoken ascription of praise. Here the canon ends, and the third part of the Mass commences.

THIRD PART OF HOLY MASS: THE COMMUNION.

As the preface forms the introduction to the canon, so with the *Pater noster* we enter upon the third part of the Mass, the communion. Christ has made the sacrifice of Himself for us by the consecration: we can now call God our Father, we may proffer our petitions to Him with filial confidence, we are entitled to partake of celestial food at the communion. In the petition of the Lord's Prayer: "Give us this day our daily bread," we express our longing for the bread of angels, given to us in holy communion.

Raising his voice, with hands uplifted, the priest recites the *Pater noster*, inviting all who are present to take part in his supplications. At its close, the Amen having been said, in a low voice he beseeches God the Father to deliver him and all who pray with him from all evils, past, present, and future, through the intercession of the saints, and to grant peace in their days. He makes the sign of the cross with the paten, and places the sacred host upon it; then, kneeling down, he adores the host, and in remembrance of Christ, Who broke bread at the Last Supper, he breaks it, and puts a particle into the chalice. As the separation of the two species is significant of Our Lord's death, so the reunion of His body and blood is intended to remind us of His resurrection.

Hitherto the prayers said by the priest have been addressed to God the Father; he now calls upon Christ our Redeemer, saying three times the *Agnus Dei :* "Lamb of God, Who takest away the sins of the world, have mercy upon us." At the third time of repetition the words: "Grant us peace," are substituted as the conclusion. The next prayer is one for peace. At High Mass the kiss of peace is here exchanged between the celebrant and those amongst the clergy who may be assisting at the altar. In early times, when the men and women occupied separate places in the church, and all who were present took part in the communion, it was customary for all the congregation to exchange this salutation. Only those who observe mutual charity and kindness are worthy to receive the God of peace. Then the priest, bending low, his eyes reverently fixed upon the sacred host, prepares by fervent prayer to receive the Adorable Sacrament. Taking the host in his hand, he says three times, devoutly and humbly, the words of the centurion: "Lord, I am not worthy that Thou shouldst enter under my roof; say but the word, and my soul shall be healed." He then reverently consumes the sacred body and blood of the Lord, thus uniting himself intimately with Him in that close intercourse which is the meaning of the word "communion." Any of the congregation who desire to communicate then approach to receive the adorable body of Our Lord, and thus participate in the holy sacrifice.

After the communion the priest takes the ablutions of the chalice, a little wine and water being poured over the fingers which have touched the sacred host, and which he holds over the chalice; meanwhile he recites prayers relating to the reception of the Blessed Sacrament. He then goes to the book, which has been moved to the left side of the altar, and reads a versicle of Holy Scripture called the communion; this now replaces the canticle which was formerly sung during the communion of the people. Turning to the people, he repeats the salutation, "*Dominus vobiscum,*" and proceeds to read the concluding prayers.

These concluding prayers are called the *Post-communion,* because they come after the communion. In them the priest and the people return thanks for their participation in the holy mysteries, and pray that God would preserve in them the fruit of this sublime oblation, of this celestial food. The post-communions generally recall the leading idea of the festival of the day or of the season; they correspond in number to the collects and *secreta.* Before beginning them the priest says: "Let us pray"; and he reads them with extended hands.

Once more he greets the people with: "*Dominus vobiscum,*" and then from the middle of the altar he announces to them that the service is at an end, letting them depart with the words: "*Ite, missa est*" ("Go, the Mass is ended"). Whenever the *Gloria* is omitted, as in Advent and in Lent, "*Benedicamus Domino*" ("Let us bless the Lord"), is substituted for "*Ite, missa est.*"

The priest next gives his blessing to the people, and concludes the whole ceremony by reading from the gospel side of the altar the beginning of St. John's Gospel. As in the *Credo* so here, in reverence to the mystery of the incarnation, at the words: "And the Word was made flesh," both priest and people kneel. At the end the congregation express their heartfelt gratitude for the benefit of the divine revelation and the mystery of redemption, which are expounded in the Gospel according to St. John, by the response: "*Deo gratias*" ("Thanks be to God").

THE CEREMONIAL OF MASSES FOR THE DEAD.

As the ceremonies of holy Mass are somewhat different in Masses for the dead, it will be well not to pass them by without mention.

At the foot of the altar the psalm *Judica me* is omitted, for it expresses the joy of those who go up to the house of the Lord, and the Church mourns because the souls of the departed for whom she prays are still detained in the cleansing fire, and cannot as yet ascend the holy mount to the tabernacle of God.

At the *Introit* the priest does not make the sign of the cross upon himself, but over the book, as if the soul of the departed was before him, and at the very outset he would bestow on him his benediction, and obtain for him eternal rest and perpetual light. The *Gloria* is omitted both here and later on in the *Lavabo*, since it is an expression of joy.

For the same reason the *Gloria* is not said, to denote our sorrow that the holy souls are not yet permitted to stand before the throne of the Lamb and unite their voices to the angels' song of praise. Instead of the Gradual and joyous *Alleluia*, the Church prays in the *Tractus* that the departed may be released from the bonds of their sins and enjoy the bliss of eternal light. The *Dies iræ* forms a solemn and sorrowful sequence; it appeals for pardon to the just Judge, and entreats mercy for the departed.

Before the Gospel the priest does not, as usual, say: "The Lord be in my heart and on my lips," etc., nor in solemn requiem Masses does the deacon ask his blessing; the missal is not kissed after the Gospel has been read, nor are the words: "By the words of the Gospel," etc., said. The *Credo* is also omitted, everything that savors of a festival being excluded. The Church mourns on behalf of her departed children, for whom the holy sacrifice is celebrated, and who cannot enjoy the divine blessing in full, or receive the kiss of reconciliation which makes them forever at peace with God.

The water which is mingled with the wine in the chalice is not previously blessed, because the water represents the faithful, and the dead, for whom the oblation is offered, are no longer subject to the jurisdiction of the Church, but are answerable to divine justice alone.

The termination of the *Agnus Dei* is different: twice " Give them rest " is said, and lastly, " Give them eternal rest." The wish expressed in this prayer for the repose of our departed brethren is of a threefold nature: namely, release from punishment, the entrance of the soul into glory, and, finally, the glorification of the body, which is necessary for the consummation of bliss. The prayer for peace and the kiss of peace are omitted, because the Church militant alone is in a state to need them.

Instead of "*Ite, missa est,*" at the conclusion of the Mass, "*Requiescant in pace*" (" May they rest in peace "), is said, and the server answers: "Amen." The blessing is not given to the congregation, for all the benefit and benediction of the Mass is appropriated to the departed.

With this brief explanation of the ceremonies of holy Mass the present treatise will be concluded. The writer has but one request to make—and he makes it humbly and earnestly—that those into whose hands this book may come will read it deliberately and attentively. He ventures to hope that, by increasing in the hearts of those who read it devotion and love for holy Mass, it may induce them to assist more frequently and more reverently at the holy sacrifice.

An attentive perusal of this book will surely have convinced the reader that to hear Mass piously is indeed a good work, one which will merit for him an unspeakably great reward. And the Masses which the instructions and explanations contained in this book may perhaps have been instrumental in leading him to hear will afford him solace and support in the hour of death, and will augment the measure of his felicity to all eternity. Those, on the other hand, who have slighted holy Mass, who have heard it perfunctorily, or omitted it on the most frivolous pretext, will, when death comes, see how much they have lost through their negligence and carelessness; they will be sorry when it is too late, when they have to expiate their sin in another life.

May the all-merciful God, for the sake of His only-begotten Son, vouchsafe, by the power of the Holy Ghost, to enlighten the understanding, to strengthen the will, to touch the heart, of all who read these pages, so that they may ever assist at the holy sacrifice with heartfelt reverence and devotion. And the writer begs that he may not be wholly forgotten in their pious prayers.

APPENDIX OF PRAYERS.

FIRST METHOD OF HEARING MASS.

FOR THOSE WHO WISH TO UNITE THEIR PRAYERS WITH THOSE OF THE PRIEST.

PRAYER BEFORE MASS.

Eternal Father, I offer to Thee the sacrifice which Jesus Christ, Thy beloved Son, offered to Thee by the oblation of Himself upon the cross, and which He is now about to renew upon the altar. I offer it to Thee as a just tribute of adoration and praise, in thanksgiving for the innumerable benefits Thou dost bestow on me, to propitiate Thy justice, which I have outraged, to make due atonement for my sins, to plead for myself, for holy Church, for all mankind, and for the souls of the just suffering in purgatory.

AT THE COMMENCEMENT OF THE MASS.

How can I venture, O my God, to appear before Thy face, and take part in the sublime and spotless sacrifice which is soon to be offered to Thy divine majesty? I am but dust and ashes, a poor and miserable mortal. Nay, more, I have often and grievously offended against Thee, the infinite God; my soul is burdened with many sins and stained with guilt. But if in Thy justice Thou art angry with me, I take refuge in Thy merciful loving-kindness, trusting that for the sake of Jesus Christ, Our

Lord, my sinful soul can and shall be cleansed in His precious blood. Behold me prostrate before Thee, in deep compunction for my sins, because I have thereby offended against Thee, Who art my strict judge, and also my loving Father, my greatest benefactor, the highest good, most perfect, most worthy of my love. I confess before Thee, O infinite and eternal God, and before the whole company of heaven, the Blessed Virgin Mary, the glorious archangel Michael, blessed John the Baptist, the holy apostles Peter and Paul, and all the angels and saints, that I have sinned through my fault, my grievous fault; but I beseech Thee to pardon me for Christ's sake, through the intercession of the Blessed Virgin Mary and all the angels and saints of heaven, that with a joyful heart I may offer to Thee this holy sacrifice in union with the priest. I am fully resolved never again to offend against Thee, but, with the assistance of Thy grace, to serve Thee faithfully unto my life's end.

JOIN WITH THE PRIEST IN RECITING THREE TIMES:

Kyrie eleison.
Christe eleison.
Kyrie eleison.

AT THE GLORIA.

Glory be to God in the highest, and on earth peace to men of good will. With all the angelic choirs we praise Thee, we adore Thee for Thy great glory and majesty. We bless Thee, we thank Thee, Eternal Father, for the decree of Thy mercy and charity, whereby Thou hast given Thy only-begotten Son for our salvation. We bless Thee, we thank Thee, O Lord Jesus Christ, Son of God, Our Saviour, for Thy infinite condescension in becoming man for us, in suffering and dying for us, and now renewing upon the altar the mystery of our redemption. We bless Thee, we thank Thee, O life-giving Spirit, for the plenteousness of grace wherewith, for the sake of Christ's merits, Thou dost live and operate in the holy Catholic Church, and in all her faithful children. Manifest in our souls the power of Thy grace; cleanse and sanctify them, that they may form a diadem of glory for Our Lord and Saviour Jesus Christ; that we may honor Him to all eternity, and in His presence praise and magnify God with all angels and saints in the courts of heaven. Amen.

AT THE COLLECTS.

Almighty and everlasting God, Who hast given to Thy servants, in the confession of the true faith, to acknowledge the glory of the eternal Trinity, and to adore the unity in the power of Thy majesty: grant that by steadfastness in this faith we may ever be defended from all adversities. Through Jesus Christ, Our Lord.

Lord Jesus Christ, Who wert subject to Mary and Joseph, and by Thy sublime virtues didst sanctify family life, grant that, by the intercession of the parents who watched over Thee, we may be imitators of the Holy Trinity on earth and be admitted to their blessed company in heaven. Who livest and reignest forever. Amen.

FOR THE EPISTLE. (COL. iii. 12–17.)

Brethren, put ye on therefore, as the elect of God, holy and beloved, the bowels of mercy, benignity, humility, modesty, patience: bearing with one another, and forgiving one another, if any have a complaint against another; even as the Lord hath forgiven you, so do you also. But above all these things have charity, which is the bond of perfection. And let the peace of Christ rejoice in your hearts, wherein also you are called in one body; and be ye thankful. Let the word of Christ dwell in you abundantly, in all wisdom. Teaching and admonishing one another in psalms, hymns, and spiritual canticles, singing in grace in your hearts to God. All whatsoever you do, in word or in work, do all in the name of the Lord Jesus Christ, giving thanks to God and the Father by Him.

AT THE GOSPEL.

Speak, Lord, for Thy servant heareth. To whom shall we go: Thou hast the words of eternal life. Purify, O Lord, my heart; enlighten my understanding, animate my will, that Thy divine Word may be to me a seed which shall strike root, spring up, and bear fruit a hundredfold, —the fruit of virtue and holiness—to Thy glory and my eternal salvation.

(St. Luke ii. 42–52.) When Jesus was twelve years old, they going up into Jerusalem, according to the custom of the feast, and having fulfilled the days, when they returned, the child Jesus remained in Jerusalem, and His parents knew it not. And thinking that He was in the company, they came a day's journey, and sought Him among their kinsfolk and acquaintance. And not finding Him, they returned into Jerusalem, seeking Him. And it came to pass, that, after three days, they found Him in the temple, sitting in the midst of the doctors, hearing them, and asking them questions. And all that heard Him were astonished at His wisdom and His answers. And seeing Him, they wondered. And His Mother said to Him: Son, why hast Thou done so to us? Behold Thy father and I have sought Thee sorrowing. And He said to them: How is it that you sought Me? Did you not know that I must be about My Father's business? And they understood not the word that He spoke unto them. And He went down with them, and came to Nazareth, and was subject to them. And His Mother kept all these words in her heart. And Jesus advanced in wisdom and age, and grace with God and men.

AT THE CREDO.

When the Creed is read, repeat it silently, with reverence and faith.

AT THE OFFERTORY.

Accept, O Lord, this offering of bread and wine, which we make to Thee by the hands of Thy priest. It will soon be changed, as Thy well-beloved Son has ordained, into His true flesh and blood, and so it becomes a real sacrifice, the only sacrifice worthy to be offered to Thy divine majesty. Grant that these gifts as coming from us may find acceptance in Thy sight; grant that they may avail to wipe out our countless sins and shortcomings, that they may ascend as an odor of sweetness to the throne of Thy grace, and may thence descend in a copious shower of blessings for our health and salvation, and that of the whole world.

With this oblation we lay our heart and our whole self upon the altar in union with Thy beloved Son. Purify us, sanctify us, dispose of us and of all we have according to Thy good pleasure. From Thy divine hand we will take whatever Thy wise providence shall appoint: toil and weariness, trial and sorrow, sickness and death, for we know that Thou dost guide and direct all things for our greater good and our eternal welfare, and dost only afflict and chastise us for our ultimate advantage. Give us patience and pious resignation to Thy holy will, and the grace to persevere unto the end in the way of Thy commandments.

In this solemn moment we will put far from us all earthly thoughts and desires, and ascend in spirit to heaven, and there take our stand among the blessed company of angels and saints, by whom, and for whom, this sacrifice of praise is offered to Thee, O Lord, in thanksgiving for all the favors thou hast bestowed on them, for the merits they have gained, the heroic acts of virtue they have performed through the help of Thy grace, for the unspeakable glory and felicity which Thou hast given to them as their portion forever. May all these happy denizens of heaven, especially the one whose memory the Church celebrates to-day, or whose relics repose upon this altar, vouchsafe to intercede for us before Thy throne, that what we do to their honor may avail for our profit and salvation.

AT THE PREFACE.

With recollection of mind we lift up our hearts to Thee, O Lord, and render thanks anew to Thy divine majesty. For it is meet and just, right and salutary, that we should always and in all places give thanks to Thee. There is no time, no place, wherein we are not recipients of Thy bounteous gifts; there is no time, no place, wherein Thou, O merciful Father, dost not look upon us, ready to pour out upon us the riches of Thy grace, desirous to make us partakers in the infinite treasure of the merits of Thy Son. May we ever have a lively sense of Thy watchful care over us, of Thy ever-present majesty, for in Thee we live, and move, and are. May we never grow weary of Thy praise here on earth, and hereafter may we continue to laud and magnify Thee with the blessed company of heaven, who cease not to cry: "Holy, holy, holy, Lord God of hosts; heaven and earth are full of Thy glory. Hosanna in the highest. Blessed is he that cometh in the name of the Lord. Hosanna in the highest."

AT THE CANON.

The nearer the solemn moment approaches, my God, when Thy only-begotten Son in His divinity and humanity becomes present upon this altar under the form of bread and wine, the deeper is the awe and reverence I feel. Following the example of the priest, I enter into myself, and in silent supplication lay before Thee my desires and my necessities.

By the infinite merits of this Thy Son, Our Lord Jesus Christ, we beseech Thee, O merciful Father, look down upon Thy holy Church, protect her, extend her, govern her; bless and guide her visible head, our Holy Father the Pope, our prelate, and all her faithful children. Have mercy upon all our parents and friends, all for whom it is our desire or our duty to pray, especially NN. Keep all evil far from us, preserve us all that is good, and, above all, grant to us Thy blessing and Thy love, and grace to persevere unto the end.

Be mindful, O Lord, of the bitter sufferings and death of Thy Son, Our Lord, of the merits and virtues of the Blessed Virgin, of the holy apostles and martyrs and other saints, who during their earthly pilgrimage served Thee faithfully and found favor in Thy sight. All these, our brethren in glory, now plead on our behalf. Grant that by their intercession and the power of Christ's blood we may be delivered from eternal damnation and admitted to the company of the elect in heaven. The same Saviour Who redeemed them and purchased for them everlasting felicity shed His blood for us also. The sacrifice of atonement once offered on Calvary is now about to be renewed in an unbloody manner upon the altar in our sight. Look down, O heavenly Father, upon the face of Thy Christ, upon His wounds and precious blood, and grant us help in time of need.

AT THE CONSECRATION.

At the elevation of the host: Jesus, to Thee I live; to Thee I die. Jesus, in life and in death I am Thine.

At the elevation of the chalice: Jesus, have pity upon

me; Jesus, be merciful to me. Jesus, grant me forgiveness of sin, and bring me to life eternal.

AFTER THE CONSECRATION.

And now, my God, in accordance with His own command, we call to mind the bitter passion, the glorious resurrection and ascension, of Thy only-begotten Son, Our Lord; we present Him to Thee, as the victim of the New Testament, veiled under the lowly form of bread and wine. Vouchsafe to look upon it propitiously, and for the sake of this sublime sacrifice look also upon us, Thy unworthy children, and accept our gift, as Thou wert graciously pleased to accept the sacrifice of Thy just servant Abel, of the faithful patriarch Abraham, and of Melchisedech, the high priest.

We humbly beseech Thee that, together with this holy sacrifice, our hearts may be lifted up to Thy throne on high; admit them, with Thy beloved Son, to Thy paternal love; grant that we may be filled with all heavenly benediction, for the sake of Christ Jesus, Our Lord, Who has made us to be His brethren, and members of His mystical body.

Be mindful also, O Lord, of the souls of those who have gone before us with the sign of faith, and who sleep the sleep of peace. To these and to all that rest in Christ grant for His sake refreshment, light, and eternal rest.

And to us sinners, Thy servants, grant in the time to come, through the intercession of Thy holy martyrs and saints, some share in their felicity, not considering our merits, but pardoning us according to Thy mercy and clemency. Through Christ, and with Him, may we praise and glorify Thee in time and in eternity. Following His divine command and precept, we venture to approach Thee with filial confidence, and say: " Our Father," etc,

AT THE AGNUS DEI.

Lamb of God, Who takest away the sins of the world, have mercy upon us.

Lamb of God, Who takest away the sins of the world, have mercy upon us.

Lamb of God, Who takest away the sins of the world, grant us peace.

BEFORE THE COMMUNION.

(If you do not intend to receive holy communion, endeavor to awaken within your heart the desire to receive it as soon and as worthily as possible, and ask this grace of God.)

My God and my Redeemer, Thou hast enjoined upon us, under pain of eternal perdition, to receive the adorable sacrament of Thy body and blood, saying: "Except you eat the flesh of the Son of man, and drink His blood, you shall not have life in you." But Thou hast also taught us by the mouth of Thy apostle: "Whosoever shall eat this bread, or drink the chalice of the Lord unworthily, shall be guilty of the body and of the blood of the Lord. . . . He eateth and drinketh judgment to himself." Never, O my Saviour, let me so far forget the debt of love I owe Thee as to incur the guilt of profaning the adorable sacrament of Thy love. Grant me grace to approach this heavenly banquet of Thy body and blood with a heart purified by confession and penance, so that I may worthily participate in the rich fruits of grace and sanctity of which it is the source.

AT THE COMMUNION OF THE PRIEST.

Lord, I am not worthy that Thou shouldst come under my roof, say but the word and my soul shall be healed. [Three times.]

Since, O my Saviour, I cannot actually receive Thee as the food of my soul in the Adorable Sacrament, I will at least communicate spiritually, and thus gain some measure of profit.

Prostrate before Thee in spirit, I declare my firm and steadfast belief that Thou art really and actually here present in the Most Holy Sacrament under the form of bread—present in Thy flesh and blood, Thy body and soul, Thy divinity and humanity, living, glorified, immortal. I believe this because Thou hast said it, and Thou, the Eternal Truth, hast commanded us to believe it.

Who am I that I should venture to draw nigh to Thee? I am poor and weak, a wretched sinner who has often offended against Thee, the infinite God. Thou hast done all that Thy omnipotence, Thy wisdom, Thy love could devise to load me with benefits, and I have returned them with ingratitude. But now from the bottom of my heart I repent of my base unthankfulness and many sins, because they have displeased Thee, my merciful Father, Who art the supreme good, beautiful in Thy perfection. I love Thee, O my God, I love Thee above all; I will never forsake Thy love, nor offend against Thee again.

Would that I could now clinch my resolution by receiving the sacrament of Thy love. I long for the blissful moment when I shall be permitted to receive Thee. But now at least let me approach in spirit to kiss the sacred wounds Thou didst receive for my sake; in spirit hide myself in Thy pierced side, Thy divine heart, that I may live not only by what Thou hast done for me, but may live with Thee and for Thee, as Thy child, Thy brother, as a member of that mystical body of which Thou art the head. Thy infinite goodness and power, Thy gracious invitation, Thy unfailing promise, encourage me to hope that Thou wilt not despise Thy poor suppliant, but wilt receive me in mercy, and enrich me with Thy grace and Thy love.

PRAYER AFTER THE COMMUNION OF THE PRIEST.

We humbly beseech Thee, O Lord our God, that we, whom Thou hast called to the participation of the heavenly banquet of Thy body and blood, may by Thee be fashioned after Thy divine heart, that we may be made meek and humble of heart, and learn to abhor the vain frivolities of the world.

Grant, O Lord, that the effect of this Most Holy Sacrament may so operate in our soul and our body that in all our actions we may no longer follow the natural impulses of our heart, but may in all things obey the inspirations of Thy grace, and ever give thanks to Thee for this celestial gift. Through Jesus Christ Our Lord. Amen.

AT THE ITE, MISSA EST, AND THE BLESSING.

O Holy Trinity, may this sacrifice be pleasing to Thee. Look not upon my unworthiness, but upon the merits of Christ, and make us through Him to find mercy and forgiveness. May God Almighty, the Father, the Son, and the Holy Ghost, bless us and all whom we love. Amen.

AT THE LAST GOSPEL AND THE CONCLUSION OF MASS.

I give Thee thanks, Eternal Father, that Thou hast permitted me to assist once more at this sublime sacrifice, enabling me thereby to pay the homage that is meet to Thy infinite majesty, to render Thee adequate thanks for the countless benefits Thou hast bestowed on me, and to offer Thee abundant satisfaction for my manifold sins, as well as for the transgressions of the whole world. It is only through Thy grace and bounty that I have been capable of doing this; and for this I offer Thee my heartfelt thanks. I thank Thee also for all the gifts and graces which, in virtue of this holy sacrifice of the Mass, Thou hast bestowed and will yet bestow upon me for the profit of my soul, and for all the benefits Thou hast conferred upon others in answer to my prayers. Forgive the wandering thoughts, the inattention of which I have been guilty during the celebration of the holy mysteries. And I ask of Thee this one grace: May we never fall away from Thy love, but increase in it more and more, and frequently unite ourselves in all we do or suffer to the intentions of Thy only-begotten Son, Jesus Christ, Our Lord.

SECOND METHOD OF HEARING MASS.

OF WHICH THE PRINCIPAL MYSTERIES OF THE HOLY SACRIFICE FORM THE SUBJECT.

TO DIRECT THE INTENTION SAY:

My God, I desire to assist at this holy Mass in order: 1. To adore, praise, and bless Thee in concert with all the angels who are here present; 2. To give Thee thanks for all the benefits Thou hast conferred on me; 3. To make satisfaction for my sins; 4. To obtain the assistance that I need both for my soul and my body.

OR THIS PRAYER MAY BE USED BEFORE HIGH MASS:

In the spirit of profound humility and fervent charity I, Thy unworthy servant, offer to Thee, almighty, eternal God, my Lord and heavenly Father, this most holy sacrifice, which Thy divine Son Himself presents to Thee through the instrumentality of the priest. I offer it to Thee in union with that sublime oblation which Jesus Christ made to Thee at the Last Supper, and afterwards upon the cross, with tears and sweat of blood, and strong cries. I offer it to Thee for Thy honor and glory, as a tribute of praise to Thy infinite perfections, and as a recognition of Thy sovereign dominion over heaven and earth. I offer it to Thee in testimony of my subjection, as a public profession of the Catholic faith, by which alone we can be saved, and as a memorial of the passion and death of Christ. I offer it to Thee in thanksgiving for the institution of the Adorable Sacrament of the Altar, and for all the benefits bestowed on me and on mankind in general. I offer it to Thee in atonement for my sins, and the sins of all men, whether living or dead. I offer it to Thee for the exaltation of the holy Catholic Church, for the preservation of the peace of Christendom, for the conversion of heretics and unbelievers. I offer it to Thee for all ecclesiastical superiors, for all Catholics, for my relatives, friends, and benefactors, for all who have asked my prayers, or for whom I ought to pray, and for those who are my enemies and persecutors. Finally, I offer it to Thee for all unrepentant sinners, for the dying, and for the souls in purgatory.

Most merciful God, by the virtue of this holy Mass, and of all other Masses which shall be offered this day, for the sake of the inestimable value of Thy precious blood, I entreat Thee to grant me: 1. The special grace that I ask of Thee in this Mass; 2. Help and consolation, grace and blessing, both for time and for eternity; 3. All that is most conducive to the salvation of my soul; 4. A good life and a happy death. Finally, I ask Thee to give me Thyself, to be my eternal joy and beatitude.

AT THE FOOT OF THE ALTAR.

Poor and sinful creature that I am, O just and merciful God, I fear, on account of the number and magnitude of my transgressions, to appear before Thy divine majesty; I fear to utter Thy praise with lips so defiled with sin, because both sin and the sinner are an abomination in Thy sight.

Wherefore I confess to Thee, the omnipotent and all wise God, to the Blessed Virgin Mary, to my guardian angel, and to all the heavenly host, that I, to my sorrow, have committed many and grievous sins up to this time. For all these sins, whether known or unknown, I am very sorry, and I repent of them with my whole heart, not so much through dread of the penalties, temporal and eternal, which I have incurred thereby, as because I have offended against Thee, my God, Who art the supreme Good. I make a firm resolution never to offend Thee again by my sin, and to love Thee, and Thee only, to all eternity.

After this confession I will go up to the altar in spirit with the priest, and with him I will say:

V. Thou wilt turn again, O God, and quicken us.

R. And Thy people shall rejoice in Thee.

V. Show us, O Lord, Thy mercy.

R. And grant us Thy salvation.

V. O Lord, hear my prayer.

R. And let my cry come unto Thee; for a contrite heart Thou wilt not despise, and Thou wilt not reject the prayer of the humble.

AT THE GLORIA.

Most Holy Trinity, one God, with deepest reverence I praise and worship Thy supreme majesty, Thy eternal Godhead. Thou art more beautiful and precious to me than all things that are in heaven and on earth. I rejoice, O most high God, in Thy infinite greatness, power, wisdom, sanctity, goodness, mercy, and justice. I desire from the bottom of my heart that all men may know Thee, love Thee, and magnify Thee to all eternity.

Willingly would I accept labor and suffering, nay, gladly would I even shed my blood, if by this means I could cause Thee to be no more sinned against, but praised and glorified as is meet.

I thank Thee as best I can, most good and bounteous God, for all the benefits which hitherto I have received from Thy fatherly hand. I give myself to Thee, body and soul; I offer to Thee all the good that I have ever done, all the pains I have ever endured for love of Thee, as well as all the work and suffering that may yet be in store for me. But since this gift is far too poor and mean, as a proof of my gratitude I offer Thee all that the just on earth, all that the saints in heaven, and pre-eminently the glorious queen of heaven, have done and suffered for Thy love.

Finally, I offer Thee all that Jesus Christ did and endured for us as an oblation worthy of Thy acceptance, and pleasing in Thy sight. At the same time I humbly pray Thee to receive this gift of infinite value from the hand of Thy divine Son, that thus I may render Thee thanks, may praise and glorify Thee in a fitting manner, through Jesus Christ, our advocate with Thee.

AT THE GOSPEL.

My God and my Lord, Who art infinitely wise, unerring in Thy judgment, infallible in Thy words, Who art Thyself very truth and eternal wisdom, I accept all the teaching of the Catholic Church, with full knowledge and free will, without any reserve. I acknowledge and attest before the whole world, before all the heavenly host, that I firmly believe all that the holy Church proposes to be believed. Although there is much which I am unable to comprehend, yet I receive and believe it all, in the firm conviction that it is revealed to us by Thee, my God, Who canst not deceive nor be deceived. And in order to show that it is my fixed determination never to deny this faith, and rather to lay down my life than to secede from the Catholic Church, I now solemnly promise, in the presence of Thy divine majesty, to remain steadfast to the faith of Thy Church until my last breath. Thou art all truth, O my God, Who hast said: "In the beginning was the Word, and the Word was with God, and the Word was God." (St. John i. 1.) I earnestly entreat Thee, my God, to preserve me in this faith; to strengthen and increase it in my heart; to keep far from me all temptations contrary to it; to accept as a full profession of this faith my last communion, and the kiss my dying lips press upon the crucifix; finally, in virtue of this faith, according to Thy promise, to grant me admittance into everlasting bliss. Amen.

AT THE OFFERTORY.

Almighty Father, holy and eternal God, accept this sacred host which I offer to Thee, the living and true God, by the hands of the priest, as a satisfaction for my countless sins, negligences, and imperfections, and also for the temporal and eternal welfare of all orthodox believers, whether living or dead.

At the same time I offer to Thee, O heavenly Father, my understanding and my memory, beseeching Thee to enlighten and sanctify them, that henceforth nothing may occupy my mind and thoughts but what is pleasing unto Thee.

To Thee I surrender my will, uniting it so closely with Thy will that I may seek after nothing but Thee, love nothing but Thee, desire nothing but what Thou dost will, whensoever and wheresoever it may please Thee.

To Thee I give my body and soul, all that I am, all that I have, with all my powers. Take me for Thy own,

O my God, and give me Thyself! I am Thine; Thine in life and in death; let me not perish eternally. Amen.

AT THE PREFACE.

Almighty, eternal God, our Lord and heavenly Father, look with the eyes of Thine immeasurable mercy upon our misery, our destitution, our sorrows. Have compassion upon all faithful Christians, for whom Thy only-begotten Son, our dear Lord and Saviour Jesus Christ, of His own free will delivered Himself into the hands of sinners, and shed His precious blood upon the cross. For the sake of this Our Lord Jesus Christ avert from us the chastisements which we have well deserved; all dangers, present and future; disturbances, wars, famine, sickness; and let our days be peaceful. Enlighten our rulers, both ecclesiastical and secular; strengthen them in all that is good, that in whatever they do they may promote Thy glory, our salvation, and the general welfare of Christendom.

Grant us, O God of peace, to be united in one faith without schism or divisions. Bring us to true repentance and amendment of life, kindle in us the fire of Thy love; make us hunger and thirst after justice, that, as Thy obedient children, we may be pleasing and acceptable to Thee in life and in death. We also pray, for it is Thy will that we should thus pray, for our friends and our enemies, for those who are well and those who are sick, for all our fellow-Christians who are in trouble and afflicted, for the living and for the dead. To Thee we consecrate all we do or leave undone, our work and our conversation, our life and our death. Grant that we may enjoy Thy favor here, and hereafter, with Thine elect, laud, magnify, and bless Thee in the land of peace and everlasting bliss. We ask this, O Lord, our heavenly Father, for the sake of Thy beloved Son, Our Lord and

Saviour, Who with Thee and the Holy Ghost liveth and reigneth world without end. Amen.

AT THE CONSECRATION.

I adore Thee upon the altar, Christ Jesus, born of the Virgin Mary, sacrificed upon the cross for man's salvation. Hail, Jesus, my Lord, my Saviour, my God, my supreme good. I believe in Thee, O truth infallible! I hope in Thee, O infinite bounty! I love Thee, my God and my all!

Hail, precious blood, that flowed from the wounds of my crucified Saviour, and is now reunited to His sacred body in this adorable sacrament. Cleanse, purify, enlighten, strengthen my soul, and preserve it to life eternal. Amen.

AFTER THE CONSECRATION.

Most loving and merciful Father, I beseech Thee no longer to look upon me, an unhappy sinner, but upon Him Who has taken upon Himself my transgressions, Jesus, Thy beloved Son, Who now, in His office of mediator between Thee and me, is present upon this altar in His Godhead and humanity, in His body and soul, in His flesh and blood.

Consider, O Father of mercy, the infinite value of this oblation, and for the sake of this precious body and blood give us remission both of the guilt and the penalty of our sins, and pour out upon us in copious measure Thy celestial gifts and graces.

Look in mercy, O most compassionate Father, upon the suffering souls in purgatory, and relieve those who are most forsaken and destitute of assistance.

[Here commend to God the souls for whom you ought to pray, and those whose speedy release you have most at heart.]

Look also in Thy clemency upon the souls who are

most dear to Thee, to Thy divine Son and His blessed Mother, and accept in expiation of their guilt the superabundant satisfaction made by Thy Son in His bitter agony and death upon the cross. Grant that one drop of His precious blood may be given for their relief, and procure for them admittance into eternal felicity. Amen

AT THE PATER NOSTER.

O Father of mercies and God of all consolation, Thou alone art worthy to receive all honor, praise, love, and obedience—Father, Whose property it is always to have mercy and to spare!

Father, Who art in heaven and on earth, in heaven in Thy glory and majesty, on earth in Thy goodness and justice, to Thee we raise our eyes, our hands, our hearts. Have compassion upon Thy exiled children, who send up their sighs to Thee, in this valley of tears.

Father, hallowed be Thy name by me and by all men; by the just and by sinners, by believers and by unbelievers. Hallowed be Thy name in all our thoughts, words, and works, that all we do and suffer may be to the glory of Thy name and that of Thy Son.

Father, Thy kingdom come! Thou art our sovereign Lord and King, the God of our heart. Take from us the concupiscence of the flesh, the concupiscence of the eyes, the pride of life. Dwell in us, reign in us according to Thy good pleasure, and lead us in the way of Thy commandments to Thy heavenly and eternal kingdom.

Father, Thy will be done, whether it be painful or pleasant to us, whether it bring to us prosperity or adversity, life or death. Father, Thy will be done in us as perfectly as it is done in heaven, as perfectly as it was done by Thy divine Son when He became obedient even to the death of the cross.

Father, give us our daily bread! From Thy fatherly hand we look to receive all that we need here below for soul and body. Bestow Thy gifts upon us, and grant us grace so to seek things temporal that we may not thereby lose things eternal.

Father, forgive us our debts, that is, our sins, and the punishments due to them. Forgive us our mortal and our venial sins; for out of love to Thee we repent of them with our whole heart. Forgive us our daily faults and frailties as often as we turn to Thee with contrite hearts. Father, forgive us all the guilt of our sins, especially at the hour of our departure out of this world; forgive us, as we forgive those who have offended against us.

Father, lead us not into temptation! Let us not be overcome when assailed by the tempter; stand by us with the all-powerful help of Thy grace. Let Thy holy angels ever guard and protect us.

Father, deliver us from evil—from all evils, temporal and spiritual, past, present, and to come. We ask this of Thy boundless mercy; we ask it through Jesus Christ, Our Lord. Amen.

AT THE COMMUNION.

Make a spiritual communion in the following manner:

I adore Thee, Lord Jesus Christ, true God and true man, Who art here present upon the altar under the veil of the sacramental species. With deepest reverence I fall before Thy face. I am sorry from the bottom of my heart for having displeased Thee, my God and my sovereign Good. I now renounce all sin, I resolve to banish all evil inclinations and desires from my heart, in order to prepare for Thee a fit dwelling-place in a heart set free from sin.

Since I am not worthy to receive Thy body and blood in the Most Holy Sacrament this day, I entreat Thee to look upon me with Thy clemency and come to me spiritually. O sweet and loving Jesus, come to me in Thy love and Thy goodness; come with Thy celestial gifts and graces to satisfy this hungry soul of mine!

Jesus, beloved of my heart, grant that the fire of Thy divine charity may consume in me all that is sinful, worldly, earthly. Jesus, beloved of my soul, give me to rejoice in Thy presence, strengthen me to lead a Christian life, and persevere in Thy grace unto my life's end.

Jesus, the ruler of all my powers, Thou knowest the secrets of my heart; Thou knowest all my crosses and sorrows, my desires and interests, my needs and necessities. To Thee I commend myself, body and soul, and all who are near and dear to me; to Thy care I intrust all that I am, all that I have. Do with me according to Thy good pleasure; I have no other wish than that Thy most holy will be done in me, and all who are related to me, at all times and in all places.

Above all, I beseech Thee, most loving Jesus, do not permit me, or any one dear to me, to fall into mortal sin; give us grace to be diligent in the practice of Christian virtues, to bear all things and do all things out of love to Thee, to desire nothing but Thee, to lead a pious life, to die in Thy grace, and to be happy for all eternity. Amen.

AT THE BLESSING.

God the Father, bless us; God the Son, protect us; God the Holy Ghost, enlighten us! May we be strengthened and confirmed in all good in virtue of the bitter passion of Christ; through the intercession of the saints may we be preserved from all sin and all evil. Amen.

THIRD METHOD OF HEARING MASS

IN HONOR OF OUR LORD'S BITTER PASSION.

TO DIRECT THE INTENTION.

I purpose to assist with devotion at this holy Mass, and in union with the priest, to offer it up to God, first, in memory of the Passion of my Saviour, and as an act of thanksgiving; secondly, to make satisfaction for my manifold sins; thirdly, to obtain a fervent love for Jesus crucified; fourthly, to implore the grace of unflinching patience in trials and sufferings; fifthly, to obtain a happy death in the arms of my divine Saviour.

AT THE COMMENCEMENT OF MASS.

Call to mind the sadness of Jesus, His prayer in the Garden, His sweat of blood.

1. O Jesus, who wert sorrowful even unto death, for the sake of the fear, the distress, the anguish, the agony of Thy heart, inspire me with a salutary fear of God, which will preserve me from mortal sin, whatever my dangers and temptations may be. Be with me in my last agony, lest my soul be overwhelmed with fear and horror.

2. O Jesus, Who didst fall upon Thy face upon the ground, my sins thus bowed Thee down, oppressed Thee thus heavily. Alas! I grieve from the bottom of my heart that I should ever have offended against Thee, my God, the supreme Good, worthy of all love. I entreat Thee, O Jesus, to offer to Thy heavenly Father the threefold prayer which Thy lips uttered in the Garden

of Olives, and grant me grace nevermore to offend against Thee.

3. O Jesus, covered with a sweat of blood, I lay all my sins and iniquities in the blood that flowed from Thy sacred body; wash me, O Jesus, in Thy blood; adorn me with it as with the wedding-garment, arrayed in which I must one day appear before Thee, to be thereby recognized as Thy servant, and admitted to the number of Thine elect. Amen.

AT THE GLORIA, THE COLLECTS, AND THE EPISTLE.

Consider (1) how Jesus was led as a prisoner into the town; (2) how He was buffeted and struck in the face; (3) how He was mocked in the high priest's house.

1. O my captive Jesus, Who of Thy own free will didst allow Thyself to be taken captive as a malefactor by wicked men, Who wert bound, dragged through the brook Cedron, and led through the streets of Jerusalem—I devoutly venerate the ropes and fetters that bound Thee, and I desire earnestly with the apostle Paul to be a prisoner of Jesus Christ. Bind me hand and foot with the cords of Thy love; let all the powers of my body and soul be held captive to Thee; attach me so firmly to Thyself, that nothing may ever separate me from Thee.

2. O most patient Jesus, for the sake of the blows, the buffets, the strokes Thou didst receive because of me, deliver me from the temporal and eternal punishment of my sins. And if it be Thy holy will and conducive to my salvation that I should suffer the penalty of sin here upon earth, I beseech Thee so to fortify me with Thy grace that I may be ready to exclaim: Burn, cut away all that is evil here in time, but spare me in eternity!

3. O most long-suffering Jesus, by the shameful spitting and buffeting whereby Thy divine countenance was

cruelly disfigured; by the mockery, the blasphemies, the outrages hurled at Thee by wicked men, all of which Thou didst endure in silence with amazing patience—I pray Thee to pardon my sins, both open and hidden; extinguish within me anger, hatred, desire of revenge; give me the strength I need to bear patiently and silently, for love of Thee, all the contempt and injury to which I may be exposed.

AT THE GOSPEL AND THE CREDO.

Think to thyself how Jesus was (1) falsely accused; (2) clothed with ignominy; (3) declared guilty of death.

1. O most meek Jesus, Who wert so innocent, so stainless, so far removed from all sin, Thou wert yet falsely accused. Alas! against me my sins rise up, and accuse me before the tribunal of Thy divine justice. Woe to me, unhappy sinner, unless Thou in mercy spare me I shall be lost forever. Wherefore with deep contrition I cast myself at Thy feet, and earnestly implore Thee: Have mercy upon me! Have mercy upon me, O Jesus, according to Thy great mercy!

2. O Jesus, worthy of all honor and worship, Thou wert slandered and reviled at the judgment-seat of Thine enemies, although Thou didst ever seek and maintain the glory of Thy heavenly Father; grant me the courage I need, that I may never, under any circumstances, act in a manner contrary to Thy honor and that of Thy Father; that I may never suffer any oath or blasphemous word to be uttered in my presence, but may do all to the glory of God, and make it my aim to promote His glory and defend His holy name from insult.

3. O Jesus, Thou Who art perfect innocence wert with gross injustice declared deserving of death, whilst I by my sins have frequently merited eternal damnation.

Merciful Jesus, I beseech Thee, enter not into judgment with Thy servant! I take as my advocate Thy mother and mine, the Mother of Dolors, and as my intercessors my guardian angel and my patron saint; they will not allow the sentence of condemnation to be passed on me. Amen.

AT THE OFFERTORY.

Consider how Jesus was (1) scourged; (2) crowned with thorns; (3) condemned to death.

1. O most pure and chaste Jesus, how cruelly wert Thou scourged! From the head to the feet Thy tender body is one vast wound. I, alas! deserved to be thus scourged on account of my sins, and Thou, Who art innocence itself, didst receive that terrible castigation in my stead. Behold, O heavenly Father, the wounds of Thy dear Son, my Saviour; and accept His precious blood to wipe out my transgressions. O Jesus, covered with wounds and blood, give me a chaste heart and a pure mind; let me never do or permit others to do anything that is contrary to the modesty becoming to a Christian.

2. O Jesus, Whose regal diadem is love, to Thee belongs by right a golden crown of glory, and to me, on account of my vanity and pride, the thorny crown of shame and contempt. O Jesus, my King, press upon my proud temples Thy crown of love and of suffering, and let me become like unto Thee, meek, patient, and lowly of heart!

3. O Jesus, Who being entirely innocent, wert yet condemned to death, how shall I feel when, after my death, the sentence is given which will decide my fate for all eternity? I earnestly beseech Thee, by Thy precious blood and Thy sacred wounds, by Thy stainless innocence and by the immaculate heart of Mary, grant that

when I stand before Thy judgment-seat I may hear the consoling words: "Come, blessed of My Father, enter thou into the joy of thy Lord." Amen.

AT THE PREFACE AND THE CANON.

Think how Jesus (1) took the cross upon His shoulders; (2) carried it to the place of execution; (3) was nailed to the cross.

1. Hail, fair and holy cross! Thou art become beautiful and precious because of the divine limbs that hung upon thee, the crimson tide from Jesus' veins that dyed thy stem. I humbly venerate thee, I lovingly embrace thee, I gladly take thee on my shoulders. My Jesus, do Thou lay upon me poverty and misery, sickness and persecution, whatever may be Thy holy will. Strengthened by Thee, suffering with Thee, Whom I behold bearing the cross, weighed down beneath its load, I hope to bear every trial with patience, nay, with joy, even unto my life's end.

2. O wondrous cross, I welcome thee, I embrace thee a thousand times. Be thou to me a sure defence in every conflict with the enemies of my salvation, visible or invisible. O precious cross, be to me a tree of life, in whose shadow I may rest in the hour of sorrow and adversity, whose sweet fruit shall give refreshment to my weary heart. By thee, life-giving cross, I shall be lifted upwards; by thee, as by a ladder, I shall be enabled, in my last hour, to ascend to heaven.

3. Fasten me, O Jesus, to Thy cross by these nails, the fear of God and the love of God. Impress Thy cross as a seal upon my heart; imprint it in the centre of my soul. My sole desire, my last entreaty is this: that in life and in-death I may rest in the arms of Jesus, stretched out for my sake upon the cross of pain. Amen.

AT THE CONSECRATION.

Picture to thyself Christ upon the cross, and say:

Jesus, my God and Saviour, Who art here present upon the altar, I believe that, according to Thy own infallible word, Thou art that very same Son of God Who, for the salvation of all mankind, hung upon the cross. Draw me upward towards Thee, away from the entanglements of this miserable world, clasp me in Thy loving arms, hide me in Thy sacred wounds, adorn me with Thy virtues, confirm me with Thy grace. O good Jesus, hear and answer me! Let me never be separated from Thee.

Imagine thyself watching the blood of Jesus as it drops from the cross, and say:

This blood upon the altar, O Jesus, is the self-same blood that flowed from the wounds of Thy sacred body upon the cross. O blessed Jesus, let not this precious blood have been shed in vain for me a sinner. Let it be for my safety and salvation, and for that of all men both living and dead. Amen.

AFTER THE CONSECRATION.

Think upon the agony which Jesus endured for three hours upon the cross, and say:

1. By the bitter anguish of soul which Thou, O Lord Jesus, didst endure for me whilst hanging on the cross, especially in that final struggle in which Thou didst overcome death, have pity on me in my last struggle, when soul and body shall be torn asunder.

2. O Jesus, Who didst suffer such torments upon the cross, by the merits of Thy passion and death, whereby Thou didst make full atonement for the sins of the world, forgive me my sins and misdeeds; deliver me from the

guilt and punishment of sin by the rich ransom Thou hast paid for me.

3. O Jesus, forsaken even by God in Thy last agony, upon Thy cruel sufferings and death I rest all my hope and confidence; Thy cross is my refuge; in it alone I hope to find life and salvation. When I think upon Thy three hours' agony, not even the multitude of my iniquities have power to terrify me. For was it not in order that I might have a happy death, that I might not be lost forever, that Thou didst hang upon the cross, that Thou didst suffer such unutterable pain and torture? I cannot, I will not despair, since Thy cross, Thy wounds, Thy blood, are my ransom. By Thy cross I will put to flight all my spiritual enemies; to Thy sacred wounds I will appeal when I stand before Thy dread tribunal; with Thy blood, the most precious of all treasures, I will purchase admittance into the courts of heaven. Amen.

AT THE PATER NOSTER.

Reflect upon the seven words of Christ upon the cross, and say:

1. O most merciful Jesus, Who whilst hanging upon the cross didst say: "Father, forgive them," I pray Thee to forgive me my sins, and make me ready to forgive, so that for love of Thee I may fully and freely pardon all who have ever done me wrong.

2. O most merciful Jesus, Who didst say to the repentant thief: "This day thou shalt be with Me in paradise," grant me the grace so to live, that when, in the hour of my death, I fix my eyes upon Thy cross, I may hear within my heart those words of consolation addressed to me also: "This day thou shalt be with Me in paradise."

3. O most loving Jesus, Thou didst say to Thy mother: "Woman, behold thy Son!" and to the disciple: "Be-

hold thy mother!" With filial confidence I implore Thee to give me Thy sorrowful Mother as my mother, and ask her intercession to deliver me from all evil, to confirm me in grace, and ensure for me a happy death.

4. O Jesus, abandoned by Thy Father, Thou didst exclaim: "My God, My God, why hast Thou forsaken Me?" By thy sad dereliction, I beseech Thee to be my support and strength in time of distress, and, above all, at my latter end.

5. O Jesus, in Thy hour of desolation Thou didst cry: "I thirst!" I too thirst for the living water which flows from Thy pierced side. For this one thing I ask, that the last refreshment and quickening draught my soul shall receive on earth may be the adorable sacrament of Thy sacred body and blood.

6. O most obedient Jesus, Whose dying lips uttered the words, "It is consummated!" let me not depart hence, I implore Thee, before I have accomplished all that is pleasing to Thee and befitting a good Christian, in regard to both the things of time and of eternity.

7. O Jesus, Who at the moment of death didst cry aloud, "Father, into Thy hands I commend My spirit!" with all intensity of devotion and earnest entreaty I beseech Thee to grant me the grace, that the last prayer my lips may utter may be this: "Jesus, to Thee I live; to Thee I die. Jesus, in life and in death I am Thine. Jesus, Mary, Joseph, into your blessed hands I commend my spirit. Amen."

AT THE COMMUNION.

Take your stand with Mary and John beneath the cross, and say:

O Jesus, crucified for me, Thy attitude upon the cross is expressive of charity and full of mercy for me;

Thy head is bowed down to give me the kiss of peace; Thy arms are extended to embrace me; Thy feet are made fast with nails to await my coming; Thy whole body is stretched out for my redemption; and each one of Thy wounds is a voice calling to me: "Come unto Me, all you who labor and are burdened."

I come at Thy call, O blessed Jesus; I come with the penitent Magdalen to cast myself at Thy feet; for love of Thee I repent of all my sins, I bewail them with tears, because they are displeasing to Thy infinite goodness and sanctity. I come with Thomas, no longer incredulous, but believing, to touch the sacred wounds of Thy hands, Thy feet, Thy side; with him I exclaim: My God and my Lord, my Saviour and my Redeemer, hide me in Thy wounds, keep me in Thy wounds, sanctify me by Thy wounds; let them be my meat and drink, let me never depart thence, but in them let me die, and thus enter upon a blissful eternity! Finally, I come with John, the beloved disciple, not only to lean my head upon Thy breast, but to lay my heart within Thy most loving heart. In that furnace of love, O Jesus, my Saviour, may my cold heart gain heat and be inflamed! And in this wise, every time that I receive holy communion, let my heart be united to Thy heart, that I may become one with Thee: I shall then no longer live to myself, but to Thee, or rather Thou wilt live in me, until at length I die in Thy love, in order to live with Thee, to love Thee, to magnify Thee to all eternity. Amen.

AT THE CONCLUSION OF MASS.

Contemplate in spirit the body of Jesus in the arms of His Mother, and addressing yourself to Mary, say:

O most afflicted and sorrowful Mother, I beseech thee by thy seven dolors, and especially by the sword of sorrow that transfixed thy soul when the body of Jesus was taken down from the cross and laid in thy arms, offer to thy Son this Mass which I have just heard, with my poor prayers, in union with thy tears, thy sorrows, the grief of thy heart, and by thy intercession obtain for me an answer to my petitions. Amen.

FOURTH METHOD OF HEARING MASS.

OFFERED IN BEHALF OF THE POOR SOULS.

BEFORE MASS.

O most merciful Lord Jesus Christ, Who didst institute the holy sacrifice of the Mass for the salvation and relief of both living and dead, I offer to Thee this holy Mass, and the prayers which I shall say during this Mass for the soul of NN., as well as for all other souls now suffering the torments of the purgatorial fire. I beseech Thee, O good Jesus, to present unto Thy heavenly Father this same sacrifice, together with my poor prayers, and the intercession of the saints whom I invoked, in order that, by the virtue and efficacy of the same, the soul specially commended to Thee, and all other suffering souls, may by Thy powerful assistance experience an alleviation of their pains. Amen.

AT THE INTROIT.

Take your stand in imagination before the throne of the Holy Trinity, in the company of the souls of the departed, and offer to the three Persons of the Godhead the following prayers:

PRAYER TO GOD THE FATHER.

O Father of compassion and God of all consolation, show mercy to those who are now in purgatory, that place of sadness and of desolation. Behold, O merciful Father, the souls who are suffering there; they were created by Thee to Thy likeness. It is to wipe out the debt they have incurred by their sins that Thy beloved Son presents to Thee the precious blood, infinite in value, which flowed from His sacred wounds. Vouchsafe to accept it propitiously, and of Thy great clemency take pity on the suffering souls, more especially the one for whom I pray.

PRAYER TO GOD THE SON.

O Jesus, the source of all bounty and compassion, how canst Thou, in the sacrament of Thy love, bear the sight of these suffering and forsaken souls any longer? Most tender-hearted Jesus, remember that these are the very souls for whom Thou didst become man, for whom Thou didst endure such grievous pains for whom Thou wast immolated upon the cross. Jesus, Lover of souls, grant that Thy cross and passion may afford speedy relief to the soul of NN., and all others who are yet suffering in the place of expiation. Amen.

PRAYER TO GOD THE HOLY GHOST.

Holy Spirit, God of love and of consolation, how countless are the souls that are tormented in the fires of purgatory! O Father of the afflicted, listen, I pray Thee, to the bitter groans and sighs of these unhappy souls, and help them in their dire distress. O Holy Spirit, Who art of all comforters the best, sweet help of souls, these souls for whom I pray are Thine through baptism, they are espoused to Thee by faith and love, they are inheritors of the kingdom of heaven. Wherefore refresh them with but one drop of heavenly dew, open the doors of their prison, conduct them to Thy throne above, and bestow on them the crown of glory. Amen.

AT THE EPISTLE.

Call upon the blessed Mother of God, the holy angels-guardian, and the saints to unite their intercession to your petitions.

O Mary, Mother of mercy, hear the cries which the souls of thy departed servants, for whom thy dear Son paid so high a price, even His precious blood, send up to thee from the prison wherein they groan. O Mary, most afflicted Mother, behold their tears, listen to their sighs, and plead for them with thy divine Son, Who refuses no request that thou dost proffer. Show to them, thy unhappy children, Jesus, the blessed fruit of thy womb. O clement, O kind, O sweet Virgin Mary! Amen.

Holy angels-guardian, whose office it is to further the salvation of mankind, look upon the souls whom God committed to your charge. Innumerable are the groans, the petitions, they send up to you in heaven. How ardently they long to be with you there! Implore Almighty God to grant them the remission of the punishment still due to them; console them, encourage them, refresh them, and finally conduct them to everlasting joys. Amen.

O you, the blessed in heaven, who are the chosen friends of God, behold with tender compassion the pains which the souls of your brethren and sisters in Jesus Christ are now enduring. They are entitled to a place by your side in the kingdom of heaven. Present yourselves before the throne of the Triune God; once more offer Him your good works, your sufferings, your death, in union with the passion and death of Christ; raise your voice in importunate entreaty, until, through your intercession, they are released from the fiery prison, and admitted to be your companions in heaven. Amen.

AT THE OFFERTORY.

Betake yourself to Calvary, and there remind the Eternal Father of all that Jesus suffered for the holy souls.

Accept, O heavenly Father, this sacred oblation of bread and wine which the priest makes upon the altar for Thy glory and for the profit of all faithful Christians, living and dead. I offer it to Thee for the souls of NN. and all others yet captive in the cleansing flames. I place in spirit upon the altar all the torments, the anguish they endure; their sighs and tears, their wailing and lamentation, their anxious longing to be in heaven, in order that, united to the merits, the passion, the precious blood of Christ, they may be a sacrifice of propitiation before Thee.

Be mindful, O merciful father, that Thy only-begotten Son vouchsafed to endure cruel torments and the ignominious death of the cross, and take pity on the souls for whom I now pray, as well as all who are suffering in purgatory, especially those who are nearest to the time of their deliverance.

Behold, O compassionate Father, His head crowned with thorns, His pallid countenance, His eyes glazed in death, His features covered with blood, and take pity on those unhappy souls of whose sufferings I have been the cause.

Behold, O loving Father, His arms extended wide, His hands and feet transfixed with cruel nails, His side, His sacred Heart pierced by a lance, and take pity on the suffering souls who are the most grievously tormented in the flames of purgatory.

Behold, O merciful Father, how the whole of His sacred body is torn and mangled from head to foot; every limb is tortured, every drop of blood is drawn from His veins; and take pity on the poor souls who have yet to suffer for the longest period of time.

Behold, O kind Father, what agony of body, what anguish of soul Thy most innocent Son endured; how, in addition, He was reviled, mocked, calumniated, and finally forsaken by heaven and earth, by angels and men; nay, even by Thee His Father, and take pity on the hapless souls who have none to succor them.

Look upon this, Almighty Father, and remember at the same time the intolerable torments and pains which the suffering souls bear with perfect submission to Thy holy will, uniting them in intention to the obedience and charity of Thy divine Son, and offering them to Thee with the heartfelt and fervent entreaty that Thou wouldst grant them grace and mercy and release them from their present misery. Amen.

AT THE CONSECRATION.

Implore Jesus, by the shedding of His precious blood, to send help to the holy souls.

AT THE ELEVATION OF THE SACRED HOST.

Jesus, my God and Saviour, I firmly believe that Thou art here present upon the altar in the consecrated Host, with Thy divinity and humanity, Thy soul and body, Thy flesh and blood. I adore this sacred blood which Thou hast shed to the last drop for our salvation; and I beseech Thee to apply it to the souls in purgatory as their all-sufficient ransom.

AT THE ELEVATION OF THE CHALICE.

O my sweet Saviour, again I bow down to venerate Thy precious blood now contained in that chalice. A single drop of that divine blood would suffice to extinguish the flames of the purgatorial fire. Wherefore, O tender-hearted Jesus, make the suffering souls feel the all-prevailing power of that adorable blood and set the unhappy captives free. Amen.

AFTER THE CONSECRATION.

All hail, sacred blood of my Redeemer! This blood here present is none other than the blood which flowed to the ground on the Mount of Olives, wrung from every pore in the Saviour's body during His death-agony. By Thy sweat of blood, O Jesus, let Thy blood be for the cleansing of the souls of the departed.

It is the same blood as that which flowed from the Saviour's mangled body during the cruel scourging in the court of Pilate's house. Oh, how precious is that blood! Jesus, covered with innumerable wounds, offer, we pray Thee, but one drop of that all-prevailing blood to Thy heavenly Father, to make satisfaction for the debt the holy souls still owe to His justice.

It is the same blood as that which was drawn from the sacred head of the Saviour when the crown of thorns pierced His aching brow. Jesus, my sovereign Lord and King, give, we pray Thee, but one drop of that precious blood to each one of the suffering souls, as the price wherewith they may purchase heaven.

It is the same blood as that which was shed from the transfixed hands and the riven side of the crucified Saviour. O dearest Jesus, let the sacred stream that issued from Thy wounds be poured upon the devouring flames to quench their glowing heat, to set free the souls thus tortured, and gain for them admittance to the realms of eternal bliss. Amen.

AT THE COMMUNION.

Commend the holy souls to Jesus for the sake of His five sacred wounds.

O my crucified Jesus, I adore and humbly venerate the wound of Thy right hand, and in virtue of it I commend to Thee the souls of my departed parents, relatives, benefactors, friends, and enemies. For the sake of the blood that flowed from that wound, and the pain that it caused Thee, have compassion upon them, and gladden them by a sign of Thy favor.

O most benign Jesus, I adore and devoutly venerate the wound of Thy left hand and in virtue of it I commend to Thee those souls who are in the greatest need of assistance. For the sake of the blood that flowed from that wound, and the pain that it caused Thee, extend Thy hand in clemency towards these souls, and deliver them from their prolonged agony.

O most charitable Jesus, I adore and profoundly venerate the wound of Thy right foot, and in virtue of it I commend to Thee the souls for whom it is Thy will that I should pray. For the sake of the blood that flowed from that wound, and the pain it caused Thee, grant that they may soon hear Thy lips utter those happy words: "This day you shall be with Me in paradise."

O most bounteous Jesus, I adore and venerate with all the fervor of my soul the wound of Thy left foot, and by virtue of it I commend to Thee the souls who had the greatest devotion to Thy passion, and to the dolors of Thy sorrowing Mother. For the sake of the blood that flowed from that wound, and the pain it caused Thee, show Thy liberality by remitting the punishment yet due to them.

O most merciful Jesus, I adore and venerate with all my heart the sacred wound of Thy side, and in virtue of it I commend to Thee the souls for whose intention I assist at this Mass. For the sake of the water and the blood that flowed from that wound, and the terrible agony which Thou didst endure for three hours upon the cross, vouchsafe in answer to the prayers of Thy sorrowful Mother to extinguish the flames wherein they are tormented, and take them, together with those who suffer with them, to the never-ending joys of Thy presence. Amen.

AFTER THE COMMUNION.

Commend the holy souls to the Heart of Jesus, open to receive them, and implore Him to admit them into the kingdom of heaven.

O most sweet Jesus, Who for love of us didst not merely give Thyself to us in the sacrament of Thy love, thereby to unite our heart most intimately with Thine, but after Thy death didst cause it to be opened, that it might be to all faithful Christians a gate through which they pass to their celestial country: I beseech Thee, by the boundless charity of Thy pierced heart, Thou wouldst open wide these heavenly portals to the suffering souls, to give them admittance into Thy kingdom.

Listen, O gentle Jesus, to the voice that ascends to Thee from the prison-house of fire where these holy souls are confined; listen to their constant cry: " Open to us, O Lord, open to us Thy heart! From the depths of our misery, from this fiery furnace, we cry to Thee, merciful Jesus; hear our petitions, incline Thine ear to the voice of our supplication; for with Thee is propitiation, with Thee alone is plenteous redemption!"

Wherefore, O good Jesus, we beseech Thee, let not Thy heart, which bears the wound of love, be any longer closed against these unhappy supplicants. By the anguish and distress, the desolation and faintness which Thy sacred Heart experienced during the time of Thy passion, and especially upon the cross; by the seven dolors of Mary's sorrowing heart,—the heart on which, when taken down from the cross, Thy lifeless body rested,—vouchsafe, we pray Thee, to open this gate of salvation, Thy adorable Heart, to all the faithful departed who are yet detained amid the cleansing flames.

May their souls, and above all the souls for whom my suffrages are now offered, enter through that gate into the heavenly city. And through their intercession on my behalf may I obtain the grace to live piously, die happily, and after death be speedily released from purgatory, that I too may pass through that golden portal, Thy pierced heart, unto the abode of eternal felicity. Amen.

PS. CXXIX.: DE PROFUNDIS.

Out of the depths have I cried to Thee, O Lord: Lord, hear my voice.

Let Thine ears be attentive to the voice of my supplication.

If Thou, O Lord, shalt mark our iniquities: O Lord, who shall stand it?

For with Thee there is merciful forgiveness: and by reason of Thy law, I have waited for Thee, O Lord.

My soul hath relied on His word: my soul hath hoped in the Lord.

From the morning watch even until night, let Israel hope in the Lord.

Because with the Lord there is mercy, and with Him plenteous redemption.

And He shall redeem Israel from all his iniquities.

V. Eternal rest give to them, O Lord.

R. And perpetual light shine upon them.

[50 days' indulgence, three times daily, for the psalm and versicle.

Plenary indulgence, once a year.—Leo XIII., Feb. 2, 1888.]

DEVOTIONS FOR CONFESSION.

Preparation.

PRAYER FOR THE GRACE OF TRUE REPENTANCE.

(ST. FIDELIS OF SIGMARINGEN.)

O Lord Jesus Christ, Who dost graciously receive those who truly sorrow for sin, grant me by Thy grace that for love of Thee, and with a good intention, I may feel profound contrition of heart. Awaken within me a pure and fervent desire to increase in love to Thee, which is the foundation and source of true compunction. Enlighten my understanding, that I may consider and understand how hateful sin is in Thy sight. Assist my memory, that I may see how often I have offended against Thee, and the circumstances that have aggravated my offences. Fill me with an abhorrence of every sin, stir my inmost soul, that I may feel the deepest sorrow and repentance for my misdeeds. Take from me all pride of heart, and dispose me to piety and devotion. Grant that I may lift my eyes to Thy majesty with love and thankfulness, on account of Thy exceeding great charity towards us, and Thy unswerving faithfulness. And, thus meditating, may I be impelled to love Thee above all things to adore Thee, to endeavor to please Thee and to serve Thee as Thou dost command. Make me conscious of my own nothingness, the infidelities of which I have been guilty, my ingratitude and injustice in Thy sight, so that I may learn to despise myself, and strive earnestly to make due reparation to Thee.

Help me, O my God, to make a firm resolution by Thy grace to avoid these faults in future, and rather to die than to offend against Thee with deliberation and forethought. Enable me, O Jesus, to make reparation to Thee for the affronts I have put upon Thee, and grant that henceforth I may glorify Thee as much by my pious conduct as I have hitherto dishonored Thee by my transgressions.

PRAYER TO THE HOLY GHOST FOR LIGHT. (ST. PETER DAMIAN.)

O Holy Ghost, God Almighty, one with the Father and the Son, and proceeding from both in an ineffable manner, vouchsafe to descend into my heart, and by Thy marvellous power dispel the darkness that still reigns there through my evil nature, so that I may discern the works that it produces, that I may bewail them deeply, and confess them humbly.

Come down, Eternal Lord and Life-giver, and with the fire of Thy charity melt the ice that is in my breast. Soften my stony heart; fill me with sorrow and repentance, that I may deplore my sins with abundant tears. Woe is me, miserable sinner that I am; how many sins I daily commit for which I ought to weep, and yet not a tear do I shed for them! Let the dew of Thy grace distil upon me from above, that my soul, which is dry and parched through having wandered far from the fount of life, may awake to new life under Thy vivifying influence. My heart is ready, O God, my heart is ready. Behold, all the secrets of my soul are open before Thee;

and with longing desire I await the time until Thou condescend to visit me.

[Here examine your conscience.]

ACT OF CONTRITION. (ST. BERNARD.)

I believe, O Lord, that Thou art my God and my Lord; I know it, and acknowledge it. In many and great things I have offended against Thy majesty; my sins are multiplied in number above the sand of the seashore—to this, alas! my unholy life bears only too sure testimony. But I take refuge in Thy mercy; I repent and am exceedingly sorry for all that I have done amiss; above all, because I have displeased Thee, the most holy God, by my sins, and defiled my soul, which was made after Thy image. Forgive me, forgive me all my transgressions; I will amend my life; I am fully resolved never again to swerve from the way of Thy commandments. Cast me not away, I humbly beseech Thee, for I know that I can find a refuge nowhere but with Thee, Whom I love above all things. Cast me not away because of my iniquities, but chastise me according to the multitude of Thy tender mercies. This I earnestly implore and confidently ask of Thy eternal loving-kindness. Amen.

RESOLUTION OF AMENDMENT. (ST. FRANCIS DE SALES.)

O Lord my God, never again will I, with the help of Thy grace, wander again in the paths of sin. I have loved them too well, but now I abhor them, and turn to Thee, O Father of mercy. To Thee alone will I live and die. In order to blot out my past iniquities I will accuse myself of them fearlessly, and tear them out of my soul even to the last and least. I will spare no effort, but strive to the utmost of my power to eradicate every fibre, especially of those sins which have the most power over me. And for this end I will employ every means of grace, according to the counsels given me, nor will I ever allow myself to think that I have done enough in reparation of my grievous misdeeds.

PRAYER BEFORE CONFESSION. (ST. FRANCES CHANTAL.)

O my God, Most Holy Trinity! I have sinned before Thee. Once more I desire to express my sincere contrition for all my transgressions; I weep for them with all my heart, from love to Thee, Who art the supreme Good, perfect in holiness. O my God, pour the oil of Thy compassion plenteously upon my wounds, that I may recover from my hurt. Thou art, and ever will be, my only hope; heal and restore me, O Lord, with the assistance of Thy grace. Guided by Thy spirit, I will henceforth endeavor to amend my ways, and serve Thee beneath the standard of the cross unto my life's end, that I may thus merit finally to praise and magnify Thee throughout eternity.

O Mary, my dearest mother, help me to observe and accomplish rightly all that thy divine Son has appointed for the forgiveness of sin.

AFTER CONFESSION.

PRAYER TO GOD THE FATHER.

How great is Thy goodness towards me, my God and my Father! Through the merits of Jesus Christ, Thou hast given me absolution of my sins, by the voice of the priest who is Thy representative. I now dare to hope that I may again be regarded as Thy well-beloved child. All thanks, praise, and glory be to Thee, Father of mercy, for this great grace, which I have deserved so little. I will not be forgetful of what Thou hast done for me, and I will keep strict watch over myself, that I may not fall into the same sins again. Give Thy blessing to this my resolution, O Lord, and grant me strength to keep it faithfully until death. I ask this for the sake of the blood Christ shed for me, and through the merits of Mary, the Mother of grace, and the intercession of all the saints. Amen.

PRAYER TO GOD THE SON.

How great are the thanks I owe to Thee, my dear Lord and Saviour Jesus Christ! I venture with all confidence to hope that, through the merits of Thy most precious blood, I have obtained the pardon of my sins. I thank Thee from the bottom of my heart, and I trust that it may be granted me to praise Thy mercy forever in heaven. Although I have hitherto offended Thee so often, for the future I will do so no more. I am steadfastly resolved thoroughly to amend my life. Thou art alone worthy of my love, therefore I will love Thee above all things, and never separate myself from Thee by sin. I now ratify all my former promises; rather will I die than offend against Thee by mortal sin. But Thou, O Jesus, knowest my frailty; give me grace to be faithful to Thee until death, and in the hour of temptation let me have recourse to Thy assistance.

PRAYER TO GOD THE HOLY GHOST.

Holy and divine Spirit, I believe that Thou art true God, one God with the Father and the Son. I adore Thee, I acknowledge Thee as the author of all the light whereby I have to-day been enabled to see how grievous a wrong I have committed in offending Thee, and how great is the obligation I am under to love Thee. I thank Thee for thus enlightening me, and again I declare how deeply I regret all that I have done amiss in Thy sight. If I had been dealt with as I deserved, I should have been thrust out into exterior darkness; but Thou hast

shown me by Thy forbearance that Thou dost not yet
regard me as a reprobate. Enlighten me further, O
blessed Spirit! Make me more and more sensible of
Thy infinite goodness, and give me good dispositions to
love Thee henceforth with my whole heart. Pour out
upon me the plenitude of Thy grace, that, taken captive
by it, I may be constrained to love Thee, and Thee alone.
I ask these blessings in the name of Jesus Christ and by
His merits. Henceforth I will belong wholly to Thee,
Whom I love as the supreme Good, the God of my heart;
receive this gift that I make of myself, and let me never
fall away from Thy love. Amen.

CONCLUDING PRAYER.

Graciously receive, O sacred Heart of Jesus, my confession and my penance, poor and imperfect though they are; and through Thy perfect charity supply, I pray Thee, all that is lacking to the depth of my contrition, and the sincerity of my desire to do penance.

O Mary, immaculate Mother of our Redeemer! On thee God has ever looked with complacency; to thy maternal care I commend the devotions I have just performed, beseeching thee to unite them to the infinite merits of the Passion of thy dear Son, and thus offer them as an oblation to the God and Father of mercies. Obtain for me the grace to bring forth worthy fruits of penance, that I may ever walk in the way of God's commandments, so as to please Him, to edify my neighbor, and work out my own salvation.

May the blessing of the Triune God, Father, Son, and Holy Ghost, be upon me and remain with me: Amen. May His grace ever live and work in me; may the protection of the Blessed Virgin Mary ever be my shield; may my holy angel guardian, to whose care I am committed, be with me and watch over me unto my life's end! Amen.

DEVOTIONS FOR COMMUNION.

Before Communion.

ACTS OF FAITH, HOPE, AND CHARITY. (ST. ALPHONSUS.)

O dearest Jesus, Son of the most high God, Who for love of me didst suffer death upon the cross, overwhelmed with anguish and with the contempt of men, I believe that Thou art here present in the Adorable Sacrament of the Altar, and I am ready to lay down my life in defence of this truth. O most loving Saviour, I hope that of Thy bounty, for the sake of the merits of that precious blood shed for me this day upon the altar, Thou wilt come to visit me, to inflame my heart with the fire of Thy love, and to give me the grace I need to continue Thy faithful and obedient servant unto my life's end.

My God, only true lover of my soul, what couldst Thou have done which Thou hast not done to compel me to love Thee? Not satisfied with dying for me, O Jesus, Thou hast vouchsafed, in addition, to institute this holy sacrament to be my spiritual food, that Thou mayst hereby give Thyself wholly to me, and unite Thyself as closely as possible with me, miserable and ungrateful as I am. Thou dost Thyself invite me to approach and receive Thee, and Thou desirest ardently that I should be united to Thee.

O charity inconceivable, that a God should give Himself wholly unto me! O my God, supreme and infinite Good, worthy of a love infinite as Thine own, I love Thee above all things, I love Thee with my whole heart, I love

Thee more than my life, I love Thee because Thou art alone worthy of my love. I love Thee because Thou desirest that I should love Thee with all my powers. Away from me, then, all affections that savor of earth; all the love of my heart shall be given to Jesus. To-day He is going to give me Himself; I, on my part, will give Him my whole self. Permit me to love Thee, O Jesus; I desire nothing but to possess Thee; I will do nothing but what will please Thee. I love Thee, my Saviour, and I unite my feeble love to the love which the angels and saints feel for Thee, to the love of Mary, Thy blessed Mother, to the love of God, Thy Eternal Father. Would that all men loved Thee! Would that I could induce all the world to love Thee, to love Thee as Thou deservest!

ACT OF HUMILITY. (ST. ALPHONSUS.)

Behold, O Jesus, I come to Thee in order that my soul may feed upon Thy sacred body. But what art Thou, O my God, and what am I? Thou art a God of infinite goodness, and I am a miserable worm, laden with innumerable sins, whereby I have again and again separated myself from Thee. I am not worthy, O my God, to enter Thy presence; I deserve to be banished to hell, and there, far from Thee, forsaken by Thee, to burn to all eternity. But Thou, Who art infinite in mercy, dost bid me come to Thee that I may receive Thee into my heart.

Behold, O Lord, I come, humble and ashamed on account of the manifold offences which I have committed against Thee, and yet full of confidence in Thy mercy and Thy love. How bitterly I grieve, O sweet Saviour, for having so often sinned against Thee. Thou hast made the sacrifice of Thy life for me, and I have abandoned Thee for what is worthless; again and again I have outraged Thy grace and Thy love. I sorrow most deeply for the transgressions against Thee, both great and small, of which I have been guilty; they are the greatest of all evils, because they have displeased Thee, O infinite goodness, and I abhor them from the bottom of my heart. I venture to hope that Thou hast pardoned them; but if I am mistaken, I implore Thee, O Jesus, forgive me now, before I receive Thee into my heart. Let me at any rate be in a state of grace when Thou comest to dwell within my breast.

ACT OF DESIRE. (ST. ALPHONSUS.)

Come, Lord Jesus, come unto the heart which is ardently longing to receive Thee. Thou art my only, my supreme good, my love, my life, my all in all. I desire to receive Thee this morning with the love of those saints who were most inflamed with love to Thee; I desire to receive Thee as Thy blessed Mother received Thee; I desire to unite my communion with her communions. O Mary, ever-blessed Virgin, my dearest Mother, do thou give Thy Son to me. Let me receive Him from thy hand. Tell Him that I am thy faithful servant, and then, when He vouchsafes to come to me, He will embrace me with greater tenderness and affection.

Lord, I am not worthy that Thou shouldst enter under my roof; say but the word and my soul shall be healed. [Three times.]

May the body of Our Lord Jesus Christ preserve my soul unto life everlasting. Amen.

AFTER COMMUNION.

ACT OF FAITH. (ST. FRANCIS OF ASSISI.)

Thou didst behold me, O my God, standing in Thy presence as a beggar at the gate of the rich man, and Thou didst bestow on me the treasures of Thy grace.

Thou gavest me Thy precious body and blood, like a robe of charity, to cover my nakedness and my shame. I stood before Thee as a slave in the presence of his master; Thou gavest me my liberty, that I might be free to love Thee. I stood before Thee a wretched sinner; Thou hast pardoned my sins, and blotted them out with Thine own blood. Now I stand before Thee as a friend, face to face with his friend; I desire to be so united to Thee in charity that I may never swerve from Thy side. I stand before Thee as a child before his father, humbly asking that I may one day enter upon the inheritance of which I am the heir. Amen.

ACT OF ADORATION. (ST. FRANCIS DE SALES.)

How can I ever sufficiently praise and magnify Thee, my Lord and Saviour Jesus Christ, Who of Thy sovereign condescension hast at this time come to abide in so humble a dwelling-place as this poor heart of mine! Thou art here present within my breast in Thy Godhead and Thy humanity, Thy body and soul, Thy flesh and blood. I truly possess Thee, Who art my Lord and my God, my Redeemer and my Sanctifier, my chief aim and final end, my only consolation and sure repose, all that I hope for, all that I desire.

I adore Thee, most loving Jesus, good shepherd of my soul! Thy sublimity and majesty fill me with awe whilst I rejoice in the tenderness of Thy mercy, and from the abyss of my own nothingness I worship Thee in all humility. I adore Thy sacred body and blood, which Thou hast given to be to me the bread of life, the pledge of intimate union with Thee. I adore Thy sacred head, for my sake crowned with thorns; I adore Thy sacred eyes, which shed so many tears for me; Thy sacred lips, by which I have been taught the way of truth; Thy sacred countenance, disfigured with rude blows; Thy sacred feet, pierced by cruel nails and fastened to the tree of shame; Thy sacred arms, extended wide in the loving desire to clasp me in their embrace; Thy sacred side, riven by the soldier's lance, that out of it might flow the water and the blood that are the witnesses to our redemption. I adore the exceeding charity of Thy tender heart, which loved me unto death, even the ignominious death of the cross. I adore Thy most holy body, O my Lord and Saviour, torn with countless wounds, enduring unspeakable torments, for my salvation; I adore Thy most sacred soul, troubled and sorrowful unto death in the Garden of Olives that I might attain to eternal life.

I worship Thee, O my Jesus, with holy reverence; I will cleave to Thee faithfully, with loyal and loving adoration, all my life long, and will call upon Thee in the hour of death. Grant Thy blessing to the resolutions I have made, that I may stand firm when the evil one assails me with a storm of temptation.

ACT OF THANKSGIVING. (ST. THOMAS OF AQUIN.)

I give Thee thanks, O Lord, heavenly Father, almighty, eternal God, that Thou hast vouchsafed, for no merit of my own, but for the mere condescension of Thy mercy, to satisfy me, a sinner, and Thine unworthy servant, with the precious body and blood of Thy Son, Our Saviour Jesus Christ. I implore Thee, let not this holy communion be to me an increase of guilt unto my punishment, but an availing plea unto pardon and forgiveness. Let it be to me the armor of faith and shield of good-will; grant that it may work the extinction of my vices, the rooting out of concupiscence and lust, and the increase within me of charity and patience, of humility and obedience. Let it be my strong defence against the snares of my enemies, visible and invisible; the stilling and calm of my impulses, carnal and spiritual; my indissoluble union with Thee, the one and true God, and a blessed consummation at my last end.

And I beseech Thee that Thou wouldst vouchsafe to bring me, sinner as I am, to that ineffable banquet where Thou, with the Son and the Holy Ghost, art to Thy saints true and unfailing light, fulness of content, joy forevermore, gladness without alloy, consummate and everlasting bliss. Through Jesus Christ, Our Lord. Amen.

PETITION. (ST. BONAVENTURE.).

Wound my inmost heart, O dearest Lord Jesus, with the blissful and salutary wound of Thy love, that true, pure, and most holy love, which causes my soul to glow and be consumed with ardent longing to possess Thee. Grant that my soul may evermore hunger for Thee, Thou bread of angels, the refreshment of holy souls, our daily, supersubstantial bread, containing in itself all sweetness, all savor, all that is delightful and attractive.

For Thee, on Whom the angels desire to look, my soul continually yearns, and my inmost being longs to be satisfied with the blissful enjoyment of Thy presence. Henceforth my soul thirsts for Thee alone, Who art the source of life, the fount of wisdom and knowledge, the well-spring of eternal brightness, the river of joy, the fulness of the riches of the dwelling-place of the Most High. For Thee I long, for Thee I sigh, after Thee alone I seek, that, finding Thee, I may draw nigh to Thee, gaze upon Thee, converse with Thee and of Thee. May every thought and action of my soul be to the praise and glory of Thy holy name, in all humility and submission, love and gladness, zeal and fervor, and steadfast endurance unto the end.

Be Thou, O Jesus, henceforth and for evermore my hope and my trust, my joy and rejoicing, my sovereign treasure; in Thee is my rest and support, my peace and refreshment, my meat and my drink, my sweetness and consolation, my sure refuge, my ready help, my real wisdom, my true riches, my unfailing inheritance, my portion to all eternity. Amen.

CONCLUDING PRAYER.

Pour forth Thy blessing, O Lord, upon Thy holy Church; upon our Holy Father the Pope, our bishop, and all our clergy; upon our country; upon those who are in authority, either ecclesiastical or civil; upon our parents or children, our relatives, friends, benefactors, and enemies. Comfort the sick, the poor, the dying; give the grace of conversion to sinners, heretics, unbelievers, apostates.

Remember in Thy mercy the souls who are suffering in purgatory, and grant them eternal rest. Deliver those who long to be released, and admit them to everlasting felicity. Amen.

PRAYERS TO OBTAIN A PLENARY INDULGENCE.

I. FOR THE EXALTATION OF THE CATHOLIC CHURCH.

O most gracious Lord Jesus Christ! Thou didst choose the holy Catholic Church as Thy bride, and for the great love wherewith Thou lovedst her Thou didst lay down Thy life for her; for her Thou didst shed Thy precious blood. In union with all faithful children of the Church, I beseech Thee to take her under Thy special protection; shield her from the assaults of the powers of hell, maintain her in unity, enrich her with graces and heavenly benedictions, cause her to shine with the light of holiness, extend her, exalt her, and

make all orthodox Christians to do Thy holy will, and serve Thee faithfully until they arrive at everlasting joys.
Our Father and Hail Mary twice.

2. FOR THE CONVERSION OF UNBELIEVERS, HERETICS, AND SINNERS.

Most compassionate Jesus, source of all goodness and mercy, God of all consolation, Who willest that all men, even those outside the fold of Thy Church, should be saved; Who desirest not the death of the sinner, but that he should be converted and live: I beseech Thee to cause the marvellous light of the Catholic faith, in which alone is salvation, to arise upon all pagans, Mohammedans, Jews, and heretics, that they may be brought to know Thee, to love Thee, and to serve Thee. Look with compassion upon all sinners, who have lost Thy sanctifying grace, and give them true conversion of heart. Remember, O my crucified Lord, that for them Thou didst endure the death of the cross, for them Thou didst shed Thy precious blood. Let not the infinite merits of Thy **passion and** death be unavailing for them. Let them **not be** banished to the regions of despair, where Thy **name is** continually blasphemed and cursed. O most merciful Jesus, soften their hard hearts by the wondrous power of Thy cross, that they may willingly take upon themselves Thy sweet yoke, and may learn to believe in **Thee,** to hope in Thee, to love Thee for evermore. **Amen.**
Our Father and Hail Mary twice.

3. FOR CONCORD AMONGST CHRISTIAN PRINCES.

O my crucified Saviour, Who hast reconciled heaven with earth and God with man, behold how frequently the blood of Christian people is shed in devastating wars! Hear how that blood cries to Thee from the ground: Have pity, have pity, O most compassionate Jesus! I implore Thee, O blessed Prince of peace, for the sake of Thy precious blood, the price of our reconciliation, and for the sake of Thy five most sacred wounds, make all Christian princes and governors to be of one mind; unite them by a bond of mutual charity, and grant to us an inviolable peace, in order that we may be able to devote ourselves more freely and fully to Thy service. Hear and answer our petitions, O God of clemency, and we will extol Thy mercy to all eternity. Amen.

Our Father and Hail Mary twice.

4. AN OFFERING OF THE INDULGENCE FOR THE SOULS IN PURGATORY.

I beseech Thee, O Jesus, my God and Saviour, by Thy infinite bounty and loving-kindness, to apply the prayers I now offer and the plenary indulgence attached to them, to the soul of NN., that it may be to his profit, and that he, being thereby delivered from the pains of purgatory, may fervently love Thee, and may laud and magnify Thee before the throne of Thy majesty. Grant also that the soul for whom I pray may obtain for me the special grace I need, and plead for me, that I may be permitted to expiate my sins in this life, and, after a happy death, may be admitted to the company of the blessed in heaven. Amen.

STANDARD CATHOLIC BOOKS

PUBLISHED BY

BENZIGER BROTHERS,

CINCINNATI: NEW YORK: CHICAGO:
343 Main St.   36 & 38 BARCLAY ST.   178 Monroe St.

ABANDONMENT ; or, Absolute Surrender of Self to Divine Providence. By Rev. J. P. CAUSSADE, S.J. 32mo,   *net*, 0 40

ANALYSIS OF THE GOSPELS of the Sundays of the Year. By Rev. L. A. LAMBERT, LL.D. 12mo,   *net*, 1 25

ART OF PROFITING BY OUR FAULTS, according to St. Francis de Sales. By Rev. J. TISSOT. 32mo,   *net*, 0 40

BIBLE, THE HOLY. With Annotations, References, and an Historical and Chronological Index. 12mo, cloth,   1 25
Also in finer bindings.

BIRTHDAY SOUVENIR, OR DIARY. With a Subject of Meditation for Every Day. By Mrs. A. E. BUCHANAN. 32mo, . 0 50

BLESSED ONES OF 1888. By ELIZA A. DONNELLY. 16mo, illustrated,   0 50

BLIND FRIEND OF THE POOR: Reminiscences of the Life and Works of Mgr. de SEGUR. 16mo,   0 50

BROWNSON, ORESTES A., Literary, Scientific, and Political Views of. Selected from his works, by H. F. BROWNSON. 12mo,   *net*, 1 25

BUGG, LELIA HARDIN. The Correct Thing for Catholics. 16mo,   0 75

——— A Lady. Manners and Social Usages. 16mo,   1 00

CANONICAL PROCEDURE in Disciplinary and Criminal Cases of Clerics. By the Rev. FRANCIS DROSTE. Edited by the Right Rev. SEBASTIAN G. MESSMER, D.D. 12mo,   *net*, 1 50

CATECHISM OF FAMILIAR THINGS. Their History and the Events which led to their Discovery. 12mo, illustrated,   1 00

CATHOLIC BELIEF; or, A Short and Simple Exposition of Catholic Doctrine. By the Very Rev. JOSEPH FAÁ DI BRUNO, D.D. Author's American edition edited by Rev. LOUIS A. LAMBERT. 200th Thousand. 16mo.
Paper, 0.25 ; 25 copies, 4.25 ; 50 copies, 7.50 ; 100 copies,   12 50
Cloth, 0.50; 25 copies, 8.50; 50 copies, 15.00; 100 copies,   25 00

"When a book supplies, as does this one, a demand that necessitates the printing of one hundred thousand [now two hundred thousand] copies, its merits need no eulogizing."—*Ave Maria.*
"The amount of good accomplished by it can never be told."—*Catholic Union and Times.*

STANDARD CATHOLIC BOOKS.

CATHOLIC FAMILY LIBRARY. Composed of "The Christian Father," "The Christian Mother," "Sure Way to a Happy Marriage," "Instructions on the Commandments and Sacraments," and "Stories for First Communicants." 5 volumes in box, 2 00

CATHOLIC HOME ANNUAL. A Charming Annual for Catholics. 0 25

CATHOLIC HOME LIBRARY. 10 volumes. 12mo, each, 0 50
Per set, 3 00

CATHOLIC MEMOIRS OF VERMONT AND NEW HAMPSHIRE. 12mo, cloth, 1.00 ; paper, 0 50

CATHOLIC WORSHIP. The Sacraments, Ceremonies, and Festivals of the Church explained. BRENNAN. Paper, 0.15 ; per 100, 9.00. Cloth, 0.25 ; per 100, 15 00

CATHOLIC YOUNG MAN OF THE PRESENT DAY. By Right Rev. AUGUSTINE EGGER, D.D. 32mo, paper, 0.15 ; per 100, 9.00. Cloth, 0.25 ; per 100, 15 00

CHARITY THE ORIGIN OF EVERY BLESSING. 16mo, 0 75

CHRIST IN TYPE AND PROPHECY. By Rev. A. J. MAAS, S.J. 2 vols., 12mo, *net*, 4 00
"By far the most serviceable manual that has hitherto appeared in the English language on a most important subject."—*London Tablet.*

CHRISTIAN ANTHROPOLOGY. By Rev. J. THEIN. 8vo, *net*, 2 50

CHRISTIAN FATHER, THE : what he should be, and what he should do. Paper, 0.25 ; per 100, 12.50. Cloth, 0.35 ; per 100, 21 00

CHRISTIAN MOTHER, THE : the Education of her Children and her Prayer. Paper, 0.25 ; per 100, 12.50. Cloth, 0.35 ; per 100, 21 00

CIRCUS-RIDER'S DAUGHTER, THE. A novel. By F. v. BRACKEL. 12mo, 1 25

CLARKE, REV. RICHARD F., S.J. The Devout Year. Short Meditations. 24mo, *net*, 0 60

COCHEM'S EXPLANATION OF THE MASS. With Preface by Rt. Rev. C. P. MAES, D.D. 12mo, cloth, 1 25

COMEDY OF ENGLISH PROTESTANTISM, THE. Edited by A. F. MARSHALL, B.A. Oxon. 12mo, *net*, 0 50

COMPENDIUM SACRAE LITURGIAE Juxta Ritum Romanum una cum Appendice De Jure Ecclesiastico Particulari in America Foederata Sept. vigente scripsit P. WAPELHORST, O.S.F. 8vo, *net*, 2 50

CONNOR D'ARCY'S STRUGGLES. A novel. By Mrs. W. M. BERTHOLDS. 12mo, 1 25

COUNSELS OF A CATHOLIC MOTHER to Her Daughter, 16mo, 0 50

CROWN OF THORNS, THE; or, The Little Breviary of the Holy Face. 32mo, 0 50

DATA OF MODERN ETHICS EXAMINED, THE. By Rev. JOHN J. MING, S.J. 12mo, *net*, 2 00

DE GOESBRIAND, RIGHT REV. L. Christ on the Altar. Instructions for the Sundays and Festivals of the Year. Quarto cloth, richly illustrated, gilt edges, 6 00

—— Jesus the Good Shepherd. 16mo, *net*, 0 75

—— The Labors of the Apostles: Their Teaching of the Nations. 12mo, *net*, 1 00

—— History of Confession; or, The Dogma of Confession Vindicated. 16mo, *net*, 0 75

EGAN, MAURICE F. The Vocation of Edward Conway. A novel. 12mo, 1 25

—— The Flower of the Flock, and the Badgers of Belmont. 12mo, 1 00

—— How They Worked Their Way, and Other Stories, 1 00

—— A Gentleman. 16mo, 0 75

ENGLISH READER. Edited by Rev. EDWARD CONNOLLY, S.J. 12mo, 1 25

EUCHARISTIC GEMS. A Thought about the Most Blessed Sacrament for Every Day, By Rev. L. C. COELENBIER. 16mo, 0 75

EXAMINATION OF CONSCIENCE for the use of Priests who are making a Retreat. BY GADUEL. 32mo, *net*, 0 30

EXPLANATION OF THE BALTIMORE CATECHISM of Christian Doctrine. By Rev. THOMAS L. KINKEAD. 12mo, *net*, 1 00

EXPLANATION OF THE GOSPELS of the Sundays and Holydays. From the Italian, by Rev. L. A. LAMBERT, LL.D. With An Explanation of Catholic Worship. From the German, by Rev. RICHARD BRENNAN, LL.D. 24mo, illustrated.
Paper, 0.25; 25 copies, 4.25; 50 copies, 7.50; 100 copies, 12 50
Cloth, 0.50; 25 copies, 8.50; 50 copies, 15.00; 100 copies, 25 00

"It is with pleasure I recommend the 'Explanation of the Gospels and of Catholic Worship' to the clergy and the laity. It should have a very extensive sale; lucid explanation, clear style, solid matter, beautiful illustrations. Everybody will learn from this little book."—ARCHBISHOP JANSSENS.

FABIOLA; or, The Church of the Catacombs. By CARDINAL WISEMAN. Illustrated Edition. 12mo, 1 25
Edition de luxe, 6 00

STANDARD CATHOLIC BOOKS.

FINN, REV. FRANCIS J., S.J.   Percy Wynn ; or, Making a Boy
  of Him.   12mo,   0 85
——— Tom Playfair; or, Making a Start. 12mo,   0 85
——— Harry Dee; or, Working it Out. 12mo,   0 85
——— Claude Lightfoot ; or, How the Problem was Solved.
  12mo,   0 85
——— Ethelred Preston; or, The Adventures of a Newcomer.
  12mo,   0 85
——— Mostly Boys.   16mo,   0 85
  Father Finn's books are, in the opinion of the best critics, standard works
  in modern English literature ; they are full of fascinating interest, replete with
  stirring and amusing incidents of college life, and admirably adapted to the
  wants of our boys.

FIVE O'CLOCK STORIES ; or, The Old Tales Told Again.
  16mo,   0 75

FLOWERS OF THE PASSION. Thoughts of St. Paul of the Cross.
  By Rev. LOUIS TH. DE JÉSUS-AGONISANT. 32mo,   0 50

FOLLOWING OF CHRIST, THE. By THOMAS À KEMPIS.
  With reflections. Small 32mo, cloth,   0 50
  Without reflections. Small 32mo, cloth,   0 45
  Edition de luxe. Illustrated,   from 1 50 up.

FRANCIS DE SALES, ST. Guide for Confession and Communion. Translated by Mrs. BENNETT-GLADSTONE. 32mo, 0 60
——— Maxims and Counsels for Every Day. 32mo,   0 50
——— New Year Greetings. 32mo, flexible cloth, 15 cents ; per
  100,   10 00

GENERAL PRINCIPLES OF THE RELIGIOUS LIFE. By
  Very Rev. BONIFACE F. VERHEYEN, O.S.B. 32mo,   *net*, 0 30

GLORIES OF DIVINE GRACE. From the German of Dr. M.
  JOS. SCHEEBEN, by a BENEDICTINE MONK. 12mo,   *net*, 1 50

GOD KNOWABLE AND KNOWN. RONAYNE. 12mo, *net*, 1 25

GOFFINE'S DEVOUT INSTRUCTIONS on the Epistles and
  Gospels. With Preface by His Eminence Cardinal GIBBONS.
  Illustrated edition. 8vo, cloth, 1.00; 10 copies, 7.50 ; 25 copies,
  17.50 ; 50 copies,   33 50
    This is the best, the cheapest, and the most popular illustrated
  edition of Goffine's Instructions.

"GOLDEN SANDS," Books by the Author of :
    Golden Sands. Third, Fourth, Fifth Series. 32mo, each, 0 60
    Book of the Professed. 32mo.
        Vol. I.   ⎫   ⎧ *net*, 0 75
        Vol. II. ⎬ Each with a steel-plate Frontispiece. ⎨ *net*, 0 60
        Vol. III. ⎭   ⎩ *net*, 0 60
    Prayer. 32mo,   *net*, 0 40
    The Little Book of Superiors. 32mo,   *net*, 0 60
    Spiritual Direction. 32mo,   *net*, 0 60
    Little Month of May. 32mo, flexible cloth,   0 25
    Little Month of the Poor Souls. 32mo, flexible cloth,   0 25

STANDARD CATHOLIC BOOKS. 5

GREETINGS TO THE CHRIST-CHILD. A Collection of Christmas Poems for the Young. 16mo, illustrated, 0 50

GROU, REV. J., S.J. The Characteristics of True Devotion. Translated from the French by the Rev. ALEXANDER CLINTON, S.J. A new edition, by Rev. SAMUEL H. FRISBEE, S.J. 16mo, *net*, 0 75

——— The Interior of Jesus and Mary. Edited by Rev. SAMUEL H. FRISBEE, S.J. 16mo, 2 vols., *net*, 2 00

HAMON'S MEDITATIONS. See under MEDITATIONS. 5 vols. 16mo, *net*, 5 00

HANDBOOK FOR ALTAR SOCIETIES, and Guide for Sacristans and others having charge of the Altar and Sanctuary. 16mo, *net*, 0 75

HANDBOOK OF THE CHRISTIAN RELIGION. For the use of Advanced Students and the Educated Laity. By Rev. W. WILMERS, S.J. From the German. Edited by Rev. JAMES CONWAY, S.J. 12mo, *net*, 1 50

HAPPY YEAR, A; or, The Year Sanctified by Meditating on the Maxims and Sayings of the Saints. By ABBÉ LASAUSSE. 12mo, *net*, 1 00

HEART, THE, OF ST. JANE FRANCES DE CHANTAL. Thoughts and Prayers. 32mo, *net*, 0 40

HIDDEN TREASURE; or, The Value and Excellence of the Holy Mass. By ST. LEONARD OF PORT-MAURICE. 32mo, 0 50

HISTORY OF THE CATHOLIC CHURCH. By Dr. H. BRUECK. With Additions from the Writings of His Eminence Cardinal Hergenröther. Translated by Rev. E. PRUENTE. 2 vols., 8vo, *net*, 3 00

HISTORY OF THE CATHOLIC CHURCH. Adapted by Rev. RICHARD BRENNAN, LL.D. With a History of the Church in America, by JOHN GILMARY SHEA, LL.D. With 90 Illustrations. 8vo, 2 00

HISTORY OF THE MASS and its Ceremonies in the Eastern and Western Church. By Rev. JOHN O'BRIEN, A.M. 12mo, *net*, 1 25

HOLY FACE OF JESUS, THE. A Series of Meditations on the Litany of the Holy Face. 32mo, 0 50

HOURS BEFORE THE ALTAR; or, Meditations on the Holy Eucharist. By Mgr. DE LA BOUILLERIE. 32mo, 0 50

HOW TO GET ON. By Rev. BERNARD FEENEY. 12mo, paper, 0 50; cloth, 1 00

HUNOLT'S SERMONS. Sermons by the Rev. FRANCIS HUNOLT, Priest of the Society of Jesus and Preacher in the Cathedral of

Treves. Translated from the original German edition of Cologne, 1740, by the Rev. J. ALLEN, D.D. 12 vols., 8vo, 30 00
Per set of 2 vols., *net*, 5 00
Vols. 1, 2. The Christian State of Life.
Vols. 3, 4. The Bad Christian.
Vols. 5, 6. The Penitent Christian.
Vols. 7, 8. The Good Christian.
Vols. 9, 10. The Christian's Last End.
Vols. 11, 12. The Christian's Model.

His Eminence Cardinal Satolli, Pro-Delegate Apostolic: "... I believe that in it is found realized the desire of the Holy Father, who not long ago in an encyclical urged so strongly the return to the simple, unaffected, but earnest and eloquent preaching of the word of God. . . ."

His Eminence Cardinal Gibbons, Archbishop of Baltimore: . . . "Contain a fund of solid doctrine, presented in a clear and forcible style. These sermons should find a place in the library of every priest. . . ."

His Eminence Cardinal Vaughan, Archbishop of Westminster: "... I cannot praise it too highly, and I think it might find a place in every priest's library."

His Eminence Cardinal Logue, Archbishop of Armagh, Primate of all Ireland: "... What is of real service is some work in which the preacher can find sound, solid matter. I believe Father Hunolt's Sermons furnishes an inexhaustible treasure of such matter. . . ."

IDOLS; or, The Secret of the Rue Chaussée d'Antin. A novel. By RAOUL DE NAVERY. 12mo, 1 25

INSTRUCTIONS ON THE COMMANDMENTS and the Sacraments. By ST. LIGUORI. 32mo. Paper, 0.25; per 100, 12 50
Cloth, 0.35; per 100, 21 00

KONINGS, THEOLOGIA MORALIS. Novissimi Ecclesiæ Doctoris S. Alphonsi. In Compendium Redacta, et Usui Venerabilis Cleri Americani Accommodata, Auctore A. KONINGS, C.SS. R. Editio septima, auctior, et novis curis expolitior, curante HENRICO KUPER, C.SS.R. The two vols. in one, half morocco, *net*, 4 00

LEGENDS AND STORIES OF THE HOLY CHILD JESUS from Many Lands. Collected by A. FOWLER LUTZ. 16mo, 0 75

LEPER QUEEN, THE. A Story of the Thirteenth Century. 16mo, 0 50

LIBRARY OF THE RELIGIOUS LIFE. Composed of "Book of the Professed," by the author of "Golden Sands," 3 vols.; "Spiritual Direction," by the author of "Golden Sands"; and "Souvenir of the Novitiate." 5 vols., 32mo, in case, 3 25

LIFE AND ACTS OF LEO XIII. By Rev. JOSEPH E. KELLER, S.J. Fully and beautifully illustrated. 8vo, 2 00

LIFE OF ST. ALOYSIUS GONZAGA. From the Italian of Rev. Father CEPARI, S.J. Edited by Rev. F. GOLDIE, S.J. Edition de luxe, richly illustrated. 8vo, *net*, 2 50

LIFE OF THE EVER-BLESSED VIRGIN. From Her Conception to Her Assumption. 12mo, imitation cloth, 0 30

LIFE OF FATHER CHARLES SIRE. By his brother, Rev. VITAL SIRE. 12mo, *net*, 1 00

LIFE OF ST. CLARE OF MONTEFALCO. By Rev. JOSEPH A. LOCKE, O.S.A. 12mo, *net*, 0 75

LIFE OF THE VEN. MARY CRESCENTIA HÖSS.
 12mo, *net*, 1 25
LIFE OF REV. MOTHER ST. JOHN FONTBONNE. By
 Abbé Rivaux. 12mo, *net*, 1 25
LIFE OF ST. FRANCIS SOLANUS, APOSTLE OF PERU.
 16mo, *net*, 0 50
LIFE OF ST. GERMAINE COUSIN. 16mo, 0 50
LIFE OF ST. IGNATIUS OF LOYOLA. By Father Genelli.
 12mo, *net*, 1 25
LIFE OF ST. CHANTAL. See under St. Chantal. *net*, 4 00
(LIFE OF) MOST REV. JOHN HUGHES, First Archbishop of
 New York. By Rev. H. A. Brann, D.D. 12mo, *net*, 0 75
LIFE OF FATHER JOGUES. By Father Felix Martin, S.J.
 From the French by John Gilmary Shea. 12mo, *net*, 0 75
LIFE OF MLLE. LE GRAS. 12mo, *net*, 1 25
LIFE OF MARY FOR CHILDREN. By Anne R. Bennett, née
 Gladstone. 24mo, illustrated, *net*, 0 50
LIFE OF RIGHT REV. JOHN N. NEUMANN, D.D. By Rev.
 E. Grimm, C.SS.R. 12mo, *net*, 1 25
LIFE OF OUR LORD AND SAVIOUR JESUS CHRIST and of
 His blessed Mother. Adapted by Rev. Richard Brennan,
 LL.D. With nearly 600 illustrations. No. 1. Roan back, gold
 title, plain cloth sides, sprinkled edges, *net*, 5 00
 No. 3. Morocco back and corners, cloth sides with gold stamp,
 gilt edges, *net*, 7 00
 No. 4. Full morocco, richly gilt back, with large figure of Our
 Lord in gold on side, gilt edges, *net*, 9 00
 No. 5. Full morocco, block-paneled sides, superbly gilt, gilt
 edges, *net*, 10 00
LIFE OF OUR BLESSED LORD. His Life, Death, Resurrection. 12mo, imitation cloth, 0 30
LIFE, POPULAR, OF ST. TERESA OF JESUS. By L'Abbé
 Marie-Joseph. 12mo, *net*, 0 75
LIGUORI, ST. ALPHONSUS DE. Complete Ascetical Works of.
 Centenary Edition. Edited by Rev. Eugene Grimm, C.SS.R.
 Price, per volume, *net*, 1 25
 Each book is complete in itself, and any volume will be sold separately.
 Volumes 1 to 22 are now ready.

Preparation for Death.
Way of Salvation and of Perfection.
Great Means of Salvation and Perfection.
Incarnation, Birth, and Infancy of Christ.
The Passion and Death of Christ.
The Holy Eucharist.
The Glories of Mary, 2 vols.
Victories of the Martyrs.

True Spouse of Christ, 2 vols.
Dignity and Duties of the Priest.
The Holy Mass.
The Divine Office.
Preaching.
Abridged Sermons for all the Sundays.
Miscellany.
Letters, 4 vols.
Letters and General Index.
Life of St. Alphonsus, 2 vols.

STANDARD CATHOLIC BOOKS.

LINKED LIVES. A novel. By Lady Gertrude Douglas. 8vo, 1 50

LITTLE COMPLIMENTS OF THE SEASON. Simple Verses for Namedays, Birthdays, Christmas, New Year, and other festive and social occasions. By Eleanor C. Donnelly. 12mo, *net*, 0 50

LITTLE MANUAL OF ST. ANTHONY. Illustrated. 32mo, cloth, 0 60

LITTLE MANUAL OF THE SODALITY OF THE CHILD JESUS. 32mo, 0 20

LITTLE PICTORIAL LIVES OF THE SAINTS. With Reflections for Every Day in the Year. Edited by John Gilmary Shea, LL.D. With nearly 400 illustrations. 12mo, cloth, ink and gold side, 1 00
10 copies, 6.25; 25 copies, 15.00; 50 copies, 27.50; 100 copies, 50 00

The book has received the approbation of the following prelates: Archbishop Kenrick, Archbishop Grace, Archbishop Hennessy, Archbishop Salpointe, Archbishop Ryan, Archbishop Gross, Archbishop Duhamel, Archbishop Kain, Archbishop O'Brien, Archbishop Katzer, Bishop McCloskey, Bishop Grandin, Bishop O'Hara, Bishop Mullen, Bishop Marty, Bishop Ryan, of Buffalo; Bishop Fink, Bishop Seidenbush, Bishop Moreau, Bishop Racine, Bishop Spalding, Bishop Vertin, Bishop Junger, Bishop Naughten, Bishop Richter, Bishop Rademacher, Bishop Cosgrove, Bishop Curtis, and Bishop Glorieux.

LITTLE PRAYER BOOK OF THE SACRED HEART. Prayers and Practices of Blessed Margaret Mary. Sm. 32mo, cloth, 0 40
Also in finer bindings.

LITTLE SAINT OF NINE YEARS. From the French of Mgr. De Segur, by Mary McMahon. 16mo, 0 50

LIVES, SHORT, OF THE SAINTS; or, Our Birthday Bouquet. By Eleanor C. Donnelly. 16mo, 1 00

LOURDES. Its Inhabitants, Its Pilgrims, Its Miracles. By R. F. Clarke, S.J. 16mo, illustrated, 0 75

LUTHER'S OWN STATEMENTS Concerning his Teachings and its Results. By Henry O'Connor, S.J. 12mo, paper, 0 15

MANIFESTATION OF CONSCIENCE. Confessions and Communions in Religious Communities. By Rev. Pie de Langogne, O.M.Cap. 32mo, *net*, 0 50

MANUAL OF THE HOLY FAMILY. Prayers and Instructions for Catholic Parents. 32mo, cloth, 0 60
Also in finer bindings.

MANUAL OF INDULGENCED PRAYERS. A Complete Prayer Book. Arranged and disposed for daily use by Rev. Bonaventure Hammer, O.S.F. Small 32mo, cloth, 0 40
Also in finer bindings.

MARCELLA GRACE. A novel. By Rosa Mulholland. With illustrations after original drawings. 12mo, 1 25

MARRIAGE. By Very Rev. Père Monsabré, O.P. From the French, by M. Hopper. 12mo, *net*, 1 00

STANDARD CATHOLIC BOOKS. 9

MARRIAGE, Popular Instructions On. By Very Rev. F. GIRARDEY, C.SS.R. 32mo, paper, 0.25; per 100, 12.50; cloth, 0.35; per 100, 21 00

The instructions treat of the great dignity of matrimony, its indissolubility, the obstacles to it, the evils of mixed marriage, the manner of getting married, and the duties it imposes on the married between each other and in reference to their offspring.

MEANS OF GRACE, THE. A Complete Exposition of the Seven Sacraments, of the Sacramentals, and of Prayer, with a Comprehensive Explanation of the "Lord's Prayer" and the "Hail Mary." By Rev. RICHARD BRENNAN, LL.D. With 180 full-page and other illustrations. 8vo, cloth, 2.50; gilt edges, 3.00; Library edition, half levant, 3 50

"The best book for family use out."—BISHOP MULLEN.
"A work worthy of unstinted praise and heartiest commendation."—BISHOP RYAN, of Buffalo.
"The wealth of matter, the admirable arrangement, and the simplicity of language of this work will make it a valuable addition to the household library."—BISHOP BRADLEY.

MEDITATIONS (BAXTER) for Every Day in the Year. By Rev. ROGER BAXTER, S.J. Republished by Rev. P. NEALE, S.J. Small 12mo, *net*, 1 25

MEDITATIONS (HAMON'S) FOR ALL THE DAYS OF THE YEAR. For the use of Priests, Religious, and the Laity. By Rev. M. HAMON, SS., Pastor of St. Sulpice, Paris. From the French, by Mrs. ANNE R. BENNETT-GLADSTONE. With Alphabetic Index. 5 vols., 16mo, cloth, gilt top, each with a Steel Engraving, *net*, 5 00

"The five handsome volumes will form a very useful addition to the devotional library of every ecclesiastic."—HIS EMINENCE CARDINAL LOGUE.
"Hamon's doctrine is the unadulterated word of God, presented with unction, exquisite taste, and freed from that exaggerated and sickly sentimentalism which disgusts when it does not mislead."—MOST REV. P. L. CHAPELLE, D.D.
"We are using them daily, and are delighted with them."—MOTHER M. BLANCHE, Mother House Sisters of Charity, Mt. St. Joseph, O.
"Having examined the 'Meditations' by M. Hamon, SS., we are pleased to recommend them not only as useful and practicable for religious, but also for those who in the world desire by means of mental prayer to advance in the spiritual life."—SISTERS OF ST. JOSEPH, Flushing, L. I.

MEDITATIONS (PERINALDO) on the Sufferings of Jesus Christ. From the Italian of Rev. FRANCIS DA PERINALDO, O.S.F. 12mo, *net*, 0 75

MEDITATIONS (VERCRUYSSE), for Every Day in the Year, on the Life of Our Lord Jesus Christ. By the Rev. Father BRUNO VERCRUYSSE, S.J. 2 vols., 4 00

MEDITATIONS ON THE PASSION OF OUR LORD. By a PASSIONIST FATHER. 32mo, 0 40

MISTRESS OF NOVICES, The, Instructed in her Duties. From the French of the ABBÉ LEGUAY, by Rev. IGNATIUS SISK. 12mo, cloth, *net*, 0 75

MOMENTS BEFORE THE TABERNACLE. By Rev. MATTHEW RUSSELL, S.J. 24mo, *net*, 0 40

MONK'S PARDON. A Historical Romance of the Time of Philip IV. of Spain. By RAOUL DE NAVERY. 12mo, 1 25

MONTH OF THE DEAD. 32mo, 0 75

MONTH OF MAY. From the French of Father DEBUSSI, S.J., by ELLA MCMAHON. 32mo, 0 50

MONTH, NEW, OF MARY, St. Francis de Sales. 32mo, 0 40

MONTH, NEW, OF THE SACRED HEART, St. Francis de Sales. 32mo, 0 40

MONTH, NEW, OF ST. JOSEPH, St. Francis de Sales. 32mo, 0 40

MONTH, NEW, OF THE HOLY ANGELS, St. Francis de Sales. 32mo, 0 40

MR. BILLY BUTTONS. A novel. By Walter Lecky. 12mo, 1 25

MÜLLER, REV. MICHAEL, C.SS.R. God the Teacher of Mankind. A plain, comprehensive Explanation of Christian Doctrine. 9 vols., crown 8vo. Per set, *net*, 9 50
    The Church and Her Enemies. *net*, 1 10
    The Apostles' Creed. *net*, 1 10
    The First and Greatest Commandment. *net*, 1 40
    Explanation of the Commandments, continued. Precepts of the Church. *net*, 1 10
    Dignity, Authority, and Duties of Parents, Ecclesiastical and Civil Powers. Their Enemies. *net*, 1 40
    Grace and the Sacraments. *net*, 1 25
    Holy Mass. *net*, 1 25
    Eucharist and Penance. *net*, 1 10
    Sacramentals—Prayer, etc. *net*, 1 00

—— Familiar Explanation of Catholic Doctrine. 12mo, 1 00

—— The Prodigal Son; or, The Sinner's Return to God. 8vo, *net*, 1 00

—— The Devotion of the Holy Rosary and the Five Scapulars. 8vo, *net*, 0 75

—— The Catholic Priesthood. 2 vols., 8vo, *net*, 3 00

MY FIRST COMMUNION: The Happiest Day of My Life. BRENNAN. 16mo, illustrated, 0 75

NAMES THAT LIVE IN CATHOLIC HEARTS. Cardinal Ximenes—Michael Angelo—Samuel de Champlain—Archbishop Plunkett—Charles Carroll—Henry Larochejacquelein—Simon de Montfort. By ANNA T. SADLIER. 12mo, 1 00

NATALIE NARISCHKIN, Sister of Charity of St. Vincent of Paul. By Lady G. FULLERTON. 12mo, *net*, 0 75

NEW TESTAMENT, THE. 32mo. Limp cloth, *net*, 0.20; levant, *net*, 1.00; French calf, red edges, *net*, 1 60

OFFICE, COMPLETE, OF HOLY WEEK, according to the
Roman Missal and Breviary, in Latin and English. New
edition, revised and enlarged. 24mo, cloth, 0.50 ; cloth, limp,
gilt edges, 1 00
Also in finer bindings.

O'GRADY, ELEANOR. Aids to Correct and Effective Elocution.
12mo, 1 25
——— Select Recitations for Schools and Academies. 12mo, 1 00
——— Readings and Recitations for Juniors. 16mo, *net*, 0 50
——— Elocution Class. A Simplification of the Laws and Principles of Expression. 16mo, *net*, 0 50

ON CHRISTIAN ART. By EDITH HEALY. 16mo, 0 50

ON THE ROAD TO ROME, and How Two Brothers Got There.
By WILLIAM RICHARDS. 16mo, *net*, 0 75

ONE AND THIRTY DAYS WITH BLESSED MARGARET
MARY. 32mo, flexible cloth, 0 25

ONE ANGEL MORE IN HEAVEN. With Letters of Condolence by St. Francis de Sales and others. White mar., 0 50

OUR BIRTHDAY BOUQUET. Culled from the Shrines of Saints
and the Gardens of Poets. By E. C. DONNELLY. 16mo, 1 00

OUR LADY OF GOOD COUNSEL IN GENAZZANO. By
ANNE R. BENNETT, née GLADSTONE. 32mo, 0 75

OUR OWN WILL, and How to Detect it in Our Actions. By the
Rev. JOHN ALLEN, D.D. 16mo, *net*, 0 75

OUR YOUNG FOLKS' LIBRARY. 10 volumes. 12mo. Each,
0 50 ; per set, 3 00

OUTLAW OF CAMARGUE, THE. A novel. By A. DE LAMOTHE.
12mo, 1 25

OUTLINES OF DOGMATIC THEOLOGY. By Rev. SYLVESTER
J. HUNTER, S.J. 3 vols., 12mo, *net*, 4 50

PARADISE ON EARTH OPENED TO ALL ; or, A Religious
Vocation the Surest Way in Life. 32mo, *net*, 0 40

PEARLS FROM FABER. Selected and arranged by MARION J.
BRUNOWE. 32mo, 0 50

PETRONILLA, and other Stories. By E. C. DONNELLY. 12mo, 1 00

PHILOSOPHY, ENGLISH MANUALS OF CATHOLIC.
    Logic. By RICHARD F. CLARKE, S.J. 12mo, *net*, 1 25
    First Principles of Knowledge. By JOHN RICKABY, S.J.
    12mo, *net*, 1 25
    Moral Philosophy (Ethics and Natural Law). By JOSEPH
    RICKABY, S.J. 12mo, *net*, 1 25
    Natural Theology. By BERNARD BOEDDER, S.J. 12mo, *net*, 1 50
    Psychology. By MICHAEL MAHER, S.J. 12mo, *net*, 1 50
    General Metaphysics. By JOHN RICKABY, S.J. 12mo, *net*, 1 25
    A Manual of Political Economy. By C. S. DEVAS, Esq., M.A.
    12mo, *net*, 1 50

PICTORIAL LIVES OF THE SAINTS. With Reflections for Every Day in the Year. Edited by JOHN GILMARY SHEA, LL.D. 50th Thousand. 8vo, 2 00
5 copies, 6.65; 10 copies, 12.50; 25 copies, 27.50; 50 copies, 50 00

PRAYER-BOOK FOR LENT. Meditations and Prayers for Lent. 32mo, cloth, 0 50
Also in finer bindings.

PRAXIS SYNODALIS. Manuale Synodi Diocesanæ ac Provincialis Celebrandæ. 12mo, *net*, 0 60

PRIEST IN THE PULPIT, THE. A Manual of Homiletics and Catechetics. Adapted from the German of Rev. I. SCHUECH, O.S.B., by Rev. B. LUEBBERMANN. 8vo, *net*, 1 50

PRIMER FOR CONVERTS, A. By Rev. J. T. DURWARD. 32mo, flexible cloth, 0 25

PRINCIPLES OF ANTHROPOLOGY AND BIOLOGY. By Rev. THOMAS HUGHES, S.J. 16mo, *net*, 0 75

REASONABLENESS OF CATHOLIC CEREMONIES AND PRACTICES. By Rev. J. J. BURKE. 12mo, flexible cloth, 0 35

RELIGIOUS STATE, THE. With a Short Treatise on Vocation to the Priesthood. By ST. ALPHONSUS DE LIGUORI. 32mo, 0 50

REMINISCENCES OF RT. REV. EDGAR P. WADHAMS, D.D., First Bishop of Ogdensburg. By Rev. C. A. WALWORTH. 12mo, illustrated, *net*, 1 00

RIGHTS OF OUR LITTLE ONES; or, First Principles on Education in Catechetical Form. By Rev. JAMES CONWAY, S.J. 32mo, paper, 0.15; per 100, 9.00; cloth, 0.25; per 100, 15 00

ROSARY, THE MOST HOLY, in Thirty-one Meditations, Prayers, and Examples. By Rev. EUGENE GRIMM, C.SS.R. 32mo, 0 50

RUSSO, N., S.J.—De Philosophia Morali Prælectiones in Collegio Georgiopolitano Soc. Jes. Anno 1889-90 Habitae, a Patre NICOLAO RUSSO. Editio altera. 8vo, half leather, *net*, 2 00

ST. CHANTAL AND THE FOUNDATION OF THE VISITATION. By Monseigneur BOUGAUD. 2 vols., 8vo, *net*, 4 00

ST. JOSEPH, THE ADVOCATE OF HOPELESS CASES. From the French of Rev. Father HUGUET. 24mo, 1 00

SACRAMENTALS OF THE HOLY CATHOLIC CHURCH, THE. By Rev. A. A. LAMBING, LL.D. Large Edition, 12mo, *net*, 1 25
Popular Edition, illustrated, 24mo.
Paper, 0.25; 25 copies, 4.25; 50 copies, 7.50; 100 copies, 12 50
Cloth, 0.50; 25 copies, 8.50; 50 copies, 15.00; 100 copies, 25 00
"Am glad you have issued so practical a work, in a shape in which it ought to reach every Catholic family."—CARDINAL SATOLLI, Delegate Apostolic.

STANDARD CATHOLIC BOOKS. 13

SACRED HEART, BOOKS ON THE.
    Devotions to the Sacred Heart for the First Friday of Every Month. By P. HUGUET. 32mo,   0 40
    213. Imitation Levant, limp, gilt centre, round corners, edges red under gold,   1 35
    Imitation of the Sacred Heart of Jesus. By Rev. F. ARNOUDT, S.J. From the Latin by Rev. J. M. FASTRE, S.J. 16mo, cloth,   1 25
    Month of the Sacred Heart of Jesus. From the French of Rev. Father HUGUET. 32mo,   0 75
    New Month of the Sacred Heart, St. Francis de Sales. 32mo, 0 40
    One and Thirty Days with Blessed Margaret Mary. From the French by a Visitandine of Baltimore. 32mo, flexible cloth,   0 25
    Pearls from the Casket of the Sacred Heart of Jesus. A Collection of the Letters, Maxims, and Practices of the Blessed Margaret Mary Alacoque. Edited by ELEANOR C. DONNELLY. 32mo,   0 50
    Month of the Sacred Heart for the Young Christian. By BROTHER PHILIPPE. From the French by E. A. MULLIGAN. 32mo,   0 50
    Sacred Heart Studied in the Sacred Scriptures. By Rev. H. SAINTRAIN, C.SS.R. 8vo,   *net*, 2 00
    Revelations of the Sacred Heart to Blessed Margaret Mary; and the History of her Life. By Monseigneur BOUGAUD. 8vo,   *net*, 1 50
    Six Sermons on Devotion to the Sacred Heart of Jesus. From the German of Rev. Dr. E. BIERBAUM, by ELLA MCMAHON. 16mo,   *net*, 0 60
    Year of the Sacred Heart. Drawn from the works of PÈRE DE LA COLOMBIÈRE, of Blessed Margaret Mary, and of others. 32mo,   0 50

SAINTS, THE NEW, OF 1888. By Rev. FRANCIS GOLDIE, S.J., and Rev. Father SCOLA, S.J. 16mo, illustrated,   0 50

SECRET OF SANCTITY, THE. According to ST. FRANCIS DE SALES and Father CRASSET, S.J. 12mo,   *net*, 1 00

SERAPHIC GUIDE. A Manual for the Members of the Third Order of St. Francis.   0 60
    Roan, red edges,   0 75
        The same in German at the same prices.

SERMONS, HUNOLT. See under HUNOLT.

SERMONS ON THE BLESSED VIRGIN. By Very Rev. D. I. MCDERMOTT. 16mo,   *net*, 0 75

SERMONS for the Sundays and Chief Festivals of the Ecclesiastical Year. With Two Courses of Lenten Sermons and a Triduum for the Forty Hours. By Rev. JULIUS POTTGEISSER, S.J. From the German by Rev. JAMES CONWAY, S.J. 2 vols., 8vo, *net*, 2 50

SERMONS, SHORT, FOR LOW MASSES. A complete, brief course of instruction on Christian Doctrine. By Rev. F. X. SCHOUPPE, S.J. 12mo, *net*, 1 25

SERMONS, SIX, on Devotion to the Sacred Heart of Jesus. From the German of Rev. Dr. E. BIERBAUM, by ELLA McMAHON, 16mo, *net*, 0 60

SHORT CONFERENCES ON THE LITTLE OFFICE OF THE IMMACULATE CONCEPTION. By Very Rev. JOSEPH RAINER. With Prayers. 32mo, 0 50

SHORT STORIES ON CHRISTIAN DOCTRINE: A Collection of Examples illustrating the Catechism. From the French by MARY McMAHON. 12mo, illustrated, *net*, 0 75

SMITH, Rev. S. B., D.D. Elements of Ecclesiastical Law.
    Vol. I. Ecclesiastical Persons. 8vo, *net*, 2 50
    Vol. II. Ecclesiastical Trials. 8vo, *net*, 2 50
    Vol. III. Ecclesiastical Punishments. 8vo, *net*, 2 50

———— Compendium Juris Canonici, ad usum Cleri et Seminariorum hujus regionis accommodatum. 8vo, *net*, 2 00

———— The Marriage Process in the United States. 8vo, *net*, 2 50

SODALISTS' VADE MECUM. A Manual, Prayer Book, and Hymnal. 32mo, cloth, 0 50
Also in finer bindings.

SOUVENIR OF THE NOVITIATE. From the French by Rev. EDWARD I. TAYLOR. 32mo, *net*, 0 60

SPIRITUAL CRUMBS FOR HUNGRY LITTLE SOULS. To which are added Stories from the Bible. By MARY E. RICHARDSON. 16mo, 0 50

STORIES FOR FIRST COMMUNICANTS, for the Time before and after First Communion. By Rev. J. A. KELLER, D.D. 32mo, 0 50

STORY OF JESUS SIMPLY TOLD FOR THE YOUNG. By ROSA MULHOLLAND. 24mo, illustrated, 0 50

SURE WAY TO A HAPPY MARRIAGE. A Book of Instructions for those Betrothed and for Married People. From the German by Rev. EDWARD I. TAYLOR. Paper, 0.25; per 100, 12.50; cloth, 0.35; per 100, 21 00

TALES AND LEGENDS OF THE MIDDLE AGES. From the Spanish of F. DE P. CAPELLA. By HENRY WILSON. 16mo, 0 75

THINK WELL ON'T; or, Reflections on the Great Truths of the Christian Religion. By the Right Rev. R. CHALLONER, D.D. 32mo, flexible cloth, 0 20

THOUGHT FROM ST. ALPHONSUS, for Every Day of the Year. 32mo, 0 50

THOUGHT FROM BENEDICTINE SAINTS. 32mo, 0 50

THOUGHT FROM DOMINICAN SAINTS. 32mo,   0 50
THOUGHT FROM ST. FRANCIS ASSISI and his Saints.
    32mo,   0 50
THOUGHT FROM ST. IGNATIUS. 32mo,   0 50
THOUGHT FROM ST. TERESA. 32mo,   0 50
THOUGHT FROM ST. VINCENT DE PAUL. 32mo,   0 50
TRUE SPOUSE OF CHRIST. By St. Alphonsus Liguori.
    2 vols., 12mo, *net*, 2.50; 1 vol., 12mo,   1 50
TRUTHS OF SALVATION. By Rev. J. Pergmayr, S.J. From
    the German by a Father of the same Society. 16mo,   *net*, 0 75
TWELVE VIRTUES, THE, of a Good Teacher. For Mothers,
    Instructors, etc. By Rev. H. Pottier, S.J. 32mo,   *net*, 0 30
VISIT TO EUROPE AND THE HOLY LAND. By Rev. H. F.
    Fairbanks. 12mo, illustrated,   1 50
VISITS TO THE MOST HOLY SACRAMENT and to the Blessed
    Virgin Mary. For Every Day of the Month. By St. Alphonsus
    de Liguori. Edited by Rev. Eugene Grimm. 32mo,   0 50

WARD, REV. THOMAS F. Fifty-two Instructions on the Principal Truths of Our Holy Religion. 12mo,   *net*, 0 75
    ——— Thirty-two Instructions for the Month of May and for the Feasts of the Blessed Virgin. 12mo,   *net*, 0 75
    ——— Month of May at Mary's Altar. 12mo,   *net*, 0 75
WAY OF INTERIOR PEACE. By Rev. Father De Lehen,
    S.J. From the German Version of Rev. J. Brucker, S.J.
    12mo,   *net*, 1 25
WENINGER'S SERMONS.
    Original Short and Practical Sermons for Every Sunday of the Year. Three Sermons for every Sunday. 8vo,   *net*, 2 00
    Sermons for Every Feast of the Ecclesiastical Year. Three Sermons for Every Feast. 8vo,   *net*, 2 00
    Conferences specially addressed to Married and Unmarried Men. 8vo,   *net*, 2 00
WHAT CATHOLICS HAVE DONE FOR SCIENCE, with
    Sketches of the Great Catholic Scientists. By Rev. Martin S.
    Brennan. 12mo,   1 00
WOMEN OF CATHOLICITY: Margaret O'Carroll—Isabella of
    Castile—Margaret Roper—Marie de l'Incarnation—Margaret
    Bourgeoys—Ethan Allen's Daughter. By Anna T. Sadlier.
    12mo,   1 00
WORDS OF JESUS CHRIST DURING HIS PASSION, explained
    in their Literal and Moral Sense. By Rev. F. X. Schouppe, S.J.
    Flexible cloth,   0 25
WORDS OF WISDOM. A Concordance of the Sapiential Books.
    12mo,   *net*, 1 25
ZEAL IN THE WORK OF THE MINISTRY; or, The Means by
    which every Priest may render his Ministry Honorable and
    Fruitful. From the French of L'Abbé Dubois. 8vo,   *net*, 1 50

THE BEST, THE CHEAPEST, THE MOST POPULAR
EDITION OF

GOFFINE'S DEVOUT INSTRUCTIONS

On the Epistles and Gospels for the Sundays and Holydays; with the Lives of many Saints of God, Explanations of Christian Faith and Duty, and of Church Ceremonies, a method of hearing Mass, Morning and Evening Prayers, and a Description of the Holy Land. With a Preface

By His Eminence Cardinal Gibbons.

8vo, cloth, 704 pages, with nearly 150 illustrations. $1 00

As a work of spiritual reading and instruction "Goffine's Devout Instructions" stands in the foremost rank. In it the faithful will find explained in a plain, simple manner the doctrines of the Church, her sacraments and ceremonies, as set forth in the Epistles and Gospels of the Sundays and holydays.

A greatly improved edition of this work is now published, with large clear type and beautiful illustrations, at such a low price that every Catholic family may possess it.

| 25 Cents each in paper. | LIBRARY OF CATHOLIC INSTRUCTION. Special Prices for Quantities. | 50 Cents each in cloth. |

Church Ceremonies, and Explanation of the Ecclesiastical Year. From the French of the Abbé Durand. 16mo, illustrated.

The Sacramentals of the Holy Catholic Church. By Rev. A. A. Lambing. 16mo, illustrated.

Explanation of the Gospels and of Catholic Worship. By Rev. L. A. Lambert and Rev. R. Brennan. 16mo, illustrated.

Catholic Belief. By Very Rev. Fáa di Bruno. 16mo.

| 25 Cents each in paper. | CATHOLIC FAMILY LIBRARY. Special Prices for Quantities. | 35 Cents each in cloth. |

Popular Instructions on Marriage. By Very Rev. F. Girardey, C.SS.R. 32mo.

Instructions on the Commandments and Sacraments. By St. Alphonsus Liguori. 32mo.

The Christian Father. What He should be, and what He should do. 32mo.

The Christian Mother. The Education of Her Children, and Her Prayer. 32mo.

A Sure Way to a Happy Marriage. A book for those betrothed and for married people. 32mo.

www.ingramcontent.com/pod-product-compliance
Lightning Source LLC
Chambersburg PA
CBHW022141300426
44115CB00006B/286